Helping Patients and Their Families Cope with Medical Problems

*A Guide to Therapeutic
Group Work
in Clinical Settings*

Howard B. Roback, Ph.D.

Editor

Helping Patients and Their Families Cope with Medical Problems

Jossey-Bass Publishers

San Francisco • Washington • London • 1984

HELPING PATIENTS AND THEIR FAMILIES COPE
WITH MEDICAL PROBLEMS
*A Guide to Therapeutic Group Work
in Clinical Settings*
by Howard B. Roback, Ph.D., Editor

Copyright © 1984 by: Jossey-Bass Inc., Publishers
433 California Street
San Francisco, California 94104
&
Jossey-Bass Limited
28 Banner Street
London EC1Y 8QE

Library of Congress Cataloging in Publication Data
Main entry under title:

Helping patients and their families cope with medical
    problems.

    (The Jossey-Bass social and behavioral science
series) (The Jossey-Bass health series)
    Includes bibliographies and index.
    1. Sick—Psychology. 2. Sick—Family relationships.
3. Group counseling. 4. Medical personnel and patient.
I. Roback, Howard B. II. Series. III. Series: Jossey-
Bass health series. [DNLM: 1. Family therapy.
2. Disease—Psychology. WM 430.5.F2 H4835]
R726.5.H45 1984 615.8'51 83-49267
ISBN 0-87589-600-6 (alk. paper)

Manufactured in the United States of America

The paper in this book meets the guidelines for
permanence and durability of the Committee on
Production Guidelines for Book Longevity of the
Council on Library Resources.

JACKET DESIGN BY WILLI BAUM

FIRST EDITION

Code 8412

A *joint publication in*
The Jossey-Bass
Social and Behavioral Science Series
and
The Jossey-Bass Health Series

*Dedicated to my most important
group, my family*

Preface

Group approaches to medical and surgical patients have progressed enormously since Boston internist Joseph Pratt's pioneering efforts with tuberculosis patients in the early 1900s. Unfortunately, the communication of many of today's exciting conceptual and technical advances in group treatment for people with specific medical disorders has not kept pace with the burgeoning interest in these advances. Much of this lag is probably due to the fact that many experts in this field are more concerned with clinical practice than with writing or research. Also, group leaders are drawn from diverse professional backgrounds (for example, nursing, psychology, psychiatry, nonpsychiatric medical fields, social work, and rehabilitation) and tend to publish in their own professional journals.

One result of this communication deficiency is that leaders of groups for patients with specialized medical conditions often cannot benefit from the prior experience of their colleagues. For instance, some group leaders have found that hemodialysis patients often develop a hostile dependency on the life-preserving machine. This may later develop into a passive-aggressive reaction and cause such patients to avoid obtaining essential medical treatment. Obviously, this is a situation that is important to anticipate and recognize in a kidney disease group. Further, group leaders may be unaware of innovative techniques that are proving effective with such patients.

The aim of this book is to convey information and knowledge gained by group specialists working with medical patient populations. The authors all use a group or family approach in treating persons with specific medical disorders; they also have special techniques and important clinical observations to share with other workers in the field.

The opening chapter provides relevant background information, including common psychological strategies used by patients for coping with chronic or progressive medical disorders, how patients' coping styles interact with their developmental level, the role and history of disease management groups, and the benefits and difficulties of membership in such groups. Following this chapter are two major clinical sections. Part One focuses on groups composed of medical-surgical patients, and Part Two concentrates on family support groups.

The medical conditions discussed in Part One are primarily those commonly seen in hospitals, clinics, and medical centers throughout the country for which group therapy is increasingly becoming a part of the total treatment program. While not intended to be a comprehensive listing of medical disorders presenting significant psychosocial demands, they are representative of medical conditions in which substantial clinical group work is being conducted. The disorders are grouped for clarity in four large and, in some instances, overlapping categories.

Chapters Two through Four discuss medical patients whose physical symptoms have no discernible organic cause (somatic patients), patients for whom potentially serious medical complications are secondary to a functional disorder (victims of anorexia nervosa), and persons who may have legitimate physical concerns but whose conditions may also be psychologically influenced (chronic pain patients). Chapters Five through Eight review patients with medical disorders involving significant physical limitations (amputees and patients with spinal cord injuries) or medical disorders requiring the patients to remain near medical care (patients with renal disease who are dependent on a dialysis machine and patients with serious chronic lung disease).

Chapters Nine through Twelve focus on medical patients living with uncertain prognoses (survivors of a myocardial infarction and adolescent and adult cancer patients) or confronted with imminent death. Chapters Thirteen and Fourteen discuss patients with chronic medical conditions characterized by highly unpredictable flare-ups (patients with multiple sclerosis and sickle cell anemia); such patients must adjust to their inability to plan life activities in an orderly fashion.

Family members both influence and are influenced by a patient's illness and adaptation to it. It is often important to educate a patient's family about the course of the illness and treatment requirements. Family members must also learn to cope constructively with the stressful impact of the disorder on the family and to channel their complex emotional responses in ways that help the ill relative. In examining these issues, Part Two emphasizes the impact of environmental disasters or catastrophic illnesses on families and patients.

Chapter Fifteen discusses working with family members of victims of devastating environmental events. Helping families following the death of a newborn child in a neonatal intensive care unit is the subject of Chapter Sixteen. When family members never have the opportunity to take their child home, parental and sibling grief reactions are intense and often go unrecognized by physicians and friends. The difficulties families have in coping with a close relative who has a catastrophic illness such as cancer are explored in Chapter Seventeen. Chapter Eighteen deals with family members of patients having Alzheimer's disease. Alzheimer's disease is discussed in its own chapter because this disease differs from cancer in that Alzheimer patients never have remission and have no chance of cure. Also, in cancer (except brain cancer), the patient is essentially unchanged mentally and behaviorally, whereas the mind and behavior of the Alzheimer patient are radically altered. A perspective on support groups for parents of children with cancer is provided in Chapter Nineteen.

The reader will recognize that a number of chapters deal with cancer-related issues. This emphasis is intentional and reflects on both the high incidence of these disorders and their pervasive emotional consequences. There are many other situations in which group work with families of patients would be practicable, and it is hoped that many of the principles presented in Chapters Fifteen through Nineteen will be applied in other therapeutic situations. The final chapter in Part Two discusses common issues confronting group leaders working in medical settings. These issues include clinical, research-theoretical, and professional-personal matters of concern to the contributing authors.

The book is primarily a clinical one and should prove a valuable resource for practitioners and trainees in family practice medicine, internal medicine, psychiatry, psychology, nursing, social work, rehabilitation counseling, pastoral counseling, and other related disciplines in the health delivery field. Although this book is primarily targeted to health professionals who lead groups for medical patients and their families, it is clearly appropriate for a much broader population of treatment providers. For instance, care givers will become aware of psychological issues that are common among patients with specific illnesses. This knowledge will enable care givers to anticipate the concerns of their patients and thus maximize care.

Acknowledgments

In editing an interdisciplinary book such as this one, I have heavily relied on numerous colleagues from diverse disciplines to obtain essential information and practical assistance. These persons include: Miles Crowder, M.D.; Marc Hollender, M.D.; Howard Kirshner, M.D.; James Nash, M.D.; and Jane Weinberg, M.D. Of course, responsibility for technical accuracy rests with the editor.

Colleagues who generously helped the editor cope with "chapter burnout" by reading and criticizing various chapters of the book include: Stephen Abramowitz, Ph.D.; Jeff Binder, Ph.D.; Nancy Crow, M.A.; Christine Davidson, Ph.D.; Brenda Dew, Ph.D.; David Folks, M.D.; Linda Hawkins, M.D.; Mark Kelly, Ph.D.; Carole Kirshner, M.A.T.; Perry Nicassio, Ph.D.; Maud Pincus, M.A.; Merrill Roback, M.Ed.; Sherry Rochester,

Ph.D.; Helen Romfh, A.C.S.W.; Mark Goldstein, M.D.; and DeAnna Mori, B.A.

Special acknowledgment is due my graduate students, Suzanne Chabaud and Carrie Cornsweet, and my psychology intern, Gloria Waterhouse, Ph.D., for their many important contributions to this volume. Their efforts clearly improved the product as well as provided me with considerable intellectual stimulation.

My secretary, Laurie LaFleur, was a dedicated and untiring coworker in all phases of this book's preparation. She provided ideas, skilled proofreading, and competent management of the multitude of details involved in preparing an anthology. The secretarial assistance of Rhonda Johnstone, Gloria Martin, and Diane Williamson is also acknowledged and appreciated.

I also wish to express my gratitude to my wife, Ellen, and my children, Michelle and H. B., for their enthusiastic encouragement.

Several contributors wished to acknowledge the helpfulness of colleagues in preparing their chapters or providing related contributions. These include Lucy Barksdale, R.N. (by Susan Lewis, Chapter Eleven); Charles Zanor, Ph.D., Jeanne Hopkins, R.N., Stephen Goldsmith, M.D., and Robert Baxter, M.D. (by Stephen Armstrong, Chapter Seven); Arlene MacBride, who was the coinvestigator of the survey described by Joy Rogers (Chapter Six); Richard Elliott, M.D., the group coleader with Helen Whitman (Chapter Ten), who provided a verbatim transcript, and Mrs. Audrey Hessig, who provided the follow-up (Chapter Ten). Andrew Razin (Chapter Nine) acknowledges the contributions to the Cardiac Stress Management Program of Lenore Zohman, M.D. (director of the Montefiore Hospital Cardiac Rehabilitation Exercise Laboratory), and Jessica Schairer, M.D., Charles Swencionis, M.D., and Herbert Weiner, M.D., whose inputs helped to shape the program.

Nashville, Tennessee   Howard B. Roback, Ph.D.
February 1984

Contents

The Editor

Howard B. Roback, Ph.D., is professor of psychiatry (psychology) at Vanderbilt University School of Medicine. He received his B.A. degree (1962) from Case Western Reserve University in psychology, his M.A. degree (1964) from Ohio University in clinical psychology, and his Ph.D. degree (1970) from York University in clinical psychology.

Roback's main research activities have been in the process and outcome of group psychotherapy with specialized populations. He is coeditor of *Group Psychotherapy Research: Commentaries and Selected Readings* (1979). His research and clinical papers appear in many professional journals, including *Archives of General Psychiatry, American Psychologist, American Journal of Psychiatry, Journal of Consulting and Clinical Psychology,* and *Journal of Abnormal Psychology.*

Roback is chief psychologist and director of group psychotherapy training at the Vanderbilt Adult Psychiatric Outpatient Clinic. He was formerly on the staff of the Clarke Institute of Psychiatry, University of Toronto School of Medicine, where he was actively involved in inpatient group psychotherapy training.

Contributors

Stephen Armstrong, Ph.D., is associate clinical professor of psychology, Tufts University School of Medicine, and clinical psychologist, Baystate Medical Center, Springfield, Massachusetts.

Thomas W. Campbell, M.D., is clinical assistant professor of psychiatry, Vanderbilt University School of Medicine, and candidate at the St. Louis Psychoanalytic Institute.

Mark A. Chesler, Ph.D., is associate professor of sociology, University of Michigan.

Myron G. Eisenberg, Ph.D., is chief psychologist, Veterans Administration Medical Center, Hampton, Virginia, and associate professor of psychiatry (psychology), Eastern Virginia Medical School.

Sona Euster, A.C.S.W., is administrative supervisor of social work, Columbia Presbyterian Hospital, New York, New York.

Charles V. Ford, M.D., is professor of psychiatry, Vanderbilt University School of Medicine.

Paul E. Garfinkel, M.D., FRCP(C), is professor of psychiatry, University of Toronto School of Medicine.

James P. Gustafson, M.D., is associate professor of psychiatry, University of Wisconsin Center for Health Sciences.

Nelson H. Hendler, M.D., M.S., is assistant professor of psychiatry, and consultant to the Pain Treatment Center, Johns Hopkins University School of Medicine, and clinical director, Mensana Clinic, Stevenson, Maryland.

Mary A. Jerse, M.D., was resident in psychiatry at the University of Wisconsin Center for Health Sciences prior to her death in 1983.

Lissa Robins Kapust, A.C.S.W., is clinical social worker on the Behavioral Neurology Unit of Beth Israel Hospital, Boston.

Susan Lewis, Ph.D., is assistant professor of psychiatry (psychology), Vanderbilt University School of Medicine.

Daniel M. McDonnell, M.S.W., is executive director, St. Mary's Hospice, Tucson, Arizona.

Robert J. Marcovitz, Psy.D., is clinical assistant professor of psychiatry, Jefferson Medical College, Philadelphia.

E. Mansell Pattison, M.D., is professor and chairman of psychiatry, Medical College of Georgia.

Marcia Pavlou, Ph.D., is with the Department of Psychology and the Multiple Sclerosis Center of Rush Presbyterian St. Luke's Medical Center, Chicago.

Janet Polivy, Ph.D., is associate professor of psychology and psychiatry, University of Toronto.

Andrew M. Razin, Ph.D., M.D., is director of the psychiatric consultation-liaison service, North Central Bronx Hospital, and assistant clinical professor, Albert Einstein College of Medicine, Yeshiva University.

Joy Rogers, R.N., is mental health consultant in social and community psychiatry and lecturer, University of Toronto School of Medicine.

Stephen B. Shanfield, M.D., is associate professor of psychiatry, University of Arizona College of Medicine.

Edward Walwork, A.C.S.W., is medical social worker, Neonatal Intensive Care Unit, Milwaukee County Medical Complex.

Sandra Weintraub, Ph.D., is head of neuropsychology on the Behavioral Neurology Unit, Beth Israel Hospital, Boston, and instructor in neurology (neuropsychology), Harvard Medical School.

Helen H. Whitman, R.N., is supervisor nurse on the Clinical Oncology Unit, University of Wisconsin Center for Health Services.

Margaret Yoak, M.A., M.S., is research assistant in the Department of Sociology, University of Michigan.

Helping Patients and Their Families Cope with Medical Problems

A Guide to Therapeutic Group Work in Clinical Settings

1

Howard B. Roback, Ph.D.

▦ ▦ ▦ ▦ ▦ ▦ ▦ ▦ ▦ ▦ ▦ ▦ ▦

Introduction:
The Emergence of
Disease-Management
Groups

What is the fiercely independent, hard-driving, fifty-two-year-old business leader M.K., who recently underwent coronary by-pass surgery for intractable angina, really saying when he exclaims, "I'll be back working at full steam within a week!"? Assuming that he complies with his therapeutic regimen, is judged medically ready to leave the hospital, and does not display obvious signs of distress, most staff members would be satisfied that they had done their job. However, the patient's expressed plan for a speedy—and premature—return to his previous frantic pace suggests great emphasis on the mechanism of denial. M.K.'s pollyannish refusal to recognize the need to restrict physical activity could have cost him his life.

Fortunately, M.K. was in a hospital where patients in the coronary care unit were routinely assigned to a therapeutic

group, coled by a psychiatrist and a nurse, aimed at improving
the patients' functioning after being discharged. Patients were
encouraged to discuss concerns about sexual activity, work performance, future heart attacks, family relationships, and related
issues. M.K. joined the group with reluctance and quickly felt
intimidated by the discussions. On several occasions he threatened to drop out of the group, and only the persuasions of his
primary physician kept him attending. When asked by one of
the therapists what it was about the group that made him most
uncomfortable, M.K. hesitantly revealed that his own father had
died of heart disease at forty-eight years of age and that his father's brother died of a heart attack at age fifty-three. His therapists judged that it was best to avoid discussing the patient's
terror of dying because of the attendant risk of his becoming a
"cardiac cripple." Due to M.K.'s obsessive cognitive style, the
cotherapists with group support and input focused on the benefits of surgery and other factors that M.K. could personally control. (For instance, his work pace, diet, and exercise could
greatly influence his future health.) He benefited significantly
from these discussions and became appropriately receptive to
medical recommendations. As a result of the group intervention, M.K. was successfully prevented from setting a course that
would have led to his own destruction.

Medical care traditionally focuses on the physical illness
of the patient. Psychiatric consultation is typically sought for
patients whose symptoms have no detectable organic cause, patients whose preexisting psychopathology aggravates their physical disorder or interferes with their hospital adjustment, and
patients experiencing overwhelming distress because of their illness. However, the concerns of other patients about their illnesses
are likely to go undetected and unexamined. Because family
members and friends are also likely to focus on a patient's illness, neglecting emotional problems may result in a deterioration of the patient's physical and psychological state.

Many health care professionals now recognize the importance of providing psychological interventions for "normal" as
well as psychologically impaired persons who have suffered the
devastating blow of learning that they have a debilitating, pain-

ful, or terminal illness, or that a close family member has such an illness. Caring for the psychosocial needs of medical patients and their families has become a concern of therapists in most disciplines involved with health care delivery—many of whom prefer to administer care in a group format. Group leaders come from varied professions, such as nursing, medical social work, clinical psychology, psychiatry, medicine, pastoral counseling, and other related fields. They vary greatly in their grasp of group principles and their knowledge of individual reactions to physical illness.

This chapter draws from diverse sources in an attempt to make interchanges among therapists of different disciplines more productive. The chapter discusses common psychological responses to physical illness, provides a history of group approaches with medical patients, describes group mechanisms among medical-surgical patient groups, describes important functions of group leaders, and concludes with the advantages and pitfalls of homogeneous groups.

Psychological Response to Physical Illness

In a thorough and insightful discussion of reactions to physical illness, Cassell (1979) cites four psychological changes that often accompany illness: loss of connectedness, loss of a sense of omnipotence, failure of reason, and loss of control.

Loss of Connectedness. This first change refers to a person's increasing withdrawal from his usual life-style (interests, social network, and relationships with family members) when experiencing a progressive illness. This increasing isolation, or, as Cassell prefers, "disconnection," may be sudden or gradual. It may result from family members and friends abandoning the patient or the patient rejecting them. Cassell believes that helping patients maintain their social contacts is extremely important; without this connectedness, they are likely to give up and yield to their illness.

Loss of a Sense of Omnipotence. To varying degrees, people harbor a belief in their own indestructibility; otherwise, as Cassell puts it, who would ride a motorcycle? This sense of

omnipotence is indicated by the mechanism of denial demonstrated by the cardiac bypass patient mentioned earlier. Cassell
notes that the reaction that is opposite to denial is often panic.
A challenge for the practitioner is to prevent patients from ex-
ceeding their physical limits without reinforcing their underlying fears.

Failure of Reason. Cassell points out that patients tend
to dwell on their illnesses but do not have the knowledge necessary to comprehend the complexities involved. For this reason,
their world seems out of control. In addition, in profound physical disturbances, patients' cognitive processes are often affected without their realizing it. Because knowledge is an important means of controlling our world, Cassell believes physicians
should share with patients information about the cause, process,
and outcome of their illness rather than leaving them with an
uncertain or errant understanding of their condition.

Loss of Control. The ability to control one's existence
and to feel intact are basic human needs. Patients who feel helpless and dependent typically feel worthless. For instance, patients who can no longer do their job because of their illness
lose not only income but also a sense of control over their
world. Cassell states that treating the illness is one challenge for
the physician, but helping patients "regain control over their
lives" is the final task (1979, p. 129). Brehm's reactance theory
(Berkowitz, 1975; Brehm, 1966), drawn from the field of social
psychology, emphasizes this same idea but also predicts how individuals confronted with this loss of control are likely to be
affected. Interested readers may wish to acquaint themselves
with Brehm's work.

In addition to Cassell's four characteristic reactions to
physical illness, several other clinicians have focused on defense
mechanisms commonly used by physically ill patients: denial,
intellectualization, regression, projection, displacement, and
introjection. Denial, in which a person blocks out awareness of
some painful reality, may initially have adaptive value. Walker
(1981) refers to the patient who calmly and efficiently tends to
his affairs prior to entering the hospital and only later faces his
fears. Denial can be quite maladaptive, however, if it leads to

noncompliance with medical care. This was the coping mechanism employed by the bypass patient in the opening example.

A second common reaction is intellectualization, in which patients attempt to reduce anxiety about their illness by learning as much as possible about it. Abram (1981) interprets this as though the patient were saying, "If I know enough about my condition, it won't exist," while Blumenfield (1977) views this form of intellectualization as an attempt by the patient to control her illness.

Regression is another common reaction to both acute and chronic illness. In this case, the patient becomes childlike, dependent, and demanding and tries to shed adult responsibilities. This response may be reinforced by the patient's family members.

Other common defenses include projection (attributing the cause of illness to the environment or other persons), displacement (focusing on less threatening symptoms rather than those that are most worrisome), and introjection (blaming oneself for the illness, which often leads to severe depression).

The depression commonly found in patients with physical diseases is often related to grief over the loss of bodily functions, psychological well-being, bodily integrity, and a satisfying life-style. Depression in patients with debilitating or terminal illnesses may also stem from grief over the possible loss of independence or anticipated parting from loved ones. It is of great importance that physicians and other workers treating medical patients also recognize that patients may develop distorted body images. Such misconceptions may permeate all aspects of their social and vocational lives (Roback, Kirshner, and Roback, 1981).

Children's reactions to physical illness and hospitalization are influenced by numerous factors, including their individual developmental level and coping skills, the nature of the stress, and the reactions of their family and the hospital staff to the stress (Christ, 1977). Christ points out that a seven-month-old infant cannot understand explanations of present and future events related to an illness; at this age, white coats are associated with vaccinations and other injections and are likely to elicit a healthy wail. Since children are primarily attached to their mothers at this stage, Christ recommends a live-in arrangement for the mother of a hospitalized child. The author strongly advocates that people who work with ill children be aware of the major concerns and anxieties characteristic of each developmental level, as well as usual coping strategies.

Family members of patients having debilitating, painful, or terminal illnesses are often left to their own devices in coping with their emotions, which vacillate between sadness, hopelessness, encouragement, guilt, and rage. This is particularly true of families who have a child with a terminal illness. Gilder and others (1978, p. 277) describe the intense frustration and rage often experienced by parents of children with leukemia because they cannot control their child's deteriorating condition. The authors emphasize that these family members "may rail against God or vent their fury at doctors and nurses."

A tragic illustration of a family's need for assistance appeared in the *Nashville Tennessean* newspaper on February 4, 1982, under the headline "St. Jude Gunman Slain." Police had stormed St. Jude Children's Research Hospital in Memphis and killed a gunman who was holding captive several hospital employees and the physician who had treated the gunman's son for leukemia; the boy had died two years earlier at six years of age. The gunman's ex-wife described her husband as a "very sad and lonely man" who had never been able to accept the death of their son. This incident, while rare, reveals the severe turmoil that family members of a deceased patient can maintain for years.

It has become increasingly apparent that patients and their families need a safe place to talk about issues related to the patients' illnesses. These issues include the personal meaning given to the illness, the patients' fantasies about their condition ("Am I dying?"), the threat to patients' sense of body integrity, previous experiences with the illness, necessary life-style changes for patients and their families, coping with restrictions in life-style, and whether the disorder will necessitate a short-term or long-term adjustment for the family unit (Wood and others, 1978; Abram, 1981). Stressors on medical patients and their family members may include somatic changes (for amputees and paraplegics), life-style changes (for patients with diabetes or multiple sclerosis), dependence on machines (for patients with serious renal disease), the threat of death, and severe pain. Some patients must contend with several of these events as well as with the loss of a job and economic insecurity, prolonged hospitalization and separation from family members, and the complete disruption of daily routines. Depending on the needs of the individual patient, recommended treatment may be behavioral therapy, hypnotherapy, individual psychotherapy, or group intervention. In some instances, these treatments may be administered concurrently with the patient's other care (such as medical treatment and vocational retraining).

Over the past two decades, small groups have had increasingly encouraging results in helping medical patients and their families effectively cope with stress secondary to illness or accident (Cunningham, Strassberg, and Roback, 1978; Marram, 1973). The recent emphasis on group treatment in this context is an extension of the promise this modality showed when used with medical patients at the beginning of the twentieth century. Group therapy for medical-surgical patients and their families has evolved slowly, and the story of its evolution is an interesting one.

Historical Perspective

The first group efforts with medical patients are usually attributed to an American internist, Joseph Hersey Pratt, of Massachusetts General Hospital. In a 1907 article, Pratt wrote about his group experience (the "class method") with tuberculosis patients. Pratt was concerned about the failure of traditional individual treatments for these patients and the personal discouragement and shame experienced by both the patients and their families (Pattison, 1973). He firmly believed that these patients required almost constant bed rest in an outdoor setting, but that it was difficult to get patients to comply with this essential treatment. Suspecting that educating patients might enhance their compliance, he decided on his class method as the most economical way to teach them. Although Pratt employed lectures and apparently had no conception of group dynamics, he was struck by the camaraderie that developed among class members and the emotional support that they provided one another in coping with both their debilitating disease and their treatments. Pratt felt that the patients had found a "common bond in a common disease" and that the group experience had contributed enormously to the success of his treatment program.

Pratt further described his approach in papers published in 1908 and 1922. Essentially, Pratt's group members met every Friday in a large, cheerful room at Massachusetts General Hospital. Patients were weighed in by a nurse who also recorded their pulse rate and temperature. The patients then interacted with one another while Pratt and one of his assistants scrutinized the patient information. Each patient's weight and time spent out of doors were conspicuously displayed and the name of the person who gained the most weight was placed on the "honor roll." Pratt then gave his class of twenty to twenty-five members advice and encouragement in an inspirational talk lasting no more than two or three minutes. The "star patients" (those who had gained the most weight and spent the most time out of doors) then gave testimonials for the rest treatment.

In a 1908 *British Medical Journal* article, Pratt described his treatment goals and findings more explicitly, stating that his aim was to restore the members to the "ranks of wage earners with the disease entirely arrested." Of the thirty-eight group members who remained in his group until recovery or death from 1905 to 1908, twenty-nine recovered and nine died. Of the twenty-nine whose wage-earning potential had been restored, twenty were known to be well and working, while eight were apparently lost to follow-up.

Pratt's class method seemed to be well received by both the medical and nonmedical community, and his approach was successfully applied to patients with peptic ulcers. Pratt felt that practitioners who failed to replicate his success probably lacked knowledge of his method, did not have sufficient financial support to underwrite the program, or needed a trained nonphysician to help lead the group. As a pragmatist, he believed that the work was too arduous for a physician in active practice and that nonphysicians who had a substantial knowledge of patients' medical conditions, a clear idea of treatment needs, and a definite method of treatment could use the class method effectively.

Pratt's approach was adopted by American psychiatrists in the early 1920s. Psychiatrists such as L. Cody Marsh and E. W. Lazell lectured to institutionalized psychotic patients about their illness in classroom style, sometimes by means of loudspeakers (Anthony, 1972).

In the mid-1930s, with the rise of the psychoanalytically oriented groups of Louis Wender and others, Pratt's approach lost its dominance. However, his influence was still felt: Wender began each session with a didactic lecture on psychodynamics or dreams. The group therapy movement at this time was also influenced by Paul Schilder, who focused on the importance of member-to-member interaction; by Trigant Burrow, who believed that the group rather than the individual was the proper focus of treatment; and by Jacob Moreno, who was more concerned with social interaction than with the psychoanalytic approach (Appley and Winder, 1973; Whiteley and Gordon, 1979).

In 1937, Robert Buck published a paper in the *Annals of Internal Medicine* on his use of the class method with hypertensive patients. He viewed the approach as having three major functions: (1) encouraging patients to use common sense in dealing with health needs, (2) prescribing a diet of baked potatoes, dark bread, fresh fruit, and so on, and (3) providing education and psychotherapy. To this third end, Buck gave talks on pathological physiology, the significance of physical and nervous strain in the development of symptoms, the important role of the emotions in hypertension, and the importance of relaxation. In addition, older members of the group gave testimonials. Buck's goals were to reduce blood pressure and to improve the patients' total well-being. After several months in the program, patients reported relief of such symptoms as insomnia, dizziness, and shortness of breath. Sixty-seven percent of the patients who attended three or more classes experienced a drop in blood pressure ranging from 18 to 46 millimeters of mercury. Buck focused on friendly competition among group members as well as on the morale gained from working toward a common end as key therapeutic factors.

In his 1943 review of group psychotherapy practice prior to 1940, Giles Thomas appealed to psychiatrists to increase their use of group approaches because of their economic and therapeutic advantages. He believed that "the functionally incapacitated individual becomes a drag on our national effort" (p. 166) and argued that group treatment was economically necessary in wartime conditions and justified by its therapeutic potential. Like Pratt and Wender, however, Thomas had no clear concept of the therapeutic forces at work in therapy groups.

The psychoanalytic approach to group psychotherapy continued to dominate, with some modifications, during and after World War II. Psychiatrists and psychologists were becoming influenced by the group approach of Bion and others in Great Britain who focused on the "here and now" interactions taking place in groups. Like Trigant Burrow, Bion viewed the group as a single entity rather than a collection of individuals. Modern group psychotherapy is still polarized between those who focus on the members of the group and those who focus on the group itself (Freedman, Kaplan, and Sadock, 1972; Whiteley and Gordon, 1979).

In the 1950s, group dynamicists with backgrounds in psychology and sociology started applying their concepts and findings from small nontreatment groups to therapy groups. Concepts such as cohesiveness, clique formation, and norm development seemed to have their counterparts in psychotherapy groups. Research strategies were also adopted from studies on nontherapeutic small groups and modified for application to the therapy groups. In 1956, Stein reviewed the literature on group therapy with psychosomatic patients and reached the following conclusion: "It can be stated quite definitely that experience with the use of group psychotherapy in the treatment of psychosomatic disease has amply demonstrated its effectiveness, which is also in accord with the therapeutic formulations relative to psycho-somatic disorders and psychotherapy" (p. 56).

In the 1960s, there was greater emphasis on conceptualiz-ing group processes, group practices proliferated, and clinical practice with special populations such as nonpsychiatric medical patients gained momentum (Appley and Winder, 1973). A new wave of experiential-humanistic groups appeared in the 1960s (see Kaplan and Sadock's *New Models for Group Therapy*, 1972, for more information on this topic).

During the 1970s, specialized group techniques came to be widely used in nonpsychiatric medical settings. In 1978, Cunningham, Strassberg, and Roback reviewed the literature on group psychotherapy for medical patients published after Stein's 1956 paper. Although the studies documented often lacked objective evaluations of the processes used and their ef-fectiveness, frequent reports of favorable outcomes argued for the continued use of such groups. In a 1979 paper, Karasu re-viewed the effectiveness of various psychotherapeutic modali-ties (including individual, group, and family psychotherapy) with medically ill patients and noted "consistently impressive results with group therapy" (p. 7).

Although there is currently no comprehensive theory of group therapy, many group leaders have found principles and concepts from the maturing field of group dynamics to be help-ful in explaining the processes in their therapeutic groups.

Group Mechanisms

There are major differences in group work with tradition-al psychiatric populations and medical-surgical patients. In the former, one is often treating the patient's long-standing social maladjustment, while in the latter, the therapist attempts to help a basically normal individual learn to cope with stress sec-ondary to his medical problems. Marram (1973, p. 26) stated it well when she described the goal of medical-surgical groups as being to "preserve mental health versus treating full-fledged men-tal illness." That is, the group leader's goal is primarily preventa-tive. Nonetheless, I believe that most group leaders and theoreticians would agree that the theoretical framework provided by Yalom (1975) for understanding therapeutic forces operating in traditional therapy groups is also useful for leaders of medical-surgical patient groups. Cunningham, Strassberg, and Roback applied this framework directly to studies of disease-management groups in their 1978 review (pp. 136–137):

1. *Instillation of hope.* In groups that attempt to aid the patient in management of any chronic disease, the presence of group members who have been successful in dealing with the problem and who are not currently in debilitating distress greatly enhances the hopeful feelings of new members. This development of faith in treatment is not only therapeutic in itself, but may keep the patient in treatment until other medical and psychologic therapies can take effect. It may also enhance the therapeutic impact of other experiences in the group setting, increasing such nonspecific factors as expectation for improvement.

2. *Universality.* The therapeutic value of universality lies in an individual's sense of relief in recognizing that he is not alone in his misery. For example, members of a group for patients with life-threatening disorders have been found to believe that since other members shared their medical problems, they would be understanding and helpful listeners.

3. *Imparting of information.* Symptoms and treatments are frequently confusing and distressing to the patient and his family. Often, factual information removes misconceptions and relieves anxieties. Such information can come from the group leaders as well as from other group members. For example, Hollon's (1972) chronic hemodialysis patients and their families exchanged solutions to everyday problems of living with kidney disease, and wives of patients collaborated with a dietitian to write a cookbook.

4. *Altruism.* Patients with major medical problems seldom have much reason or opportunity to help others. However, a chance to be of help can do a great deal to relieve feelings of hopelessness and uselessness. A therapy group composed of pa-

tients with similar medical problems often provides many group members with the perfect opportunity to provide aid, insight, and comfort to each other (Asch and Calhoun, 1966).

5. *Corrective recapitulation of the primary family group.* While this factor may have more relevance for groups aimed at personality change, the treatment of psychologically determined physical problems must often focus on family histories to be successful. Reid (1962) believes that the group can serve as a corrective "good family" for patients whose own families have contributed to the development of their psychophysical problems.

6. *Development of socializing techniques.* Traditionally, therapy groups have served as a setting in which individuals could learn and practice new ways of dealing with other people in an atmosphere of understanding and support. Therapy groups provide an opportunity for many types of medical patients to learn new social skills necessitated by the nature of their physical condition. For example, patients with terminal or severely disfiguring illnesses can learn how others are likely to react to their condition and the most effective ways to maintain comfortable relationships with these and other people in their lives.

7. *Imitative behavior.* Patients in therapy groups are often able to benefit, vicariously, from the therapeutic experiences of other group members. This can be particularly important for those patients whose psychological defenses make it difficult for them to recognize maladaptive patterns in their own lives. For example, Reid (1962) found that chronic, disabled asthma patients could safely learn the relationship between their own symptoms and stresses in their lives when they saw such relationships in other group members.

8. *Interpersonal learning.* Perhaps the most significant advantage of group therapy over individual therapy is the opportunity it provides for patients to receive feedback as to how others perceive them. For example, chronic medical complainers have been able to learn the reaction of others to their overutilization of the "sick" role.

9. *Group cohesiveness.* Cohesiveness refers
to the group members' feelings that their group is
important and worth their participation. Group cohesiveness has been shown to decrease the social
isolation experienced by Parkinson's disease patients as a result of their own and others' embarrassment at their symptoms (Chafetz and others,
1955).

10. *Catharsis.* Several authors mentioned
catharsis and ventilation as important curative factors in their groups. Cancer patients found relief
in expressing themselves freely concerning their
own deaths and the process of dying in their
group; they had previously repressed these feelings
because they feared it would upset their families
(Parsell and Tagliereni, 1974).

11. *Existential factors.* The problem of finding meaning in life is especially important for medical groups, since members may have to live with
disabilities that make many former sources of satisfaction unavailable to them. A ward of post-polio
patients confined to respirators (Asch and Calhoun, 1966) discussed the issue of finding meaning
in their survival of the disease and tried to activate
new interests in life. Group members developed interest in the stock market, in reading, and even in
gardening in the hospital windows. Eventually, several group members decided to leave their bodies
to science in order to give meaning to their deaths.

These group mechanisms (except for the corrective recapitulation of the primary family group, the development of
socializing techniques, and interpersonal learning) are particularly helpful for patients and family members in acute turmoil but
not so severely overwhelmed that they require individual crisis
intervention. It should also be noted that techniques such as
interpreting interpersonal dynamics (intermember transference-
countertransference reactions) and analyzing defenses found in
psychoanalytically oriented group psychotherapies would be de-
emphasized in most disease-management groups and family
support groups, since personality reorganization is not considered a primary goal.

There is less consensus on the applicability of the concepts, theories, and findings from the scientific study of small groups (such as family groups, educational groups, political groups, work groups, and social groups) to groups for medical-surgical patients. I believe that properties that can be generalized across all groups are also pertinent to intervention groups for these populations because the major objectives of most disease-management groups include sharing information, improving problem-solving skills, and providing emotional support. Particularly relevant to these objectives are several key concepts from the field of group dynamics, including social motives, reference groups, conformity, social comparisons, cohesiveness, clique formation, and scapegoating. Group leaders who are familiar with such concepts will be more aware not only of mechanisms operating within the therapy groups but also of those operating within patients' social systems that influence their ability to cope with their illness. That is, the group leader must also be aware of how group members, as ill people, affect their social field and are in turn affected by it.

Social Motives. One major issue confronting students of group behavior is the process by which people acquire their social motives or need for group affiliation. Learning theory postulates that the infant becomes attached to its mother because her physical features become associated with the satisfaction of certain drive states, such as hunger and thirst. Through this process, the child develops strong affectional needs for the mother that generalize to other people. The instinctive-component theory suggests that certain aspects of the mother (such as her physical warmth) set off certain social responses in the infant, such as sucking, smiling, and clinging. These theories and others are presented in detail by Middlebrook (1974), who believes that the formation of this initial attachment is critical to normal social development, which includes a strong affiliation motive.

Middlebrook cites personal events such as the loss of a loved one, national tragedies such as the assassination of President Kennedy, and many replicated experiments (including Schachter's 1959 stress experiments) to illustrate the relationship between heightened stress or fear and an increase in the affiliation motive. According to Middlebrook, two frequently advanced explanations of the desire to be with others in times of stress and fear are social comparison (a need to determine the appropriate level of emotion to display in a situation by viewing the response of others) and fear reduction (the possible reduction in fear caused by the mere presence of others during times of stress, in addition to that caused by any reassurance that these others may provide).

Experiments by other investigators have supported these ideas and have added two qualifications to the general conclusion that the need to affiliate increases proportionately with emotional upset. These qualifications relate to appropriateness and the degree of upset. If a person believes his upset to be inappropriate to the situation, he will likely avoid others (Berscheid and Walster, 1978). In addition, extreme upset frequently leads an individual to prefer to be alone, perhaps because of a fear that the intensity of emotional upset will be heightened even further by interaction with others.

Reasons for affiliation during nonstressful times are numerous. Acceptance within a group can be a means of verifying one's social acceptability (most people believe that they can find one person to like them, but to be liked by a group really indicates that they are OK). Recreational or special interest groups can satisfy a need for interpersonal contacts without the demands of intimacy. Social prestige can be obtained through membership in groups with high social prestige. In addition, groups can provide protection, help to alleviate loneliness, and can foster hope in those who feel that they can solve otherwise insurmountable problems through group membership. Obviously, just as reasons for affiliation differ from person to person, so does the strength of the affiliation need.

The following is an example of how heightened stress can stimulate the affiliation motive:

I.N., a forty-eight-year-old manufacturer's representative, felt overwhelmed and alone when he learned of his wife's breast cancer and her need for a bilateral modified radical mastectomy. After his wife's surgery, I.N. vacillated between being overly protective and highly irritable toward his wife; he was unable to provide her with any consistent support or comfort. He felt unable to share his own concerns for fear of upsetting his wife, close relatives, and friends. As the stress mounted, I.N. sought out and affiliated with a group for spouses of partners with breast cancer, which met at a nearby hospital. Subsequently, I.N. persuaded his wife to join him in a family-oriented support group for cancer patients and their partners.

Reference Groups. Although people may be members of many different groups, relatively few of the groups are likely to be recognized as reference groups. A reference group is one in which obtaining or maintaining membership is very important to the individual, who evaluates his own behavior according to the anticipated reactions of the other group members (Marram, 1973). Reference groups (such as a group of friends, a professional organization, or a religious group) often help to provide a basis for identity, self-esteem, and a sense of belonging. Expulsion from a reference group for nonconformance to group norms or expectations is usually very threatening to a group member. Therapy groups commonly become reference groups for individuals.

The following is an example of a medical patient changing reference groups:

M.S., a forty-five-year-old housewife, had been active for the past seven months in a therapeutic group for patients with multiple sclerosis. Her physical condition was worsening, and she realized that soon she would be confined to a wheelchair. She stopped calling close personal friends of many years and also discouraged them from contacting her. She started replacing old friends with persons in her therapeutic group and with other persons she knew who had major medical problems. There was a shift taking place in M.S.'s reference groups; she was disconnecting from her previously valued, long-standing social group to a new social group composed of physically ill people. Fortunately, when the group recognized this phenomenon taking place, they helped M.S. work out her conflicts about being around well people, both in the present and in the future, when she would be less mobile. This conflict resolution was very important, since some medical patients with a progressive illness totally isolate themselves from physically healthy people and seek out the companionship of physically ill people, who they feel understand their plight and concerns.

Conformity. Reference groups influence the behavior and attitudes of their members by both direct and subtle pressures to conform to group standards. Conformity to group norms is strong in most groups. As Cartwright and Zander (1968, p. 139) put it, "Even among dedicated nonconformists one finds a monotonous similarity of hair styles." Although research on small groups does suggest some correlation between personality traits and conformity, personality factors are not powerful predictors of conformity behavior.

The more productive approach has been to examine factors intrinsic to the group context. For instance, Shaw (1971) cites the classic work of Asch (1951) conducted with male Swarthmore students. Each subject was asked to judge which of three vertical lines was the same length as a standard. The subject was not aware that the other group members were paid accomplices whose job was to convincingly call out incorrect answers. The object of the manipulation was to determine how people responded to group pressures to conform. Asch found that group pressure was significantly more effective when the group had a unanimous point of view than when one or more of the confederates gave the correct response.

This finding underscores the fact that social support (that is, at least one other person sharing a person's point of view) can diminish the conformity effect. Other factors that influence conformity include relations among group members, the attractiveness of the group to the individuals, and the prior success of the group in achieving its goals.

The following is an example of conformity in a medical patient group:

> Susan, an attractive twenty-three-year-old female, was a member of an outpatient anorexia nervosa–bulimia group. Group norms included the expectation that members would not focus on their eating disorder per se but rather would examine their personal feelings, with particular attention devoted to the manner in which they coped with stress. Susan had found self-examination and exploration of her intense feelings toward her parents extremely difficult, even though she felt emotionally very close to the other group members. After increasing amounts of group pressure (through nonacceptance) were placed on her to conform to group norms, she reluctantly started to open up about her problems in handling criticism by her parents. She ultimately perceived an association between heated arguments with her parents and periods of binging and purging. Had Susan not felt close to the other group members, it is quite possible that she would have responded to the group pressure by quitting the group.

Social Comparisons. Individuals rely upon reference groups to make judgments about themselves, their values, and their beliefs (Festinger, 1954). Whenever we feel uncertain about the validity of our perceptions, these opinions are evaluated by comparing them with the views of others in similar situations.

An example of the process of social comparison within a medical patient group follows:

> R.F., a single, twenty-one-year-old, rugged outdoorsman was paralyzed from the waist down following a motorcycle accident. Due to his injury, he was unable to have an erection, and it was unlikely that he would ever be able to have one. He was placed in a paraplegic group, where after several sessions of nonparticipation he angrily blurted out, "I'm not a man any longer, I might as well be dead." He stared at the ground and his speech low-

ered as he stated, "I must be going nuts." Persons who had been dealing with their paralysis and accompanying sexual problems for a longer period of time quickly pointed out that they, too, had initially felt frustrated, angry, and confused over the severe wound to their sense of masculinity. They later learned alternate techniques for functioning sexually. After the patient learned that his response to this situation was normal and after he learned alternate sexual techniques through group discussion and films, his psychological functioning improved significantly.

Cohesiveness. The concept of cohesiveness, which holds a central place in the small-group field, refers to the relative attractiveness of a group for its members. According to Whiteley and Gordon (1979, p. 65):

> Group cohesiveness varies with (1) the *incentive properties* of the group (attractiveness of or similarities between members, the attractiveness of group goals, activities, the nature of its leadership, atmosphere or prestige); (2) the *motivations of members* (needs for affiliation, friendship, rewards, recognition); (3) their *expectancies* concerning outcome (a subjective estimate of the probability that membership will insure the realization of goals or the satisfaction of needs); and (4) the *comparison* level (a general conception of what outcomes group membership should provide on the basis of other group experience). In turn, the more cohesive a group, the more it can (1) hold its members; (2) exert power over them; (3) count on their participation and loyalty; (4) affect their feelings of personal security; and (5) influence their self-evaluations.

According to Yalom (1975), cohesiveness in therapy groups is not a curative factor per se but is a "necessary precondition for effective therapy" (p. 47). He cites studies with group therapy patients (Dickoff and Lakin, 1963) and encounter group participants (Lieberman, Yalom, and Miles, 1973) indicating a strong relationship between cohesiveness and patient outcome.

The favorable impact of being part of a cohesive group for medical patients is illustrated by the following example:

> R.H., an eighteen-year-old female, had recently been hospitalized for study of her many symptoms and was finally diagnosed as diabetic. R.H. was alternately angered by the intrusion of the disease into her life and frightened by what being a diabetic would mean. She was referred to a group for young adults with diabetes, which was coled by a social worker and a psychologist. During the screening interview, R.H. shared her fears that she would be unable to attend college, that her body would betray her, and that she would constantly look drunk and crazy so that no one would want to come near her. R.H. was initially apprehensive about group membership but found herself relaxing as other members voiced fears and feelings that paralleled her own. R.H. was particularly pleased to learn that several group members were attending a local college and living the life that she had planned for herself prior to the diagnosis of diabetes. The group became quite meaningful to R.H., and to date she has fully complied with her prescribed diet and insulin administration. She has also formed a strong support system with several group members while maintaining her other social relationships.
>
> R.H. initially felt betrayed by her body and thus was angry and frustrated. Also, she felt inferior to others because she was physically sick (that is, different). Without being part of this cohesive group, she might well have become isolated and not complied with her medical treatment. In the group, she observed others coping and succeeding with life and controlling their disease.

Clique Formation. In group dynamics, clique formation refers to the cohesiveness of two or more members, but not necessarily to the group as a whole. Subgrouping is often destructive to the group, particularly if the involved members tend to emphasize their separateness from the larger group. An example in a therapy group would be two or more patients regularly going out for a drink after the group session but excluding other members from such participation.

An example of clique formation in medical patient groups follows:

> S.B. and J.A. were the only members of a group of leukemia patients who were unmarried and living alone. Their shared status was the basis for a strong sense of mutual identification. Although this sharing helped them survive many personal crises, they began to set themselves apart from the rest of the group and exhibit behaviors such as whispering to each other during group sessions. Further, S.B. and J.A. began to gain less and less from group membership. Only when another member pointed out their behavior did the two realize that they had essentially separated themselves from the larger group, threatened other members by their separation, and failed to realize fully the rewards of group membership. More importantly, they achieved the understanding that their fear of full membership in the group derived from their unwillingness to accept that they, too, were leukemia patients.

Scapegoating. When a group contains more than one subgroup, the likelihood of an individual being isolated or even becoming the scapegoat for the group increases (for example, he may become the target of displaced aggression, which may be communicated directly or through making him the butt of malicious jokes).

An illustration of scapegoating follows:

> J.B.'s rapidly deteriorating condition fostered fear and repulsion in the other members of his group because of their own anticipated deterioration. The group suppressed these feelings by essentially ignoring J.B. Gradually, J.B. began to feel that he was useless to the group and he completely withdrew. The therapist pointed out that J.B. and the rest of the group were mutually responsible for

sentencing J.B. to isolation. Both J.B.'s fears of detachment from the functioning world and the
group's sense of foreboding, graphically represented by J.B.'s condition, became critical issues
for the entire group. Working through these issues
restored the cohesiveness the group had experienced prior to the threat of J.B.'s diminishing
health.

Scapegoating typically brings to mind displaced aggression—negative comments directed toward a scapegoat rather
than toward the real object of a person's displeasure. While a
dramatic illustration of scapegoating, the example of J.B. is
atypical in that it is usually the sicker patients in a medical
group who deal with their upset and frustration by scapegoating the healthier patients rather than vice versa.

As stated previously, the information presented in this
section is not intended to cover all of the many facets of the
field of group dynamics. Therapeutic groups designed to assist
medical-surgical patients and their families conform to the general definition of formal groups; they consist of two or more
persons who perceive one another as participants in a common
activity, who interact dynamically with one another, and who
communicate their responses verbally (Barnlund and Harman,
1960). Only concepts and findings from the scientific study of
small groups that can be generalized and thus have implications
for these groups have been introduced.

Implications. A skillful group therapist must be able to
anticipate the various challenges typically posed by the therapeutic group process. An awareness of the interplay of group
and individual factors can be important in creating an environment conducive to learning. Such awareness can also help the
therapist to prevent these factors from interfering with learning.
An effective therapist will want to develop group norms that
(1) foster self-examination, (2) discourage scapegoating or
harmful comments by group members, (3) promote the comparison of group members' adaptive styles and their effectiveness, and (4) encourage experimentation with new coping
styles, both in and out of the therapy group.

Group members will engage in self-observation and try

out new behavior only after they develop a sense of security in the group—security that the group will be a durable source of hope, satisfaction, and help to them. A period of testing and building of trust is required before group members realize that the group will still be there for them despite their disclosure of their more disturbing fantasies, urges, dreams, and behavior. Some therapists, in order to promote trust and to help members pass through this testing period quickly, use suggestion to influence patients' attitudes toward the group before their first session. This may take the form of comments such as "I'm sure you'll like the other group members" or "In addition to your shared difficulties, you have many other things in common."

At all times, a therapist wants to minimize a perception of the group as a collection of conflicting parts rather than a cohesive whole. Medical-surgical patients share their unhappiness with the disruption of their lives caused by their illness, and this promotes cohesiveness within their therapy groups. Although each member may react differently to the reality of this disruption, the fact that it remains a shared experience helps cohesiveness to develop quickly because group members typically search for common experiences.

Small-group research suggests that an optimal level of tolerable stress keeps the group on the edge of learning, but beyond that point members are likely to withdraw from the group. If the group activity is completely nonstressful, it becomes comparable to a social group that provides no challenge for growth. Thus, findings from group dynamics on stress are directly relevant to therapeutic groups. Learning about individual reactions to different levels of stress can provide the therapist with an important therapeutic tool. In the clinical context, the therapist can induce a certain degree of stress in the group by making observations that are not so threatening that the group will fall apart but incisive enough that the members will want to deal with them. The therapist can pace the level of stress, adjusting the degree of confrontation according to his estimation of the tolerance level of the group. Useful questions for the therapist to ask himself might be: How much do I want to reveal about what I see operating in this group? Am I going to say everything or am I going to pace it? What is the group ready to hear and to learn?

Factors such as conformity and cohesiveness affect groups deeply and are strongly interrelated. It is helpful in understanding the complexity of group therapy to think about those interactions, as well as the interplay between individual and group factors. For instance, self-disclosure or self-examination is a personal function, while cohesiveness is a group factor that can promote an individual's motivation for self-exploration. Conformity provides another example. Some persons will come to a group as rigid individualists ("I don't care what you think or believe; I'm going to hold on to my beliefs and I won't listen to what you have to say"), and others will come ready to acquiesce to the group. Such self-perceptions will affect the group process and must be dealt with by the therapist and the group. In the chapters that follow, the authors will discuss ways of dealing with such situations. While there is no complete theory of human interaction or group dynamics, the material presented in this section has conceptual as well as practical value, particularly by providing a framework for understanding the process issues facing the group at any specific time in its evolution.

The Group Leader

In discussing types of group leadership, Shapiro (1978, p. 116) states, "Each leader brings his or her unique skills, personality, beliefs and values to the group. . . . For this reason, any classification system will do injustice to individual group therapists." This view is supported by the research on encounter groups conducted by Lieberman, Yalom, and Miles (1973). They found little similarity in the leadership styles or treatment effectiveness of group leaders adhering to identical theoretical perspectives. However, a close correlation was found between leader behavior and outcome. Two leader orientations were associated with higher casualty rates than others: "energizing" and "laissez-faire." The energizer was defined as a charismatic, verbally aggressive, confrontational leader who saw himself, as did the group members, as an extremely powerful figure. Casualties resulted when negative feedback from the leader or from group members to other group members was not regulated through protective norms.

Lieberman and his associates also found that a greater number of casualties resulted when group norms were unclear; that is, when the leader took a laissez-faire attitude. This and other research (see Hartley, Roback, and Abramowitz, 1976) emphasizes the powerful negative effect that an inadequately led group can have on individual members.

Shapiro (1978) states that group leaders generally play five important roles: (1) information disseminator, (2) catalyst, (3) orchestrator, (4) model for learning, and (5) dispenser of reinforcement and environment manipulator.

Information Disseminator. According to Shapiro, the leader must present information "individualized to the recipient's needs and motivational levels" (p. 124), particularly early in the group and again at its termination. However, information must be disseminated in moderation, because a reliance upon this role can lead to a classroom lecture situation and the likely development of a hostile dependency on the therapist. In contrast, too little information dissemination can lead to what Shapiro refers to as "wasteful nondirectiveness" (p. 124).

Catalyst. In this role the group leader serves as both a "spark plug" for the group and an ensurer of group movement toward desired goals. The therapist tries to motivate participants to risk revealing their personal beliefs and fantasies, points out subtle nonverbal communications, and reflects group levels of involvement.

Orchestrator. In this role, the group leader attempts to bring members' problems and needs into contact with group resources (that is, members who can be helpful). If this role is properly fulfilled, Shapiro believes that it increases members' participation in problem solving; this leadership function becomes unnecessary after members have acquired the ability to communicate spontaneously with one another.

Model for Learning. The group leader demonstrates openness to new learning, spontaneity, caring, sincerity, appropriate assertiveness, communication of empathy, and nondefensiveness. Members can acquire these behaviors through imitative learning and use them to further their own growth (for instance, by openly and nondefensively examining their own behavior).

Dispenser of Reinforcement and Environment Manipulator. Shapiro (1978), like others, notes that moderate levels of anxiety are necessary to optimize the amount of learning that takes place. Since ambiguity and anxiety are linearly related, the therapist can raise anxiety by lowering the degree of structure in the situation and reduce anxiety by adding structure. The means for controlling structure is through selective reinforcement. The author recommends such behaviors as head nodding, verbal acknowledgment, giving attention, and smiling. Overmanipulation will cause group members to mistrust the therapist, while too little will likely produce a laissez-faire, understructured atmosphere.

Based upon his group research, Lieberman (1980) believes that all leaders, regardless of their theoretical orientation, engage in four fundamental functions: emotional stimulation, support, meaning attribution, and executive tasks. Leaders vary, however, in the emphasis they place on each function.

Emotional Stimulation. A basic function of a group therapist is to help make group members emotionally involved and responsive. However, the tactics for doing so vary widely among leaders and include self-disclosing, challenging, expressing anger or warmth, and so forth. Lieberman (1980) also notes the use of role-playing techniques, simulated games, and various structured exercises. Leaders preferring low levels of stimulating behavior are more likely to use techniques such as elicitation and questions.

Support. This function is necessary to help group participants deal with the heightened emotional atmosphere often found in groups. Specifically, support and caring are offered to help members manage the anxiety inherent in the change process.

Meaning Attribution. Lieberman's research indicates that all leaders of people-changing groups attempt to "provide members with some means of translating feelings and behavior into ideas" (1980, p. 511). Some leaders use educational methods, others label experiences as they occur, and still others utilize exercises intended to provide participants with new ideas about themselves and their behavior.

Executive Tasks. Each group is a social system and as such must be organized toward attaining its goals. The leader's role includes direct executive tasks such as establishing rules (when and where the group is to meet), helping to determine group goals, and keeping the group focused. Indirect executive functions include selecting members, preparing persons to enter the group, and determining the group composition. Lieberman (1980, p. 512) notes that "composing the group membership in some ordered way has been clinically and empirically demonstrated to be a powerful strategy for affecting the productivity of a change group."

Yalom (1975, p. 105) makes the important point that "underlying all considerations of technique there must be a consistent, positive relationship between therapist and patient. The basic posture of the therapist to his patient must be one of concern, acceptance, genuineness, and empathy." The leader's personality is of critical importance and can either enhance or detract from his techniques. In his excellent chapter on the group therapist, Shapiro (1978) lists and discusses ten personality traits characteristic of an effective group therapist: honesty, integrity, patience, courage, flexibility, warmth, empathy, intelligence, timing, and self-knowledge. These personality attributes are self-evident and will not be discussed. It is important to monitor continuously the impact of a leader's personality on the effectiveness of his therapeutic methods.

Advantages and Pitfalls of Homogeneous Groups

In her fine book on groups, Marram (1973) states that the strength of special-problem groups is their homogeneity. The members share common problems and thus can share mutual concerns and fears while simultaneously feeling understood and accepted. This is particularly true of cancer patients, who often feel others are incapable of really understanding what they are experiencing. Homogeneous groups also allow patients to give up the "silent sufferer" role. Many patients with chronic illness such as cancer are reluctant to share their distress with family members or friends for fear of upsetting them.

I believe that an additional value of homogeneous medical patient groups is that they provide unique learning environments for their members. A group comprised of patients with markedly different disorders or a group of physically healthy persons would not concentrate sufficiently on particular concerns associated with specific disorders (for example, the concern of the patient with the spinal cord injury about his future sexual functioning). Obviously, the issues and goals of treatment for patients with peptic ulcers would be very different from those for patients with leukemia. Since homogeneous groups are likely to be composed of persons afflicted to varying degrees, they also offer patients the opportunity to learn from each other at different levels of adaptation.

Exposure to different personality styles and thus to different ways of viewing and coping with the same illness may cause group members to relinquish stereotypical beliefs about how one copes with a given disease. For example, a group identity of "We are all cancer victims" would ideally change to "We are all unique persons with unique ways of looking at and dealing with our cancer." This is an important point, since a leader's emphasis on shared problems to the neglect of individual differences would rob the group of valuable resources. It would perhaps also permit members to evade issues crucial to successful adjustment to an illness. For example, there are a number of reasons why a person may have difficulty in dealing with a particular disorder, but the real issue may be how this person copes with threatening situations. Some people become guilty, others explosive, and others withdrawn.

A medically ill person's reaction to his disturbance is a complicated outgrowth of his pre-illness coping strategies, his self-concept (particularly, his physical self-concept), his attitude and that of his reference groups toward illness, his previous experience with his disorder, his fantasies about it, and so forth.

These individual factors must not be overlooked by the group leader. It is important to recognize that members of the group are not just persons having difficulty coping with the same illness. They are individuals whose personal histories have not prepared them to deal effectively with a major threat in their lives and who thus require retraining in order to deal with current and future threatening situations. Learning to be problem solvers in dealing with threatening situations is of particular value to individuals with progressive diseases, who must continue to face new threats and challenges in the future.

Homogeneous medical patient groups have inherent problems as well as advantages. Foremost is the danger that the group will become overly cohesive around a negative theme, such as "No one understands us." Members may present a unified front against society and possibly even reject the physically healthy therapist! In other words, the individual's primary reference group may be drawn from the world of illness, which reinforces withdrawal from the pre-illness interpersonal field. As Cassell (1979, p. 111) so empathically states, "It is sad but inevitable when patients die from diseases that we cannot control, but it is an absolutely unnecessary tragedy when the same patients die alone and disconnected from their social world, like a sailor fallen overboard at night."

References

Abram, H. "The Psychology of Chronic Illness." *Reflections,* 1981, *16,* 26-34.

Anthony, E. J. "The History of Group Psychotherapy." In H. Kaplan and B. Sadock (Eds.), *The Origins of Group Psychoanalysis.* New York: Dutton, 1972.

Appley, D., and Winder, A. *T-Groups and Therapy Groups in a Changing Society.* San Francisco: Jossey-Bass, 1973.

Asch, M. J., and Calhoun, S. "Group Therapy with Patients in a Respiratory Center." *International Journal of Group Psychotherapy,* 1966, *16,* 373-376.

Asch, S. "Effects of Group Pressure upon the Modification and Distortion of Judgments." In H. Guetzkow (Ed.), *Groups, Leadership and Men.* Pittsburgh: Carnegie Press, 1951.

Barnlund, D. C., and Harman, F. S. *The Dynamics of Discussion.* Boston: Houghton Mifflin, 1960.

Berkowitz, L. *Advances in Experimental Social Psychology.* New York: Academic Press, 1975.

Berscheid, E., and Walster, E. *Interpersonal Attraction.* Menlo Park, Calif.: Addison-Wesley, 1978.

Blumenfield, M. "The Psychological Reactions to Physical Illness." In R. Simons and H. Pardes (Eds.), *Understanding Human Behavior in Health and Illness.* Baltimore: Williams & Wilkins, 1977.

Brehm, J. W. *A Theory of Psychological Reactance.* New York: Academic Press, 1966.

Buck, R. W. "Class Method in Treatment of Essential Hypertension." *Annals of Internal Medicine,* 1937, *11,* 514-518.

Cartwright, D., and Zander, A. (Eds.). *Group Dynamics: Research and Theory.* New York: Harper & Row, 1968.

Cassell, E. J. "Reactions to Physical Illness and Hospitalization." In G. Usdin and J. M. Lewis (Eds.), *Psychiatry in General Medical Practice.* New York: McGraw-Hill, 1979.

Chafetz, M. E., and others. "Short-Term Group Psychotherapy of Patients with Parkinson's Disease." *New England Journal of Medicine,* 1955, *253,* 961-964.

Christ, A. "Reactions of Children to Illness, Hospitalization, Surgery, and Physical Disabilities." In R. Simons and H. Pardes (Eds.), *Understanding Human Behavior in Health and Illness.* Baltimore: Williams & Wilkins, 1977.

Cunningham, J., Strassberg, D., and Roback, H. "Group Psychotherapy for Medical Patients." *Comprehensive Psychiatry,* 1978, *19,* 135-140.

Dickoff, H., and Lakin, M. "Patients' Views of Group Psychotherapy: Retrospections and Interpretations." *International Journal of Group Psychotherapy,* 1963, *13,* 61-73.

Festinger, L. "A Theory of Social Comparison Processes." *Human Relations,* 1954, *7,* 117-140.

Freedman, A., Kaplan, H., and Sadock, B. *Modern Synopsis of Psychiatry.* Baltimore: Williams & Wilkins, 1972.

Gilder, R., and others. "Group Therapy with Parents of Children with Leukemia." *American Journal of Psychotherapy,* 1978, *32,* 276-287.

Hartley, D., Roback, H., and Abramowitz, S. "Deterioration Effects in Encounter Groups." *American Psychologist*, 1976, *31*, 247-255.

Hollon, T. H. "Modified Group Therapy in the Treatment of Patients on Chronic Hemodialysis." *American Journal of Psychotherapy*, 1972, *26*, 501-510.

Kaplan, H., and Sadock, B. (Eds.). *New Models for Group Therapy*. New York: Dutton, 1972.

Karasu, T. B. "Psychotherapy of the Medically Ill." *American Journal of Psychiatry*, 1979, *136*(1), 1-11.

Lieberman, M. "Group Methods." In F. Kanfer and A. Goldstein (Eds.), *Helping People Change*. New York: Pergamon Press, 1980.

Lieberman, M., Yalom, I., and Miles, M. *Encounter Groups: First Facts*. New York: Basic Books, 1973.

Marram, G. *The Group Approach in Nursing Practice*. St. Louis: Mosby, 1973.

Middlebrook, P. *Social Psychology and Modern Life*. New York: Knopf, 1974.

Parsell, S., and Tagliereni, E. M. "Cancer Patients Help Each Other." *American Journal of Nursing*, 1974, *74*, 650-651.

Pattison, E. M. "Group-Treatment Methods Suitable for Family Practice." *Public Health Review*, 1973, *2*, 247-265.

Pratt, J. H. "The Class Method of Treating Consumption in the Homes of the Poor." *Journal of the American Medical Association*, 1907, *49*, 755-759.

Pratt, J. H. "Results Obtained in the Treatment of Pulmonary Tuberculosis by the Class Method." *British Medical Journal*, 1908, *2*, 1070-1071.

Pratt, J. H. "The Principles of Class Treatment and Their Application to Various Chronic Diseases." *Hospital Social Services*, 1922, *6*, 401-411.

Reid, J. "Group Therapy with Asthmatic Patients." *Geriatrics*, 1962, *17*, 823-830.

Roback, H., Kirshner, H., and Roback, E. "Physical Self Concept Changes in a Mildly, Facially Disfigured Neurofibromatosis Patient Following Communication Skill Training." *International Journal of Psychiatry in Medicine*, 1981-82, *11*, 137-143.

Schachter, S. *The Psychology of Affiliation*. Stanford, Calif.: Stanford University Press, 1959.

Shapiro, J. *Methods of Group Psychotherapy and Encounter*. Itasca, Ill.: Peacock, 1978.

Shaw, M. *Group Dynamics*. New York: McGraw-Hill, 1971.

Stein, A. "Psychosomatic Disorder." In S. R. Slavson (Ed.), *The Fields of Group Psychotherapy*. New York: International Universities Press, 1956.

Thomas, G. "Group Psychotherapy: A Review of the Literature." *Psychosomatic Medicine*, 1943, *5*, 166–180.

Walker, J. I. *Clinical Psychiatry in Primary Care*. Menlo Park, Calif.: Addison-Wesley, 1981.

Whiteley, J., and Gordon, J. *Group Approaches to Psychiatry*. Boston: Routledge & Kegan Paul, 1979.

Wood, P. E., and others. "Group Counseling for Cancer Patients in a Community Hospital." *Psychosomatics*, 1978, *19*, 555–561.

Yalom, I. *The Theory and Practice of Group Psychotherapy*. New York: Basic Books, 1975.

Part One

▦ ▦ ▦ ▦ ▦ ▦ ▦ ▦ ▦ ▦ ▦ ▦ ▦

Group Treatments for Patients with Specific Medical Problems

Part One focuses on therapeutic groups for medical-surgical patients, in which family members often participate. Chapters Two through Four concern patients whose medical conditions are somewhat psychologically determined. In Chapter Two, Charles Ford, who has extensive experience working with somatizing patients, cites studies showing that a significant proportion of patients who present physical symptoms have no corresponding evidence of disease. Ford discusses two major patterns of somatization (hypochondriasis and Briquet's syndrome) and their treatment implications. Ford's chapter also stresses how differences in techniques used with somatizing patients differ from those used with traditional psychiatric patients.

Janet Polivy and Paul Garfinkel are among North America's foremost authorities on anorexia nervosa, a functional disorder that can lead to life-threatening medical conditions. In Chapter Three, they discuss their experience in using treatment groups as part of a multifaceted treatment program for patients with anorexia nervosa. The authors also attempt to identify patient characteristics associated with successful treatment.

Chronic pain patients, whose response to physical pain is determined by various psychological factors, are discussed in Chapter Four, which was written by Nelson Hendler. Hendler, an authority on chronic pain, discusses both inpatient and outpatient groups for this challenging population. Differences in leadership roles within the two groups are emphasized.

Chapters Five through Eight review group approaches for patients with medical disorders involving significant physical limitations (spinal cord injury and amputation) and restrictions due to the need for proximity to special medical care, such as renal patients dependent on dialysis machines and patients with serious chronic lung disease.

Group techniques in working with spinal-cord-injured patients are addressed in Chapter Five by Myron Eisenberg, who has received numerous professional and civic awards for his work with these patients. He presents a stage theory approach for understanding adjustment to physical disability and then describes both a patient-family and sexual counseling group program for these patients.

Chapter Six, by Joy Rogers, describes a unique endeavor in which consultants experienced in psychosocial interventions and research collaborated with the staff of an inpatient amputee rehabilitation unit to explore the emotional needs of their patients, develop an innovative program, evaluate its impact, and then incorporate the program into the overall treatment method of the rehabilitation unit.

In Chapter Seven, Stephen Armstrong presents a systems approach for working with renal disease patients. Armstrong candidly discusses the difficulties of being a psychotherapist on a medically oriented team, the importance of attending to staff as well as patient needs and problems, and how to prevent interdisciplinary difficulties from interfering with the group's prog-

ress. This chapter should prove a valuable resource for persons planning to establish groups for hemodialysis patients.

Chapter Eight by Mansell Pattison focuses on group work for patients having chronic lung disease. The particular group population with whom Pattison works includes many persons with preexisting psychopathology who are poorly prepared for coping with the stress of a severe illness and the necessary hospitalization.

Groups for patients living with uncertain prognoses or imminent death are discussed in Chapters Nine through Twelve.

In Chapter Nine, Andrew Razin describes his "cardiac stress management training" program for modifying Type A behavior in patients with coronary artery disease. Razin, who is a highly regarded researcher as well as a superb clinician, also presents findings from the evaluations of his program.

In Chapter Ten, Mary Jerse, Helen Whitman, and James Gustafson discuss their group work with cancer patients and their families. Through its eight-year history, the Wisconsin cancer group has served as a model for other groups of its kind. Group sessions, which are conducted among patients in an inpatient oncology ward, focus on affective issues rather than on providing information about the disease and its treatment. A transcript of a group session is presented and discussed.

Susan Lewis's chapter on adolescents with cancer, Chapter Eleven, highlights the developmental issues to which group leaders must be sensitive in working with this population. For example, prolonged dependence, impact on body image, and worries about sexual relationships are particularly important to adolescent cancer patients.

Stephen Shanfield and Daniel McDonnell, in Chapter Twelve, address the role of group interventions in caring for dying persons. Like Lewis, these authors discuss the role of developmental issues in group work with their target population, the dying elderly. McDonnell is executive director and a group leader at St. Mary's Hospice (formerly Hillhaven Hospice), which was the first freestanding hospice in the United States. Shanfield is a psychiatric consultant to the hospice and is well-known for his work with dying patients and their families.

The final two chapters in Part One discuss patients with

chronic medical conditions characterized by a highly unpredictable pattern of acute crises and remissions: multiple sclerosis (Chapter Thirteen by Marcia Pavlou) and sickle cell anemia (Chapter Fourteen by Robert Marcovitz). Pavlou, who is associate director of the Rush Multiple Sclerosis Center, has organized and conducted groups for MS patients for a number of years. She has investigated such topics as psychological factors and the outcome in MS, the child in the MS family, and, more pertinent to this book, the outcome of counseling MS groups. She provides many insightful comments about the unspoken fears and concerns harbored by marital couples in which one member has MS. The group appears to be a valuable setting for expressing and resolving these issues.

Marcovitz's chapter describes the experience of working with a group of patients with sickle cell anemia, a population that has received limited attention from psychosocial care givers. Perhaps their most unique problem is the painful sickle-cell crisis, which has unpredictable onset, intensity, and duration. Problems attendant to working with this population are addressed.

2

Charles V. Ford, M.D.

▦ ▦ ▦ ▦ ▦ ▦ ▦ ▦ ▦ ▦ ▦ ▦ ▦

Somatizing Disorders

Somatization is remarkably prevalent in our society. Most simply, it can be defined as the use of the body, through physical symptoms, to serve intrapsychic needs, to communicate with others, or to obtain some personal gain such as the manipulation of interpersonal relationships. From this perspective, somatization is a form of behavior rather than a diagnosis and no specific etiology is implied. In fact, somatization may or may not occur with an organic disease. An example of the former is someone who uses disease (for example, diabetes) for interpersonal gains, and an example of the latter is the classic hypochondriac. This concept of somatization is essential to the themes presented in this chapter, because the question of whether somatization is "all in the head" then becomes irrelevant. The issue under examination becomes illness behavior itself rather than a controversy over whether a disease is present.

It is noteworthy that a significant proportion of patients who present symptoms to a physician have no evidence of disease. Depending on the practice or clinic, this proportion may be as high as 40 percent (Culpan and Davies, 1960; Garfield and others, 1976; Hilkevitch, 1965). Across all forms of medical services (psychiatry excluded), a figure of 10 percent would be a reasonably conservative estimate of the proportion of persons presenting symptoms who have no objective evidence of disease (Ford, 1983). It has also been demonstrated that a relatively small proportion of the population accounts for a disproportionate amount of the medical services used (Hinkle and Wolff, 1958). On the average, 25 percent of all persons use 50 percent of all medical care provided.

The above figures reflect the fact that physicians spend a significant amount of their time with patients who demonstrate somatization. These doctor-patient interactions are frustrating, and the treatment techniques employed by the physician with a bioscientific perspective of illness are usually ineffective and occasionally lead to iatrogenic disease.

Nonphysicians who are in the helping professions often encounter somatizers because these individuals are usually dependent and needy in a variety of ways. As soon as a somatic complaint is voiced, however, the person is usually urged to see a physician. Such an opportunity to "refer away" these demanding, difficult persons may be accompanied by a concealed sigh of relief. The result is that physicians, whose training is largely biomedical and scientific, find themselves caring for patients who believe that their problems are medical but who in actuality have difficulties that are primarily psychosocial in nature.

Clinical Features of Somatization

Two major forms of recurrent somatization are well recognized. Describing these disorders in detail is beyond the scope of this chapter, but brief descriptions of the major categories of somatization will clarify some practical issues of treatment.

One form of recurrent somatization is that of hypochondriasis. Patients with this condition repeatedly return to their physicians, each new symptom provoking the fear of a serious illness. The hypochondriac is only temporarily reassured and then again becomes preoccupied with symptoms. As a group, these patients are generally emotionally constricted and are frequently latently depressed. Hypochondriacs often have characteristics of "alexithymia," a term introduced by Sifneos (1972) to describe persons who do not possess a vocabulary to describe their feelings. Another similar term, "emotional illiteracy," was previously used by Freedman and Sweet (1954) to describe these individuals.

Alexithymics demonstrate a mechanical type of thought process that is preoccupied with concrete details rather than abstract feelings. For example, if one of these patients were asked how he felt at the time of his mother's death, he might describe arrangements for the funeral or the medical cause of death. Persons who are alexithymic are not psychologically minded, have an impoverished fantasy life, and, interestingly, tend not to remember their dreams. While these patients are aware of the physiological concomitants of their affects, they cannot label these somatic sensations with words. Consequently, it can be readily seen how such persons might use somatic symptoms to acknowledge and communicate feelings of distress.

The etiology of alexithymia has not been established, but it may be determined by cultural, socioeconomic, or underlying neurophysiological factors (Lesser, 1981). Many patients with chronic pain syndromes also have features consistent with the common clinical profile of alexithymia and hypochondriasis. Reports describing group therapy for chronic pain patients (see Chapter Four) suggest many similarities (and some differences) to descriptions of group therapy for somatizing patients (Hendler and others, 1981; Marbach and Dworkin, 1975; Pinsky, 1978).

A second major group of somatizing patients are those with Briquet's syndrome (hysteria). These patients, usually women, have many dramatic symptoms, which at times suggest conversion disorders. The boundaries of Briquet's syndrome are indistinct and often become blurred with those of other simulated diseases, including malingering and factitious illness. A history of hospitalizations and surgical operations, particularly of the pelvic organs, is common among hysterics. In addition, hysterics often have periods of emotional distress or behavioral disturbances that may bring them, at least temporarily, into psychiatric treatment. These persons frequently receive prescriptions for psychotropic medications; thus, problems with habituation to narcotics, sedatives, or minor tranquilizers are not uncommon. Women with Briquet's syndrome often come from unstable childhood homes, and their marriages, often multiple, are conflicted. Sexual problems are very common.

These two forms of somatizing behavior, hypochondria and hysteria, can be differentiated as polar extremes in processing information (cognitive style) and expressing emotions. Hypochondriacs are preoccupied with details, worried about the implication of every new piece of information, and constricted in their emotional expression. Conversely, the hysteric denies or represses factual information, makes decisions impulsively, and responds to situations with a dramatized emotionality that is not deeply experienced; bodily symptoms are frequently a part of this emotionality.

These differences in the types of somatization have theoretical and practical implications for the treatment of affected patients, including group therapy. In general, those techniques that increase the perception or expression of emotion are useful for hypochondriacs but are contraindicated for hysterics (Murphy, 1982). Hysterics must learn to tone down their emotionality and instead use intellectual mechanisms to solve life problems.

Dividing patients into two major groups as above is done for didactic purposes but is obviously simplistic. In the practical clinical situation, a patient may evidence characteristics of both groups. In addition, many patients (with either hysterical or obsessive traits) may have borderline disorders manifested by unstable and emotionally labile relationships with other people, low ego strength, masochistic behavioral tendencies, and acting-out behavior (Schreter, 1979). Irrespective of the different personality types represented by somatization, most of these patients have some intrapsychic conflict. Issues of conflict include dependency, sexuality, low self-esteem, and troubled interpersonal relationships.

Etiological Explanations of Somatization

There are a number of proposed explanations for somatization. Each will be discussed separately, but they are by no means mutually exclusive.

1. The patient may be unable to identify emotions as such. Some individuals have difficulty in recognizing and verbally expressing their affective states (alexithymia, or emotional illiteracy).

2. The body may be used symbolically to communicate emotions or ideas (conversion disorders). When other culturally or interpersonally acceptable means of communicating certain emotions or statements of protest are blocked, a person may resort to symbolic body language. For example, a wife's anger toward her husband that cannot be directly expressed may be symbolized by posterior cervical pain (a pain in the neck).

3. Body symptoms may be used to manipulate and control relationships. For example, an elderly woman might use chest pain in an effort to block a daughter's vacation (and therefore separation).

4. Medical complaints can be used as a coping device to deal with environmental stresses. The continuation of physical symptoms after recovery from an industrial accident may be an effort by a marginally employable worker to keep receiving disability payments.

5. Physical symptoms can serve as a solution to an intrapsychic conflict. Chronic pain may serve an underlying need to suffer in a neurotically guilty individual.

6. Somatization may be used to establish and maintain relationships. For example, a person who as a child received only perfunctory care except when sick—at which time the parents and other care givers provided concern, sympathy, and increased attention—may, as an adult, employ somatic symptoms to obtain attention and sympathy.

Rationale for Group Therapy
as a Treatment for Somatization

There are many reasons, both theoretical and practical, to propose group therapy as an adjunctive treatment for chronic somatization. Groups can gratify the dependency needs of these patients, increase interpersonal skills, and provide a nonthreatening environment in which to learn to experience and verbalize emotions and wishes more directly. Social and affiliative needs can be gratified by group meetings, thereby reducing the need to somatize in order to establish relationships. Within a supportive environment, patients can be confronted by each other about their use of somatic symptoms to communicate with and manipulate others.

Although individual psychotherapy provides similar opportunities, group experience not only is far more cost-effective but also has several other advantages. Patients are less dependent on the therapist. A group also increases the opportunities for a variety of emotional responses to and interactions with different persons. Group meetings provide a setting for learning social skills and an opportunity to interact with others in more ways than is possible with individual therapy (Schreter, 1980).

As a rule, therapists have found that seeing somatizing patients in groups is less tiring and more enjoyable than seeing them in individual therapy (Ford and Long, 1977; Valko, 1976). One possible reason for this difference is that group members interact enough to lessen the duties of the therapist.

Techniques Used in Group Therapy for Somatizers

The following discussion differentiates group therapy techniques used for somatizing patients from those traditionally used for psychiatric patients. It is essential to realize that, with few exceptions, somatizing patients do not see themselves as having a primary psychiatric disorder. The psychological distress that is acknowledged by these persons is seen as a function of their somatic symptoms or the response of other people to their symptoms. Somatizers do not demonstrate resistance in the classical sense but rather respond to their own style of perception, which is primarily somatic and not intrapsychic. To argue with these patients that their symptoms are psychological is pointless and counterproductive: The somatizer knows exactly where it hurts!

Referring a patient to group therapy may initially provoke resistance. While most somatizing patients will accept the idea that there is a relationship between physical symptoms and emotions, they are usually reluctant to engage in any form of treatment that is perceived as psychiatric. A more productive therapeutic approach—and one that is intellectually honest—is to present the idea that life stresses frequently lead to somatic symptoms (tears are a concrete demonstration of a somatic response to an emotion). In addition, the idea that somatic distress leads to psychological problems is readily acknowledged by the somatizing patient. The therapist can then propose that the patient meet regularly with other persons who have similar problems.

To increase the likelihood of the patient accepting therapy, several changes from procedures typically followed in psychiatric clinic groups should be made. The first involves the name of the group; it should emphasize educational and medical issues rather than psychiatry. Something like "stress management group" is far superior to "psychosomatic group." To avoid the impression that a psychiatric referral is being made covertly, the group should not meet in a psychiatric clinic but rather in medical or surgical clinics (Friedman and others, 1979).

Another important issue in effecting a successful referral is that the therapist meet individually with a patient several times before the patient enters the group. This arrangement is especially important if the group is well established so that the rapport developed with the therapist can be transferred to the group. In addition, the patient will feel more secure in having a friend and ally at the initial group meetings. Thus, referring the somatizing patient to group therapy is more supportive and less confrontative than the referral procedure used for patients with neuroses or acting-out character disorders.

An evaluation of the patient's character and prominent ego defense mechanisms is desirable before referring the patient to a group. When possible, hysterical and hypochondriacal patients should be referred to different groups.

The number of members needed for a group is flexible. However, experience indicates that for obsessive hypochondriacal patients, an ideal group size is somewhat more than the traditional eight members. This increase is due to the fact that these patients are relatively nonverbal and frequently miss scheduled meetings (Ford and Long, 1977). A larger group is

necessary in order to provide a "critical mass" for patient interaction. Groups comprised of hysterical (Briquet's syndrome) patients can have fewer members because these patients maintain
a much higher degree of personal and emotional involvement in
group interactions (Valko, 1976).

Different schedules for group meetings have been reported. Ford and Long (1977) found that a weekly meeting of
about 75 minutes proved the most comfortable for both patients and therapists. The group reported by Roskin and others
(1980) met weekly for 90 minutes, while the group described
by Schreter (1980) met for 90 minutes biweekly. A coleader is
very helpful and enables meetings to be held when one of the
therapists is away or ill. Both closed (Mally and Ogston, 1964;
Peters and Grunebaum, 1977) and open (Ford and Long, 1977;
Schoenberg and Senescu, 1966; Schreter, 1980) group formats
have been described in the literature. Closed groups (no new
members enter the group after it forms) have an advantage in
that all members work together at similar stages of therapy.
However, open groups may be necessary because of high drop-
out rates (see the discussion below) and the need for an ongoing
resource for patient referral.

Effective group leaders come from a wide variety of professional health care disciplines. Represented are medicine (including psychiatry), nursing, psychology, and social work. The
professional degree of the leader is less important than the individual's capacity to engage the patients, to facilitate group interactions, and to skillfully and subtly translate to the patients
their underlying motivations for somatizing behavior. There are
obvious advantages to having a nonphysician as group leader,
since patients are not as likely to focus group discussions on
questions about medical problems.

The basic therapeutic strategy is that of education: teaching the somatizing patient new ways to relate to other people.
The assumption is that if the patient can communicate feelings
and wishes more directly, then somatizing behavior will become
unnecessary and gradually be discarded. This strategy does not
ignore the relationship between psychosocial stress and somatizing behavior, but neither is it directly confrontative or inter-

pretive. The process of therapy is seen as one of maturation rather than obtaining insight. Concomitant with maturation in the form of more direct verbal communication is the goal of having the patients become less dependent on others to satisfy their own needs. Somatizing patients repeatedly imply that because of their illness, others (including family and professional care givers) are responsible for taking care of them and for making them feel better.

To initiate group treatment for patients complaining of physical symptoms, didactic material can be provided over several sessions or at the beginning of each session (Buchanan, 1978). This technique, which has been well received by patients, initially gives the group the atmosphere of a class, a feature that is ego-syntonic to the patients. Topics presented can include the concept of pain, emotional responses to illness, grief responses, and addictive medications. Questions and answers after the didactic portion of the session almost invariably lead to group discussions and interactions.

Topics discussed early in group treatment inevitably center on several recurrent themes, including a sense of suffering that is not understood by others (including physicians), irritation and excessive anger at physicians for failing to achieve a cure, and doubts about how talking about these issues can be of any value. It is necessary that each patient tell his story of physical suffering and frustration with the medical profession. The therapist can help elicit these histories by assuming a nonjudgmental manner and making no effort at interpretation.

Techniques used for hysterical patients differ from those used for obsessive patients. Hysterical patients must be continually redirected to the details and facts of their life, and emphasis must be placed on problem solving through cognitive means. Efforts to increase expressions of emotion in these patients, who are already dominated by their emotionality, are contraindicated (Murphy, 1982). Conversely, the obsessive (and frequently alexithymic) hypochondriacal patient may express little or no affect and rarely uses words that reflect feeling states. The therapist must continuously look for clues about the underlying emotional state of the patient. This information must be skillfully translated to the patient in a nonthreatening manner. Initially words such as *anger* or *depression* may be rejected by the patient, who may be willing only to acknowledge feeling states such as irritation, annoyance, "feeling blue," or "having low spirits."

Early in the therapeutic process, it is useful to use the patient's language in order to establish communication (for example, "It must cause you pain when your daughter neglects you" or "I bet you get pretty sore when someone treats you like that"). Later in the therapy, after emotional feelings have been acknowledged, the therapist can start to use more direct words to identify the patient's affective state.

The somatizing patient characteristically lacks social skills; therefore, the group leader must facilitate group interactions. Such interactions develop spontaneously and more quickly in groups of identified neurotic patients, but somatizing patients are much more likely to attempt to maintain dyadic relationships with the therapist, particularly if the therapist is a physician. In such a situation, the therapist must continuously resist attempts by patients to make the group a series of individual doctor-patient relationships in which the patients constantly pose medical questions and make requests of the physician. To counteract such attempts, the therapist should redirect questions to other group members or ask other group members to reflect on the situation described.

Although most somatizing patients resist any attempt to label their symptoms as imaginary or simulated, they will accept to some degree that physical symptoms can be related to stress. The group leader can look for relationships between symptoms and life events and make group interventions that increase awareness of the relationship between psyche and soma. For example, the therapist might ask Mrs. Jones if she thinks that Mrs. Smith's headache might be related to the fact that Mrs. Smith's daughter, without warning, left the grandchildren with her for the weekend. Such an intervention may lead to a discussion of a lack of assertiveness, feelings of being used, and silent resentment—themes familiar to most somatizing patients. A more direct interpretation to the effect that the headaches symbolized rage toward an exploitative daughter would fall on deaf ears and possibly mobilize resistance.

One technique described by Peters and Grunebaum (1977) is essentially that of paradoxical intention. The therapist outdoes the patient's negativity through empathy, dramatization, hyperbole, and irony. For example, the authors reported that the more they challenged the value of talking about the hopelessness and seriousness of a patient's problems, the more the patients focused on how helpful talking could be. By sidestepping a patient's negativity, the therapist avoids the role of rescuer. Consequently, the patients are forced to adopt other attitudes and views with the net result being a new range of behavior.

Although most authors employ the nonconfrontative techniques described above, at least one report suggests that a more confrontative, insight-oriented approach in groups can be useful for somatizing patients. Schoenberg and Senescu (1966) reported success by a group leader who largely directed the group toward analyzing the somatic complaints as deviations from the group contract. These authors noted that for many of their patients, the group represented the first opportunity to discuss feelings such as anger, jealousy, envy, and inferiority in a setting where they were not humiliated. Some patients were able to recognize the compulsive and irritating nature of their complaints after observing similar behavior in other patients.

Short-term, intensive group therapy for patients with refractory "functional" physical complaints has been described by Melson and others (1982). These authors described a psychodynamic approach in which issues of resistance, transference, and termination are actively considered throughout therapy. A total of eighty-four therapy hours were condensed within a three-week period at an outpatient treatment center. Results as demonstrated by standardized psychological tests were impressive, and are discussed on p. 55.

The experience of Valko (1976) with hysterics is also somewhat novel. He initiated the group experience for these patients by providing information about the nature of the patients' illness and its name—Briquet's syndrome. Getting patients to talk proved to be no problem, and frequently the therapist had to intervene to keep just one person talking and to keep the group's attention focused on the matter being discussed. Emphasis was placed on the fact that stress preceded the onset of physical symptoms. It was pointed out to patients that stress often led to nervousness, which in turn led to physical symptoms. Subsequently, the group process frequently revolved around problem solving, for example, helping a group member learn how to handle nervousness or a disabling physical symptom.

Group Progress and Therapeutic Problems

Initial group meetings with hypochondriacal patients are characterized by a passive-aggressive withholding and questions about the efficacy of the entire therapeutic venture. This approach can be summarized by the attitude "I am here, I don't know why because it won't do me any good, but you can't make me talk." This period of the group process is the most difficult for the therapist, who must continuously elicit participation from group members. As mentioned above, this initial problem can be alleviated by providing group members information on physiological and psychological responses to psychosocial stress.

A common second phase of the group process is attempts by group members to create dyadic relationships with the therapist and to compete with each other for attention. Individuals attempt to establish that "I am the sickest of all and have suffered immensely." At this point the group leader should reflect common experiences back to the group so that group members can recognize that others have had similar experiences. With this recognition, some bonding of group members will begin to occur and the group will start to form a sense of unity. This process generally requires several weeks, and group identity may remain fragile for a considerable length of time.

The focus of discussion then shifts from the individuals' sense of suffering and mistreatment to a generalized external cause of the difficulties. The health care professional is usually cited as the cause, because she is seen as having taken the patient's money and failed to deliver the desired services. That the patient's demands are unconsciously determined and have been misstated as somatic complaints to health care personnel does not change the individual's feelings of injustice.

At this point in the evolution of the group process, the therapist is often caught in a double bind. There is the wish to further group unity and keep patients talking even though the discussion appears to be antitherapeutic. Skill is required to maintain the patients' verbal expressions of frustration while not appearing to reinforce the inappropriate projection of their difficulties. That is not to say that there is no reason for the patients' frustrations or no mistreatment by medical personnel. Rather it is important to gently redirect attention to the fact that the anger experienced by the patients is a pervasive feeling and that it is related to the fact that their desire to be taken care of by others has been frustrated. The group leader's task is made easier, in contrast to that of the individual psychotherapist, by the fact that patients can frequently see in others the personal behaviors and feelings that they hide from themselves.

Inevitably—and more quickly if the therapist is a physician—the group will begin to express feelings of not receiving enough help from the leader. This response will come in the form of complaints that symptoms persist or requests for medication. Again, such behavior must be handled with skill and more subtly than with neurotic patients; direct transference interpretations are not likely to be accepted or even understood by these psychologically unsophisticated patients. At this time, the patients should be reminded that a cure was not promised and that the goals of the group are, instead, to help patients learn to live with some degree of discomfort. When deserved, praise can be used as a reward to encourage patients to persevere. (For example, "I know that you're frustrated because you still have pain, but you showed great strength by helping out at your nephew's Bar Mitzvah last week despite your headache. Perhaps you'll feel better as you learn more about how to handle stress.")

The process of therapy must be continually directed toward making the patients increasingly independent, including the acknowledgment of personal responsibility for feeling states. The patients' efforts to make other people responsible for them, including how they feel, must be deflected, and the group should be asked repeatedly about how an individual might handle a specific problem other than by referring it to a physician.

Expressing emotion directly in group meetings provokes extreme anxiety in many patients. If anger or other intense emotional outbursts occur, it is not uncommon for several group members to miss the next scheduled meeting. When the group does all gather again, it may ignore or not even remember events leading to the poorly attended meeting. Because of this low tolerance to emotion, the therapist must adjust the level of emotional expression permitted in group meetings (Ford and Long, 1977). With too little affect, therapy does not proceed. With too much, massive resistance is elicited and therapy quickly comes to a halt. Similarly, the therapist must be cautious in confronting patients with intense emotions that are implied by their statements or by overt behavior. During one group meeting, an alexithymic man turned red and angrily jumped to his feet. When confronted, he denied being angry but later allowed that he might have been a little irritated. Helping patients to identify emotions is an essential part of the therapeutic process, but doing so too vigorously may be counterproductive.

The essence of the therapeutic process is the continuous investigation of day-to-day life and the patients' emotional and behavioral responses to stresses that are commonly encountered. First the therapist learns to recognize the characteristics of the somatizing behavior; then other patients begin to identify it, and finally the individual patient becomes more emotionally expressive. Gradually, usually very slowly, there is a change in behavior. This change is initially reflected by increased assertiveness and a more direct expression of affects, especially anger. Verbal expressions and changes in relationships with others that reflect an increased sense of self-esteem indicate that therapy has been successful. *These changes may occur without the patients ever having fully understood the nature of the problem or the therapeutic process.*

Poor attendance and dropping out of therapy are common problems among hypochondriacal patients in therapy groups (Ford and Long, 1977), despite the best efforts of the therapists (and other group members). Others appear to be threatened by emotion (be it ever so slight) demonstrated by group members or the sadness of some of the patients' situations. Excuses such as doctor's appointments, illnesses, and transportation problems are common; relatively few patients attend all scheduled sessions.

A frequent phenomenon in groups for somatizing patients is that of contact between group members outside group meetings. Such contact might be regarded as acting out and therefore be discouraged in an insight-oriented group for neurotic patients. However, among somatizing patients, any effort to increase their social contacts and to provide mutual support represents therapeutic progress. Group members may begin to make arrangements to assist each other in getting to group meetings or to call each other at times of personal crises (Mally and Ogston, 1964; Schreter, 1980; Valko, 1976). These steps can be the beginning of the patients' recognition of the importance of a social network in which there is a give and take.

Progress among alexithymic hypochondriacal patients is often maddeningly slow. Patients may attend sessions for weeks, months, or even years and demonstrate relatively little change in behavior. Like watching a child grow, the changes may be so slow as to be almost imperceptible. Only in looking back is it apparent that changes have occurred. In most cases, somatizing patients who continue with group therapy improve to some degree. At times, as documented below, the improvement is dramatic.

The group process described by Valko (1976) for his group of patients with hysteria is quite different from that described above for hypochondriacal-alexithymic patients. These Briquet's syndrome patients were much more talkative and therapeutic progress was very rapid. Group meetings were described as similar to small meeetings of Alcoholics Anonymous. Mutual support seemed to be a very important component for the rapid improvement in many of these patients. Patients quickly began to exhibit more self-confidence, an improvement in mood, and an increased concern about personal appearance. As with the hypochondriacal patients, the support created outside of group meetings appeared to be a very important aspect of the treatment process.

The average length of treatment for each patient with Briquet's syndrome was only a little over five months. An attempt to terminate the group because of the apparent improvement in most patients resulted in the reappearance of symptoms in several patients approximately four months later. At this time, the group was reorganized and again symptoms were relieved fairly rapidly. It was discovered that in order to maintain remission of symptoms, a maintenance program of group meetings scheduled approximately once a month was necessary.

Efficacy of Group Therapy for Somatization

One of the problems in measuring improvement in psychotherapy is the lack of objective criteria. Although such subjective issues as happiness, increased comfort in interpersonal relationships, and life satisfaction may be very genuine, it is difficult to quantify them. One objective measure that can be used to evaluate the efficacy of group therapy for somatizing patients is the amount of medical care sought by these patients before and after a treatment program. Using such an objective measure, several authors have reported impressive therapeutic benefits. The cost-effectiveness of such treatment in reducing unnecessary medical care is obvious.

Patients of the group treated by Mally and Ogston (1964) used medical clinics on average less than half as often as when they were attending group meetings. The number of clinic visits by group members reported by Schoenberg and Senescu (1966) after group therapy dropped even more dramatically, from an average of about twelve clinic visits per year per patient to an average of approximately three visits per year. Patients treated by Schreter (1980) with group psychotherapy also reduced their medical visits dramatically. For example, one patient who had made twenty-three emergency room visits in the year before beginning his group experience required only two emergency visits for the treatment of a pilonidal cyst during the two years of his group attendance. Another patient who was diabetic had made fifty-six unscheduled medical contacts during the year before she entered the group, including seven presentations in insulin coma. With group treatment she stabilized on bimonthly scheduled medical visits and group sessions and required only one emergency room visit for the treatment of a burn.

The patients of Ford and Long (1977) who were seen in group therapy over an extended period of time appeared to make modest therapeutic gains. A few, but not all, patients decreased their use of other medical facilities. It was noted that patients in this group were of low socioeconomic status and had many concurrent problems; when improvement did occur, it usually followed a fairly lengthy period of group treatment. Peters and Grunebaum's (1977) patients who were treated by group therapy also demonstrated behavioral changes following group treatment. These authors noted that although the women still complained of hypochondriacal symptoms and were still attached to their masochistic life-styles, there was evidence that they had made many gains in the quality of their lives.

Using standardized psychological tests to evaluate the results of their intensive group psychotherapy program for patients with functional complaints, Melson and others (1982) reported impressive results. Scores on the Minnesota Multiphasic Personality Inventory (MMPI) were significantly improved, as were scores on the California Personality Inventory (CPI) and the Cornell Medical Index (CMI). These improvements involved not only test measures of somatization but also measures of overall psychological functioning and sense of wellbeing. Patients also saw themselves as more in charge of their lives, as demonstrated by a difference in scores on the Locus of Control test ($p \leqslant 0.001$).

The results of Valko (1976) in treating patients with Briquet's syndrome were dramatic. In a relatively short time, these patients, who most psychiatrists would have regarded as having severe characterological disorders, dramatically decreased their use of psychotropic medications, their frequency of psychiatric visits (excluding group treatment), and their use of physical symptoms. Valko's patients continued to show symptomatic relief after the group experience, although some booster sessions were necessary to maintain remission.

However, some somatizing patients have used group therapy in an antitherapeutic fashion (Ford and Long, 1977). Typically, these patients have been pressured to seek psychiatric treatment by their primary care physicians. In one situation, an internist told a patient that he would stop seeing her if she did not regularly attend the group meeting. She subsequently attended meetings reluctantly and with passive-aggressive anger. At the end of several months, she announced to the group that her symptoms were no better and therefore her problem was physical and "not in my head." She discontinued the group abruptly and resumed a series of manipulative encounters with her internist.

Personal Reflections

As a physician who has seen somatizing patients in a primary care setting, as a consultant, and as a therapist, I can testify to the frustration and irritation (even anger) that these patients can elicit in others. Even when the somatizer is willing to accept psychiatric treatment, traditional individual psychotherapy may be almost painful for the therapist because of the patient's failure to maintain a dialogue. Successful management of the somatizer largely depends on transforming the treatment of these patients into an intellectually rational and enjoyable experience for the therapist. For me, using a theoretical model that emphasizes the patients' inability to communicate emotions directly provides rational indications for specific therapeutic interventions.

Group therapy, although no magical answer for the complex problems presented by these patients, has proven to be an effective adjunctive treatment and one that is personally gratifying to the therapist. The therapy sessions are more social than the intense intellectual activity required for insight-oriented psychotherapy. Relationships with patients tend to be more personal, and there is a pleasant satisfaction in hearing hearty hellos from patients as I pass them in the hospital corridors.

Psychotherapy with these patients is different, but it is treatment and, given time, it is effective.

Summary

Somatizing patients constitute a large proportion of the typical medical practice. However, on the whole, medical interactions with these patients are frustrating because they present with symptoms of disease although their problems are actually psychosocial. In general, the traditional bioscientific model of medical practice is not applicable to these patients, and alternative treatment methods must be considered.

One treatment strategem is to eliminate the need for somatization by developing other, more direct, more mature means of communicating emotional states. Group therapy is proposed as an effective way to improve patients' ability to recognize and communicate feeling states and to simultaneously gratify, at least partially, dependency wishes. The techniques suggested for groups of somatizing patients provide a supportive educational experience rather than any psychological insight.

Group therapy for chronic somatizing patients has been demonstrated to be a cost-effective treatment. Reports indicate that patients not only experience increased pleasure in life but also significantly decrease their use of medical services.

References

Buchanan, D. C. "Group Therapy for Chronic Physically Ill Patients." *Psychosomatics,* 1978, *19*, 425-431.
Culpan, R., and Davies, B. "Psychiatric Illness at a Medical and a Surgical Outpatient Clinic." *Comprehensive Psychiatry,* 1960, *1*, 228-235.
Ford, C. V. *The Somatizing Disorders: Illness as a Way of Life.* New York: Elsevier, 1983.
Ford, C. V., and Long, K. D. "Group Psychotherapy of Soma-

tizing Patients." *Psychotherapy and Psychosomatics,* 1977, *28,* 294-304.

Freedman, M. B., and Sweet, B. S. "Some Specific Features of Group Psychotherapy and Their Implications for Selection of Patients." *International Journal of Group Psychotherapy,* 1954, *4,* 355-368.

Friedman, W. H., and others. "Group Therapy for Psychosomatic Patients at a Family Practice Center." *Psychosomatics,* 1979, *20,* 671-675.

Garfield, S. R., and others. "Evaluation of an Ambulatory Medical Care Delivery System." *New England Journal of Medicine,* 1976, *294,* 426-431.

Hendler, N., and others. "Group Therapy with Chronic Pain Patients." *Psychosomatics,* 1981, *22,* 333-340.

Hilkevitch, A. "Psychiatric Disturbance in Outpatients of a General Medical Outpatient Clinic." *International Journal of Neuropsychiatry,* 1965, *1,* 372-375.

Hinkle, L. E., and Wolff, H. G. "Etiologic Investigations of the Relationships Between Illness, Life Experiences and the Social Environment." *Annals of Internal Medicine,* 1958, *49,* 1373-1388.

Lesser, I. M. "A Review of the Alexithymia Concept." *Psychosomatic Medicine,* 1981, *43,* 531-543.

Mally, M. A., and Ogston, W. D. "Treatment of the 'Untreatables.'" *International Journal of Group Psychotherapy,* 1964, *14,* 369-374.

Marbach, J. J., and Dworkin, S. F. "Chronic MFO, Group Therapy and Psychodynamics." *Journal of the American Dental Association,* 1975, *90,* 827-833.

Melson, S. J., and others. "Short-Term Intensive Group Psychotherapy for Patients with 'Functional' Complaints." *Psychosomatics,* 1982, *23,* 689-695.

Murphy, G. E. "The Clinical Management of Hysteria." *Journal of the American Medical Association,* 1982, *247,* 2559-2564.

Peters, C. B., and Grunebaum, H. "It Could Be Worse: Effective Group Psychotherapy with the Help-Rejecting Complainer." *International Journal of Group Psychotherapy,* 1977, *27,* 471-480.

Pinsky, J. J. "Chronic, Intractable, Benign Pain: A Syndrome and Its Treatment with Intensive Short-Term Group Psychotherapy." *Journal of Human Stress,* 1978, *4,* 17-21.

Roskin, G., and others. "Psychiatric Treatment of Chronic Somatizing Patients: A Pilot Study." *International Journal of Psychiatry in Medicine,* 1980, *10,* 181-188.

Schoenberg, B., and Senescu, R. "Group Psychotherapy for Patients with Chronic Multiple Somatic Complaints." *Journal of Chronic Diseases,* 1966, *19,* 649-657.

Schreter, R. K. "Treating the Untreatables: Identifying the Somaticizing Borderline Patient." *International Journal of Psychiatry in Medicine,* 1979, *9,* 207-216.

Schreter, R. K. "Treating the Untreatables: A Group Experience with Somaticizing Borderline Patients." *International Journal of Psychiatry in Medicine,* 1980, *10,* 205-215.

Sifneos, P. E. *Short-Term Psychotherapy and Emotional Crisis.* Cambridge, Mass.: Harvard University Press, 1972.

Valko, R. J. "Group Therapy for Patients with Hysteria (Briquet's Disorder)." *Diseases of the Nervous System,* 1976, *37,* 484-487.

3

Janet Polivy, Ph.D.
Paul E. Garfinkel, M.D., FRCP(C)

▦ ▦ ▦ ▦ ▦ ▦ ▦ ▦ ▦ ▦ ▦ ▦

Anorexia Nervosa

Anorexia nervosa is a psychosomatic disorder characterized by an exaggerated desire for thinness and by severe weight loss. Many patients periodically overeat and then try to prevent weight gain by fasting, vomiting, excessive exercising, and diuretic or laxative abuse. In this chapter, we review group therapy techniques used with these patients and describe our own attempts to apply group treatments to anorexic patients.

Until the early 1970s, this condition was relatively rare, but over the last decade it has become increasingly common (see Jones and others, 1980; Kendall and others, 1973). Anorexia nervosa affects mainly adolescent females, although some male patients have this condition. The ratio of male to female patients is usually cited as approximately 1 to 20, but the recent increase in the incidence of the disorder has occurred among females only (Bruch, 1978; Garfinkel and Garner, 1982b; Jones and others, 1980). Current estimates of incidence range from about 1 in 250 to 1 in 100 adolescent girls (Crisp, Palmer, and Kalucy, 1976; Nylander, 1971). While the disorder formerly occurred predominantly among people in the upper classes, females of all social classes now seem to be at risk. Finally, anorexia nervosa has traditionally been viewed as a maturational disorder with the typical age of onset being between twelve and twenty-five (Halmi, Powers, and Cunningham, 1975), but more recently increasing numbers of older patients (aged twenty-five to thirty-five) have been presenting with the disorder.

The symptoms usually required for a diagnosis of anorexia nervosa focus on eating and body weight together with the drive for thinness. Commonly used diagnostic criteria are those advocated by Garrow and others (1975) and the *Diagnostic and Statistical Manual* (American Psychiatric Association, 1980). These include the following: an intense fear of being fat that does not diminish with weight loss; a weight loss of at least 25 percent of original (premorbid) body weight or to a level 25 percent below normal for height and age; a distorted body image; refusal to maintain body weight over a minimal normal weight; no known medical or other psychiatric conditions that could be responsible for the symptoms; and physical symptoms like amenorrhea, lanugo hair, bradycardia, periods of overactivity, and episodes of bulimia or vomiting. Many of these symptoms appear to be side effects of starvation and weight loss.

Psychological Aspects

The essential psychological feature of anorexia nervosa is a relentless pursuit of thinness or a phobia of being fat, which is rooted in earlier deficits in self-esteem, self-control, and attitudes toward the body (Bruch, 1973; Garner and others, 1982). Bruch (1973, 1978) has pointed out that anorexics typically have extremely low self-esteem and suffer from feelings of worthlessness and a lack of control over their lives. She has related the well-documented distorted perceptions these individuals have of their bodies to their poor self-images and the lack of a coherent sense of self. Feelings of a lack of control over themselves or their environments have likewise been linked to distorted self-perception (Garner and others, 1976). Bruch has suggested that problems in body awareness go beyond distorted self-perception and include a variety of interoceptive deficiencies, among them the inability to recognize such internal states as hunger or emotional level. This deficit leads to concomitant difficulties in a variety of situations that require a reliance on internal signals, such as sexual activity. As a result of these deficiencies, anorexics are frequently preoccupied with conformity, conscientiousness, and perfection ("doing the right thing"). Exaggerated pressures to conform and achieve, not to please the self but to please others, have been linked by both sociocultural (Garner and Garfinkel, 1980) and familial studies (Garfinkel and others, in press) to the development of this illness in girls whose self-worth is highly bound to external standards for performance and achievement.

Crisp (1970) has emphasized the psychobiological regression of many of these patients; they seem to be actively avoiding physical and emotional maturity as a means of adapting to these deficits in ego functioning. Selvini Palazzoli (1974) has also described the anorexics' feeling of ineffectiveness and has further related this to a sense of intrapsychic and interpersonal distrust, attitudes that prevent the formation of close relationships and produce fears of losing control. These psychological problems are increased by the effects of starvation. Starvation leads to a preoccupation with thoughts of food, hoarding, sleep disturbance, poor concentration, obsessiveness, decreased sexual drive, and social withdrawal (Garfinkel and Garner, 1982b; Keys and others, 1950). Anorexics interpret many of these features as threats to an already tenuous sense of self-control and thus respond by increasing efforts to control their weight.

Treatment

Treatment must focus on both the nutritional-metabolic and psychological components of the illness. The issues of weight and eating must be addressed. Malnutrition ultimately threatens the patient's life, while in less extreme form it decreases the individual's ability to benefit from therapy. Moreover, most patients must overcome their phobia about body size by actually gaining weight. Most investigators believe the starvation syndrome must be corrected early in treatment (Garfinkel, Garner, and Moldofsky, 1977). Many earlier treatment approaches addressed only this aspect of the disorder, as if the problem were entirely an eating disorder in which remission would be achieved if normal weight was regained. Treatment programs emphasizing high-calorie supplements, bed rest, and the administration of chlorpromazine may be conducted without any psychological therapies (Van Buskirk, 1977). Many behaviorally oriented treatment programs focus only on the issues of weight and eating (Stunkard, 1972), which is exemplified in reports by Agras and others (1974) and Halmi, Powers, and Cunningham (1975). The groups described in these latter reports used reinforcement programs both in and out of the hospital; successful treatment was defined in terms of weight gain and an increase in appropriate eating behavior. Garfinkel and his colleagues (Garfinkel, Garner, and Moldofsky, 1977; Garfinkel, Moldofsky, and Garner, 1977a, 1977b; Moldofsky and Garfinkel, 1974) have repeatedly found that behavior modification can be a useful adjunct to an integrative program aimed at treating both malnutrition and psychological disturbances, although as a technique in and of itself (focused only on weight gain), it does not seem to be especially effective.

While some psychological features of the disorder improve when weight increases, others are accentuated (such as the fear of loss of control) and require psychotherapeutic attention. Traditional psychotherapies have long focused on the underlying psychopathology in anorexia nervosa patients, and many earlier writers advocated psychotherapy without tending to the corresponding metabolic-nutritional difficulties. These therapies produce results that are no better than those therapies that focus entirely on starvation. For example, Thomae (1963) described thirty anorexic patients who were treated with either classical psychoanalysis (nineteen) or dynamic interpretative psychotherapy (eleven). After three years, one patient had died, ten had recovered completely, four had only slight symptoms, nine had more serious ones, and six cases showed no improvement. Russell (1973), Bruch (1973), and Garfinkel and Garner (1982b) all felt that while the success of treatment can to some extent be gauged by a return to normal body weight, improvements in the patient's psychological state are of at least equal importance. Studies show that at least 25 to 50 percent of anorexic patients display severely restricted interpersonal relationships and episodes of depression and other sequelae, and about 9 percent die from the illness (Garfinkel and Garner, 1982b; Garfinkel, Garner, and Moldofsky, 1977; Van Buskirk, 1977).

Because of these long-term problems, many physicians now advocate a multifaceted approach to treatment that combines aspects of many different therapies (see Garfinkel and Garner, 1982b). For example, Lucas, Duncan, and Piens (1976) describe a combined approach aimed at correcting both inanition and psychological conflicts, which they found superior to tube feeding, behavior therapy, or psychotherapy alone. Their therapy had four facets: separation from the home and its conflicts, treatment of the malnutrition, individual psychotherapy that was initially supportive but became increasingly conflict oriented, and family therapy for those patients who would be returning to a family setting. Lucas and his colleagues reported that the majority of their patients had both maintained substantial weight gains and improved in their general adjustment up to three years after treatment.

Combined treatment strategies aimed both at weight gain and at psychological issues seem to produce the best results when weight and adjustment are the criteria of success. Even with combined treatments, however, many patients still do not respond well to any available therapy.

Rationale for Group Treatment Approaches. In Chapter One, Roback discusses Yalom's ten curative factors in group therapy. Kaul and Bednar (1978) reduced these ten factors to four sources of learning unique to group therapy. These four distinct sources are (1) the opportunity to participate in a social microcosm; (2) interpersonal feedback both similar to and different from that provided in individual therapy; (3) consensual validation (or Yalom's universality), which comes from learning that others have had the same feelings, doubts, and problems and provides not only comfort but also mutual trust and interpersonal intimacy; and (4) the beneficial effect of functioning both as helpee and helper, which enhances self-esteem and allows patients to attribute therapeutic gains at least partially to their own efforts.

Anorexia nervosa patients have several characteristics that seem suited to the specific benefits of group treatment. Anorexic patients are particularly prone to feelings of uniqueness, ineffectiveness, and low self-esteem, and generally lack information about such topics as nutrition, sexuality, their bodies, and the demands and responsibilities of maturity. Group therapy can provide models of coping (particularly in regard to factors pertinent to anorexics, such as weight, eating, and maturity), consensual validation of the problems faced by anorexics, peer feedback, and the increased self-esteem and feeling of control available to patients who can participate more actively in treatment. Groups also seem able to address the lack of assertiveness characteristic of many anorexic patients.

Many of the particular problems of anorexia nervosa patients thus seem both amenable and well suited to group treatments like group psychotherapy and specific-focus groups like assertiveness or self-help groups. Group therapy may be especially beneficial for the many anorexic patients who are not eligible for family therapy, either because they have already separated from their families or because their families are uncooperative or otherwise unavailable.

For patients who are admitted to the hospital, several types of group therapies may be beneficial. However, as with most psychologically focused interventions, these groups seem most likely to be useful when the cognitive and behavioral effects of starvation have been reduced. We have thus limited our groups to anorexic patients whose weights have begun to rise consistently, although other group therapists do not limit their groups in this way. Weight gain per se is thus not the goal of any of our anorexia nervosa groups; instead, it is dealt with individually by the patients and their primary therapists. In fact, we know of no groups for anorexic patients that focus on weight gain. However, a group may reassure patients about the need to gain weight and the need to accept changes in their bodies as nutritional rehabilitation occurs.

Types of Groups for Anorexic Patients. Several kinds of therapy groups have been tried or discussed for use with anorexic patients. Assertiveness training groups, for example, permit patients to express positive and negative affects more directly in a controlled setting, which prepares them for such situations in their day-to-day lives out of the hospital. Our experience has been that groups of this nature that meet for six to eight sessions are often useful for teaching patients much needed skills in expressing their emotions and asserting their own needs. As Grossniklaus (1980) indicated, assertiveness groups may also enable patients to have more confidence in acting on their own internal demands rather than purely in response to others.

Three forms of groups have been described for parents of anorexic patients in addition to family therapy. According to Sclare (1977), Hamilton and Hamill have described a group therapy program for anorexics that is supported by a second, concurrent set of groups for their parents. Piazza, Piazza, and Rollins (1980) have used a weekly group of parents to support hospitalized anorexic patients and to help the parents themselves in working with the inpatient staff. Such groups may help in communication and prevent the patients from leaving the hospital prematurely, which is more likely to occur when parents are uncertain or lack information. We have also found that parents' groups are useful, as Rose and Garfinkel (1980) reported. These were supportive, educational groups for people for whom family therapy was not feasible. A social worker experienced in family therapy served as the primary therapist, and a former anorexic was the cotherapist. The therapists' impression of the usefulness of such groups was borne out by the parents, whose ratings at the conclusion of the therapy indicated that they did indeed find it useful.

A less therapeutically oriented group, which nonetheless seems to benefit anorexic patients, is the ward meeting or inpatient community group. Crisp (1980) has described this as part of his treatment program for hospitalized anorexic patients. Although our inpatient unit is not exclusively an anorexia nervosa treatment center, for the past several years the majority (eight of eleven patients) have usually been anorexic or bulimic. Our twice-a-week community meetings for the inpatients, run by a social worker and the nursing staff, allow patients to discuss interpersonal as well as ward issues. While the focus is on community living, many patients seem to derive several of the benefits that Yalom (1970) ascribes to group psychotherapy. Specifically, the instillation of hope, universality, altruism, socialization skills, and catharsis appears to be fostered by inpatient community meetings in which most of the patients have similar disorders.

Although we have not had any direct experience with such groups, a number of self-help groups for anorexics have developed across North America over the last few years. The Anorexia Aid Society and similar organizations offer information and group support (including regular group sessions) to anorexics and their families. The effect of such patient-organized groups is likely to be significant when it augments rather than replaces other therapies.

Group Psychotherapy with Anorexic Patients. Group psychotherapy has received remarkably little attention as a treatment for anorexia nervosa. Some characteristics of anorexia nervosa may have discouraged the use of group therapy. The narcissism, manipulativeness, and obsessive self-concern of such patients may have fostered doubts about their ability to participate in group therapy. Indeed, Crisp (personal communication, 1979) reported poor results in an attempt to establish an anorexic therapy group. He suggested that anorexics might be unable to care enough about other patients to function effectively as group members. Other professionals may avoid group therapies because of concerns about the patients competing for weight loss or hardening into the identity of being an anorexic.

Two reports have recently been published about successful psychotherapy groups for anorexic patients. Yager, Rudnick, and Metzner (1981) described a therapy group that was held for eighteen months. This therapy group was one of several concurrent treatments, so specific gains could not be ascribed to group treatment. However, the patients indicated that the group was beneficial in allowing them to meet others with similar problems, to share experiences with them, and to feel less alone (Yalom's universality). The members were comforted by the feeling of being understood, although some patients found that the focus on their anorexic problems and symptoms was problematic. Being confronted with their common "games" was not always pleasant, and some patients found the overt expression of anger in the group threatening. Nevertheless, the authors concluded that group psychotherapy can be a useful adjunctive treatment for chronic anorexic patients.

The other description of successful group psychotherapy with anorexic patients was from our unit (Polivy, 1981). Like Yager, Rudnick, and Metzner's (1981) group, our anorexic therapy groups have been primarily adjuncts to individual or other therapy, so the therapeutic effects of the groups are difficult to separate from the effects of the other treatments. As Polivy indicates, though, results were sufficiently encouraging that a second group was formed, and we have offered group therapy to our patients since the fall of 1978. The rest of this chapter examines in detail these psychotherapy groups for anorexia nervosa patients.

The Clarke Institute Groups

Due to the demanding nature of therapy with anorexic patients and the lack of anecdotal or published reports on effective group psychotherapy with the population, our groups are designed to serve primarily as adjuncts to other forms of psychotherapy (usually individual therapy). Although a few patients have used the group as their sole or primary therapy at some time, the adjunctive approach has prevailed. While a multitreatment approach makes it difficult to assess the efficacy of group therapy directly, it also eliminates the need to focus on certain treatment issues like health status and weight gain, allowing the group to concentrate on shared issues and problems. Thus, the groups are meant to provide a context for discussing feelings about anorexia nervosa and its ramifications in an atmosphere where patients feel accepted and understood. It was hoped that the group milieu would operate as Yalom (1970) and Kaul and Bednar (1978) have postulated—to provide (1) models of coping, (2) corrective and accurate emotional, physical, and interpersonal feedback, (3) consensual validation about feelings (to combat feelings of aloneness), (4) a sense of participation in the treatment process and of being helpful to others (to bolster low self-esteem), and (5) accurate information to correct misconceptions. The main focus of the sessions is on experiential (that is, feeling-related) issues pertaining to anorexia nervosa and its effects on each patient's current life. Although some patients have participated while hospitalized, the groups are primarily outpatient groups.

Members. The groups are deliberately limited to patients who have been diagnosed as having anorexia nervosa. This is intended to foster cohesiveness and consensual validation; to promote acceptance of confrontation by or comments and criticism from other group members; and to foster a feeling of being with others who truly understand one's own emotions and experiences. For the same reasons, patients of similar ages are chosen (for example, we tried to avoid having a sixteen-year-old in a group with patients in their mid-twenties). Patients also must be able to talk in front of others and express themselves coherently. Patients with preexisting relationships with another group member or particular personality problems likely to disrupt the group (such as excessively competitive or regressive tendencies) are excluded. All patients are prescreened for these problems in interviews. Furthermore, either because of referrals or self-selection by the patients, our group members tend to be older and have longer histories of disturbance than the average anorexic population. Since these patients tend to be particularly difficult to treat, we expect group therapy to be fairly lengthy (indeed, patients tend to remain in group treatment for more than one year when they do not drop out immediately).

Group Size. Group size is limited to a maximum of five patients, four being the usual number. This allows all patients to feel that there is enough time for them to speak during each one-and-one-half hour session without having to compete or to feel guilty about speaking each week. Each group meets once a week (since the group supplements a comprehensive treatment program).

Group Process. Despite their lack of trust (Selvini Palazzoli, 1974), anorexics do not appear to adjust to group therapy differently from other psychotherapy patients. Most initial approaches are tentative, characterized by either limited input or nonrevealing chatter. As trust in both the therapist and the co-patients gradually develops, preliminary confidences are offered to "test the waters." Some patients become frightened by the developing closeness or the threat to their defenses posed by an understanding of their feelings and behavior. Those who leave group therapy at this early stage tend to have unsatisfactory experiences in individual therapy as well.

For example, one such patient left group therapy after less than two months, soon after the session in which she first displayed genuine emotion and experienced some closeness with the other patients and the therapists. She also suddenly left individual therapy at this time, signed herself out of the hospital, returned home, and resumed her previous outpatient individual therapy, which had been unsuccessful. Another patient who consistently avoided emotional contact in the group decided after several months that she only needed individual therapy. She stayed another year in individual therapy but did not manage to attain a normal weight; she also terminated individual therapy before the therapist felt she should. These and other premature terminators tend to be younger (twenty-one years or less), restricting-type anorexics who are still living with their parents.

However, most patients survive the initial phase of treatment and develop a strong commitment to the group, exhibiting the kind of cohesiveness described by Yalom (1970). One such patient was so committed that she persuaded the day care program in which she participated to change their rules so that she could continue to attend the group. This was especially remarkable for a patient who had always had problems asserting her own needs.

Interactional patterns typical of other therapy groups occur in our anorexic groups. Patients occasionally form coalitions, and individual patients attempt to ally with the therapist (in the first group) or one of the cotherapists (in the second group). Such coalitions (often involving phone calls or contacts outside of the group) are discouraged and brought out openly in the group sessions. Serious interpersonal friction has been relatively rare, and in all cases members were strongly urged to work out such problems in the group.

Confrontations between patients or between one patient and the therapist have been more common. The therapist has tried to protect patients from unwarranted and overly aggressive attacks and to confine confrontations to those patients able to handle them. Once a real attachment to the group has developed, most patients seem ready to accept confrontational feedback.

The issues of separation and termination resemble those in other group settings. Most patients recognize when they are ready to leave treatment and try things on their own. Patients are encouraged to cope without the group when they appear ready to do so or seem not to be benefiting from group treatment any longer. In two cases, termination was eased by assuring the patients that they were welcome to return to the group if they needed to. Only two patients ever required this, and in both cases drastic changes in their lives caused the patients to return to the group temporarily while they adjusted to the changes.

Difficulties. Some difficulties in treating anorexia nervosa with group therapy are relatively unique. The drives for perfectionism and control in most patients can lead to competitiveness within the group for the therapist's or the group's attention or competitiveness over being the best patient. Also, given the recent media attention, which has at times glamorized the disorder, and given the many aspects of treatment pertaining to eating and weight, there is a danger that being in a group specifically for anorexics might increase the patient's identity as being anorexic. Moreover some patients may learn undesirable behavior (such as new techniques for purging or vomiting) by associating with other anorexics; for this reason, discussions of such techniques should be discouraged. In a related vein, the empathy generated within groups composed of patients with the same disorder may cause patients to overidentify with the group or group members. If patients feel most accepted and understood in their anorexic therapy group, they may begin to feel that they should spend their time with other anorexics. This, of course, is not desirable. We have attempted to discourage such an attitude and try not to facilitate or encourage friendships among group members. All these problems can be minimized if the therapist is aware of them.

A more serious issue is the possibility that anorexic patients will use their membership in a therapy group to split their therapists, which anorexic patients are prone to do (for example, see Bruch, 1978). Patients may try to pit therapists against each other by portraying one therapist as being less understanding or by confiding secrets to only one therapist. We have attempted to avoid this problem by requiring that the therapist have each patient's permission to discuss the content of group sessions with the patient's other therapists, so that group communication does take place. In this way the idea that the patient's treatment is conducted by a coordinated team that is aware of all developments is established. The therapists also try to support and not contradict each other. It is emphasized that anything occurring in the group is strictly confidential, but that the patients' other therapists enjoy a special status. This point is underscored by openly discussing in group sessions any attempt by unauthorized persons (such as family or friends) to inquire about a patient's progress in the group. This policy seems to minimize problems with splitting, while maintaining the patients' trust in the confidentiality of group sessions.

The Group Leader. The group leader must perform several functions, including all the roles of leader discussed in Chapter One of this volume. In addition, the leader must provide information about nutrition, dieting, body shape, physiology, and sexuality; catalyze behavioral changes; orchestrate the sessions; act as a model participant; reinforce desirable behavior; provide emotional stimulation, support, and meaning; conduct the group as a social microcosm; and so on. The group leader must also be aware of the dangers confronting the group and its members and maintain contact with other members of each patient's treatment network. Given the complexity of this job, having a cotherapist in these groups is frequently desirable. While one of our groups runs very effectively with a single therapist, adding a cotherapist made starting a second group much more feasible.

In our second group both cotherapists are female psychologists with Ph.D.s. We thus have no experience in resolving interdisciplinary issues between cotherapists or in evaluating the desirability of group leaders of both sexes. However, since our other types of groups (like assertiveness, parents', and community groups) have successfully used leaders with different training, backgrounds, and orientations, it seems feasible to do so with therapy groups as well. The sex of therapists treating anorexic patients does not seem to be a significant issue for individual therapy (Garfinkel and Garner, 1982b) and probably is not a major one for group therapy. Since most anorexic patients are female, one could argue that at least one group leader should be female; a female therapist might understand more easily issues of sexuality and body image. Using cotherapists of both sexes might help promote the use of the group as a corrective recapitulation of the nuclear family experience.

Therapeutic Outcomes. As stated earlier, the therapeutic outcomes of these groups are difficult to assess because the patients have also received other therapies. Thus improvement during group therapy may be due to other treatments or the natural course of the illness. Similarly, patients who left group therapy prematurely or did not improve during treatment may have been more powerfully influenced by one of their other therapies. Given these limitations, we shall try to evaluate the success of our therapy groups as groups as well as their apparent contribution to individual outcomes.

Of twenty-four patients admitted to group therapy over the last four years, three left in less than a month because they did not feel able to participate in a group setting. Two of these have continued individual therapy and appear to have improved, while one severed all contact with our unit and her referral source and thus cannot be assessed. Of the remaining twenty-one, eight were restricting anorexics and thirteen had the bulimic variant. One patient was male, and only five were under twenty-one years of age. Five of the twenty-one patients were still participating in group therapy at the time this was written. Of the other sixteen patients, nine terminated satisfactorily and did so at times deemed appropriate by the therapists. Of these nine, eight made some improvement, although in one case this was clearly due to individual therapy, since group therapy only lasted three months and the patient (the only male in either group) was already doing well when he joined the group. In five of the remaining improved patients, at least some of the improvement seemed attributable to participation in the group, according to both the therapist and the patients, while in the other two improved patients, the value of group treatment was less obvious (although both patients said they felt the group had been of some use). The one patient who terminated unimproved had actually benefited from the group (and individual) therapy during a year of treatment but began to relapse in the face of extremely stressful life experiences. This patient left group therapy because her other problems overshadowed her anorexia nervosa, and she began to have trouble relating to the issues discussed in the group.

Of the seven patients who did not terminate satisfactorily, one died in a tragic accident after she was much improved clinically. Six patients dropped out of group therapy before the therapists felt they should. Of these, one dropped out of all treatment with our unit, went back to her hometown and former individual therapist, and later committed suicide. Four others left group therapy but remained in individual therapy for at least several more months. However, two of these were unimproved when they left individual therapy less than one year later, while the other two were both readmitted to the hospital within eighteen months. One patient, claiming to be better, dropped out of all therapy against the advice of the therapists. Because she returned to a distant city, we do not know whether she actually improved.

The patients currently in group therapy have all significantly improved. However, while three of them attribute some or much of their improvement to the group therapy, the other two patients do not appear to be deriving much benefit from it. Both of these patients seem to be gaining more from individual therapy, although both want to continue in group therapy.

In general, those patients benefiting from group therapy are somewhat older than the less successful group members and quite a bit older than the average anorexic patient, and they are often bulimic. Interestingly, although bulimic anorexics tend to have a worse prognosis than do restricters (for example, Garfinkel and Garner, 1982b), they seem to benefit just as much from group therapy. These older, bulimic patients also had a longer history of anorexia nervosa.

Because we have used group therapy strictly as an adjunctive treatment, we cannot say that group therapy sessions alone cannot be the major factor in alleviating anorexic problems. Our experience does indicate that group therapy is a viable treatment for this population because patients can interact in the ways identified as desirable by Yalom (1970) and Kaul and Bednar (1978). Furthermore, the patients develop a commitment to this treatment, remain in it for an average of one year, and feel that it is beneficial. The therapists also believe groups to be very helpful for some patients. In summary, group therapy seems useful at least as an adjunctive treatment for anorexia nervosa and possibly as the primary factor in therapy.

Future Directions

This treatment and its effects on anorexic patients have not yet been rigorously tested, which clearly needs to be done. No formal pretreatment or outcome measures were given to our patients, and ratings of improvement were imprecise and subjective. Such measures should be included in future assessments of treatment. Long-term follow-up should also be systematically conducted on anorexic patients receiving group therapy. Group therapy should also be assessed as a primary treatment for anorexic patients, especially given the increase in the incidence of anorexia nervosa. Group treatment as a primary therapy might need to be more frequent than once a week, but this would still provide more patients with treatment than individual therapy and thus be more cost-effective.

Other forms of group therapy for anorexic patients should also be explored. More structured therapy groups and time-limited groups might be of some benefit if properly focused. For example, a time-limited group might focus exclusively on one aspect of anorexic pathology such as the difficulty in identifying internal emotional or eating-related states.

Anorexia nervosa is a particularly difficult disorder to

treat effectively. Group therapy seems to offer many advantages for such patients but has rarely been used by therapists working with anorexics. Our experience suggests that group therapy is a useful treatment for this population and that these patients can both participate in it and benefit from it.

References

Agras, S., and others. "Behavior Modification of Obesity and Anorexia Nervosa." *Archives of General Psychiatry,* 1974, *30,* 279-286.

American Psychiatric Association. *Diagnostic and Statistical Manual of Mental Disorders.* (3rd ed.) Washington, D.C.: American Psychiatric Association, 1980.

Bruch, H. *Eating Disorders: Obesity, Anorexia and the Person Within.* New York: Basic Books, 1973.

Bruch, H. *The Golden Cage.* Cambridge, Mass.: Harvard University Press, 1978.

Crisp, A. H. "Premorbid Factors in Adult Disorders of Weight, with Particular Reference to Primary Anorexia Nervosa (Weight Phobia): A Literature Review." *Journal of Psychosomatic Research,* 1970, *14,* 1-22.

Crisp, A. H. *Anorexia Nervosa: Let Me Be.* New York: Grune & Stratton, 1980.

Crisp, A. H., Palmer, R. L., and Kalucy, R. S. "How Common Is Anorexia Nervosa? A Prevalence Study." *British Journal of Psychiatry,* 1976, *128,* 549-554.

Garfinkel, P. E., and Garner, D. M. *Anorexia Nervosa: A Multidimensional Perspective.* New York: Brunner/Mazel, 1982a.

Garfinkel, P. E., and Garner, D. M. *The Heterogeneity of Anorexia Nervosa.* New York: Brunner/Mazel, 1982b.

Garfinkel, P. E., Garner, D. M., and Moldofsky, H. "The Role of Behavior Modification in the Treatment of Anorexia Nervosa." *Journal of Pediatric Psychology,* 1977, *2,* 113-121.

Garfinkel, P. E., Moldofsky, H., and Garner, D. M. "The Outcome of Anorexia Nervosa: Significance of Clinical Features, Body Image, and Behavior Modification." In R. A. Vigersky (Ed.), *Anorexia Nervosa.* New York: Raven Press, 1977a.

Garfinkel, P. E., Moldofsky, H., and Garner, D. M. "Prognosis in Anorexia Nervosa as Influenced by Clinical Features, Treatment and Self-Perception." *Canadian Medical Association Journal,* 1977b, *117,* 1041-1045.

Garfinkel, P. E., and others. "A Comparison of Characteristics in the Families of Bulimic and Restricting Patients with Anorexia Nervosa and Normal Controls." *Psychological Medicine,* in press.

Garner, D. M., and Garfinkel, P. E. "Socio-Cultural Factors in the Development of Anorexia Nervosa." *Psychosomatic Medicine,* 1980, *10,* 647-656.

Garner, D. M., and others. "Body Image Disturbances in Anorexia Nervosa and Obesity." *Psychosomatic Medicine,* 1976, *38,* 227-336.

Garner, D. M., and others. "Does Anorexia Nervosa Occur on a Continuum? Differences Between Weight Preoccupation and Anorexia Nervosa." Unpublished manuscript, University of Toronto, 1982.

Garrow, J. S., and others. "Pathology of Eating, Group Report." In T. Silverstone (Ed.), *Dahlem Konferenzen, Life Sciences Research Report 2.* Berlin, 1975.

Grossniklaus, D. M. "Nursing Interventions in Anorexia Nervosa." *Perspectives in Psychiatric Care,* 1980, *18,* 11-16.

Halmi, K. A., Powers, P., and Cunningham, S. "Treatment of Anorexia Nervosa with Behavior Modification." *Archives of General Psychiatry,* 1975, *32,* 93-96.

Jones, D. J., and others. "Epidemiology of Anorexia Nervosa in Monroe County, New York: 1960-1976." *Psychosomatic Medicine,* 1980, *42,* 551-558.

Kaul, T. J., and Bednar, R. L. "Conceptualizing Group Research —A Preliminary Analysis." *Small Group Behavior,* 1978, *9,* 173-191.

Kendall, R. E., and others. "The Epidemiology of Anorexia Nervosa." *Psychosomatic Medicine,* 1973, *3,* 200-203.

Keys, A., and others. *The Biology of Human Starvation.* Vol. 1. Minneapolis: University of Minnesota Press, 1950.

Lucas, A. R., Duncan, J. W., and Piens, V. "The Treatment of Anorexia Nervosa." *American Journal of Psychiatry,* 1976, *133,* 1034-1038.

Moldofsky, H., and Garfinkel, P. E. "Problems of Treatment of

Anorexia Nervosa." *Canadian Psychiatric Association Journal*, 1974, *19*, 169-175.

Nylander, I. "The Feeling of Being Fat and Dieting in a School Population: An Epidemiologic Interview Investigation." *Acta Sociomedica Scandinevica*, 1971, *3*, 17-26.

Piazza, E., Piazza, N., and Rollins, N. "Anorexia Nervosa: Controversial Aspects of Therapy." *Comprehensive Psychiatry*, 1980, *21*, 177-189.

Polivy, J. "Group Therapy as an Adjunctive Treatment for Anorexia Nervosa." *Journal of Psychiatric Treatment and Evaluation*, 1981, *3*, 279-283.

Rose, J., and Garfinkel, P. E. "A Parent's Group in the Management of Anorexia Nervosa." *Canadian Journal of Psychiatry*, 1980, *25*, 228-233.

Russell, G. E. M. "The Management of Anorexia Nervosa." In R. F. Robertson and A. T. Proudfoot (Eds.), *Symposium on Anorexia Nervosa and Obesity*. Edinburgh: Royal College of Physicians of Edinburgh, 1973.

Sclare, A. B. "Group Therapy for Specific Psychosomatic Problems." In E. D. Witthower and H. Warnes (Eds.), *Psychosomatic Medicine: Its Clinical Applications*. Hagerstown, Md.: Harper & Row, 1977.

Selvini Palazzoli, M. P. *Anorexia Nervosa*. London: Chaucer Press, 1974.

Stunkard, A. "New Therapies for the Eating Disorders: Behavior Modification of Obesity and Anorexia Nervosa." *Archives of General Psychiatry*, 1972, *26*, 391-398.

Thomae, H. "Some Psychoanalytic Observations on Anorexia Nervosa." *British Journal of Medical Psychology*, 1963, *36*, 239-248.

Van Buskirk, S. S. "A Two-Phase Perspective on the Treatment of Anorexia Nervosa." *Psychological Bulletin*, 1977, *84*, 529-538.

Yager, J., Rudnick, F. D., and Metzner, R. J. "Anorexia Nervosa." In E. A. Serafetinides (Ed.), *Psychiatric Research in Practice: Biobehavioral Themes*. New York: Grune & Stratton, 1981.

Yalom, I. D. *The Theory and Practice of Group Psychotherapy*. New York: Basic Books, 1970.

4

Nelson H. Hendler, M.D., M.S.

▦ ▦ ▦ ▦ ▦ ▦ ▦ ▦ ▦ ▦ ▦ ▦ ▦

Chronic Pain

Patients with chronic pain problems may have a variety of etiologies for their complaint, ranging from severe and devastating trigeminal neuralgia with depression as the result of pain to "depressive equivalents," in which pain is used to express depression. Chronic pain of noncancerous origin usually begins to produce psychiatric problems in a previously well-adjusted individual by the third or fourth month. This is an important consideration, since the typical chronic pain patient who is eventually referred to group therapy is a "treatment failure." A brief case report may help to illustrate this statement:

Pam D. is a thirty-three-year-old white female who is married and has two teenage boys. She was well until four years ago, when in the course of doing farm chores, she was attacked by a bull that had escaped from her neighbor's farm. The back injuries she sustained were diagnosed as a ruptured disc, with resultant discectomy and laminectomy. After surgery, pain in the back and both legs persisted. She was reoperated, and a fusion was performed. Pain still persisted, and she had refusion, repair of a pseudarthrosis, and discectomy at a different level. Pain still persisted, and a CAT-metrizamide myelogram revealed arachnoiditis. At this time, she was referred to Johns Hopkins Hospital, where an epidural stimulator was implanted for pain relief. When this failed, she was referred to Mensana Clinic for residential treatment of her depression, marital discord, family problems, drug addiction (iatrogenic), and suicidal thoughts. After regulation of her medication, institution of appropriate antidepressant therapy, and family counseling, she was referred to outpatient group psychotherapy.

Why was group therapy elected? What could be expected from group therapy? What possible benefit could this patient derive from group therapy? The purpose of this chapter is to answer these questions.

Various claims have been made regarding the most effective treatment for patients suffering from chronic pain. Several authors have reported group therapy experiences with patients who have chronic intractable benign pain, rheumatoid arthritis, and terminal illness (Pinsky, 1978; Schwartz and others, 1978; Yalom and Greaves, 1977). These three types of patients share four features: (1) They have undergone conventional therapies without success; (2) they feel alone, isolated, and burdensome to family and friends; (3) they express anger at physicians for treatment failure; and (4) many experience reactive depressions as the result of their frustration and reduced activity. Some authors (Schwartz and others, 1978) consider these patients a heterogeneous group based on their social backgrounds, while others (Pinsky, 1978; Yalom and Greaves, 1977) conceptualize them as more homogeneous due to the similarities in their complaints. In our experience (Hendler, 1981b; Hendler and Fenton, 1979) these chronic pain patients may be divided into two broad and often overlapping categories according to their different responses to the presumed affliction of chronic pain.

Categorization of Patients

The first broad group of chronic pain patients may be called "objective-pain patients." They are characterized by the absence of preexisting psychopathology and by the presence of objective physical findings. These patients undergo stages of psychological readjustment very similar to the experiences of a dying patient (Hendler and others, 1977) and paralleling the stages described by Kubler-Ross (Kubler-Ross, 1969). In effect, their psychopathologies (anxiety, depression, guilt, marital maladjustment, substance abuse, and so forth) occur as the result of chronic pain.

The second broad group may be called "exaggerating-pain patients." These individuals usually have a dependent, anxious, histrionic, or obsessive-compulsive premorbid life-style (Shapiro, 1965) if not a frank character disorder or neurosis, and they manifest an exaggerated response to whatever minimal discomfort they may have. These patients rarely admit to guilt or depression as a result of their pain and usually suffer marital or social maladjustment prior to the onset of their pain. Even though attempts have been made to classify these patients by using a screening test, very often the boundaries between the two main categories described above blur (Hendler and others, 1979a). A copy of the screening test is included in this chapter (Appendix A). (Permission to use this test may be obtained by writing the chapter author.)

In addition, two smaller groups can be cited. A rarer subcategory consists of the undiagnosed patient. These patients had a good psychiatric adjustment prior to the pain, but the cause of the pain is undetermined. These "undetermined-pain" patients may go through the same reaction patterns to pain as do the objective individuals. The final category of patients are those that utilize their pain. These patients have psychiatric difficulties prior to the onset of pain, for which no organic basis is found. Typically, they deny any psychiatric difficulty and attribute all their problems to the pain. Frequently mood or thought processes are disturbed, and persons in this group might be called "affective-pain" patients. Their use of pain as an excuse for their behavior is an unconscious, psychological defense except in the case of malingerers. These categories and others are expanded on in other publications (Hendler, 1981a, 1981b).

This chapter summarizes the observations of group therapy sessions conducted on both an inpatient and outpatient basis from 1975 to 1982 at the Johns Hopkins Hospital Chronic Pain Treatment Center and from 1978 to 1983 at Mensana Clinic. The organization of these clinics has been described elsewhere (Hendler and others, 1979a). During this time, the author has seen over 900 patients in group therapy and supervised group therapy for another 350 patients.

At Mensana Clinic, the average stay for inpatients was 23 days, with a range from 3 to 125 days. Approximately 80 percent of the patients attended eight or more group therapy sessions, which were held three times a week.

Description of Inpatient Group

The majority of patients admitted to Johns Hopkins Hospital or to Mensana Clinic have musculoskeletal, back, or limb pain and have undergone back surgery an average of 3.7 times. All patients are required to attend group sessions; the therapist is a psychiatrist or psychiatric social worker. The average number of patients per sessions is ten, with a range from five to fourteen. If there are fewer than five patients, group therapy is not held, since the effect of a group is lost (Yalom, 1970), and the sessions quickly degenerate into question-and-answer sessions. Each session is a mixture of educational and free-interaction group therapy (Ascher, 1971) with occasional psychodramas (Moreno, 1972), but the content depends on many variables, such as the degree of incapacitation caused by the pain, the preexisting psychopathologies of group members, the male-to-female ratio of the group, and the average length of the participants' stay on the inpatient unit.

Themes of Inpatient Therapy

Though the content of group therapy sessions varies with the group, certain themes surface consistently. The twelve topics most often heard in inpatient sessions are represented by the statements quoted below.

1. "This is my last chance for help." The clinic is regarded by patients and referring physicians alike as a last resort. By the time patients have progressed from local medical care to specialist referral to university-hospital placement,

they themselves, their families, and their physicians have
become exasperated over the lack of understanding and
the lack of a diagnosis. If a cause is known, frustration
and a feeling of helplessness ensue. Some patients demand
and expect pain relief, while others are merely hopeful.

2. "It's so frustrating not to be helped [by the physicians]."
The basic assumption behind this statement is the natural
expectation that physicians can cure physical ills. When
they cannot, anger and disappointment with the medical
community usually follow.

3. "I'd try anything to get rid of the pain." Desperate patients are susceptible to the exaggerated claims of charla-
tans and have usually tried a variety of treatments. They
often exchange ideas regarding types of treatment.

4. "I can't do things because of the pain and I feel guilty,
helpless, burdensome, inadequate, frustrated, and angry."
This is a typical comment in a group of objective-pain patients and paves the way for dealing with the emotional,
rather than the practical, aspects of chronic pain.

5. "I can't do a thing at home but my spouse doesn't mind,
because I took care of him [her] when he [she] was ill."
This is a typical comment from an exaggerating-pain patient that usually evokes knowing glances from objective-
pain patients and nods of agreement from other exaggerating-pain patients.

6. "Why me?" This theme emerges quite frequently as the
chronic pain patient tries to come to grips with the reduced level of activity. The answers range from the theo-
logical ("God wouldn't allow me to suffer if He thought I
wasn't strong") to the rational ("Why was I selected?
What did I do to deserve this pain?"). Curiously enough,
Job is rarely mentioned, but anger at God is.

7. "I hate to be dependent." As the therapists explore this
theme, very often the entire dynamics of the patient's
dependency emerges. The need to rely on someone produces resentment toward the person providing the help.
Since patients depend on assistance, they usually become
fearful of expressing anger or displeasure toward the help-

ing person. Patients may also resent the fact that the helping persons are not performing tasks exactly the way they
would if they were able.

8. "No one believes me." This is an important issue, since
pain is a subjective, invisible problem. The absence of external manifestations of pain prompts derisive comments
from fellow workers and family, almost forcing the chronic pain patient to adopt outward mannerisms to communicate nonverbally the pain and subsequent disability. On
the other hand, these same external shows of discomfort
(limping, wincing, sighing, and so forth) can be used in a
manipulative, rather than a protective, fashion.

9. "I'm afraid the pain will get worse." Such fears are important considerations, since they reveal a lack of anatomical
and physiological knowledge. Very often such fears can be
resolved by educating the patients through physical therapy and medical instruction.

10. "I thought I was the only one with this problem. It's good
to know I'm not alone." Patients are greatly relieved and
reassured to learn that others have undergone similar feelings and experiences. This common bond enhances group
cohesiveness and validates members' feelings.

11. "I was beginning to believe I was imagining the pain."
Some patients experience a phenomenon similar to the
Asch effect (Asch, 1966), which is described by Roback
in the opening chapter, since they have been told by several physicians that they are imagining the pain. Because
of this repeated rejection by authority figures (doctors),
family and friends begin to question the validity of the
patients' pain, and the patients experience self-doubt. The
group process provides reaffirmation and support.

12. "I just want to be left alone." Very often patients with
chronic pain regard solicitous comments as an imposition
and feel that interacting with other people is a chore. The
isolating aspect of the pain process, that is, the inability to
participate in hobbies, sports, and even sex, tend to lead
to further self-imposed isolation.

Role of the Psychotherapist

As the composition of the group varies, so does the role of the main therapist. The group therapist functions as an instructor and pharmacologist in early groups, providing information about operations, tests, and withdrawal effects and the reasons for using various psychotropic medications. As the group progresses, the psychiatrist begins to function as a model for physicians in general, especially when he or she keeps repeating, "There is nothing I can do for your pain. Most of you will leave with exactly the same pain you arrived with." This statement is guaranteed to anger the group members, and they will respond in a variety of hostile ways, ranging from questioning their admission to being angry at physicians in general. This can provide the therapist with an opening for dealing with feelings of dependency, anger, and abandonment. At this stage of group development, the therapist may also distinguish between pain relief and pain behavior. In the most mature inpatient groups, the psychiatrist can use psychodrama warm-up techniques or full dramas to reenact conflicts (Moreno, 1972; Warner, 1972). Topics ranging from sexual and marital problems to suicidal ideation are discussed. Inpatient groups rarely, if ever, evolve to the point at which the therapist need not serve as leader.

Description of Outpatient Group

The outpatient group at Mensana Clinic is composed of either discharged patients from the clinic or those waiting for admission. The therapist is either the psychiatrist or the psychiatric social worker from the clinic, with the number of patients per group ranging from seven to ten. The group has the qualities of both a repressive-inspirational group and a free-interaction one (Ascher, 1971). Currently, there are three separate groups meeting weekly. Medical visits are conducted at the end of each group therapy.

Several variables influence the content of sessions, including the number of patients falling into these categories: recipients of workers' compensation, recipients of social security benefits, and plaintiffs in legal battles pertaining to the injury. Also important is the patients' status at the clinic—whether they are awaiting inpatient treatment or have completed it.

Themes of Outpatient Therapy

After the initial four to six weeks of organization and re-adjustment, the content of the sessions becomes more insightful and dynamic, as illustrated by the following seven themes most often discussed.

1. "I feel like a crippled person." This alteration of body image is a frequent theme, usually expressed angrily. This feeling is further underscored by reality.
2. "Vocational rehabilitation is not helping me." This reality serves to heighten the feelings expressed in (1), since chronic pain patients are often grouped with visibly disabled trainees (amputees and others confined to wheelchairs). The chronic pain patient, however, has no visible disability, and so is usually regarded suspiciously by the visibly disabled.
3. "It's difficult to learn to readjust your goals." Patients encounter the disappointments of reduced activity. This may mean an inability to participate in hobbies, sex, work, or exercise. For some, there is secondary gain; for others, there is open frustration.
4. "I'm worried about [the name of a missing group member]." This is both a sign of the formation of a cohesive group and a demonstration of concern for a group member. While this may not be unique in most groups, the length of time it takes for this feeling to be verbalized is inordinately long (six to nine months) when compared with normal outpatient groups. The slow evolution of this concern for others demonstrates the narcissism of chronic pain patients (Freud, 1963).
5. "You have to build up your activities slowly." Those predisposed to becoming more active usually express this frus-

tration as they attempt to increase their level of functioning.

6. "I'm afraid of losing my spouse." The denial of this fear seen in the inpatient group now diminishes, and patients begin to deal with this relatively common problem. Sexual factors are only partially responsible, while more emotional matters, such as loss of self-respect and sensing disdain or annoyance from a spouse, become more evident. Impotence and anorgasmy secondary to pain, spinal cord dysfunction, side effects of drugs, and anxiety and depression become topics of discussion.

7. "My attorney is not helping me get [social security disability payments, workers' compensation, a settlement]." Finances are often a major problem for chronic pain patients. Very often patients hope to return to their former companies, at their same job. However, a company will often not rehire injured workers because they are poor risks, and both union and company officials may resist creating "light-duty" jobs. They may also want patients to return to jobs with less pay without compensating them for the difference in income. Thus, patients have to rely on attorneys, and rarely do attorneys' efforts meet the expectations of injured workers.

Role of the Psychotherapist

While rapid turnover in the inpatient group usually prevents a strongly cohesive group from forming, thus forcing the therapist to take a more active role, outpatient group therapy provides a different setting. Usually by the sixth or seventh session the therapist can sense that the group desires the therapist to take a less active role (Ascher, 1971). In fact, this is more therapeutic, since reliance on physicians to help and dependency on others are central problems for most chronic pain patients. As the group becomes more cohesive, members begin to have "after-group groups" in the cafeteria and to form friendships and lend support outside of group sessions. That should be encouraged by the therapist, since this very weaning of chronic pain patients from physicians and the emergence of self-help are essential to reestablishing self-esteem and independence. As the process occurs, patients very often get angry at the therapist, which is to be encouraged (Ascher, 1971). This is a natural component of the separation process and probably relates to the dynamics of dependency; that is, the resentment is aimed at the object on whom the patients are dependent. Early in chronic pain, patients are afraid to express anger for fear the physician will abandon them. When this fear can be overcome, however, the patients are well on the way to becoming self-reliant.

Difficult Group Situations

A therapist must bear in mind several additional considerations when conducting either an inpatient or outpatient group session with chronic pain patients. First and foremost, the therapist must recognize that chronic pain patients have not been identified as psychiatric patients. Their perception of themselves is that of a person who has a physical problem, so they may resent their assignment to group therapy sessions (see also Ford's discussion in Chapter Two of group work with somatizing patients). As the result of this perception, a therapist will occasionally encounter a totally silent group, especially on an inpatient unit. This "resistance" on the part of the entire group may be attributable to several phenomena. The resentment the patients feel at being labeled psychiatric patients (why else would they be in group therapy?) may account for part of their resistance. The group retaliates by stonewalling the therapist. Then there is displacement of anger, which is especially common in a multidisciplinary Pain Treatment Center and even more so in inpatient groups. The surgeons are viewed as the real doctors, the care givers, the ones who can eliminate pain. The nurses are viewed as the constant support system, providing medication and assistance. Therefore, both the surgeons and the nurses are viewed as stereotypical helping professionals; not so the psychiatrist. He (or she) is viewed as an auxiliary member of the health care team—not necessary, not requested, and not someone who can cure. For that reason, group members find it much easier to displace their anger onto the psychiatrist rather than direct it at the surgeon or nurse.

The therapist must be aware of these covert or hidden agendas and must be able to defuse a potentially hostile or angry situation by offering empathic comments to the group. For example, resistance and subsequent silence—due to resentment for having to attend group therapy sessions in the first place—are easily dispelled by saying to the group, "I bet you really don't want to be here at group therapy." Usually, there will be immediate confirmation of this statement, and the therapist can then follow up with an open-ended question, something like "Why don't you want to be here?" This query usually elicits a series of reasons, such as "I'm not crazy," or "I came here for my back pain, not to have my head shrunk," or "Why do they [other doctors] think we have psychiatric problems?" The response to these comments can take two forms: Either clearly stating that chronic illness can create personality changes, and then asking the group if anyone had noticed changes in themselves, or by being less directive and asking if anyone has become more irritable, anxious, or depressed since they have had pain. In either fashion, the therapist can quickly lead into a discussion of the four stages of pain and how pain can lead to personal and family problems.

Handling displaced anger is usually a bit more difficult, since the therapist has to maintain balance between being a patient advocate (if the therapist agrees with a patient's complaint against a doctor or nurse, he or she may thereby offend a colleague and create staff splitting) and recognizing that the patient may be a chronic complainer (if the complaint is invalid, then the therapist would be defending a colleague against an unwarranted complaint). Either position is undesirable, since it places the therapist in the role of judge and eliminates the nonjudgmental attitude so important for therapy (Frank, 1973). Rather, it is best to ask the patient to air the complaint in full detail. The approach would follow the format described below.

Prior to beginning group therapy, it is always wise to check with the nursing staff, secretarial staff, or even housekeeping staff to see if any altercations have occurred of which the therapist is not aware. Typically, a postponed surgical procedure or lack of diagnosed physical cause will lead to an argument between patient and surgeon. Medication problems (late or missed), short or inconvenient visiting hours, and lack of response to a patient's request for help can lead to nurse-patient arguments. Armed with the knowledge that some tiff has taken place, the therapist can then more readily understand a group's silence when greeted with this resistance. If the therapist suspects the silence is the result of an argument, he or she may open with the statement, "I sense a lot of anger in the group today." Once the group confirms this statement, the therapist asks "Are you angry with me?" If there is a great deal of displacement, the group may suggest they are, for some minor flaw, such as being three minutes late while they had to wait, or leaving behind a dirty paper coffee cup or ashtray that they had to clean up. Obviously, these are not the issues. Therefore, the therapist has to be prepared to interpret the accusations leveled at him (or her), to determine if they are valid. The best construct for this is offered by Roethlisberger and Dickson (1939), who delineate three types of complaints.

The first type is one with an objective basis and an objective solution. An example of this would be a complaint such as "A doorknob is missing." Obviously, one can objectively confirm the absence of a doorknob, and the solution is equally as objective—replace the doorknob. There is no room for interpretation, nor any need for it.

The second type is more subjective, such as "It's too hot in this room." With this complaint, one can examine the thermostat and find it is set at 72 degrees Fahrenheit, which is an objective measurement. However, the solution is more subjective; for one person, 72 degrees Fahrenheit is too hot; for another, too cold. Therefore, there is an objective measure, but a subjective interpretation.

The third type is the most difficult to assess. This complaint usually manifests as subjective complaints with subjective solutions. An example of this might be "No one understands me!" There is no way to objectively interpret or respond to this complaint. When faced with the third, and even the sec-

ond type of complaint, the therapist must search for the underlying problem. The therapist must then determine whether the
group is displacing anger onto him or her by voicing subjective/
subjective or objective/subjective complaints. However, if the
group has valid objective complaints that have objective solutions about the therapist or other staff members, then the complaints should be dealt with directly. At all times integrity of
action is essential for maintaining trust. If an objective complaint with an objective solution is leveled at the therapist, then
it is incumbent on the therapist to change his or her behavior,
that is, pick up dirty coffee cups after using them, or arrive on
time if habitually late. However, if the complaints or the solutions are subjectively vague, the therapist can confidently search
for the underlying problem.

The entire issue of complaints becomes quite delicate if
an objective complaint is lodged against a fellow staff member
or colleague. These situations can be readily handled to the satisfaction of all parties if "psychodrama" is utilized. In this technique, a therapist will ask the offended group member to play
him or herself, and then ask that person to select a member of
the group who could best represent the offending staff member.
By having the therapist act as director the entire event can be
acted out, with the group or offended member offering ideas on
the accuracy of appropriateness of behavior that may serve to
help defuse the situation. Very often the act of expressing ani-
mosity to the health care provider is enough to mollify the
offended patient.

However, if there is group confirmation of the incident or
exchange then the therapist is placed in the uncomfortable situation of recognizing that the complaint against a staff member
or colleague may be quite valid, and that the initial silence of
the group was a hostile displacement onto himself. At this time,
there is only one course of action to take. The therapist must
instruct the offended party to speak with the offending staff
member directly. (See Chapter Seven, where Armstrong also advocates this approach.) Under no circumstances should the therapist offer to do this for the patient. However, the therapist
should tell the staff member or colleague in question about the

group session—not the content, but merely the process—to prepare the professional for the confrontation and to offer advice if needed or requested.

As an example of the above described events, a sequence of events from a typical complaint-registering group therapy session follows. The therapist enters the room, on time, having been admonished by other groups that they will not excuse his tardiness any more than he excuses theirs. He carefully places his coffee cup on a table—not the piano—having also been previously reproached about that as well. He is pleased with himself for these minor conciliations, and hopes the group will notice and compliment him. This would serve to indicate to the group that he respects them as individuals. Instead, he is greeted with an icy silence. The therapist is puzzled, since he has not heard news of any altercations on the ward. After three minutes of silence it is apparent that there is some underlying problem. The therapist asks if there are any problems with his behavior: "Are you angry with me?" There is no reply to this icebreaker, which signals an ominous situation. A direct approach is required now, so the therapist asks "Has something happened that I don't know about?" This is followed by still more silence. This prompts an even more direct effort: "Did something happen on the ward?"

One or more group members will encourage the offended party to speak up: "Go on, George, tell him!" George is still silent. Then the therapist reassures the group that he is not a judge, and that his sole responsibility is to listen to others without prejudice. He conveys to the group that he cannot help if he does not know what the problem is. More silence prevails. Finally, the therapist explains that he is not a staff advocate and that complaints really can exist that need to be corrected. He cites as an example his own behavior with lateness and coffee cups. Thus reassured that staff members can be wrong, George is again encouraged to speak and this time he tells of the offensive behavior of a nurse who chased his family off the ward during visiting hours. This complaint has two components: (1) the manner in which the nurse asked his family to leave (objective event/subjective interpretation) and (2) the fact that she asked them to leave because she thought visiting hours were over, when indeed, as written in the Pain Treatment Center Guide, there was still another hour (objective event/objective interpretation).

Based on this transaction the therapist asks George to act out what happened. George selects another patient, who witnessed the exchange, to play the nurse. After enacting the scene, the therapist allows George to say to the psychodramatic nurse what he really wanted to say at the time of the incident. George pours forth abuse. The therapist then asks the group how they feel the situation should be rectified. Some group members suggest that the nurse should be reprimanded by the therapist or the surgeon on the unit; others excuse her by attributing her behavior to being tired or having a bad day; still others feel she should apologize to George. George agrees with the last suggestion. The therapist then advises George to speak to the nurse directly.

However, the therapist's work has just begun. He approaches the nurse after the session, and recounts what transpired. She becomes indignant. First, she resents having been discussed in a group therapy session in her absence. She then offers her version of what transpired with George. She feels he was offensive, but finally admits she had been in error about the visiting hours and offers the excuse that she had been misinformed about them by other staff members. After some further discussion, she coldly thanks the therapist for telling her of the group session. The therapist later learns that she apologized to George for her error. Her relationship with the therapist remains formal and remote.

Situations like the one described here happen often in multidisciplinary pain treatment centers by virtue of the very nature of the patients and the necessary involvement of a number of health professionals. This setting provides fertile ground for staff splitting, missed communications, and competing staff factions (Hendler and others, 1979b). However, with adequate ward management techniques and a willing, cooperative staff, the occasional complaint-registering group therapy session can prove constructive rather than destructive.

Problem Patients

In a chronic pain treatment center context, there are five major character disorders that are disruptive to the usual group processes: (1) paranoid patients, (2) histrionic patients, (3) intellectually impaired patients, (4) obsessive-compulsive patients, and (5) passive-dependent patients. Each of these disorders will be discussed separately.

Paranoid Patient. When a therapist is faced with a paranoid patient in group therapy, especially in conjunction with patients who complain of chronic pain, it is important to consider the differential diagnosis for patients who present with this manifestation. In and of itself, paranoia is not a diagnosis, but rather is a symptom of a variety of diagnoses. These diagnoses include, but are not limited to, paranoid schizophrenia, paranoid personality, psychotic depression, amphetamine abuse, some forms of temporal lobe epilepsy, hallucinogenic drug use, and alcohol abuse. In extreme cases, where a patient voices delusions of grandeur, feelings of persecution, and hostile threats and appears to be suffering auditory hallucinations, it is imperative to hospitalize the patient, for his and others' protection. However, many paranoid delusions are more subtle, and a therapist has to be careful to differentiate between those patients with paranoid delusions and those patients who are highly suspicious.

A truly paranoid person in a chronic pain patient group is quite disquieting because some of the paranoid concerns, especially the feelings of persecution, may have some basis in reality. For example, the feeling of being spied upon by one's employer may be justified, as it is not uncommon for companies in certain industries to hire detectives to observe employees claiming a physical disability or seeking workers' compensation. The fact that these feelings are carried to the extreme is anxiety producing and disruptive for the group because the group members feel that under slightly different circumstances they could experience the very same difficulties. Therefore, when faced with the paranoid patient in a group setting the therapist must become quite directive. He or she should feel comfortable asking the paranoid patient to discontinue any discourses about conspiracies, harming other people, messages from God, or extreme religious experiences. Since these experiences lack the commonality that makes sharing them therapeutic, and voicing them only serves to raise the anxiety of other group members, gently controlling the paranoid patient does help the group function better. The therapist should bear in mind, however, that the paranoid patient who is asked not to voice his or her extreme opinions in the group should have the opportunity to express these views privately with the therapist immediately after group, so the paranoid patient does not feel additionally persecuted. Merely having the opportunity to speak with the therapist after group may make the paranoid patient feel somewhat special, and consequently willing to curtail discussion of paranoid delusions.

However, the therapist should be aware that it is quite possible the group may ostracize or isolate the paranoid patient, taking their lead from the therapist, who is making efforts to maintain group cohesiveness by reducing the input of this type of patient. As long as individual sessions are offered to the paranoid patient the isolation that he may feel from the group may be lessened.

Histrionic Patient. Another patient that tends to be quite disruptive of smooth group functioning is the histrionic patient. This type of patient makes every effort to call attention to herself or himself, and tends to monopolize group conversations. Frequently, histrionic patients will emotionally and dramatically outline their most intimate secrets on their first or second visit to the group, keeping the other members' attention focused on them. However, after this grand performance the histrionic patients will begin to have second thoughts about revealing too much of themselves too soon and may not return for subsequent sessions.

If a therapist is aware of this type of behavior, he or she can prevent a histrionic personality from revealing too much before bonds of trust between group members are established. When the histrionic patient begins speaking the therapist should limit the content and amount of time in order to eliminate the expose-and-retreat behavior. A histrionic patient may also attempt to monopolize the group and influence group dynamics by wearing seductive clothing or engaging in diversionary behavior while another group member is speaking. Firm, consistent, and understanding intervention on the part of the therapist will limit this type of distracting behavior.

Intellectually Impaired Patient. Occasionally a group will find that they have an intellectually impaired member. This impairment may manifest itself by concrete thought processes, inability to abstract concepts, and a tendency to have some degree of perseveration. Also this type of group member may interrupt the group with some tangential comment after finding that they cannot understand a theme or topic that the group may be discussing. A gentle reminder by the therapist, such as "Mary, we're not talking about that just now, but we would like to hear about this later in the group," will help keep the group on the topic and not destroy continuity.

Obsessive-Compulsive Patient. The obsessive-compulsive patient can also be disruptive to group functioning. This type of patient tends to challenge the therapist and demand precise answers. In patients with chronic pain this is particularly difficult since very often the questions they ask cannot be answered in precise terms. A typical question may focus on methods of relieving pain, such as operations, medications, and various other techniques. The obsessive-compulsive patient has a tendency to demand facts and figures and to persevere tenaciously when a topic has been introduced that is of interest to them. These patients respond better to group and peer pressure than to direct therapist-patient exchanges. Allowing the group to inform the disruptive individual that their behavior is interfering with the therapeutic benefit of the sessions is much more productive for the entire group process, and voids the battle for control that very often arises between the therapist and an obsessive-compulsive patient.

Passive-Dependent Patient. Finally, the passive-dependent patient can be somewhat disruptive of group function, only because of his or her own lack of functioning. These patients may sit quietly through many group sessions and be regarded as a cipher by other group members. Very often the therapist feels he must intervene and become directive with this type of patient. However, after several attempts on the part of the therapist to involve the passive-dependent group member, the group itself usually senses the need to do so and assumes this role.

While the difficult patients discussed here are not unique to chronic pain patient groups, the frequency with which these character disorders occur in chronic pain patients seems to be higher than in the general psychiatric population. It is for this reason that these disorders have been discussed in detail. Obviously other types of personality disorders may be found in patients with chronic pain, but only the prevalent types have been discussed here.

Efficacy of Group Therapy

To determine the efficacy of group therapy, a small number (twenty-three) of patients who had little or no relief from their pain and had no need for surgical intervention were selected consecutively on discharge from the clinic. They were randomly assigned either to group psychotherapy with pharmacological management by the psychiatrist or to individual follow-up by the same psychiatrist. After three months, eight of the eleven patients in group therapy remained in therapy, and seven of the eight claimed to have abstained from narcotic and hypnotic use. This is in contrast to the group of twelve patients assigned to see the same psychiatrist on an individual basis. Seven of the twelve patients admitted to obtaining hypnotics, narcotics, or benzodiazepines from other physicians. By the end of three months, six of the twelve had discontinued sessions. In a much more comprehensive report, Hall and his associates (1979) compared the efficacy of combined group therapy and tricyclic antidepressants versus supportive individual psychotherapy, analytically oriented therapy, and management by a surgical specialist who prescribed narcotics or antidepressants. Using the Zung rating scale to indicate the severity of depression, Hall's group found that group therapy combined with tricyclic antidepressant administration was the more effective therapy for the chronic pain patient.

Summary

As outlined in this chapter, the time course of group therapy (that is, whether it is short- or long-term) determines the
content. Regardless of content, however, the support derived
from a homogeneous (chronic pain patient) group setting is
most therapeutic and uses a physician's time very efficiently
and productively. The use of group therapy for long-term (one
or two years') support after discharge from a chronic pain treatment center or as a treatment method in lieu of hospitalization
helps to develop self-reliance.

Appendix A
Hendler 10-Minute Screening Test
for Chronic Back Pain Patients

Instructions: Each question is asked by an examiner, and
the patient is given points according to the response that he
makes. The number of points to be awarded for the various responses is shown in the column at the right. At the end of the
test, the examiner calculates the total number of points. The
results are interpreted as explained in the key.

			Points
1.	How did the pain that you now experience occur?		
	a.	Sudden onset with accident or definable event	0
	b.	Slow, progressive onset without acute exacerbation	1
	c.	Slow, progressive onset with acute exacerbation without accident or event	2
	d.	Sudden onset without an accident or definable event	3
2.	Where do you experience the pain?		
	a.	One site, specific, well-defined, consistent with anatomical distribution	0
	b.	More than one site, each well-defined and consistent with anatomical distribution	1

    c. One site, inconsistent with anatomical considerations, or not well-defined   2

    d. Vague description, more than one site, of which one is inconsistent with anatomical considerations, or not well-defined or anatomically explainable   3

3. Do you ever have trouble falling asleep at night, or are you ever awakened from sleep? If the answer is "no," score 3 points and go to question 4. If the answer is "yes," proceed:
What keeps you from falling asleep, or what awakens you from sleep?

3a. a. Trouble falling asleep every night due to pain   0

    b. Trouble falling asleep due to pain more than three times a week   1

    c. Trouble falling asleep due to pain less than three times a week   2

    d. No trouble falling asleep due to pain   3

    e. Trouble falling asleep which is not related to pain   4

3b. a. Awakened by pain every night   0

    b. Awakened from sleep by pain more than three times a week   1

    c. Not awakened from sleep by pain more than twice a week   2

    d. Not awakened from sleep by pain   3

    e. Restless sleep, or early morning awakening with or without being able to return to sleep, both unrelated to pain   4

4. Does weather have any effect on your pain?

    a. The pain is always worse in both cold *and* damp weather.   0

    b. The pain is always worse with damp weather *or* with cold weather.   1

    c. The pain is occasionally worse with cold or damp weather.   2

    d. The weather has no effect on the pain.   3

5. How would you describe the type of pain that you have?
   a. Burning; or sharp, shooting pain; or pins and needles; or coldness; or numbness   0
   b. Dull, aching pain, with occasional sharp, shooting pains not helped by heat; or, the patient is experiencing hyperesthesia   1
   c. Spasm-type pain, tension-type pain, or numbness over the area, relieved by massage or heat   2
   d. Nagging or bothersome pain   3
   e. Excruciating, overwhelming, or unbearable pain, relieved by massage or heat   4
6. How frequently do you have your pain?
   a. The pain is constant.   0
   b. The pain is nearly constant, occurring 50%-80% of the time.   1
   c. The pain is intermittent, occurring 25%-50% of the time.   2
   d. The pain is only occasionally present, occurring less than 25% of the time.   3
7. Does movement or position have any effect on the pain?
   a. The pain is unrelieved by position change or rest, and there have been previous operations for the pain.   0
   b. The pain is worsened by use, standing, or walking; and is relieved by lying down or resting the part.   1
   c. Position change and use have variable effects on the pain.   2
   d. The pain is not altered by use or position change, and there have been no previous operations for the pain.   3
8. What medications have you used in the past month?
   a. No medications at all   0
   b. Use of non-narcotic pain relievers; non-benzo-

| | diazepine tranquilizers; or use of antidepressants | 1 |

    c. Less than three-times-a-week use of a narcotic, hypnotic, or benzodiazepine   2

    d. Greater than four-times-a-week use of a narcotic, hypnotic, or benzodiazepine   3

9. What hobbies do you have, and can you still participate in them?

    a. Unable to participate in any hobbies that were formerly enjoyed   0

    b. Reduced number of hobbies or activities relating to a hobby   1

    c. Still able to participate in hobbies but with some discomfort   2

    d. Participate in hobbies as before   3

10. How frequently did you have sex and orgasms before the pain, and how frequently do you have sex and orgasms now?

    a^1. Sexual contact, prior to pain, three to four times a week, with no difficulty with orgasm; now sexual contact is 50% or less than previously, and coitus is interrupted by pain   0

    a^2. (For people over 45) Sexual contact twice a week, with a 50% reduction in frequency since the pain   0

    a^3. (For people over 60) Sexual contact once a week, with a 50% reduction in frequency of coitus since the onset of pain   0

    b. Pre-pain adjustment as defined above (a^1-a^3), with no difficulty with orgasm; now loss of interest in sex and/or difficulty with orgasm or erection   1

    c. No change in sexual activity now as opposed to before the onset of pain   2

    d. Unable to have sexual contact since the onset of pain, and difficulty with orgasm or erection *prior to* the pain   3

Points

    e. No sexual contact prior to the pain, or absence of orgasm *prior to* the pain   4

11. Are you still working or doing your household chores?

    a. Works every day at the same pre-pain job or same level of household duties   0

    b. Works every day but the job is not the same as pre-pain job, with reduced responsibility or physical activity   1

    c. Works sporadically or does a reduced amount of household chores   2

    d. Not at work, or all household chores are now performed by others   3

12. What is your income now compared with before your injury or the onset of pain, and what are your sources of income?

    a. Any one of the following answers scores   0

        (1) Experiencing financial difficulty with family income 50% or less than previously

        (2) Was retired and is still retired

        (3) Patient is still working and is not having financial difficulties

    b. Experiencing financial difficulty with family income only 50%-75% of the pre-pain income   1

    c. Patient unable to work, and receives some compensation so that the family income is at least 75% of the pre-pain income   2

    d. Patient unable to work and receives no compensation, but the spouse works and family income is still 75% of the pre-pain income   3

    e. Patient doesn't work, yet the income from disability or other compensation sources is 80% or more of gross pay before the pain; the spouse does not work   4

13. Are you suing anyone, or is anyone suing you, or do you have an attorney helping you with compensation or disability payments?

Points

   a. No suit pending, and does not have an attorney   0

   b. Litigation is pending, but is not related to the pain.   1

   c. The patient is being sued as the result of an accident.   2

   d. Litigation is pending or workers' compensation case with a lawyer involved   3

14. If you had three wishes for anything in the world, what would you wish for?

   a. "Get rid of the pain" is the only wish.   0

   b. "Get rid of the pain" is one of the three wishes.   1

   c. Doesn't mention getting rid of the pain, but has specific wishes usually of a personal nature such as for more money, a better relationship with spouse or children, etc.   2

   d. Does not mention pain, but offers general, nonpersonal wishes such as for world peace   3

15. Have you ever been depressed or thought of suicide?

   a. Admits to depression; or has a history of depression secondary to pain and associated with crying spells and thoughts of suicide   0

   b. Admits to depression, guilt, and anger secondary to the pain   1

   c. Prior history of depression before the pain or a financial or personal loss prior to the pain; now admits to some depression   2

   d. Denies depression, crying spells, or "feeling blue"   3

   e. History of a suicide attempt prior to the onset of pain   4

POINT TOTAL

Key to Hendler Screening Test for Chronic Back Pain

A score of 18 points or less suggests that the patient is an objective-pain patient and is reporting a normal response to chronic pain. One may proceed surgically if indicated, and usually finds the patient quite willing to participate in all modalities of therapy, including exercise and psychotherapy. Occasionally, a person with conversion reaction or posttraumatic neurosis will score less than 18 points; this is because subjective distress is being experienced on an unconscious level. Persons scoring 14 points or less can be considered objective-pain patients with more certainty than those at the upper range (14–18) of this group.

A score of 15–20 points suggests that the patient has features of an objective-pain patient as well as of an exaggerating-pain patient. This implies that a person with a poor premorbid adjustment has an organic lesion that has produced the normal response to pain; however, because of the person's poor pre-pain adjustment, the chronic pain produces a more extreme response than would otherwise occur.

A score of 19–31 points suggests that the patient is an exaggerating-pain patient. Surgical or other interventions may be carried out with caution. This type of patient usually has a premorbid (pre-pain) personality that may increase his likelihood of using or benefiting from the complaint of chronic pain. The patient may show improvement after treatment in a chronic pain treatment center, where the main emphasis is placed on an attitude change toward the chronic pain.

A score of 32 points or more suggests that a psychiatric consultation is needed. These patients freely admit to a great many pre-pain problems, and show considerable difficulty in coping with the chronic pain they now experience. Surgical or other interventions should not be carried out without prior approval of a psychiatric consultant. Severe depression, suicide, and psychosis are potential problems in this group of affective pain patients.

References

Asch, S. "Opinions and Social Pressure." In S. Coopersmith (Ed.), *Frontiers of Psychological Research*. San Francisco: W. H. Freeman, 1966.

Ascher, E. *Group Psychotherapy in the Practice of Medicine.* Vol. 10. Hagerstown, Md.: Harper & Row, 1971.

Frank, J. D. *Persuasion and Healing: A Comparative Study of Psychotherapy.* Baltimore: Johns Hopkins University Press, 1973.

Freud, S. "The Theory of Libido: Narcissism." In *A General Introduction to Psychoanalysis.* New York: Washington Square Press, 1963.

Hall, R. C., and others. "A Comparison of Tricyclic Antidepressants and Analgesics in the Management of Chronic Post-Operative Surgical Pain." Paper presented at the annual meeting of the Academy of Psychosomatic Medicine, San Francisco, Oct. 31, 1979.

Hendler, N. *Diagnosis and Nonsurgical Management of Chronic Pain.* New York: Raven Press, 1981a.

Hendler, N. "Psychiatric Aspects of Chronic Pain." In J. J. Youmans (Ed.), *Textbook of Neurosurgery.* (2nd ed.) Philadelphia: Saunders, 1981b.

Hendler, N., and Fenton, J. A. *Coping with Chronic Pain.* New York: Clarkson N. Potter, 1979.

Hendler, N., and others. "EMG Biofeedback in Patients with Chronic Pain." *Diseases of the Nervous System,* 1977, *38,* 505-509.

Hendler, N., and others. "A Preoperative Screening Test for Chronic Back Pain Patients." *Psychosomatics,* 1979a, *20,* 800-808.

Hendler, N., and others. "The Expanded Role of the Psychiatric Liaison Nurse." *Psychiatric Quarterly,* 1979b, *51* (2), 135-143.

Kubler-Ross, E. *On Death and Dying.* New York: Macmillan, 1969.

Moreno, J. L. *Psychodrama.* Vol. 1. (4th ed.) Beacon, N.Y.: Beacon House, 1972.

Pinsky, J. J. "Chronic, Intractable, Benign Pain: A Syndrome and Its Treatment with Intensive Short-Term Group Psychotherapy." *Journal of Human Stress,* 1978, *4* (3), 17-21.

Roethlisberger, R. J., and Dickson, W. J. *Management and the Worker.* Cambridge, Mass.: Harvard University Press, 1939.

Schwartz, L. H., and others. "Multidisciplinary Group Therapy for Rheumatoid Arthritis." *Psychosomatics,* 1978, *19,* 289-293.

Shapiro, D. *Neurotic Styles.* New York: Basic Books, 1965.

Warner, G. E. *Psychodrama Training Tips.* Hagerstown, Md.: Maryland Psychodrama Institute, 1972.

Yalom, I. D. *The Theory and Practice of Group Psychotherapy.* New York: Basic Books, 1970.

Yalom, I. D., and Greaves, C. "Group Therapy and the Terminally Ill." *American Journal of Psychiatry,* 1977, *134,* 396-400.

5

Myron G. Eisenberg, Ph.D.

▦ ▦ ▦ ▦ ▦ ▦ ▦ ▦ ▦ ▦ ▦ ▦ ▦

Spinal Cord Injuries

Physiologically, injury or disease to the spinal cord can result in paraplegia (paralysis of the upper limbs) or quadriplegia (paralysis of all four limbs). Depending upon the nature and level of the lesion, a variety of complications can occur. Reflex activity may be severe enough to cause violent, uncontrollable muscle spasms of the trunk and legs. This condition may prevent a full range of motion, which in turn can lead to the formation of contracture deformities. Another common problem among the cord injured is that of autonomic dysreflexia, a condition that can increase blood pressure to the point of producing a stroke and, if not treated immediately, death.

Many cord-injured individuals have lost normal skin sensation; they are essentially anesthetic below the level of the injury. As a result, prolonged pressure from sitting or lying too long in one position may lead to the development of decubiti, or pressure sores. Lack of voluntary control of the bladder results in the inability to void, treatment for which requires the use of a urinary drainage system and a leg bag; bowel dysfunction frequently necessitates the use of mechanical aids to induce bowel movements. Paralysis of the intercostal and abdominal muscles curtails respiratory capacity. Erectile and ejaculatory incompetence and sterility are also common among the cord injured.

These physiological impairments often have massive psychological ramifications that can threaten the life goals, endanger the defense systems, and disrupt the role functions (that is, a wife may have to assume tasks formerly performed by the husband) of the cord injured and their families.

The road to emotional recovery or adjustment for the spinal-cord-injured person is perilous and tortuous. Contrary to popular belief, however, important psychological processes are not necessarily manifested as disintegrative personality crises requiring intensive psychological intervention. Rather, the little everyday problems of routine personal management and medical care may provide the clue to an emotional crisis. Such things as a patient's refusal to cooperate in treatment procedures, the development of psychosocial or psychoneurotic reactions, and exaggerated or bizarre demands are but a few examples of minor problems that, unless recognized and dealt with, could lead to severe crises.

All of the changes experienced by the spinal-cord-injured person are not biological and psychological. Some are sociological, while others are what can be termed architectural. For example, the spinal-cord-injured person's opportunity to meet and socialize with other persons is severely compromised. Because of the lack of transportation, inaccessible public bathroom facilities, and other architectural barriers, cord-injured persons repeatedly confront and deal with the permanence and severity of their disabilities.

The attitudes of people also hinder the reentry of the spinal cord injured into society. These barriers are created by the cord injured themselves as well as by their able-bodied peers. The able bodied are often reluctant to interact with the spinal cord injured. Some investigators hypothesize that this reluctance might arise out of fear of confronting someone whose battered body vividly reminds the viewer of the fragility of the human condition. As a result, many able-bodied persons try to distance themselves physically and emotionally from the spinal cord injured. Others deal with their discomfort by being solicitous. However, this attitude creates a superior-inferior relationship that lowers the cord-injured individual's self-esteem.

Many cord-injured persons acknowledge their annoyance, frustration, and outright anger in continually having to deal with the staring and devaluating pity they meet almost daily. Many of these patients have long before completed their rehabilitation and have done so successfully. Nonetheless, their need to examine and reexamine their feelings about being disabled must be dealt with indefinitely. It is not at all unusual to find that questions raised and presumably put to rest surface repeatedly in therapy. A poignant example of this difficulty follows. These words were spoken by a middle-aged professor of English, injured since adolescence, who is considered by nearly all who know him as being satisfactorily adjusted to the injury.

> Here I am, a forty-six-year-old college professor, the author of a number of books, the father of two splendid sons, the husband of a lovely wife, the recipient of a number of academic awards and honors—and a man whose dreams at night still make him alien to what the world defines as success. How shall I tell my "normal" colleagues that I still dream about running on the beach, that even at the age of forty-six I desperately want to swing a baseball bat once again, that I lie awake at night wondering what I would do with normal legs. I want to run on the beach, I want to jump a rope, I want to ride a bike, I want to climb a mountain —not a metaphor for achievement, just a real honest-to-God mountain—I want to ride a horse. I want to make love differently, I want to drive differently. I want to know my children differently. The list could easily be extended, but perhaps it is enough to note simply that I want to know the world differently [Kriegel, 1981, pp. 54-55].

To deal rationally with these problems, it is essential to know the background and personality of typical spinal-cord-injured victims and to know about the progression of emotional states often experienced by these people in the course of recovery and rehabilitation. Also important to consider is a method of determining the unique individual emotional factors that lead to a particular crisis. Finally, some guidelines will be discussed for assisting patients so as to prevent or minimize the development of crises as well as to hasten the patients' mastery of their condition. This text will explore attaining these goals within the context of group therapeutic interventions.

Characteristics of the Typical Spinal-Cord-Injured Person

Although a severe spinal injury may occur to any individual in any role or life situation, at any age, and with any personality constellation, most such injuries involve individuals with certain personality and social characteristics—specifically, adult males between the ages of fifteen and forty who earn their living in some active outdoor or unskilled vocation (Gunther, 1969). Many of them are passive-aggressive characters with a strong desire to express the aggressive side of their ambivalent emotional conflicts. They are people of action rather than contemplation, with few inner emotional resources for gratification. They frequently lack the capacity for fantasy as a means of discharging their impulses. In general, in personality orientation and makeup, they resemble adolescents. Although some recent investigators (Trieschmann, 1980) challenge this stereotypical image, evidence for these generalizations can be found in an analysis of the cord-injured individual's developmental and social history before the injury as well as from psychological implications of the physical circumstances at injury, from repeated mental-status interviews, and from psychological testing. These findings are supported by case histories obtained from the private sector (Gunther, 1969) and the public (such as Veterans Administration hospitals and military facilities). However, much of the information is impressionistic and based on clinical experience and is not empirically based.

A second group of characteristics delineating this type of patient are the personality dilemmas imposed by the nature of the lesion itself, regardless of the premorbid personality pattern.

Spinal cord injury is a serious, far-reaching, life-threatening experience. Individuals with such a lesion never fully resume their former life or their former personality patterns and adaptations. The injury almost completely limits the discharge of aggressive energy, severely restricts activity, and requires the patient to rely largely on verbal channels for relating to others and for expressing feelings. Thus, inner resources such as intellectual interests and fantasizing become especially important. Despite the presence of such resources, patients adjusting to a spinal cord injury can encounter hopelessness, dependency, and negativistic and even self-destructive feelings. These common reactions may arise in part from patients' desperate need to assert mastery over their immediate environment, thereby denying the restrictions imposed by the lesion. Ultimately, this may represent a need to counteract a painful sense of utter helplessness. Finally, and especially in the male, these lesions tend to impose severe problems in the areas of self-esteem and social and vocational roles, as well as in the area of sexual identity and function.

In summary, people with spinal cord lesions tend to be young adult males with aggressive conflicts and constricted egos that encourage acting-out behavior. The lesion itself prevents individuals from using previous modes of behavior and confronts them with painfully unacceptable impulses, to which they frequently respond with verbal provocation and disturbed behavior. Ironically, those who are least well endowed to meet the massive challenge imposed by a spinal cord injury are frequently the very people who incur it. Therefore, people with spinal cord injuries impose difficult and challenging medical, psychological, and social problems for any rehabilitation staff.

Assessing Where the Patient Is
in the Adjustment Process

There is some controversy about whether the adjustment process can be adequately characterized by any model because of its complexity and the large variations from person to person. The following discussion attempts to establish a framework for describing emotional reactions commonly observed among persons with spinal cord injuries.

Discussing stages of adjustment often leads one to conclude that these stages must occur in some orderly sequence. This, however, is not the case. Although a general movement toward acknowledging the disability is a characteristic of stage theory approaches to disability, the most striking single feature of the overall adaptive sequence is its cyclical nature. Cycles occur less frequently until, when adaptation is complete, they become virtually unnoticed.

Therapeutic interventions of either a group or individual nature may be complicated by the cyclic nature of the adjustment process. For this reason, it is important to keep themes open that were previously addressed and thought to be resolved. Just as able-bodied persons experience changes in their psychosocial status as they meet new people, are exposed to new situations, and experience success and failure, cord-injured persons also undergo profound changes in their psychosocial status. The rate at which these changes occur for such patients, however, appears to be faster than the rate for the able bodied. One reason for this is the extreme changes brought on by the injury.

Based on a framework suggested by Davis (1963) and Schontz (1976), a scheme describing reactions to disability is considered here. The first stage, shock, can be described as a depersonalized emergency reaction marked by feelings of detachment. Individuals often report feeling as though they were observing events in which they were not actively participating. Emotionally, shock is either numbing, with patients reporting they feel nothing at all, or pleasant, with patients feeling calm and detached. Cognitive events during shock are usually nonverbal with cognitive flooding; for example, persons report their whole life passing before them. This stage normally lasts a few weeks, but durations as short as several days have been reported in some patients.

The second stage, impact, is observable behaviorally when an individual panics. The disorganization and helplessness that might have been expected to surface during shock manifest themselves during this stage. The emotional content of the impact stage is best described as despair. Behaviorally, actions are most consistent with the psychiatric diagnosis of reactive depression. Generally, the impact stage does not end suddenly. Grief and a sense of loss are only gradually replaced by attempts to evaluate the situation, explore its implications, and adjust to its demands. This stage typically lasts several months. The repeated reliving of the impact experience frequently occurs during this adaptive sequence.

> I didn't want anyone . . . to know how I felt when I saw myself for the first time. There was no noise, no outcry. I didn't scream with rage when I saw myself. I just felt numb. That person in the mirror couldn't be me. I felt inside like a healthy, ordinary, lucky person—oh, not like the one in the mirror!
>
> Over and over again I forgot what I saw in the mirror. It could not penetrate into the interior of my mind and become an integral part of me. I felt as if it had nothing to do with me; it was only a disguise. But it was not the kind of disguise which is put on voluntarily by the person who wears it. My disguise had been put on me without my consent—like the ones in fairy tales and it was I myself who was confused by it.
>
> Every time I looked at myself in a mirror it was like a blow on the head. I was left dazed and dumb and senseless, every time, until slowly, my persistent illusion of well-being and of personal beauty spread all through me and I was all unprepared and vulnerable again [Hathaway, 1943, pp. 46-47].

The next stage typically observed is a type of avoidance referred to by some as retreat. One extreme form of retreat is complete denial, refusal to admit that the implications of the disability exist. During this stage, patients characteristically attempt to fend off the finality of the diagnosis. As patients begin to enlarge their focus from themselves to their environment and others in it, this stage begins to resolve. However, some patients never pass through this phase successfully. They remain fixated on problems created by the injury, always focusing on what they have lost and never thinking of those physical and emotional attributes that remain intact.

The final stage, adaptation, is longest in duration. It is often at this stage that patients are involved in group therapy. Once the physical deficit is acknowledged, the disabled typically begin to hope that mastery of a new situation will solve all of their problems. Paraplegics, for example, may begin to accept their condition by believing that once they can move around in a wheelchair or drive a car, the struggle will be over. Experienced rehabilitation workers know, however, that increased mobility creates difficulties and frustrations not foreseen by the patients.

For example, patients may face financial problems when purchasing adaptive equipment. Often the expense of the hospitalization and rehabilitation drains the family of its savings, leaving little for devices that would increase patients' independence. Because mobility means reentering the outside world, patients must learn to deal with staring and devaluating pity and with people who want to help but further compromise the patient's sense of independence in so doing.

Patients also discover that the physical environment makes few allowances for persons in wheelchairs and that the economic world regards hiring the handicapped as an act of charity. Factors such as a guaranteed income and compensation for disability or employment opportunities that exploit public pity for a person with an obvious disability must also be dealt with. The cyclic nature of the adjustment process can be seen clearly at this point. Patients, faced with these and other problems, may retreat into a previous adjustive phase. If acknowledgment of the physical impairment continues, patients may forego retreat and renew efforts to adapt. No fixed number of cycles is necessary to complete this final stage of acknowledgment. Rather, the cycles may continue indefinitely, each repetition leading to a higher and more stable level of psychological organization.

Rationale for Group Therapy

Dealing in a group setting with problems typically experienced by the spinal cord injured can be very efficient and productive. Because the group is composed of individuals with varied experiences and insights, feedback can be especially rewarding and therapeutic. The opportunity to use these varied insights and experiences as a source of support, expertise, and hope is an advantage one can experience in the group setting.

One example of this group benefit stands out: A counseling group in a ward of hospitalized, spinal-cord-injured men was trying to deal with a single, middle-aged, quadriplegic man who was keeping the others awake at night by constantly complaining and making requests. Through the discussion, he revealed that he found nighttime very frightening, because at night he felt particularly vulnerable and helpless. As a result, he worried excessively about himself and his future. This led to his making constant requests of the staff, which kept him distracted and reduced his anxiety. In the group, other patients further along in the adjustment process expressed having experienced similar feelings. Through this group experience, the patient learned that his feelings of fright and powerlessness were not unusual. Because of the support he received from other group members, the incidence of his complaints and other poorly masked and inappropriate requests for attention significantly decreased. After hearing other members express concerns similar to his own and receiving helpful feedback, this patient reported feeling more able to confront his disability and to solve the problems created by it.

Patients may be more willing and able to use new types of interpersonal behaviors as they become aware that such behaviors are valued by others in the group setting. The likelihood that behavior will change is a function of patients' motivation, rigidity of character structure, and interpersonal style. When change in behavior does occur, however small, a new cycle of interpersonal learning via feedback from other group members is generated. Gradually an adaptive spiral is set into motion. As patients' interpersonal distortions about their social worth diminish, their ability to form rewarding relationships is enhanced. Anxiety decreases and self-esteem rises.

The range of group counseling approaches with the spinal cord injured is as great as the skills and creativity of the counselor. Groups can be used at any phase of the rehabilitation process as long as the purpose is congruent with the psychosocial

needs of the members. These needs change as the members gradually adapt to their changed body image and become increasingly responsible for maintaining themselves physically, socially,
and economically in the community. Initially, the group can
deal with such topics as exploring the impact and ramifications
of the spinal cord injury on the self-concept, defining and reestablishing familial roles and role functions, learning how to
ask for assistance in performing tasks one can no longer perform
alone, learning how to deal with potentially embarrassing experiences (such as falling out of the wheelchair, having an acci-
dental bowel movement, or asking someone to empty your leg
bag). Later, after some adjustment has been made to the injury,
topic areas may include learning how to reestablish sexual activity, acquiring new vocational skills if previously learned skills
can no longer be performed, acquiring new avocational interests, and learning how to deal with solicitous, well-meaning persons who prevent cord-injured individuals from doing things
that they still can do themselves. Using groups to deal with
these problems provides an ideal forum to promote the exchange
of information and the sharing of feelings, which, in turn, helps
spinal-cord-injured individuals feel less isolated and hopeless
during the adjustment process.

    Although real barriers do exist to their reentry into soci-
ety, some spinal-cord-injured people tend to attribute all of
their interpersonal and intrapersonal problems to their physical
impairment, making the injury the scapegoat for all their difficulties, whether they are a consequence of the disability or not.
In fact, however, by providing a basis in reality for expressing
suppressed dependency needs, disability may resolve conflict
for some patients. Viewed as a punishment for past sins, disease
or disability may alleviate guilt. If life problems were previously
unsolvable, physical disorders may provide welcome relief. Patients may view their disability as a message from God to
change their life-style, while others may see it as a spiritual test,
and still others use it to retire from a world to which they had
never been able to adjust.

    One of the group leader's primary tasks is to assist group
members through the adjustive process by helping them assess

their strengths, acquire coping mechanisms to deal with deficits, and grow emotionally through risking themselves within the supportive environment of the group. Promoting the individual's emotional growth is the primary goal of the group, regardless of the topic being discussed. To do otherwise only delays the personal adjustment process that is required if strengths and weaknesses are to be evaluated and shortcomings corrected for psychological survival. The group can provide an ideal forum for dealing with distrust, pity, dependency, and fear.

Techniques for Conducting Groups with the Spinal Cord Injured

Basic techniques used in conducting groups for the spinal cord injured are essentially the same as those used with groups comprised of able-bodied members. These may include role playing, paraphrasing and reflecting feelings, behavioral rehearsal, and video feedback. However, at least one difference exists between groups conducted for the able bodied and those for the spinal cord injured—the usefulness of employing cotherapists who themselves are cord injured and who have adequately adjusted to the disability. Such persons can offer much to the recently disabled individual. The experience and understanding of such a role model can be invaluable tools in teaching the skills needed to interact effectively with others and gain confidence in oneself.

Open Versus Closed Groups. At their inception, groups are usually designated by their leaders as being open or closed. Once begun, a closed group accepts no new members and usually meets for a predetermined number of sessions. An open group may also have a predetermined life span but does not close its doors to new members.

The most productive groups for cord-injured individuals that the author has led have been closed. The closed group helps ensure confidentiality and stability, which are often lost in the open group format. In closed groups, group cohesiveness seems to develop to a far greater extent than it does in open groups. Being comfortable enough to risk oneself by making personal disclosures is greatly facilitated in the trusting environment fostered by closed groups.

Duration and Timing of the Sessions. Most therapists agree that a period of sixty minutes is required for unfolding and working through the major themes of the session. This is also the case in working with spinal-cord-injured groups. After approximately eighty minutes, a point of diminishing returns is reached. The group becomes weary, repetitious, and inefficient. In addition, because some individuals find it difficult to assimilate the mass of information presented, it is often necessary to present material in smaller, well-structured, and focused units over a period of several weeks. This enables group members to discuss what has happened at previous sessions among themselves, thus helping each other assimilate new material, gain insight, and enrich subsequent meetings.

Selection of Patients. It is important that patients be medically stable, have initiated the process of adapting to their changed physical status, and not be brain damaged, paranoid, or actively psychotic. Such patients are generally unable to participate in the primary task of the group. They soon construct an interpersonal role that proves to be detrimental to themselves and to the group. In addition, emotionally unstable individuals often find the subject matter and frank discussion anxiety provoking.

Leadership and Group Size. Group leaders should not be restricted to practitioners of a specific discipline but rather should be chosen on the basis of their interest and knowledge. It may be necessary to ask a professional not directly involved in the program to make a presentation if highly technical information is to be discussed. For example, a physician may be asked to discuss the anatomy and physiology of sexual functioning if the group leaders do not feel comfortable doing so themselves. Also, there is some advantage in having both a male and a female therapist as group leaders if the group contains both males and females. Patients appear to find some types of material, such as that related to sexuality, more credible when presented by a person of the same sex. Basic requirements of group leaders include:

1. accurate detailed knowledge of the psychological aspects of spinal cord injury,
2. positive attitudes toward the disability,
3. an objective understanding of expressions of psychological complaints and problems, and
4. training in group therapy.

Such training can be acquired through formal course work, seminars, workshops, and internships. Audiovisual and written material can supplement the training.

Groups should not exceed ten to fifteen participants. Larger groups tend to inhibit spontaneous questions and limit contributions from participants. Groups with as few as three persons can be valuable for disseminating information, sharing experiences, and providing counseling.

In order to provide the reader with specific examples of how various groups have been conducted with spinal-cord-injured members, a patient-family group and a sex counseling and information group are presented below. The information on the patient-family group is drawn from a colleague's experience at the Ohio State University Hospital, whereas the example of a sex-counseling education group is drawn from personal experience.

Use of a Patient-Family Group

Between September 1974 and May 1976, a series of family groups were conducted at the Ohio State University Hospital in Columbus (Rohrer and others, 1980). During that time, 208 participants met in a total of twelve groups. Groups ranged in size from 10 to 21. Participation in the group program was voluntary, and a wide range of age, ethnic, economic, educational, and social groups was represented. The family group program was held every six to seven weeks for an entire day. The group leaders were a social worker, an occupational therapist, and a nurse who organized, evaluated, and adjusted the program to achieve the following rehabilitation goals:

1. increasing the patient's and family's knowledge and under-

standing of the effects of spinal cord injury upon physical, social, vocational, and psychological functioning;

2. increasing the participation of family members in the patient's rehabilitation program and decreasing feelings of isolation, hopelessness, and anxiety;

3. reestablishing communication channels among family members to supply mutual support in dealing emotionally with the disability; and

4. directing the patient and the family toward discharge and realistic planning for the future.

Patients were selected for participation in the family group based on the following criteria:

1. traumatic or congenital spinal cord injury or similar neurological disorder manifesting comparable symptoms (for example, loss of movement or sensation, lack of bowel and bladder control, or sexual dysfunction),

2. a minimum age of thirteen years,

3. medical clearance to participate in the day-long program, and

4. no behavior symptomatic of severe emotional disturbance such as psychosis, which might be disruptive to the group process.

Using these criteria, each rehabilitation team referred patients to the family group. If patients expressed an interest when asked to participate, invitations were sent to appropriate family members. However, patients could participate with or without family or intimates present. Inpatients were given priority, but outpatients were considered when group size permitted.

The family group began as patients and families signed in, received a folder of resource materials, and completed a pretest. Some family members participating were part of the nuclear unit (parents, spouses, and children), while others were part of the extended family (grandparents, aunts, uncles, and so on). Although presentations and lectures were scheduled throughout the day, an informal atmosphere was developed to encourage comments and questions. After participants introduced themselves, the program began with the film *Changes,* and then the general goals of rehabilitation were outlined. A film titled *The Effects of Spinal Cord Injury* began the medical discussion. The participating physician used the film as a basis for a detailed explanation of spinal cord physiology and the effects of spinal cord injury. The subsequent discussion usually evoked intense interest and the first active involvement by group members. The medical discussion increased participants' knowledge and understanding, thus providing a common basis for defining mutual concerns and feelings.

After the medical presentation, the group leader discussed available community medical health resources, such as home health agents and public nursing, and the value and intent of weekend leaves of absence. Because group members were interested in education and employment, the afternoon session began with a counselor from the Bureau of Vocational Rehabilitation explaining the agency's services, eligibility requirements, and application procedures. After this presentation, the group leader discussed home visits, home modifications, and architectural barriers.

The film *Last Step, First Step* was shown next to focus the group's attention on less obvious emotional responses to changes in adjustment to disability and the role of the family in the adjustment process. After this film was shown, a panel comprised of long-term disabled individuals and their family members engaged the group members in an open discussion of the adjustment to disability. All participants then completed the posttest and an evaluation form at the end of the day.

To measure the effectiveness of the family group, several evaluation methods were used: (1) a pretest-posttest series measuring knowledge, (2) an opinion questionnaire administered at the conclusion of the workshop, and (3) a follow-up questionnaire administered six months after the patient had returned to the community. Results of the pretest-posttest series indicated that patients retained more information than did family members. Patients and families generally saw the group as being effective, with positive responses ranging from 55 percent to 100 percent, with a mean of 92.7 percent. To further evaluate the effectiveness of the family group, follow-up questionnaires were sent to all of those who had participated in the groups studied. Approximately 37 percent of the families completed and returned the forms. The majority of those who returned the questionnaire felt that participation in the family group increased their understanding of disability and aided in their planning for discharge. As one spinal-cord-injured mother indicated, "It helped me and my family adjust to my changes, emotional and physical, and was very helpful in my attitude toward rearing my son." Both patients and family members related increased comfort in discussing feelings and plans. Most felt that family relationships were largely back to normal. Using information provided during the sessions, many families had constructed ramps and continued to find the family group folder distributed at the initial session a valuable resource. Contacts had often been made with public health services and the Bureau of Vocational Rehabilitation. Medical complications were reported to be minimal, and the majority of the patients had been socializing since their discharge. Many persons added comments to express their positive opinion of the family group or to describe further their activities since discharge.

From the responses on both the objective and subjective questionnaires, the patient-family group apparently met its well-specified goals. However, the group seemed to serve different purposes for persons at different stages following disability. Generally, those more recently injured benefited from the discussion of medical implications, problems, and solutions. They seemed to find expressing their feelings and fears emotionally supportive but were less likely to share openly comments about their own emotions.

Those who had been injured for longer periods of time and lived outside of the rehabilitation center seemed more willing to express and deal with their feelings about the changes in their lives created by the spinal cord injury. In addition to using the family as a forum for sharing and working through feelings, these persons received positive ego support from other members on how well they had coped with problems. Thus, the investigators found that the group addressed the needs of people at various stages of adjustment and felt that mixing recently injured individuals with those who had been disabled for longer periods was beneficial to the group process.

Group Sex Counseling Program
for the Spinal Cord Injured

Very early in the development of sex education programs for the spinal cord injured, it became apparent that group sessions were perhaps the most desirable format for providing not only information but also treatment regarding impaired sexual functioning following the injury. The advantages of utilizing such an approach become clear when viewed within Yalom's (1970) format outlining the curative factors in group therapy.

Imparting of Information. A group setting provides an efficient forum for relaying information. In providing information on sexual matters to patients, considerable attention must be paid to various physiological features of the injuries that can impair sexual functioning. To help a patient to function sexually, these issues must be thoroughly understood. Although individual differences certainly exist in areas related to sexuality, much of this material can be economically and productively presented in a group setting, thereby saving time for both the therapist and the group members.

Interpersonal Learning. In addition to helping individuals acquire new insights into sexual problems that have been resolved by others with similar impairments, the group format provides members with support, expertise, and hope as they speak with others who have resumed sexual activity. Because the more interested group members are in an issue, the more involved in a discussion they will become. Discussing sexual matters in a group setting is highly appropriate and can be particularly therapeutic. Through sexual counseling conducted in a group setting, patients gain a more objective perspective on their interpersonal behavior and learn how their interactions with others may be hindering their ability to form relationships.

In fact, by focusing on sexual concerns, one is also providing counseling that can generalize to other areas of interpersonal functioning.

Universality. Group members can be enormously relieved by discussing sexual concerns with others who have resolved these problems. Patients' sense of isolation and overwhelming concern that they alone experience sexual difficulties are diminished. Decreasing anxiety will also improve sexual functioning.

Development of Socializing Techniques. Patients may need to learn new socialization skills to establish a sexual relationship following disability. Information shared by patients who have developed such skills and who can testify to their effectiveness can help motivate newly injured individuals to learn these skills.

Imitative Behavior. Patients commonly employ the techniques found to be effective by others who have resolved similar problems.

The sex education and counseling program described below is structured, time limited, and designed for a spinal-cord-injured population. Groups composed of patients with different disabilities may not be advantageous, since it becomes more difficult to focus on a specific disability. Conflicts may arise because of the different interests of the participants, varying degrees of impairment, and the need for different kinds of information, particularly concerning physiological matters. Although the program uses films, slides, and other visual aids, these should not play a central role. Rather, the active sharing of experiences and information by participants, particularly about sexual matters, should be most important. The sex education and counseling program used by the Spinal Cord Injury Service at the Veterans Administration Medical Center in Cleveland (Eisenberg and Rustad, 1976), which is tailored to meet the needs of the individual group, is outlined below. Each session is approximately sixty to ninety minutes long. Groups are composed of males and females, and whenever possible, the sexual partners of the participants are included.

Meeting 1: Introductory Meeting. A detailed outline of the format and content of the course is presented, and patients are given the option of taking part in the group. This meeting essentially serves as a consent form in which the therapists agree to provide certain information and the group members agree to participate in the entire program.

Meeting 2: Film and Discussion. Just What Can You Do? a film of a group discussion by spinal-cord-injured individuals and their partners about sexual experiences, is shown. The film has proven valuable as an introductory presentation and served as a basis for discussion. It allows patients to observe other disabled individuals openly discussing their concerns and experiences and thus serves as a model of group interaction. It also reduces anxiety in group members about the uniqueness of their own disabilities. The film has also served as a basis for discussing the different ways in which individuals approach the discussion of sexual material. For example, some deal with it by joking and otherwise making light of serious concerns and apprehensions; others deal with sexual material by refusing to acknowledge a problem might exist or, worse still, refusing to discuss the subject with health care professionals, who then are unable to determine the extent of the problem.

Meeting 3: Male Sexual Response. The male reproductive system is reviewed and the ways spinal cord injuries can interfere with sexual functioning are explained. Reflexogenic and psychogenic erections are discussed, as are methods by which such erections can be used to satisfy both the cord-injured individual and his partner.

Meeting 4: Sex as Part of the Total Relationship. Factors not directly related to the sex act that may interfere with a satisfactory sexual adjustment are examined. Communication skills are stressed, because coping with fears related to changed physical states and adjusting to new modes of functioning can be greatly aided by an open, trusting relationship. Alternative sexual preferences such as homosexuality are also discussed in this session.

Meeting 5: Female Sexual Response. Female anatomy and physiology are discussed, as is the importance of using all the senses. This material is presented to help both male and female cord-injured individuals understand and communicate with their partners. It is also intended to reassure males that inability to obtain or maintain an erection need not prevent them from satisfying their partners or bringing them to orgasm.

Meeting 6: Techniques for Preparation, Relaxation, and Arousal. Specific techniques are described and discussed. Among topics considered are the advantages and disadvantages of catheter removal, the importance of relaxation, and the use of various activities and aids such as massage, vibrators, and alcohol in moderate amounts. The use of fantasy, written materials, manual and oral techniques, and prosthetic devices are discussed, as are alternative positions.

Meeting 7: Marriage, Divorce, and Children. Fertility rates among the cord injured and alternative methods of obtaining children such as artificial insemination, adoption, and foster child placement are discussed. Statistics on marriage and divorce among the cord injured are presented, and causes of success and failure in these marriages are investigated.

Meeting 8: Film and Discussion. Touching, an explicit film showing a quadriplegic and his girl friend engaged in sexual activity, is shown in this final session only after group members have been properly prepared. The film is used primarily to stimulate discussion and to summarize previous sessions. At the end of the final session, participants are reminded that individual counseling, neurological assessments of function, and sperm count studies are available. The opportunity to continue meeting as a group to discuss nonsexual matters is also offered.

Although most patients participating in the sex education program are male, the occasional female spinal-cord-injured veteran also receives sexual rehabilitation in this program. Questions typically raised by female group members include "Will I be able to have my own children?" and "Will men find me attractive even though I am in a wheelchair?" However, most themes and group goals are similar for group members of either sex. These include learning how to maintain a healthy and positive self-concept, learning to use most effectively those functions that are unimpaired, and developing the social skills necessary to cope successfully with the disability's sequelae.

Evaluating Rehabilitation Goals

Although psychological restoration following spinal cord injury is an important goal of rehabilitation, not everyone is able to reach the objectives set by well-meaning personnel. How, then, does one assess the meaningfulness of rehabilitation goals and whether they have been achieved? First, successful rehabilitation does not necessarily mean all goals have been achieved. When patients' preoccupations with unobtainable things are eliminated and their attention is focused on achievable goals, rehabilitation has been partly achieved. Second, the restoration of self-image, a healthy respect for oneself as a person despite physical limitations, is a major achievement. For most patients these are realistic goals for therapy. For others, though, the dearth of emotional resources before the accident makes achieving these goals difficult and in some cases impossible.

Unless properly educated, the family can undo the work of rehabilitation and unnecessarily impede the progress of the patient. For that reason it may be essential to involve the family in the group encounter. Neff and Weiss (1965) have discussed a "Penelope pattern" that may occur unless the family is taught to deal realistically and supportively with the patient:

1. Mindful of the suffering of the patient, a solicitous, guilt-ridden mother or wife may encourage a self-sufficient paraplegic to "cheat a little" and let her help feed him.
2. Family members may shower the individual with pity, undoing gains in independent living achieved in the hospital.
3. Resentment toward hospital personnel may be aired in the presence of patients, destroying their faith in their therapists.
4. Insurance litigations may be so emphasized that the patient begins to think of himself as a cash asset rather than as an individual in need of rehabilitation.

Being able to talk about these and other issues is essential to achieve adjustment. Discussions in which the cord injured can give and receive feedback and information on how to resolve these issues is perhaps best offered in a group setting.

No individuals can avoid conflicts between the needs and demands of reality and their own opposing needs. Nor would such a state be desirable, since a reasonable degree of conflict often provides the impetus for further development. Therapists working with groups must help spinal-cord-injured individuals to learn how to tolerate and deal effectively with conflict and frustration. Cord-injured individuals must learn to be reasonably independent and capable of farsighted planning. They must be motivated to receive satisfaction from fulfilling the roles they play in society, and they must develop the skills necessary for vocational self-sufficiency. They must learn to compete and cooperate, to assert themselves when necessary, and to gain satisfaction from being helpful to others. They must learn to tolerate anxiety and remain flexible, able to try out new responses when old ones fail. Probably more than anything else, they need to develop a realistic knowledge of themselves, their capabilities and limitations, needs, fears, and sources of conflict.

While preparing for each specific problem persons with a spinal cord injury may face is impossible, the basic skills involved in establishing satisfactory social relationships can be taught, and favorable emotional attitudes and personality traits can be fostered. Developing these characteristics ultimately determines the chance that the spinal-cord-injured individual has to live a satisfying and productive life.

References

Davis, F. *Passage Through Crisis: Polio Victims and Their Families.* Indianapolis: Bobbs-Merrill, 1963.

Eisenberg, M. G., and Rustad, L. C. "Sex Education and Counseling Program on a Spinal Cord Injury Service." *Archives of Physical Medicine and Rehabilitation,* 1976, *57,* 135–140.

Gunther, M. S. "Emotional Aspects." In D. Ruge (Ed.), *Spinal Cord Injuries.* Springfield, Ill.: Thomas, 1969.

Hathaway, K. B. *The Little Locksmith.* New York: Coward, McCann & Geoghegan, 1943.

Kriegel, L. "Claiming the Self: The Cripple as American Male." In M. G. Eisenberg, C. Griggins, and R. J. Duval (Eds.), *Disabled People as Second-Class Citizens.* New York: Springer, 1981.

Neff, W. S., and Weiss, S. A. "Psychological Aspects of Disability." In B. Wohlman (Ed.), *Handbook of Clinical Psychology.* New York: McGraw-Hill, 1965.

Rohrer, K., and others. "Rehabilitation in Spinal Cord Injury: Use of a Patient-Family Group." *Archives of Physical Medicine and Rehabilitation,* 1980, *61,* 225–229.

Schontz, F. *The Psychological Aspects of Physical Illness and Disability.* New York: Macmillan, 1976.

Trieschmann, R. *Spinal Cord Injuries: Psychological, Social, and Vocational Adjustment.* New York: Pergamon Press, 1980.

Yalom, I. *The Theory and Practice of Group Psychotherapy.* New York: Basic Books, 1970.

6

Joy Rogers, R.N.

▦ ▦ ▦ ▦ ▦ ▦ ▦ ▦ ▦ ▦ ▦ ▦ ▦

Amputation

As improvements in medical science continue to prolong the average life span, the incidence of lower-limb amputation as a consequence of illness will increase. A majority of the growing numbers of civilian lower-limb amputees are sixty years of age or older, with 80 percent having lost their limbs because of peripheral vascular disease. Most of these people are facing three or more disease processes, many of which have accompanying complications, while simultaneously encountering the numerous stresses associated with aging (Kostuik and others, 1975; Tunbridge Report, 1972). It is easily understandable that amputation, especially when associated with concomitant stressors, can be physically, emotionally, and financially disabling for the individual.

However, the impact of amputation goes far beyond personal considerations. Successful treatment and rehabilitation of ischemic amputees requires much more than expert surgical intervention. In addition to costly equipment for ambulation, the skills and cooperative efforts of numerous health professionals (including prosthetists, psychiatrists, nurses, social workers, and family physicians) are required to assure optimal outcome following surgery. Thus, for a variety of reasons related to patient needs, service delivery methods, and economic factors, amputation constitutes a major medical problem that warrants closer examination (Fleurant and Alexander, 1980).

Many ischemic amputees spend considerable time in the hospital trying to avoid amputation. However, once the amputation is performed, their average postsurgical length of stay in active treatment settings is fairly brief when there are no complications. Frequently an interoperative plaster dressing is applied, and patients begin ambulation, partial weight bearing, and strengthening exercises soon after surgery. Fitting of temporary and definitive prostheses, rehabilitative treatment, and early follow-up are usually performed in rehabilitation facilities that can offer inpatient or outpatient programs.

Because medical, surgical, and prosthetic treatment procedures are constantly being researched, refined, and discussed, rehabilitation programs for amputees are always revising their approaches and incorporating new techniques. However, as the following experience will illustrate, relatively few of the professionals who work directly with amputees feel that they have enough expertise, knowledge, or confidence to research or treat the psychological impact and emotional sequelae of amputation. This chapter discusses what is known about the psychosocial problems of recent amputees and describes a successful program resulting from the mounting concerns of the physician in charge of the Amputee Unit of West Park Hospital (a regional rehabilitative and extended care facility that is publicly funded) for the unmet emotional needs of her patients.

This physician became aware of the importance of the interplay between physiological and psychosocial factors in rehabilitation as the result of a suicide attempt in the unit and of experiences with patients who, despite favorable prognoses after amputation, had not responded favorably to treatment. Also, referrals to psychiatric consultation had steadily increased, and staff members were frustrated about the inadequacy of traditional consultation methods. These circumstances, along with the physician's knowledge of the work of the Social and Com-

munity Psychiatry Section of the Clarke Institute in psychosocial research and intervention with people experiencing stressful life crises, led her to request a consultation with the author.

The Psychosocial Impact of Amputation

To understand major issues and potential problem areas,
the consultant carried out a comprehensive literature review.
Unlike the wealth of information available on the medical, surgical, and prosthetic aspects of amputation, the literature on
psychosocial factors is sparse. However, researchers and clinicians have made some noteworthy contributions.

Perhaps most important is the general agreement that the
reaction to amputation of a limb involves the broad range of responses experienced by those who are grieving over an important
loss (for example, Parkes and Napier, 1975; Siller, 1976). Grief
has been described as a syndrome involving a number of common psychological and physical symptoms. Although grief reactions vary from person to person depending on many highly
individual factors (whether the loss was expected, the individual's life circumstances, the individual's previous health, and
so on), the overall pattern of mourning is the same, whether
precipitated by the loss of a limb, the death of a spouse, or the
loss of a home (Parkes, 1972).

Initially, there is usually a short period of numbness and
dazed disbelief. During this time, which may last minutes,
hours, or even days, the grieving person may seem to function
and react normally, but the reality of the loss has not yet been
accepted. This phase is usually followed by recurrent episodes
of emotional and physical turmoil elicited by reminders of the
loss. Normal emotional reactions, which can be immediate or
delayed, may include those related to depression (sorrow, crying, apathy, disturbing dreams, a lack of energy, a sense of
hopelessness or worthlessness, suicidal thoughts, and so on).
Feelings of guilt and self-blame, related to either real or imagined factors, are not unusual. For instance, amputees may feel
that if they had behaved differently (such as by getting medical
advice earlier or not using patent medicines) the amputation

might have been avoided. Anger directed at medical professionals, God, insensitive friends, or even the lost object is common,
as is a feeling of anxiety, which can manifest as difficulty in
concentrating, forgetfulness, restlessness, tension, nervousness,
fearfulness, indecisiveness, and so on. Physical symptoms may
include weakness, a change in appetite, sleep disturbances, and
unusual somatic sensations such as a choking feeling or chest
constriction. Physical health may also deteriorate. Increased susceptibility to colds or influenza and the development or worsening of conditions such as heart disease, arthritis, ulcers, and
bowel problems have been documented in studies of the recently bereaved (Vachon, 1976).

The urge to search for what has been lost is a common
feature of grief. As comprehensively illustrated by the work of
Parkes (1972), recent amputees often have disturbing dreams in
which their bodies are intact; some may ruminate about how
the limb was disposed of; and a few patients have asked the
staff to estimate the weight of the amputated leg. Most recent
amputees experience a strong sense of the continued presence
of the lost limb, known as phantom sensation. While such sensations help in learning ambulation with a prosthesis (for example, Walters, 1981), these manifestations can be quite distressing to the patient. Adapting to the change in body image is also
a recognized problem (for example, Weiss, 1958).

However, the impact of losing a limb is not limited to
grieving for a body part; the amputee must give up many aspects of life that had been taken for granted and adjust to new
realities (Parkes, 1972). Practical aspects such as finances, vocational issues, and prosthetic problems can exacerbate emotional
and social concerns such as grief reactions, lack of social support, role changes, and isolation (Anderson and Berg, 1975;
Caine, 1973; Parkes and Napier, 1975). In addition, amputees
may experience such immediate and stressful medical problems
as difficulties with the healing stump or persistent phantom
pain at the same time as they are becoming increasingly aware
of the long-term difficulties they face due to the relentless deterioration of the vascular system (Lipp and Malone, 1976).

Of course, not all recent amputees report the foregoing

reactions and circumstances. There is some documented evidence that specific psychological factors such as dependence can facilitate or inhibit physical rehabilitation (Anderson and Berg, 1975; Caine, 1973; Haber, 1958; Parkes, 1973). Somewhat more work has been carried out on the psychosocial difficulties of wartime amputees, who must contend with the unique stresses of their youth, the traumatic nature of their amputations, and their special vocational and social concerns (for example, Dembo, Ladieu-Leviton, and Wright, 1952; Frank, 1973). However, those who reported on the problems of older civilian patients (for example, Caplan and Hackett, 1963; Parkes, 1975) found that depression, helplessness, and unfavorable outcomes were widespread, even though prior long-term illness provided an opportunity for adjusting to disability before surgery.

General literature on amputation invariably underscores the importance of understanding and providing appropriate support for the potentially serious psychological problems that can interact with physiological factors to hamper the rehabilitative process (for example, Burgess and others, 1969; Klopsteg and Wilson, 1968; Rusk, 1971). Furthermore, publications drawn from the broader field of rehabilitation medicine describe the dynamics and psychosocial aspects of physical disability, as illustrated by Siller's (1976) excellent review article.

Many authors have urged drastic changes in service delivery methods within all rehabilitative environments. Kutner (1971) carefully reviews the work of others who advocate small-group approaches, staff education, active patient involvement, and the development of a health rather than a disease model of care. The use of multidisciplinary teams incorporating psychological expertise has been another predominant theme of those calling for change (for example, Parkes and Napier, 1975).

Intervention with Recent Amputees

Although there appears to be sufficient evidence that the psychosocial concerns of recent amputees deserve special attention, the literature provides only isolated examples of intervention strategies designed to alleviate these problems. In a few instances, authors have reported success in implementing group approaches that focus on understanding, expressing, and sharing feelings; enhancing peer support; and offering information and practical advice (Fischer and Samuelson, 1971; Freeman and Applegate, 1976; Kerstein, 1980; Lipp and Malone, 1976). The value of establishing ongoing liaisons between psychiatric consultants and unit staff members has also been described (Frank and Herndon, 1974; Parkes and Napier, 1975), along with the benefits of using "veteran" patients, who give new amputees support and assistance on the basis of their own experiences (Froggatt and Mawby, 1981; May, McPhee, and Pritchard, 1979). In addition, there is a body of literature that discusses how the institutional milieu can be altered to reflect community realities more closely (for example, Katrak and Baggott, 1980), particularly through the use of community-based rehabilitation programs (Hamilton, 1981), and the development of multidisciplinary teams of professionals who provide patients with support and information before surgery and implement holistic treatment strategies after surgery (Fleurant and Alexander, 1980; Parkes and Napier, 1975).

Despite these reported endeavors, many rehabilitative programs serving amputees continue to operate along traditional lines. The inertia in these service delivery systems appears to be related not only to the lack of publications by practitioners but also to the complexities of the field, which are compounded by the separation of medical specialties. As already stated, many medical and nonmedical professionals working in settings where recent amputees are treated feel too unqualified and uncomfortable to undertake either systematic psychosocial research or special therapeutic strategies. Concepts already recognized as important in the world of psychiatry are seldom adopted because psychiatric services are usually made available only via the traditional medical-model, case consultation approach. The normal course of events (as was the case originally in the setting discussed in this chapter) is that a patient displays acute emotional and behavioral problems that nonmedical staff report to the attending physician, who requests psychiatric consultation; a psychiatrist then assesses the patient and gives the diagnosis and any information on prescriptions to the attending physician; and the staff implements the medical directions.

Unfortunately, medical and nonmedical staff rarely have ongoing access to a mental health professional who can assist them in incorporating therapeutic psychosocial strategies into the overall primary care and unit programming. Such access, known as the consultation-liaison approach, not only increases the use of the consultant to the greater benefit of patients and staff, but also is more cost-effective. This is because experienced nonmedical professionals in mental health can perform most necessary consultation-liaison functions. In addition, the need for individual, case-centered consultation either by a medical or nonmedical psychiatric consultant is gradually reduced as the staff becomes more skillful and comfortable in dealing with a patient. The staff is then shown how their newly acquired skills can be used to assist others with similar problems. Other important functions performed by such consultants include identifying and helping solve problems in team functioning (which may adversely affect not only staff relationships but also patient care), advising on administrative issues, and assisting with program design, development, and evaluation (Hunter, 1982; Lipowski, 1974).

A number of experimental programs designed and evaluated by the staff in the Community and Social Psychiatry Section of the Clarke Institute illustrate the value of these consultation strategies in improving the treatment and outcome of such potentially stressful life events as the diagnosis of cancer, the death of a spouse, and the aftermath of a recent suicide (for example, Rogers and others, 1980, 1982; Vachon and Lyall, 1976). With this consultation-liaison model in mind, the author embarked on the present project: to aid in designing, implementing, and evaluating a program of intervention aimed at improving the psychosocial adjustment of recent amputees.

Program Development Procedures

While in the process of reviewing the literature, the author visited the amputee unit several times to find out about the physical characteristics of the setting, the treatment procedures, and the patient population, as well as to record impressions of the strengths, weaknesses, motivations, and concerns of the staff. The eighteen-bed inpatient unit was located in one of a cluster of old buildings erected in the early 1900s to serve as a tuberculosis sanitorium. Although the grounds were quite attractive, the buildings were seriously outdated, and the growing city of Toronto had engulfed the originally rural surroundings. As the need for a tuberculosis sanitorium declined, the hospital developed long-term care services for the chronically ill and rehabilitation programs for amputees, stroke victims, and those with various types of chest disease. When the author first visited in 1975, an extensive building program was planned to replace some of the outmoded facilities and to expand the hospital's rehabilitative facilities.

The Amputee Unit staff was obviously skilled in physical rehabilitation and prosthetics and committed to the general welfare of their patients. However, the organizational structure of the hospital followed methods that were still influenced by the old sanitorium philosophies. Policies and practices affecting both the staff and the patients were fairly rigid. Rules for the daily ward routines were rather autocratically designed and enforced (for example, the staff was not permitted to drink coffee with the patients), and staff communications followed hierarchical lines with little collaboration among professional disciplines. Some nonmedical personnel had worked at the hospital since it housed long-term tuberculosis patients, and few care givers in the hospital had training or experience in the psychosocial aspects of chronic illness or rehabilitation. Time, money, staffing constraints, and a lack of awareness had prevented the hospital from formally attending to patients' emotional and social adjustment.

The patients, both men and women, comprised a range of sociocultural backgrounds, sites and causes of amputation, and prognoses. However, most amputations were precipitated by disease. (Those with amputations resulting from industrial accidents were usually referred to a workmen's compensation facility.) Over 60 percent of the patients also suffered from one or more of the following: cardiovascular problems, diabetes, alcoholism, deafness, or unrelated minor psychiatric disabilities.

Many patients had relatively low levels of formal education, were unaccustomed to verbalizing their emotions, and were not introspective.

The fact that this was an inpatient facility certainly helped in establishing a therapeutic milieu. However, the staff, although not hostile about making changes to better meet the patients' psychosocial needs, were somewhat uneasy about psychiatry and the initiation of groups. There was a strong underlying fear that encouraging the expression and sharing of feelings would result in the eruption of torrents of emotion that the staff could not handle. Such concerns have been documented in other attempts to introduce similar interventions in nonpsychiatric settings (for example, Whitman, Gustafson, and Coleman, 1979). Additional considerations included a complete lack of funds for new programming, little unit staff time to devote to such an endeavor, and the fact that the consultant could only offer a maximum of three hours weekly for a limited time period.

At this point, the reader might wonder whether there were any options at all for program development. However, one of the major reasons for presenting this experience was to demonstrate how to capitalize on available opportunities, maximize the use of scant resources, and mobilize fairly unresponsive systems. This kind of strategy, which is known in our department as "goal-directed opportunism," only works if the consultant already possesses a firmly grounded philosophy of patient care and a broad knowledge of service delivery methods. Otherwise, the major difficulties that hinder change in many health care systems are likely to prevent establishment of an effective therapeutic milieu.

After carefully considering the major issues, staff needs, practical realities, and available alternatives, the consultant decided to employ an intervention model similar to that used previously with cancer patients (Vachon and Lyall, 1976) and independently described by Schwartz (1975), who coined the term *situation/transition* (S/T) *group*. These groups offer social support, information, and an opportunity to acknowledge and share feelings with people who have experienced similar stressful experiences. Advantages of the model include (1) a low-key, nonthreatening, open-ended approach that is less threatening to staff and patients and that accommodates a changing population; (2) the fact that, unlike other types of groups using self-help concepts, members are not pressured to espouse a particular behavioral or value system; and (3) the possible establishment of a regular group that might raise the general awareness of both staff and patients and hopefully encourage changes in the overall milieu. Although a trained group leader is essential, the skills required can be learned fairly quickly if the consultant is experienced and staff members are interested.

After deciding to launch a pilot project based on the S/T group model and obtaining the approval of the ward physician, the consultant carried out two educational seminars with the staff. An overview of the psychosocial impact of amputation was provided, along with some concrete examples of intervention strategies drawn from the literature and the consultant's own experience. The consultant then described the proposed plan, taking pains to reassure the staff that she would take responsibility for launching and leading the groups and that she would be available to assist them with the emotional concerns of their patients. The staff was asked to select a suitable time to hold a weekly group meeting and was promised that all who were interested could participate in implementing the program and reviewing its usefulness. Group meetings were then initiated (as of this writing, they are still continuing).

Description of the Groups. Attendance at the weekly one-hour sessions is voluntary but all are invited, including visiting relatives and recently discharged patients. Staff members rotate so as to increase their awareness of patient concerns while not making the group unwieldy. Initially, because both patients and staff were uneasy about the new program, attendance was low (approximately eight patients). However, once the group became a regular part of the ward routine and interesting topics (such as the fear of falling and phantom sensations) started to be discussed between sessions, attendance rose considerably. After about three months of regular meetings, average attendance grew to fourteen; a majority of the inpatients now attend.

Participation by family members and discharged patients has always been sporadic because of distance and time problems.

To establish a successful format took time and experimentation. At first, there was a general air of diffidence and awkwardness, and there were many strained silences because of the prevailing skepticism and passive resistance. The consultant-leader tended to minimize structure because of her background in group psychotherapy, while staff and patients wanted a highly structured format. For two months, compromises were made. Information on topics germane to rehabilitation was discussed, after which experiences and feelings were shared. A series of regular topics emerged, incorporating such pertinent issues as bandaging and general care of the stump, managing at home with a prosthesis, community resources for amputees, nutrition, how to stop smoking, and more emotion-laden areas such as coping with loss and the fear of dependency.

Leadership Role. The role of the group leader is vital to the success of this model. One of the earliest and most important tasks in developing this kind of program is to select, from among local staff, the person best suited to be trained as a leader. Often there will be no clear choice, such as a staff member who already possesses formal training and experience in group techniques. Therefore, selection must be based on such factors as motivation and personal attributes such as insight and capacity for learning skills. In the situation discussed here, the public health nurse, who works in the unit two half-days weekly, was selected because of her basic communication skills and interest, and also because the group offered her a unique opportunity to fulfill her educational responsibility. Although the consultant launched the group and initially acted as leader, the already nominated local leader acted as an assistant and gradually took charge as she felt more competent and comfortable. Training and supervision were accomplished through pregroup and postgroup meetings; role playing; the provision of written material; and staff seminars dealing with psychosocial reactions, emotional concerns, and phases of adjustment following a major loss. Soon after the first local staff member took over major leadership responsibilities, the head nurse was introduced to the same training procedures to assure backup and continuity.

While the leader plans and coordinates the format, the chosen topics are presented by a variety of people, including guests (for example, medical staff members, community representatives, and researchers). Within the group, the leader's role is to be accepting and nonjudgmental and to act as a catalyst rather than to direct events. Requests for information are answered directly or referred to the most knowledgeable person, but the leader also encourages veteran amputees to address the concerns of recent amputees on the basis of their own experiences. The unique value of mutual sharing and support among people in various phases of coping with a stressful life event has been demonstrated in many programs (for example, Rogers and others, 1980, 1982).

In addition, it is important that no concern or question be dismissed as being too trivial and that the preferences of patients for certain discussion topics be respected. All opportunities are taken to reinforce the realization that many people may be silently worrying about similar kinds of problems, but at the same time nobody should be pressured to speak or express his feelings. Staff discussion is deliberately minimal to encourage patient-patient interaction. However, the leader may intervene in order to clarify, ask questions, or try to draw new patients into a discussion of recent events (such as home visits) or known concerns (such as phantom sensations).

Whenever a recurrent or widespread problem related to the overall functioning of the group is identified, attempts to mobilize the members to resolve the issue should be made. For example, the consensus that newly admitted patients were ill prepared for their inpatient rehabilitation experience resulted in using portions of two meetings to develop an orientation brochure that the unit now supplies to referring hospitals for patients. The brochure addresses the widespread conviction of patients that knowing what to expect (that is, what clothes to bring, the average length of inpatient stay, the fact that a temporary prosthesis is supplied before a permanent artificial limb is fitted, and so on) alleviates part of the emotional distress that many have experienced at the beginning of rehabilitation.

Predominant Themes. While discussion topics have varied widely depending on the personalities, concerns, and length of stay of participants, several themes have recurred often enough to deserve special mention. Most patients at some time want to relate their experiences before, during, and immediately after surgery—a need that has been observed in many other populations who have suffered traumatic losses. It is widely agreed that this review of stressful events, reactions, and circumstances is very beneficial and is best carried out in a supportive and understanding milieu. Some express anger and bitterness over the failure of medical treatment prior to surgery, such as the man who complained, "I kept being shunted from one doctor to another and none of them told me what was wrong."

Other patients feel guilty about things that they should have or could have done to prevent amputation (for example, "My wife kept telling me not to use those corn plasters but I didn't listen"). Many talk about the pain they experienced but did not communicate to doctors, and the problems that friends and relatives have had in accepting their amputation. One woman was very distressed because her teenage daughter ran from the room when she saw her mother without her artificial limb. The common feeling of being unprepared for the rehabilitative process involves many issues, such as hostility and despair over the practical concerns already described and over such stressful issues as the cost of the prosthesis and the time required to learn to walk.

Patients seldom mention phantom pains and sensations spontaneously, but if the topic is raised, there is usually widespread acknowledgment of the experience and accompanying expressions of concern. Some are afraid to discuss phantom pain because they worry that pain is caused by further complications that they do not want to face. Others fear that they will be considered weak or even crazy (for example, "I kept feeling the weight of the bedcovers on a foot that wasn't there—I thought I was losing my mind"). Concerns about patients' current medical conditions, which are certainly prominent, can be lessened through ventilation, assurance, and support from other patients who are further along in the rehabilitation process. Understandably, there are fears about losing one's good leg and about the need for surgical revision (which is sometimes more upsetting than the original amputation).

Issues of forced dependency underlie many discussions, particularly for the elderly, people whose health is deteriorating, and patients who are encountering financial strains or are independent by nature. Of course, for people who have been dependent on others for some time, dependency may not pose a problem. Interestingly, patients who are caring for dependent relatives such as sick spouses seem to be motivated toward rehabilitation because of their desire to remain needed and useful. One woman, whose husband had recently suffered a stroke, made much faster progress than predicted, stating simply, "I have to be able to take care of John."

Reactions of other patients are frequently discussed. Fellow patients provide much more appropriate support and advice than the staff because they have experienced similar reactions of avoidance, dismay, veiled curiosity, excess sympathy, and awkwardness. Many stories are told about situations, such as trying to board a bus, in which people are not helpful enough. In other circumstances, amputees feel that they are provided with more help than they want, and they resent not being asked if they need assistance. The uninhibited responses of children, which are frequently recounted, are actually preferred because of their honesty and openness. Veteran amputees talking about their own experiences recommend that the neophyte employ assertiveness and a sense of humor when they are in possibly embarrassing circumstances, such as swimming or being stuck in a revolving door. The staff that is present can therapeutically reinforce feelings, as well as suggest how to deal with unwanted assistance and how to fall without injury.

The group is also an excellent vehicle for delivering the crucial message that one must take responsibility for one's health by learning about one's condition and treatment and by being assertive in alerting professionals to persistent pain, improper bandaging, or other complications. Passivity and dependency are discouraged by both staff and experienced amputees, who convey the message "It's your body, after all." In general, the major objective of the interaction is to enhance coping skills. Thus, numerous aspects of everyday living are discussed, many of which may have to be handled or viewed differently. Also, necessary limitations in regard to driving, working, finances, managing around the house, and other issues with both practical and emotional components are distinguished from imagined limitations. Being able to anticipate and discuss potentially stressful hurdles can lessen the risk of later distress, depression, and despair. It is particularly helpful to invite a discharged patient who had coped well with amputation to participate in meetings about practical methods of improving one's life-style (for example, installing special hand-operated gearshifts in cars and using special carpeting and ramps at home).

Although the group leader and the staff try to assure patients that it is normal to feel depressed or angry periodically and that emotional adjustment takes time, one of the most interesting aspects of the group dynamics is that the group itself often discourages overt, extensive expressions of depressed feelings. A number of factors contribute to this phenomenon: Some older patients (particularly men) maintain values related to stoicism and courage and do not express their feelings; many with poor prognoses or relentless physical deterioration employ denial; and others are simply not introspective or insightful. Other therapists who have developed groups for the chronically ill (Lipp and Malone, 1976) also describe their groups as limiting or suppressing negative emotions.

In fact, the general tenor of meetings is positive, constructive, and even humorous as patients relate anecdotes about recent experiences. (For example, "Yesterday my little nephew asked me if he would be able to take off one leg when he grew up.") Of course, anger, depression, and even suicidal thoughts are voiced at times, but such feelings are usually described after they occur. (For example, "A few weeks ago I was so depressed that I wanted to die, but I feel much better now.") This method of admitting negative thoughts after the fact seems to be a safe way for patients to express their vulnerabilities, and it helps to assure new patients that there is light at the end of the tunnel.

The foregoing themes are presented not only so that readers can become more aware but also so that potential leaders of amputee groups will bring up these subjects if participants do not mention them. There will always be group members who may hesitate to verbalize their concerns.

Some topics are important enough to warrant being scheduled several times as the main subject of a session. Others can be handled in an open discussion simply by asking a question, such as "Is anyone experiencing what we call phantom sensations in the area of the amputated limb? Many amputees have these sensations, which are quite normal." Another approach is to draw out a patient with a question, such as asking how he coped with his first weekend at home. When a participant asks a question, even though the leader and other staff members know the answer, it is best to encourage group members to discuss the issue by asking if others have had similar concerns or experiences. Of course, questions related to treatment and medical issues must be answered with facts, but the feelings that often underlie such requests must not be ignored. Furthermore, some group members may have hearing or language problems, and occasionally an elderly participant may display signs of confusion, forgetfulness, or a short attention span. While many of these patients obviously benefit from attending meetings, their inclusion demands clear, simple explanations that minimize the use of medical terminology while avoiding paternalistic overtones.

Staff members who participate in the groups should not let lengthy interchanges with a few amputees or with each other dominate a session, nor use explanations that ignore the emotional content of what is being discussed, nor unthinkingly defend the hospital system. The leader should always involve other patients in a discussion and acknowledge the validity of the feelings being expressed while not necessarily endorsing the facts. At times, the leader may suggest that an issue may be dealt with more appropriately on a one-to-one basis after the meeting.

Of course, this group model has only limited usefulness in assisting seriously disturbed patients. A few recent amputees will always display severe emotional reactions, psychiatric symptoms, and signs of pathological maladaptation; these patients require individual consultation and definitive treatment. The value of the group for such patients is that it allows the therapist to recognize them early and make appropriate referrals. Also, the group is useful as an adjunct to individual therapeutic strategies.

Evaluation of Patient Needs and Program Goals. Most publications dealing with the emotional problems of amputees and similarly stressed patients are written for professionals. There are few attempts to obtain systematic feedback from patients about the nature and extent of their psychosocial needs or their perception of the successfulness of intervention strategies. While studies that rely on self-report methods have limitations (for example, they are subject to the person's expectations of the situation or desire to please), subjective perception of the stressfulness of life events is known to be an important determinant of subsequent responses to stress. Thus, information provided by patients about the characteristics and extent of their problems as well as their reactions to related intervention can be of great value.

For this reason and also because the predominant group themes for our amputees differ somewhat from psychological issues emphasized in the literature (for example, there was little spontaneous discussion of grief or phantom pain), it was decided to carry out a modest research study. The goals were to determine whether the observed discrepancies were simply due to the format or whether they related to the particular patient population, and to find out whether the group was meeting identified needs. A colleague of the author, A. MacBride, designed, implemented, and evaluated this study (MacBride and others, 1980).

Accordingly, all patients (except those with severe mental disability or language problems) admitted to the unit over a six-month period were surveyed via two structured personal interviews. Fifty amputees were interviewed immediately after admission, and thirty-six were interviewed again just before discharge (of the remaining fourteen, one died, several returned to general hospitals for further surgery, and the rest were discharged with insufficient notice). The interviews provided demographic information, details of pre- and postamputation experiences, descriptions of present concerns and supports, and scores on the thirty-item Goldberg General Health Questionnaire (GHQ), a widely validated measure of distress (Goldberg, 1972).

A number of interesting findings emerged. Change in body image was a major concern of only three amputees and a minor concern of only nine others. Similarly, forced dependency, the reactions of others, and the fear of life-style changes were of concern to only a quarter of those interviewed. However, over half expressed distress over concrete factors such as phantom pain and the fear of falling; financial and health problems and worry over managing around the house were the items of next greatest concern. Of the total group, 88 percent were "satisfied" or "very satisfied" with the physical care received in general hospitals, and 100 percent were satisfied with physical care supplied in the rehabilitation setting. In contrast, only 38 percent indicated satisfaction with the emotional care received in general hospitals, while 72 percent were satisfied with such care in the amputee unit. However, responses indicated a low expectation of such care in acute hospital settings, and only 23 percent stated that their greatest period of emotional distress occurred immediately after amputation. The remainder were evenly divided between being most upset before amputation or at a later time.

A GHQ score of 5 or more indicates a level of distress requiring further psychological attention (Goldberg, 1972). At the time of admission, 74 percent of the amputees had scores of 5 or more; just before discharge, 47 percent had such scores. But when asked to rate their attitude toward their amputation on a 5-point scale from "the worst thing that could happen to me" to a "minor upset," 46 percent rated the amputation as somewhere between a "minor upset" and a "moderately stressful" experience. Interestingly, some actually described it as not stressful at all or as a relief.

The relatively mild impact of the amputation itself is probably related to the frequently lengthy disease processes and to suffering over matters other than the loss of the limb. The characteristics of this particular population also help to explain why their major concerns tended to be practical ones. The lengthy illnesses many patients had had before their amputations had allowed some patients to anticipate grief and adjust somewhat to their altered body image and their increased dependency on others. However, for many, the full impact of the

amputation did not hit home until after they entered the rehabilitation unit. Then they realized that the assurances of physicians and relatives were unrealistic and misleading. Only 16 percent felt adequately prepared for rehabilitation, while 30 percent
found the unit to be much different from what they had expected, and 54 percent had had no idea what to expect. For a
large proportion, this was the first time that they had seen prostheses and their own stump. They began to realize that learning
to manage ambulation could be a slow, painful, and often discouraging task. This probably explains the high GHQ level upon
admission.

The absence of discussion of themes such as sex and body
image may have been due to the fact that the patients were predominantly elderly and male, while the staff was mostly female.
Also, problems of language and hearing, confusion, and continuous patient turnover meant that group topics and the level of
interaction varied from week to week. However, it cannot be
concluded that all elderly amputees are mainly concerned with
practicalities while young patients are mainly concerned about
emotional issues. One independent ninety-year-old bachelor reported more distress over psychosocial concerns than all others
surveyed. Nevertheless, the modest study did provide evidence
of the importance of apportioning attention among physiological, practical, and psychological concerns, both individually and
within groups.

With regard to response to the weekly meetings, 74 percent of the patients said they enjoyed them, and 69 percent
thought that the group helped them adjust to the amputation.
Surprisingly, none expressed negative feelings, and the majority
stated that the most helpful aspects were practical information
and social support. Many patients reported that only those who
have experienced it can really understand the impact of amputation. Of course, attention to practical concerns may reflect a
displacement of intrapsychic anxieties and, as previously suggested, permit a certain level of denial to be maintained that
may well be adaptive in instances of poor prognoses (Lipp and
Malone, 1976).

These groups for recent amputees have operated continuously since 1975, a fact attesting to their usefulness for both staff and patients. Furthermore, the impact of the program on the general operation of the rehabilitative setting and the institution as a whole has been far-reaching. The staff has become much more aware, sensitive, and tolerant of the emotional and behavioral responses of their patients. The subtle interplay between psychosocial and physiological factors in the rehabilitative process is much better understood. As a result, the staff now interacts with patients more frequently and more comfortably on a day-to-day basis. Problems brought up in the group are followed up individually with patients and in case conferences and unit planning meetings with other staff. The staff is less judgmental and authoritarian, and patients are more involved and constructively self-assertive. In fact, the entire atmosphere of the unit has changed noticeably. Published articles describing program development, the survey, and patient issues (MacBride and others, 1978, 1980; Rogers, Whylie, and MacBride, 1977; Rogers and others, 1977–78; Whylie, 1981) did much to raise staff morale. As the staff's work became more widely known, rehabilitation professionals requested seminars and presentations by staff members.

Difficulties

One of the hazards of implementing S/T groups is that the apparent simplicity of the model can lead to slipshod program development. As underscored by Schwartz (1975), knowledgeable, experienced mental health professionals should oversee the launching of groups and the selection, training, and supervision of leaders. Because most staff members who work on amputee units have not received special education or training in groups or in individual dynamics, they are likely to be unfamiliar with the comparatively free-flowing atmosphere typical of the meetings. Both the style and the thrust of interactions within the groups differ sharply from routine conversations between health professionals and patients, which focus on explaining treatment, providing direction and encouragement, and requesting or giving information. When communicating with their patients, care givers tend to adopt a logical, factual (albeit kindly and pleasant) approach, which complements their "expert helper" role. However, this style is less appropriate for S/T groups because it does not facilitate open discussion. At the same time, patients who are accustomed to viewing professionals with a certain degree of awe may be uncomfortable at the first group meetings. Not surprisingly, they may feel hesitant about expressing their emotions or asserting themselves before both professionals and laypersons.

Unless the groups are led by properly trained individuals who have regular access to professional consultants, there will always be a danger that the emphasis on patient-centered interactions will slowly disappear. The format may gradually become more didactic, or the groups may evolve into either professionally dominated question-and-answer sessions or social get-togethers. If there is a constant turnover of participants, both staff members and patients, the group process must be carefully monitored, and all staff members who participate in meetings should receive both an orientation and regular follow-up seminars on communication, emotional responses to loss and illness, and psychosocial problems common to recent amputees. In addition, the leader and the staff should meet after each group session to discuss and evaluate both content and process and to develop strategies for dealing with individual and group needs. In these review sessions, the leader and the consultant can also offer immediate positive feedback to staff regarding good communication techniques, as well as make suggestions to those staff members who initiated interactions that impeded the group process.

People working with amputees who wish to launch similar groups should also be aware that only a small proportion of mental health professionals are both experienced in consultation-liaison psychiatry and familiar with the particular group modality discussed in this chapter. The aim of the S/T group model is to help patients share information, coping strategies, feelings, and support without feeling pressured to speak about themselves. In contrast, insight-oriented group therapy usually emphasizes confronting, expressing, and resolving intrapsychic conflicts.

It is important to remember that most of the patients do not see themselves as needing therapy for their emotional problems. In fact, some may be suspicious of psychiatry and actively resist being analyzed. The consultant should first dispel prevailing fears and misconceptions by adjusting her style and the group format to create a nonthreatening atmosphere. An absence of structure and a passive, questioning leadership style tend to heighten discomfort and can produce lengthy silences or an atmosphere of diffidence. By beginning each meeting with a brief description of the objectives and a reminder of the voluntary nature of the group and then holding short staff-led discussion of an area of known concern, the consultant can alleviate apprehension about her involvement while providing a jumping-off point for patient interaction. Also, it is important that the consultant gain the trust of both staff and patients by being open to all concerned, ensuring that individual requests for case-centered consultation are promptly dealt with, and showing interest and support for stated concerns. Thus, professional experience, orientation, and personality should be considered carefully when selecting a psychiatric consultant to launch this kind of program.

From time to time, group leaders and consultants may well become bored and frustrated. Since the content of the sessions is bound to become rather repetitive, an experienced clinician may view the level of interaction as somewhat superficial and thus unrewarding. At West Park, where most participants are elderly, the group usually includes at least one patient who is deaf, another who is a little confused or irascible, and some whose insight is minimal. So that both the staff and the more alert and sensitive patients derive benefit from the groups, it is essential to identify patients whose participation significantly impedes interaction and the group process. There are several ways to deal with these difficult patients. A staff member can be assigned to sit beside a patient and interpret discussions or encourage appropriate interactions; some patients can be advised that the program is not relevant to their situations; and on very rare occasions, disruptive or acutely disturbed patients can be barred from participating in the groups.

Both leaders and consultants need to support each other

so that they can maintain a balanced perspective and not become dissatisfied with their functions. Since leaders may periodically request respites from their responsibilities, more than one trained leader should always be available.

Termination

The author's original tasks at the West Park Amputee Unit were to assess psychosocial needs and recommend solutions; to design, launch, and evaluate an intervention program; and finally to terminate the consultation after teaching leadership skills to the local staff. Although everyone knew from the beginning that the consultant's involvement was temporary, withdrawal of services was naturally the most difficult phase. As in all situations involving the severing of mutually satisfying ties, both the consultant and the staff had difficulties letting go. The program was successful; everyone wanted the groups to continue; the staff felt better able to cope with and gain help for the psychosocial needs of their patients; and hospital administrators were attracted by the low cost of the model and the increased availability of consultation. The consultant was uneasy about withdrawing support not only because of the good rapport she had developed with the local staff but also because this was her creation and she was personally involved in its survival.

When faced with conflicts of this kind, it is tempting to delay termination, and there will always be those who exploit the service provider's feelings of personal responsibility by exerting pressure to stay on. At West Park, the consultant had become convinced that consultation-liaison services were an essential element of the S/T group model for reasons already explained. So she now had to convince the hospital of the importance of regular backup professional consultation for the group leaders while simultaneously preparing herself and the staff for the possibility that her persuasions might not be successful and for the certainty that she would have to withdraw eventually. Fortunately, the hospital, which was in the midst of expanding its programs and facilities, was interested in replicating the model in another unit that treated stroke victims and wanted to develop a new psychogeriatrics program.

It was not easy to alter perceptions about the apparent simplicity of the S/T group approach or to convince the administration to employ qualified consultation-liaison staff. However, after a meeting between West Park medical staff and Clarke Institute psychiatrists, the hospital accepted a service delivery proposal featuring employment of a full-time nonmedical professional experienced in consultation-liaison psychiatry. Since implementing this approach hospitalwide, the institution has pioneered numerous program initiatives and has become widely recognized for its innovative approaches to rehabilitation and psychogeriatric services.

Had this initiative not been successful, consultative services would have been withdrawn. The consultant must always prepare for the termination of time-limited programs by emphasizing the temporariness of his involvement from the onset and encouraging local staff to take over leadership and decision-making responsibilities as soon as possible. Transitions and endings are always stressful; only foresight and an early discussion of potential problems can ease their effects. However, as long as staff concerns are anticipated, the patients will experience few problems. It is the care givers who may feel abandoned, frustrated, or betrayed, and the consultant must help them to recognize that they may well manifest themselves some of the normal reactions associated with grief and loss.

Future Directions

This experience has been valuable both because of the knowledge gained and because of the unanswered questions remaining. For a primarily elderly, nonpsychologically minded population such as the one described, amputation is seldom a solitary stressor, and there is a major conscious preoccupation with current medical and practical issues rather than intrapsychic factors. Amputees are both in need of and more receptive to emotional support and understanding during the early rehabilitative phase than they are immediately after surgery. The effectiveness of the S/T group lies in its ability to focus both on areas that patients view as priorities and on equally important underlying emotional and social stressors. Advantages to patients and staff participants include the nonthreatening atmosphere; the emphasis on prevention and on the early identification of problems and personal coping; the fostering of self-help and peer support; and the benefits of openly discussing questions, fears, and concerns that otherwise would not be mentioned.

In the future, systematic research into the emotional consequences of amputation and their interplay with physiological factors within the entire rehabilitative process must be emphasized much more. Those people working in rehabilitative settings are urged to look beyond traditional consultation methods and staffing resources and to collaborate with professionals from other medical specialties when developing programming to benefit both their patients and themselves.

Self-Reflection

It is not easy for health professionals, including those in the field of psychiatry, to move out of their specialties and liaise with professionals from other disciplines. Nor is it comfortable to expose one's self, as is inevitable through S/T group participation, to the dilemmas and concerns of patients. All of one's previous assumptions about professional roles and treatment priorities may have to be reassessed as patient needs are better understood. Those whose approach to patient care relies strongly on a professional demeanor of emotional detachment and aloofness may have difficulties interacting with the group. Others may go through a phase of overidentifying with patients or experiencing fears about their own health. Staff members who participate in S/T groups require support and assistance as they reexamine their professional roles and learn to empathize while maintaining objectivity.

Those who are not comfortable with this intervention model should not feel inadequate or be pressured to continue. The group is *not* an appropriate vehicle for all providers or receivers of treatment. Also, a few professionals will always avoid S/T group participation and consequently denigrate the program. However, although group approaches such as this are not panaceas either for the staff or the patients, the author is convinced of their inherent value: The risks are minimal and the potential benefits great.

References

Anderson, K., and Berg, S. "The Relationship Between Some Psychological Factors and the Outcome of Medical Rehabilitation." *Scandinavian Journal of Rehabilitation Medicine,* 1975, *7,* 166-170.
Burgess, E. M., and others. *The Management of Lower Extremity Amputations.* Washington, D.C.: U.S. Government Printing Office, 1969.
Caine, D. "Psychological Considerations Affecting Rehabilitation After Amputation." *Medical Journal of Australia,* 1973, *2,* 818-821.
Caplan, L. M., and Hackett, T. P. "Emotional Effects of Lower Limb Amputation in the Aged." *New England Journal of Medicine,* 1963, *269,* 1166.
Dembo, T., Ladieu-Leviton, C., and Wright, B. A. "Acceptance of Loss—Amputation." In J. F. Garrett (Ed.), *Psychological Aspects of Physical Disabilities.* Washington, D.C.: U.S. Government Printing Office, 1952.
Fischer, W. G., and Samuelson, C. F. "Group Psychotherapy for Selected Patients with Lower Extremity Amputations." *Archives of Physical Medicine and Rehabilitation,* 1971, *52,* 79.
Fleurant, F. W., and Alexander, J. "Below Knee Amputation and Rehabilitation of Amputees." *Surgery, Gynaecology and Obstetrics,* 1980, *151,* 41-44.
Frank, J. L. "The Amputee War Casualty in a Military Hospital: Observations on Psychological Management." *International Journal of Psychiatry in Medicine,* 1973, *4,* 1-16.
Frank, J. L., and Herndon, J. H. "Psychiatric-Orthopedic Liaison in the Hospital, Management of the Amputee War Casualty." *International Journal of Psychiatry in Medicine,* 1974, *5* (2), 105-114.
Freeman, A. F., and Applegate, W. R. "Psychiatric Consultation

to a Rehabilitation Program for Amputees." *Hospital and Community Psychiatry*, 1976, *27* (1), 40-42.

Froggatt, D., and Mawby, R. I. "Surviving an Amputation." *Social Sciences and Medicine,* 1981, *15*E, 123-128.

Goldberg, D. *The Detection of Psychiatric Illness by Questionnaire.* London: Oxford University Press, 1972.

Haber, W. B. "Reactions to Loss of Limb. Physiological and Psychological Aspects." *Annals of the New York Academy of Sciences,* 1958, *73,* 20-21.

Hamilton, A. "Rehabilitation of the Leg Amputee in the Community." *The Practitioner,* 1981, *225,* 1487-1497.

Hunter, R. C. A. "Consultation-Liaison Psychiatry in the General Hospital." *Perspectives in Psychiatry,* 1982, *1* (3), 1-3.

Katrak, P. H., and Baggott, J. B. "Rehabilitation of Elderly Lower-Extremity Amputees." *The Medical Journal of Australia,* 1980, *1,* 651-653.

Kerstein, M. D. "Group Rehabilitation for the Vascular Disease Amputee." *Journal of the American Geriatrics Society,* 1980, *28* (1), 40-41.

Klopsteg, P. E., and Wilson, P. D. *Human Limbs and Their Substitutes.* New York: Hafner, 1968.

Kostuik, J. P., and others. *The Geographical Area Serviced by the Amputee Centre and the Cost-Effectiveness of the Rehabilitation Programme.* Mimeograph, National Sanitorium Association, Ottawa, Canada, 1975.

Kutner, B. "Social Psychology of Disability." In W. S. Neff (Ed.), *Rehabilitation Psychology.* Washington, D.C.: American Psychological Association, 1971.

Lipowski, Z. J. "Consultation-Liaison Psychiatry: An Overview." *American Journal of Psychiatry,* 1974, *131,* 632-640.

Lipp, M. R., and Malone, S. T. "Group Rehabilitation of Vascular Surgery Patients." *Archives of Physical Medicine and Rehabilitation,* 1976, *57,* 180-183.

MacBride, A., and others. "Psychosocial Stress Among Geriatric Patients on an Amputee Unit." In *Psychogeriatric Care in Institutions and in the Community: Proceedings of the Fifth Annual Meeting of the Ontario Psychogeriatric Association.* London, Ontario: Ontario Psychogeriatric Association, 1978.

MacBride, A., and others. "Psychosocial Factors in the Rehabilitation of Elderly Amputees." *Psychosomatics,* 1980, *21* (3), 258-265.

May, C. H., McPhee, M. C., and Pritchard, D. J. "An Amputee Visitor Program as an Adjunct to Rehabilitation of the Lower Limb Amputee." *Mayo Clinic Proceedings,* 1979, *54,* 774-778.

Parkes, C. M. "Components of the Reaction to Loss of a Limb, Spouse, or Home." *Journal of Psychosomatic Research,* 1972, *16,* 343-349.

Parkes, C. M. "Factors Determining the Persistence of Phantom Pain in the Amputee." *Journal of Psychosomatic Research,* 1973, *17,* 97-108.

Parkes, C. M. "Psychosocial Transitions: Comparison Between Reactions to Loss of a Limb and Loss of a Spouse." *British Journal of Psychiatry,* 1975, *127,* 204-210.

Parkes, C. M., and Napier, M. M. "Psychiatric Sequelae of Amputation." In J. Silverstone and B. Barraclough (Eds.), *Contemporary Psychiatry: Selected Reviews from the British Journal of Hospital Medicine.* Ashford, England: Headley Brothers, 1975.

Rogers, J., Whylie, B., and MacBride, A. "The Use of Groups in the Rehabilitation of Amputees." *Annals of the Royal College of Physicians and Surgeons of Canada,* 1977, *10* (1), 92-94.

Rogers, J., and others. "The Use of Groups in the Rehabilitation of Amputees." *International Journal of Psychiatry in Medicine,* 1977-78, *8* (3), 243-255.

Rogers, J., and others. "A Self-Help Program for Widows as an Independent Community Service." *Hospital and Community Psychiatry,* 1980, *31* (12), 843-847.

Rogers, J., and others. "Help for Families of Suicide: Survivors Support Program." *Canadian Journal of Psychiatry,* 1982, *27,* 444-449.

Rusk, H. A. *Rehabilitation Medicine.* St. Louis, Mo.: Mosby, 1971.

Schwartz, M. D. "Situation/Transition Groups: A Conceptualization and Review." *American Journal of Orthopsychiatry,* 1975, *45* (5), 744-755.

Siller, J. "Psychosocial Aspects of Physical Disability." In J.

Meislin (Ed.), *Rehabilitation Medicine and Psychiatry.* Springfield, Ill.: Thomas, 1976.

Tunbridge Report. *Rehabilitation: Report of a Sub-Committee of the Standing Medical Advisory Committee.* London: H. M. Stationer's Office, 1972.

Vachon, M. L. S. "Grief and Bereavement Following the Death of a Spouse." *Canadian Psychiatric Association Journal,* 1976, *21,* 35-44.

Vachon, M. L. S., and Lyall, W. A. L. "Applying Psychiatric Techniques to Patients with Cancer." *Hospital and Community Psychiatry,* 1976, *27* (8), 582-584.

Walters, J. "Coping with a Leg Amputation." *American Journal of Nursing,* July 1981, pp. 1349-1352.

Weiss, S. A. "The Body Image as Related to Phantom Sensation: A Hypothetical Conceptualization of Seemingly Isolated Findings." *Annals of the New York Academy of Science,* 1958, *74,* 25-29.

Whitman, H., Gustafson, J., and Coleman, F. "Group Approaches for Cancer Patients—Leaders and Members." *American Journal of Nursing,* May 1979.

Whylie, B. "Social and Psychological Problems of the Adult Amputee." In J. P. Kostuik and R. Gillespie (Eds.), *Amputation Surgery and Rehabilitation: The Toronto Experience.* Toronto: Churchill/Livingstone, 1981.

7

Stephen Armstrong, Ph.D.

▦ ▦ ▦ ▦ ▦ ▦ ▦ ▦ ▦ ▦ ▦ ▦ ▦

End-Stage
Renal Disease

The human kidney both balances the concentrations of bodily fluids and electrolytes and filters metabolic byproducts from the incoming blood supply. This complex balancing and filtering process depends on three factors: first, the rate at which blood is supplied to the filtering areas of the kidney; second, the hydrostatic pressure of the blood inside the filtering capillary parts of the kidney (called the "glomerulus"); and, third, the pressure difference across the filtering membrane (called the "oncotic pressure difference"). Unlike a simple filter, however, the kidney performs another function: It rebalances the composition of the returning blood plasma by means of an active, selective reabsorption of certain electrolytes and fluid across another section of very thin membrane (called the "tubular epithelium"). Because of the great volume of blood filtered in the human kidneys (more than 100 liters per day), this selective reabsorption of the filtrate must occur; otherwise, important solutes and much of the filtered fluid would be disposed of (in diluted urine) and fluid intake requirements would be radically different.

A large number of conditions can disrupt the blood supply, membrane pressures, and filtrate transportation or reabsorption. These conditions include mechanical trauma to the kidneys or vascular supply system (as happens in auto accidents or in compression wounds from high explosives), obstruction of the blood supply or filtrate, poisoning by toxins (such as are associated with analgesic abuse or heavy-metal poisoning), metabolic diseases (such as diabetes mellitus or gout), damage to the arteriolar and capillary system (as in acute postpartum renal failure), glomerular damage (as in acute bacterial infections that are transported throughout the body by the blood), or hereditary or congenital diseases (such as polycystic kidney disease).

The causes of damaging conditions now number over 100, but many of the causes and etiologies have not been elucidated. Whatever the cause may be, when kidney functioning is permanently reduced or degraded, the condition is termed *end-stage renal disease* (ESRD) (Kerr, 1979; Ledingham, 1979; Thurau, Boylan, and Mason, 1979).

Kidney diseases may be characterized as sudden-onset or chronic. Acute renal failure has a rapid onset and can usually be reversed through careful medical management. The mechanism of acute failure apparently involves changes in renal vascular resistance and a diminution in renal blood flow, but the cause of these changes is not yet clear.

On the other hand, chronic renal failure permanently reduces filtration rates, tubular reabsorption rates, and/or plasma flow. These changes may come rapidly, with obvious symptomatology, or slowly and insidiously, depending on the underlying pathological condition. The causal mechanism of permanent damage to the kidney is not known, and microscopic structural damage to individual nephrons in the kidney can vary remarkably. However, at least four factors are thought to be involved in permanent damage: increased filtration "load" per nephron, changes in reabsorption volumes or function, changes in the membrane structure itself, and changes in the capacity to transport molecules or ions within and across the membranes.

Because the kidney filters and reabsorbs fluids, electrolytes, and metabolic products, any change in kidney functioning

has a great number of consequences. In degraded kidney functioning, the homeostatic balances of water, sodium, potassium,
phosphate, and bicarbonate are upset, and nitrogen by-products
build up. Unless a substitute filter system can be provided,
death invariably results.

Before the invention of cellophane, there was no membrane that could be used in place of normal kidney tissue. Moreover, before the development of modern hematology and elec-
tronic monitoring devices, there was no way to transport blood
across a synthetic membrane under sufficient pressure to promote filtration without also causing the membrane to rupture.
Hence, prior to 1960, all kidney failure patients died.

Beginning in 1945 and continuing through the early
1960s, a series of medical experiments and clinical trials in
northern Europe and the United States laid the foundations for
modern renal practice. A twelve-page scientific report in 1960
offered the first evidence that an artificial-membrane "kidney"
might be possible (Scribner and others, 1960).

Since that date, scientific and medical advances have been
enormous. First came advances in hematology and cardiology,
which deepened understanding of blood flow and pressure. Si-
multaneous advances included the ability to place shunts into
arms or legs to allow repeated access to the patient's blood circulation and better treatment of problems with blood coagula-
tion and contamination. Moreover, infectious disease controls
also advanced, which led to the use of the body's own membranes (the peritoneal membranes, located in the abdomen)
rather than artificial membranes as the filters. Developments in
immunology and immunosuppression enabled surgeons to consider transplanting human kidneys rather than constructing artificial kidneys.

Second, beginning in the 1960s, polymer chemistry was
advanced to the point that semipermeable membranes with very
small filtering holes could be made strong enough to withstand
the necessary filtrate and blood pressures. These membranes
also began to be produced on a large scale with great precision
and extremely high quality control.

Third, the electronics industry made great strides in developing highly reliable monitors, motors, and pumps that could transport blood to and from one side of the membrane safely at precisely measured rates and pressures and transport artificial "filtrate" to the other side of the membrane at equally precise rates and pressures.

Fourth, a complex training system was developed for persons tending to the technological and medical needs of renal patients.

Fifth, the special American genius for public finance was called into play, because private financing of these medical and technical developments was inherently undemocratic. (In the late 1960s, wealthy persons with renal failure traveled around the country as medical vagabonds to purchase or beg the means of survival.) In 1972 Congress created and funded a renal health care system that included both for-profit and the more traditional not-for-profit health care sectors. At this writing, between 40,000 and 50,000 citizens obtain comprehensive health and social benefits through this system, at an annual cost of $3 to $3.5 billion.

Only eighty-odd years after the mechanism of glomerular filtration and reabsorption was first outlined (Starling, 1896, 1899), the derivative medical care system and technologies have become available in most industrialized countries. The survival rates for patients receiving these new treatments are impressive: At two years, from 70 to 90 percent of chronic hemodialysis patients survive and from 45 to 65 percent of transplantation patients survive (Kerr, 1979). These figures underline a revolution in medicine as significant as were the developments of insulin for diabetics and intensive care settings for coronary disease and trauma victims.

Because there are multiple causes of renal failure, acute and chronic management strategies are complex. In acute renal failure, the primary task is to identify the cause and to conserve the remaining renal functioning, especially in conditions that can be controlled, such as hypertension. In more advanced stages of renal disease, medical management includes hemodialysis treatments and exploring common complications such as total renovascular failure, improper sodium and water balance, anemia, chronic bone disease (osteodystrophy), glucose intolerance, elevated gastric acid levels, and peripheral neuropathy.

Both chronic hemodialysis and renal transplantation have medical complications and side effects. Chronic dialysis requires safe access to the patient's blood through repeated venipunctures. The dialysis treatment itself may be marked by discomfort, muscle cramps, nausea, rapid changes in blood pressure, and so forth. Dialysis patients are often hospitalized for a variety of procedures or to control some of the complications resulting from treatment. Transplantation procedures usually involve surgical removal of the patient's diseased kidneys, procurement of a functioning kidney (from someone recently deceased or a family member), and a surgical procedure to implant the "new" kidney. In order to prevent the patient's immunological system from rejecting the transplant, powerful immunosuppressants are used for as long as the transplant survives (unless the donor is an identical twin). The postsurgical recovery period usually lasts about one year. Complications arise if the transplant is rejected (Armstrong, Johnson, and Hopkins, 1981).

The Clinic as a Group

All of the medical care in chronic hemodialysis or transplantation is provided by persons organized into groups. In chronic dialysis the patients meet three times a week; the staff, daily. No other chronic illness requires such intense and long-standing group membership or provides so little respite from the requirements of group life.

Apart from the patients' and staff's attitudes toward the chronic illness and its treatment, two group-wide phenomena of treatment deserve mention.

The first such phenomenon is the blurring of the boundary between private (individual) treatment and public (group) treatment. While on chronic hemodialysis in the outpatient clinic, the patient does not receive private care. Instead, the clinic is a large physical space dotted with reclining chairs, machines, blood lines, beepers, and doctors or nurses walking about. Almost all clinic activity is public and observable by anyone who cares to look.

The public routine is often quite numbing and boring, and the participants—doctors, nurses, technicians, and patients —spend enormous amounts of time just looking at one another. In a sense, everyone is trapped in this public existence; there is little respite from public scrutiny. One consequence of this social organization is that all persons in the group work to establish public identities and to set up boundaries around these identities so that they can both shield and express themselves.

Of course, there is some give-and-take between the public self and the expression of one's own private thoughts and feelings. However, the group-wide tolerance for private expression is rather low, and there are few public channels through which a person may say something personal. In fact, an individual's expression of personal feelings can lead both to loss of the public self (which results in the person feeling overwhelmed) and to the exclusion of privately conceived thoughts from the group (which results in the person feeling lonely).

For instance, consider the problem of a renal patient who wants to work, which is one important way that a person maintains a public identity. Since a job affects disability benefits, an anonymous bureaucrat can stop benefits if an industrious patient accepts a job. As a consequence, such a patient may take a job that pays under the table, a secret that sometimes is revealed to the treatment staff. The treatment staff may wink at this (public) secret, but because of constraints on their public identities, they cannot publicly approve or support this deed.

Another example of public-private boundary maintenance concerns the nephrologist who asks a family member to be tissue-typed for possible kidney donation to the ill family member. To the extent that all family members are aware of the tissue-typing, this is a public request; yet it also may elicit some very deep and private loyalties or secret resentments from both the patient and the members whose typing is requested. However, family members can learn how to handle internal family tensions better through their dealings with the doctors, nurses, and other staff members.

Clinic personnel and patients rarely acknowledge that establishing and maintaining the public-private boundary for each person is important or that few avenues exist in the clinic for discussing private ideas, images, fantasies, hopes, or discouragements. Yet public events in the clinic can trigger these private musings—as happens, for example, when a patient dies or voluntarily withdraws from treatment—and it becomes evident how few are the group-wide channels through which individuals can share their thoughts or distress. At this point, the individual becomes vulnerable to loneliness or psychological isolation, and the group becomes vulnerable to rumors, emotional contagion, group-wide denial of an individual's difficulties, or scapegoating. Patients and staff with durable public-private boundaries (who, for example, can create avenues to share appropriate sadness without being overwhelmed) stabilize the entire group's public functioning.

The second group-wide phenomenon of chronic kidney disease is that the clinic is like a lifeboat culture. This lifeboat metaphor is not accepted by some writers, but I believe that it is accurate in describing the underlying group process of the clinic. First, patients can leave the clinic only by a successful kidney transplantation, which exacts its own physical price, or by death. Second, there is no escape from the repeated reminders of one's own shortened and changed life. Third, much of clinic life is unbearably routine, and it is easy to get the feeling of not going anywhere, of floating aimlessly in a situation that one cannot escape. Fourth, because of their extensive training and financial commitments or rewards, the doctors and nurses themselves cannot leave the clinic very easily unless they go to work at another clinic. Finally, the clinic is a remarkably closed and small space in which to have doctors, nurses, or patients disagreeing with one another. If a patient does not like his doctor, he cannot simply go elsewhere, and if the doctor has negative feelings about the patient, she cannot merely refer the patient to another internist or clinic. These forces all mobilize group-wide efforts to run the clinic smoothly.

Psychosocial Aspects

Even in the experimental early years of hemodialysis and transplantation, psychiatrists and others attempted to understand the emotional and behavioral concomitants to this medical treatment (for example, Kemph, 1966, 1967; Kemph, Berman, and Coppolillo, 1969). The psychosocial literature now numbers about 3,000 articles, chapters, and books, but this research effort has led to statements of surprisingly limited validity and utility in clinical practice (Armstrong, 1982).

Two factors have caused this impasse. The first factor involves what is called the "internal validity of research." Nearly 90 percent of the psychosocial studies focus exclusively on the patient or the patient's family and ignore the treatment team's contribution to adjustment. Moreover, there are no commonly accepted characteristics of a well-adjusted patient and no method for measuring adjustment. Thus, a study that supposedly demonstrates an "impairment" of adjustment (for example, Finkelstein and Steele, 1978) can be countered by a study finding no impairment (Gelfman and Wilson, 1972), which can be countered by yet another study with equivocal evidence (Greenberg, Davis, and Massey, 1973). Thus, many psychosocial studies have unacceptably ambiguous conclusions. The second factor contributing to research confusion over psychosocial adjustment involves "external validity." That is, if a group of dialysis patients are thought to be psychologically impaired, are they any more or less so than other chronically ill patients? Only one study to my knowledge addresses this problem directly (Lohmann and others, 1979).

On the whole, dialysis and transplantation patients appear to suffer a low incidence of severe psychiatric disorders, such as major depressive disorders (McKegney and others, 1981). However, the incidence of other psychological, social, or vocational problems ranges from 20 to 70 percent of the patient population, depending on the type of impairment measured (Anderson, 1975; Armstrong, 1978; Reichsman, 1981). These are very high percentages; but the nature of the impairments, their onset, and their duration are not specified.

Fortunately, researchers in other areas of the social sciences have developed a research method that combines the findings of separate studies into larger, more valid pictures, a technique called "meta-analysis" of research findings (Rosenthal, 1978). The technical features of meta-analysis are beyond this chapter's scope, but I have done an analysis of thirty-five impairment studies (Armstrong, 1982). Briefly, these studies were broken down according to the type of psychosocial functioning measured. The overall results indicate that chronic dialysis patients are not much worse off psychologically than acutely ill medical patients. However, in some specific areas, renal patients seem to have significantly more difficulty.

The first area is in medical and somatic adjustment. The repetitive and largely routine nature of hemodialysis treatments is mildly deceiving, because each routine treatment is, in itself, medically intense. Thus, chronic dialysis patients have more medical and somatic morbidity, as measured by the intensity and frequency of medical intervention, hospitalization, somatic complaints, or physicians' ratings of health or functioning.

The second area concerns vocational rehabilitation. Renal disease restricts how patients participate in the economy. Most patients have trouble maintaining full-time jobs; this fact implies a host of other family and social changes. New patients have to arrange for medical insurance and disability benefits and need assistance for transactions like bank refinancing of loans or mortgages. Spouses often look for work outside the home, and only exceptionally trained or motivated patients can break the financial dependency on the government.

The third area of impairment is in family functioning. Most families make major adjustments in order to accommodate the chronically ill patient. The marital dyad often reverses roles; because of reduced vocational prospects, families may have difficulty making developmental transitions, such as sending a youngster off to college. The family may also have a decreased ability to respond to any additional crises or problems that may occur.

One important area of family life that requires tact and support is the sexual area of the marital relationship. Despite

well-documented difficulties experienced by patients and their
partners (Abram and others, 1975; Finkelstein and Steele,
1978; Levy, 1973), many physicians simply do not ask about
this problem.

Outside of these three areas—medical adjustment, vocational rehabilitation, and family functioning—many renal patients function well. This is not to say that there are no problems, but that the problems can be managed. For instance, one
inherent psychological problem created by chronic dialysis concerns the patient's tolerance for dependency on the machine
and medical treatment, which is affected by the social expectation that patients be independent and self-supporting (Abram,
1968, 1969). Other psychological dilemmas that require attention include the bodily changes that result from renal failure:
Bones become more brittle, skin becomes more flaxen, hair becomes thinner, muscle mass may drop, and so forth (Basch,
Brown, and Cantor, 1981).

Group Therapy

Instituting group therapy at the chronic dialysis and
transplant clinic is worthwhile for several reasons. First, group
discussions help patients share some of their common problems,
which decreases patient isolation and promotes relationships
and interactions with others. By building these relationships, patients have access to each other's knowledge (and, of course,
their common misunderstandings) and intense feelings (Karasu,
1979). With increased mutual support, patients become less passive and can channel their feelings into words and shared images.
The groups can also be useful in educating the patients as critical questions are raised and answered and important coping
mechanisms are discussed. Finally, group discussion or therapy
programs allow newcomers to identify with long-term survivors.

There are two advantages of group therapy over individual therapy. First, group therapy decreases the intensity of the
transference and allows it to be partitioned within and outside
the group. This is useful for persons who may fear a therapist's
omnipotence or their own neediness. Second, being in a group
allows emotional resources to be pooled.

Since nearly all activities at the clinic are conducted in groups, a strong group format and process already exist implicitly. For instance, most clinics have an educational program for patients or families or a videotape series that describes aspects of renal disease, and the medical and nursing staffs have daily group meetings about clinic functioning.

Given the existing group orientations at clinics, one must wonder why there are not more attempts at group-wide interventions with kidney disease patients. The answer lies in part with the patients, who are notoriously reluctant to see themselves as either psychiatric patients or psychosomatic patients and hence refuse to "waste time" by staying after a hemodialysis treatment to "talk" (Abram, 1968, 1969; de Nour, 1970). The answer also lies in part with renal social workers, whose job, as mandated in the 1972 federal legislation, is to advocate for funds and work out insurance problems, and the like, but not to do group therapy.

The answer also lies with the medical staff, which tends not to equate psychologically oriented medical care with "real" medical care (Engel, 1977). Wolff (1965) points out that medical practitioners are reluctant to refer patients to a psychotherapist, especially if the medical treatment has some success; they tend to regard psychotherapy as the last line of medicine for any disorder that appears to be a physical illness. In fact, the exclusion of psychological factors from biophysical care serves to protect the medical team's group boundaries. The lack of clearly defined psychological impairments, the slow and obscure mechanism of psychotherapeutics (contrasted with the rapid and obvious mechanisms of hemodialysis), and the need to dissociate from the stress of dealing with emotional or role problems and to stay within one's own clearly defined biophysical role—these factors all contribute to the treatment team's perception of itself as psychologically invulnerable to emotional stresses and help to preserve the distinction between "real" and "psychological" medicine.

Finally, problems with funding undermine the development of group therapeutic programs. No one gets paid by the government for helping a patient's psychological state, and hemodialysis clinics cannot bill for psychotherapeutic services, so any in-center group psychotherapy program must be paid from the clinic's own fees. The supplier of the program is thus hired as a consultant. Since the reimbursement rates for all clinics are standardized and there is no competition between clinics, there is no profit incentive for a psychological program, much less a group therapeutic program, anywhere in the country.

Literature Review

Of the six published studies of group psychotherapy, three were reported just as technological and funding advances made hemodialysis a routine treatment available to more than just a few patients. Hollon (1972) had meetings with patients, families, and members of the treatment team, up to thirty persons, once a month for an hour and a half, and reported that patients and staff benefited from the educational aspects of the meetings. Sorenson (1972), who had similar large-group meetings, said that the teaching helped decrease social isolation of the spouses, the other family members, and the treatment team members.

The most experimental of these early studies was a doctoral dissertation study (Wilson, 1973; Wilson and others, 1974) in which eighteen prospective home dialysis patients were placed in either an experimental treatment group or a control no-treatment group. The treated group met for one and a half hours per week for six weeks. The authors reported few differences between the groups except that the treated group increased the amount of time spent outside the home and felt a stronger sense of internal control than before the group meetings started.

At the University of Alberta, Campbell and Sinha (1980) selected eleven chronic hemodialysis patients for group therapy, based on high depression scores on the MMPI, anger and hostility toward the treatment staff, and the absence of psychosis. The patients were divided into two groups that met every other week for ten ninety-minute sessions. A psychiatrist and two nurses led the group meetings. The psychiatrist took a "confronting attitude" and directly interpreted patient behavior; the nurses were "supportive" (Campbell and Sinha, 1980, p. 1236).

The authors reported that nine patients had a good or fair outcome from the group as measured by therapists' ratings in ten areas of functioning (for instance, fluid and diet control, a reduction in fears, and so forth). The therapists felt that the patients did not develop group trust and cohesiveness, especially toward the doctors, and they suggested such reasons as the need to deny the illness and the fact that several (nontherapy) patients died during the course of the group meetings. Other reasons could have been the planned confrontational-supportive split between the therapists and the failure to address the group's own time limit.

The most recent study of group therapy for chronic hemodialysis patients and their families involved two groups of families (multiple family groups) of up to twenty-five members (four families in each group) that met for eight weekly sessions of ninety minutes each (Steinglass and others, 1982). The families were recruited by the authors from several local clinics and were given a fee for their participation. At the end of the therapy, group members "seemed positive about the potential usefulness of the group discussions, if somewhat skeptical" (Steinglass and others, 1982, p. 12). The authors felt that the major gains were in intrafamily communication and in the direct dissemination of information between patients and other family members.

Buchanan (1975, 1981) has taken the position that "traditional, insight-oriented, interpretive" psychotherapy groups for dialysis and transplant patients are "unsuccessful" (1981, p. 268). He feels that kidney patients do not "identify" with their illness and that insight may be "too threatening." Instead, he advocates group patient education and self-help groups, which depend on patient observation, education, and cognitive learning.

Despite the paucity of evidence that emotional insight helps renal patients, I believe that psychotherapists should encourage patients to understand their illness and the groups in which they live. To be sure, patient education and self-help are important, but the unique promise of any psychotherapy is in the active comprehension of one's life.

Developing a Comprehensive Group Therapy Program

There are five steps that the therapist must take in order to construct a comprehensive group therapy program. First, the therapist must set the group focus by defining the group as time-limited. The time limit establishes what will become the central dilemma to the group—that is, the patients' wishes to be healthy, uninjured, nurtured, and gratified, all while time (and the group) move on (Mann, 1973). The ending of the group can never be undone or turned back, and even though nearly every patient knows consciously that wishes to turn the clock back are unrealistic, these wishes are still mulled over privately. Unless patients have a therapist or doctor in whom they trust and a real-life time limit, they have great difficulty talking about these private desires.

As a first step, then, I speak to each patient individually and tell about a group of patients who "get together to discuss and understand some of the problems of chronic dialysis." I use exactly that phrase throughout the treatment (and not merely to get around using the term *psychotherapy*), because the goals are, in fact, discussing and understanding important wishes that can never be gratified but can be talked through in the course of twelve weeks. I also emphasize the twelve-week time limit by counting the weeks on the calendar as I sit with the group.

The second step is to avoid having patients spend time requesting specific medical or training information of the therapist. These requests deflect the patient from trying to understand the psychological processes of their illness. The group therapist must ensure that other clinic resources—the patient education program, for instance, and the nursing staff—are available to answer questions about specific medical problems outside of the group.

The third step is to set the basic format of the group. I usually run groups for up to nine patients, once a week, for ninety minutes. Since patients will not travel to a psychiatric clinic or facility, I usually meet in the conference room at the hemodialysis clinic before patients' dialysis runs. Finally, there should be agreement about fees.

The fourth step is to help physicians understand something about psychological medicine. When formulating the goal for the patients, I also try to have the physicians accept the notion that discussing and understanding the medical treatments and patients' wishes and feelings about them are legitimate goals of the medical treatment team. On the surface, this may seem easy enough, but some physicians may not want to adopt this goal for a number of reasons.

Physicians must endorse the group because doctors tend to resist any treatment innovation that they do not understand or control. Once the physician has accepted the goal of understanding, he or she may have to talk about perceptions, beliefs, fears, and so forth. This sets a norm within the clinic that ultimately benefits the group psychotherapy.

The nephrologist's commitment to the goal of group therapy can be measured very easily and concretely by referring to three factors—the time of group meetings, the location, and fees. I was a therapist for several groups where a nephrologist changed a patient's run time or day to conflict with the group's time. In one case, when asked about this, the nephrologist said that the change was at the patient's request, and he had to be reminded that he had denied past requests from this patient and that other, nonconflicting arrangements could have been made. In other instances, nephrologists have arbitrarily taken over the group meeting room to meet with dialysis machine salespeople even though their own offices were large enough for the meeting. Finally, the issue of fees measures the level of commitment very clearly. Because patients respond to cues from physicians, if the doctors imply that the therapist's services are not worth the fee, many patients will not attend the group.

In effecting this fourth step, therefore, I have adopted the following position: First, I will not do group therapy unless the nephrologists accept the goal of understanding. Second, I ask to be included in the nephrologists' weekly patient care meetings like any other doctor. Third, I want the nephrologists to announce to all their patients the existence of the group and, once a patient is selected, to back me in encouraging the patient's attendance. Fourth, I want the nephrologists to encourage patient attendance by asking patients to talk directly with me about their concerns over the group.

The fifth step involves selecting a cotherapist. The consulting group therapist must have a trusted partner who knows the hemodialysis clinic and its operation well. Moreover, a nonmedical therapist should have a cotherapist who can interpret some of the medical problems, estimate their severity, detect distortions of information that the patients may have acquired, and the like (Armstrong, 1977). Finally, if the cotherapist is a member of the clinic's staff, he or she can help correct staff attitudes informally, outside of the group therapy meeting hours.

I usually ask the clinic's head nurse to be the group's cotherapist. Besides operating as a medical ally, the head nurse usually enjoys the confidence of the nephrologists and makes my access to clinic communications easier. Also, patients tend to attribute more power to the group, because of the head nurse's relationship to the physicians.

Groups for Adolescents

In order to provide some insight into group therapy with hemodialysis patients, the following example of a time-limited group for adolescent patients is discussed. I decided to do a group for adolescents for several reasons. First, all adolescents with ESRD face difficult developmental transitions toward independence and often feel helpless in making these steps. Second, staff members often do not countenance adolescents' rebellious or independence-directed behaviors and thus tend to undercut these patients' attempts at autonomy, making them remain "good patients"—that is, dependent patients (Armstrong, 1975). Finally, adolescent patients have typically spent a great deal of time in the clinic or hospital, have lost a year or so of schooling, and thus have poor peer supports and lack many of the social experiences of their peers.

I began first by contacting the adolescents, one by one, in the clinic while they were on the machine. The first fantasy theme emerged right off: They were fearful of being experimented on as part of some unnamed larger study. The eight adolescents each had felt coerced the month before into participating in a study of neuropsychological deficits, and they voiced their concerns about being exploited, even though they were not sure how I might accomplish this. They had trouble seeing how a new group to discuss and understand some of the problems of hemodialysis was very different from a neuropsychological deficit study.

The first test, then, concerned their perceptions of my honesty: Would I indeed let them have free choice not to enroll in the group? Would I live by my word? To counter this opening, I had several meetings with each youngster individually, exploring particularly their feelings of being exploited: Which doctors had talked to him or her? What did the doctors say about the study? Did the adolescent feel deceived? What part of the conversation with the doctors had been seen as deceptive? Had the adolescent told anyone of the feeling of being used? What did he or she think each person was being asked to do? What had the adolescent had to do in the previous study? Did he or she still harbor negative feelings about being asked to participate in that study?

At the same time, I listened for some clue to some issue that the youngster might want help with. Like other adolescents, these patients were sensitive to overtly earnest offers of help for problems, so it was important not to seem too zealous about helping them. Nevertheless, as these interviews proceeded, I was struck that these adolescents, unlike others I had met (either in school or psychiatric settings), did not tease me or show humor about people who had disappointed or exploited them previously. Instead, each youngster appeared to have gone into a very self-protective, flat, unengaged state of psychological shutdown: They were uniformly polite, isolated, and humorless.

This protective stance masked intense feelings about themselves and the group. Each youngster offered reasons for not wanting to attend the group, and each wanted to know exactly why I wanted him or her in the group. Two youngsters wanted the exclusion of other adolescents who were better adjusted to dialysis as a precondition to their own participation in the group. All of the youngsters wanted some kind of guarantee that things at the clinic would be better after the discussions.

Thus, even before the group began, the adolescents tested the therapist's motivations and powers, and tried a number of resistances. They played out the already existing splits among the adolescents at the clinic, just as normal high school kids can find ways to snub each other in excruciatingly public ways. The snubbed youngsters, who of course found out about the preconditions through the nurses, merely replied that they did not need the group. At a more unconscious group level, the adolescents—already in a relatively regressed state—carefully preserved their own territories, as if sharing things in a group would overwhelm them all, cause them to be more subjugated by the "dishonest doctors," force them to lose their fragile identities, and cheat them of the benefits of being good patients.

The six youngsters who did agree to meet were about seventeen years old and had been ill for a minimum of three years. They agreed, as one said, "to form a club." Times were set for weekly meetings at 7:30 A.M., before hemodialysis runs. In our first group meeting, the cotherapist and I were struck by how hard it was for these youngsters to talk to one another, despite the fact that they had known each other for years. One girl always responded to questions with "Hunh?" as if she were not really there. The task of understanding some of the problems was far beyond them, because they seemed to lack the basic social skills that most adolescents have by age thirteen—being able to ask questions, to share something personal, to tell a joke, to tease a grown-up, or to think about their own behavior or thoughts.

The youngsters in the hemodialysis group talked about a favorite TV show, "Movin' On," which reflected their shared anxiety and desire for escape. One youngster mentioned getting drunk and being out of control. One of the adolescents asked the therapist to provide coffee, rolls, and soft background music to soothe the group. Another stalked into the second group meeting dressed in a flashy green suit and elevated shoes and bluntly challenged the group to state "what you all are about."

When the other adolescents meekly kept quiet, he fled the group meeting, saying that he did not need to ask "anybody for anything."

In the early meetings of the group, two major themes emerged. The first theme concerned the nurses: They chatted too much among themselves and not enough with patients; they were slow in delivering lunch trays, setting up machines, and taking patients off at the end of runs; they did not communicate with or respond to patients; they were lazy and inadequate. The second theme concerned the clinic: There were not enough magazines, entertainment, books, heat lamps, peace and quiet, and so forth. The therapists let the patients articulate these themes, but the patients feared retaliation from the head nurse cotherapist in the harsh form of bad or painful venipunctures: "You'll miss the stick," they said. The underlying concern was the fear of being rejected from the clinic—and dying—for expressing any negative thoughts. The youngsters fervently rejected the therapists' clarifications about medical needs, as contrasted to psychological needs, as well as the therapists' view that they appeared to be angry about something. The adolescents further stressed that all the deficiencies that they had described were entirely accurate—all they really needed was adequate care. To them all the problems in the clinic were medical, not psychological, and there were many such problems.

Nevertheless, the group meetings provided the patients with their first opportunity to tell each other or any doctor of their negative thoughts about the clinic. Of course, the process was not all that smooth, because at first the patients could barely talk with each other, much less talk about negative thoughts. We often felt like parents encouraging a seven-year-old who had returned home from school with hurt feelings and would not talk. The group's denial of the impact of chronic hemodialysis lessened with some support, and the group boundary was solidified by attributing the blame for the hurt elsewhere.

The middle phase of the group was less labored for the therapists. Some of the group members acknowledged looking forward to the meetings, and there were fewer attempts to control the therapists.

The adolescents developed the dependency theme. One girl accused the others of "not having your heads together" about dialysis but reported that she really did not want to learn how to drive because she might have to get a part-time job to pay for the gas. Another patient renewed the request for coffee, rolls, doughnuts, and soft music. Another patient described the deficiencies of the clinic compared with another clinic he had visited where the nurses "did everything."

Before the sixth session, the nephrologists asked all clinic patients to write their state legislators to support the state dialysis program, which was threatened by funding cuts. Moreover, staff members asked patients to count brochures for the annual fund-raising drive. A rumor circulated in the group that the clinic would close in three months if extra monies were not found.

At this time the adolescents became worried about money, and the anxiety propelled them into considering problems beyond any they had concerned themselves with before. They made a number of fund-raising suggestions in the group, which marked the first time that they had really tried to work something out together. They liked the notion of a benefit basketball game with local TV personalities, but they realized that they could not play basketball. They thought of asking the technicians to put together a team to play the TV station personalities. They then thought of having a bike race to raise money. One youngster seriously mentioned sitting in chairs for periods of time for pledges of money. Chair sitting was something they all knew about, they agreed, but they could not see the terrible existential and morbid humor in the suggestion. The idea elaborated into the notion of a telethon enlisting the entire city's aid: appealing to hundreds or thousands of people for the group's great needs.

The therapists then inquired about the financial situation and killed the rumors of a possible closing. The adolescents were surprised to find that no patients were being rejected for financial reasons, that the patient load was growing, and that the clinic was not collapsing financially. The therapists asked what the donated money would be used for, who would control it, and how much would be needed. The adolescents decided that the money would be used for "patient comforts" and "parties." These desires were exaggerated when the patients (for the first time acting in concert) asked several clinic officials and National Kidney Foundation officials to help them raise money. One NKF official was quoted by several of the patients as saying that they could hold a fund-raising "carnival" and that the "only real question" was whether to have the carnival on a supermarket parking lot or at the state fairgrounds.

Of course, the fantasy of raising very large sums of money had to collapse, but the underlying desire emerged: Each patient believed that by raising such sums, he or she would be placed higher on the eligible transplant list, which in turn was fantasized to mean getting off the machine. This wish was talked about only eight weeks after each adolescent had denied having any problems with chronic hemodialysis.

The therapists pointed out their neediness and dependency as a problem of being on dialysis. By this time, however, the planned termination was approaching, and we reminded the youngsters that we had four remaining sessions. One girl then denied that she had any needs at all (the one who had hoped for the state fairgrounds): Her parents clothed her, took care of her, and gave her gas money. She did think somewhat wistfully of marrying, for then her husband could take care of her. With two sessions to go, one fellow sarcastically asked about the therapist's degree, stating that the therapist was a jerk. Group members said that they were disappointed and surprised to find out that they felt so needy. The therapists asked if it was really true that they could do little to meet their needs, even though the tasks of growing up seemed overwhelming. Three group members asked to have the group continue, but the therapists said that the group would stop at the time limit regardless of needs.

As termination neared, some members of the group made efforts to enhance their self-images. Two boys talked about re-enrolling in high school and learning a trade. One fellow thought that he might be able to work part-time in his father's shop.

Some of the disappointment about termination was displaced onto the dietitian. She had placed a sign in the clinic about dietary compliance, prefacing her comments with the phrase "Because we love you and are concerned about you." The group talked about telling her how the sign made them feel as though she really did not care for them at all. However, the confrontation ended up being fairly mature: The group merely asked the dietitian to take the sign down because it made them feel like little kids. The group began talking about whether they wanted to be treated like adults with choices to make and consequences to bear, or like children with great needs to be filled.

The final sessions were very difficult and tortured ones for the group members. The youngsters again talked about continuing, this time without the therapists, but they pointed out that they had already done their work in the group. One fellow continued to displace his anxiety and disappointment outside the group by criticizing the behavior of his nurse while he was on the machine. Nevertheless, he also started to ask the nurses about dating etiquette and started to make attempts to meet girls his own age. Another boy found himself surprisingly sleepy during the hour. Another talked about a repeated death dream that she had had as a child. Three adolescents took charge of termination by saying that they would not come to the final group meeting because they did not need the group anymore. (They did attend the final meeting, however, despite their disappointment at the group's ending and anger at losing the group.)

Additional Comments

Before we study the conduct of staff group meetings, I would like to elaborate on certain points regarding patient groups. First, groups composed of adolescents and young adults differ from those composed of older persons. For the younger dialysis patients, their experiences are more like those of a developmental fixation—a failure to form age-appropriate bonds, to engage in role-normative tasks, or to solidify an identity beyond that of patient. For older patients, dialysis provokes a regression to earlier sorts of bonds but with the capacity remaining to return to prestressor levels without having to learn new aspects of oneself in the process. In a sense, then, older patients have it easier: Often they have had chances to establish jobs and marriages, so they know more about those activities. In a different sense, though, they have it harder: They know what they have lost and how hard it is to regain it.

Second, the group therapist must be aware of how other people—nurses, aides, technicians, Kidney Foundation officials, and transplant surgeons in different cities—affect the internal processes of these patients and the group itself. At times, these other people do not subscribe to the goals of the group, and even their casual remarks can become the focus of patient resentment, antipathy, or resistance. In contrast to group therapy for psychiatric patients, however, the therapist cannot merely interpret resistance and send group members home to work it out. For many staff members and patients, the clinic is home, the primary focus in their lives, and it is harder for them to get distance and perspective on their private feelings and beliefs.

Staff Groups

The clinic itself is a sort of family system, where issues of trust, loyalty, relationship, obligation, and entitlement are played out daily between the patients and the staff. When these issues become too difficult for the staff to handle, communication breaks down, and time-limited group meetings can help both nurses and physicians understand more about the psychological aspects of treating patients with chronic renal failure. These meetings can help solidify staff boundaries, contribute to group cohesion, increase staff morale, improve work performance, and ease clinic tensions and communication difficulties.

There are several dangers in conducting such staff meetings, however. The first problem can arise from an authority split, as when physicians want the therapist to calm troubled waters but do not give the therapist the authority to do so. At this point, nurses can be genuinely confused about who is in charge and what the chain of command is. The second problem is that legitimate labor relations issues are pushed aside as morale problems, rather than working conditions, are given as the purpose of staff meetings.

Staff members present some of the same concerns for the group therapist as do patients. For instance, nurses often wonder why a group therapist is needed. Second, nurses and physicians fear that they could lose their identities if they let themselves be too open. Third, all clinic employees understand that no matter how tactfully one expresses feelings in a group, everyone has to work together the following day. Many group members fear that the consulting psychotherapist will leave them with group wounds to bind and no method for doing so.

At the request of the head nurse and with the knowledge and approval of the nephrologists, I have conducted time-limited nursing staff meetings in the format of a "group meeting to discuss some of the concerns that persons who work with dialysis patients may have." The following description of one series of such meetings will demonstrate the dynamics of the group process.

This particular group meeting was started because the head nurse had felt powerless over her staff, which she regarded as only mildly responsive to her requests. She also felt that the team was divided, backbiting, depressed, and hostile. Her previous attempts to confront the individual staff members had been met with passive resistance and caused further splitting within the staff. Besides being difficult to work with, the divided staff had been responding inadequately to patients' requests for favors and had inadvertently created a few pet patients, who were demanding more and more attention.

I had felt initially that one point needed addressing: These women had dedicated their lives to helping patients get better, but chronic hemodialysis patients simply do not get better, no matter how helpful one is. Consequently, I anticipated that the staff would be trying to manage disappointment in themselves and in the patients.

As with all new groups, the nurses were quite anxious about their first meeting. The anxiety was heightened when one nurse, who was more in touch with her ambivalent feelings about her patients, commented that she hated hurting people while she gave them dialysis treatments. Her colleagues ignored her statement, and quite taken aback by the lack of peer acknowledgment, she bolted the meeting room in tears. The other nurses ignored her departure and turned instead to inconsequential subjects. They were astounded when I pointed out that one of their fellow nurses had just left in tears, and several nurses dismissed her departure as "her way of responding" and "not worth talking about." Since the group had not yet become a trustworthy working group, I had to demur gently, saying that I was not so sure that a person's feelings were not worth talking about and that maybe we could understand later what had happened.

The group, including the nurse who had left crying, met the following week, but instead of trying to understand the previous events, they returned to discussing unimportant details of the clinic's operation. I pointed out that they seemed to be afraid of understanding what had happened the previous week. A few nurses commented that they were afraid of saying something that could be construed as wrong. The group was told that while one had to be sensitive to saying things to the persons one worked with, it could be important for the group to work on why or how one person could be so isolated. The nurses then discussed how they had been disappointed in the head nurse, who had not been effective in protecting them from the demands of the doctors or patients, and how they wished for someone, a doctor or head nurse, to protect them.

This passive, demanding, and receptive orientation was striking, in that it so clearly paralleled and mirrored exactly what the adolescent patients were saying in their group. The nurses had come to see themselves as being as helpless and ineffective as the patients—and they were the ones who worked in the clinic.

As a result of this discussion, some nurses tried to extract themselves from this dilemma over the next several weeks; as with all work groups, the results were not exactly what they had desired. For instance, one nurse gathered her adolescent patients together and invested great energy in enlivening the dialysis runs by playing checkers, charades, and so forth. She got into a cross fire because the adolescents wanted more of such attention and other nurses resented being shown in a less favorable light. This energetic nurse was fated to lose face and disappoint either her patients or her colleagues. Over the next several weeks' meetings, the nurses spent some time trying to sort out why the energetic nurse was spending time alone in the clinic and being ignored by other nurses.

Later on, the nurses began to discuss how unfair the clinic was, the benefits they did not have, their lack of bargaining power, and other complaints concerning the clinic's administration. I confronted the group by wondering why they wanted to talk about these things with me, because it sounded as though they needed a labor organizer. Immediately the people in the room became very anxious, and finally the underlying problem was revealed: The nurses were furious at the doctors. They were incensed for a number of reasons, and they began to articulate for the first time within the group and work on problems with the persons that they had to depend on and serve.

They felt that real medical dependency needs were not being met. Doctors were not available when needed, were late for rounds, ignored nurses' comments about treatments, and so forth. Nurses felt that the doctors played nurses off against each other for favors that were unnecessary but gave the doctors a feeling of special authority, such as asking a nurse to fetch an unneeded chart. The nurses also felt that they would be fired for voicing their objections, a fantasy similar to the patients' notion that they would be denied hemodialysis treatments for being at all critical of the doctors.

By the eighth weekly meeting, the nurses had invited the doctors to attend the meetings to discuss how the doctors' behavior undercut their best efforts at patient care and made them feel less effective. Two of the three nephrologists did attend. Each doctor made a commitment to back the nurses, and they complimented the nurses on their fine work. One doctor did improve his timing for rounds; the other did not. The doctors were more careful about how they talked about the nurses in front of the patients, and they made efforts to acknowledge the hard work that the nurses did. They continued to do the small things that doctors tend to do that make for differential status—the kinds of things that most people regard as minor put-downs. The nurses began to handle these situations with more equanimity; they withdrew less and even started to kid the doctors about the doctors' need for status.

By resolving things somewhat with the physicians, the nurses' group staff meeting had lived out its usefulness. Not only could the nurses work more effectively, but they also stopped a lot of the backbiting between and isolating of particular nurses. Thus, the group meetings helped both the nurses and the physicians talk about their individual experiences in treating chronic renal failure patients.

These nursing staff meetings had one consequence that could not have been foreseen. With a lot of their energies released, the staff members found that they wanted to do something creative with their young patients. These remarkable people enlisted the support of doctors, patients, technicians, and many others and established a summer camp called Camp Okawehna, which is a Seneca word for "kidney." This camp has been described in detail elsewhere (Armstrong, 1983).

I have tried to outline how group psychotherapy and group methods can be used to help both chronic renal failure patients and the staff treating them. There is, of course, no empirical evidence that understanding some of the problems of chronic hemodialysis has any benefit whatsoever. This does not mean that group methods are useless; it merely means that empirically oriented persons may feel frustrated. Yet, to a person who attends a clinic that he or she cannot voluntarily leave, a measureless glance of understanding or comprehension, an appropriate question or nod of agreement, can bring comfort and ease; these acts cannot be measured at all. To be sure, a patient's private understanding of the clinic and the illness comes with effort and some discomfort. Yet a shared understanding of the clinic and the illness can preclude the terror of dying alone or abandoned.

References

Abram, H. S. "The Psychiatrist, the Treatment of Chronic Renal Failure, and the Prolongation of Life: I." *American Journal of Psychiatry*, 1968, *124*, 1351-1357.

Abram, H. S. "The Psychiatrist, the Treatment of Chronic Renal Failure, and the Prolongation of Life: II." *American Journal of Psychiatry*, 1969, *126*, 157-167.

Abram, H. S., and others. "Sexual Functioning in Patients with Chronic Renal Failure." *Journal of Nervous and Mental Disease*, 1975, *160*, 220-226.

Anderson, K. "The Psychological Aspects of Chronic Hemodialysis." *Journal of the Canadian Psychiatric Association*, 1975, *20*, 385-391.

Armstrong, S. "The Common Structure of Treatment Staff Attitudes Toward Adolescent Dialysis Patients." *Psychotherapy and Psychosomatics*, 1975, *26*, 322-329.

Armstrong, S. "The Psychologist's Place in Chronic In-Center Hemodialysis." *Dialysis and Transplantation*, 1977, *6*, 54-55.

Armstrong, S. "Psychological Maladjustment in Renal Dialysis Patients." *Psychosomatics*, 1978, *19*, 169-171.

Armstrong, S. "Psychological Impairment in Hemodialysis and Transplantation." Paper presented at the annual meeting of the National Kidney Foundation, Washington, D.C., October 1982.

Armstrong, S. "Psychological Factors in Child and Adolescent Dialysis Patients." In N. B. Levy (Ed.), *Psychonephrology II: Psychological Factors in Hemodialysis and Transplantation*. New York: Plenum, 1983.

Armstrong, S., Johnson, K., and Hopkins, J. "Stopping Immunosuppressant Therapy Following Successful Renal Transplantation: Two Year Follow-up." In N. B. Levy (Ed.), *Psychonephrology I: Psychological Factors in Hemodialysis and Transplantation*. New York: Plenum, 1981.

Basch, S., Brown, F., and Cantor, W. "Observation on Body Image in Renal Patients." In N. B. Levy (Ed.), *Psychonephrology I: Psychological Factors in Hemodialysis and Transplantation*. New York: Plenum, 1981.

Buchanan, D. C. "Psychological Adaptation to Chronic Hemo-dialysis." Paper presented at the North Central Dialysis and Transplant Association, Kansas City, Mo., September 1975.

Buchanan, D. C. "Psychotherapeutic Intervention in the Kidney Transplant Service." In N. B. Levy (Ed.), *Psychonephrology I: Psychological Factors in Hemodialysis and Transplantation.* New York: Plenum, 1981.

Campbell, D. R., and Sinha, B. K. "Brief Group Psychotherapy with Chronic Hemodialysis Patients." *American Journal of Psychiatry,* 1980, *137,* 1234-1237.

de Nour, A. "Psychotherapy with Patients on Chronic Hemo-dialysis." *British Journal of Psychiatry,* 1970, *116,* 207-215.

Engel, G. L. "The Need for a New Medical Model: A Challenge for Biomedicine." *Science,* 1977, *196,* 129-135.

Finkelstein, F. O., and Steele, T. E. "Sexual Dysfunction and Chronic Renal Failure: A Psychosocial Study of 77 Patients." *Dialysis and Transplantation,* 1978, *7,* 44-45.

Gelfman, M., and Wilson, E. S. "Emotional Reactions in a Renal Unit." *Comprehensive Psychiatry,* 1972, *13,* 283-290.

Greenberg, R. P., Davis, G., and Massey, R. "The Psychological Evaluation of Patients for a Kidney Transplant and Hemo-dialysis Program." *American Journal of Psychiatry,* 1973, *130,* 274-277.

Hollon, T. H. "Modified Group Therapy in the Treatment of Pa-tients on Chronic Hemodialysis." *American Journal of Psy-chotherapy,* 1972, *26,* 501-510.

Karasu, T. B. "Psychotherapy of the Medically Ill." *American Journal of Psychiatry,* 1979, *136,* 1-11.

Kemph, J. P. "Renal Failure, Artificial Kidney, and Kidney Transplant." *American Journal of Psychiatry,* 1966, *122,* 1270-1274.

Kemph, J. P. "Psychotherapy with Patients Receiving a Kidney Transplant." *American Journal of Psychiatry,* 1967, *124,* 623-629.

Kemph, J. P., Berman, E. A., and Coppolillo, H. P. "Kidney Transplant and Shifts in Family Dynamics." *American Jour-nal of Psychiatry,* 1969, *125,* 1485-1490.

Kerr, D. N. S. "Acute Renal Failure." In D. Black and N. F.

Jones (Eds.), *Renal Disease.* (4th ed.) Oxford, England: Blackwell Scientific Publications, 1979.

Ledingham, J. G. G. "Chronic Renal Failure." In D. Black and N. F. Jones (Eds.), *Renal Disease.* (4th ed.) Oxford, England: Blackwell Scientific Publications, 1979.

Levy, N. B. "Sexual Adjustment of Maintenance Hemodialysis and Renal Transplantation Patients: National Survey by Questionnaire, Preliminary Report." *Transactions of the American Society of Artificial Internal Organs,* 1973, *19,* 138-143.

Lohmann, R., and others. "Psychopathology and Psychotherapy in Chronic Physically Ill Patients." *Psychotherapy and Psychosomatics,* 1979, *31,* 267-276.

McKegney, F. P., and others. "Severe Psychiatric Disorder in Dialysis-Transplant Patients: The Low Incidence of Psychiatric Hospitalization." In N. B. Levy (Ed.), *Psychonephrology I: Psychological Factors in Hemodialysis and Transplantation.* New York: Plenum, 1981.

Mann, J. *Time-Limited Psychotherapy.* Cambridge, Mass.: Harvard University Press, 1973.

Reichsman, F. "A Brief Overview of Psychosocial Research on Hemodialysis Patients." In N. B. Levy (Ed.), *Psychonephrology I: Psychological Factors in Hemodialysis and Transplantation.* New York: Plenum, 1981.

Rosenthal, R. "Combining Results of Independent Studies." *Psychological Bulletin,* 1978, *85,* 185-193.

Scribner, B. H., and others. "The Treatment of Chronic Uremia by Means of Intermittent Hemodialysis: A Preliminary Report." *Transactions of the American Society of Artificial Internal Organs,* 1960, *6,* 112-114.

Sorenson, E. T. "Group Therapy in a Community Hospital Dialysis Unit." *Journal of the American Medical Association,* 1972, *221,* 899-901.

Starling, E. H. "On the Absorption of Fluids from the Connective Tissue Spaces." *Journal of Physiology,* 1896, *19,* 312-326.

Starling, E. H. "The Glomerular Functions of the Kidney." *Journal of Physiology,* 1899, *24,* 317-330.

Steinglass, P., and others. "Discussion Groups for Chronic Hemodialysis Patients and Their Families." *General Hospital Psychiatry*, 1982, *4*, 7-14.

Thurau, K., Boylan, J. W., and Mason, J. "Pathophysiology of Acute Renal Failure." In D. Black and N. F. Jones (Eds.), *Renal Disease*. (4th ed.) Oxford, England: Blackwell Scientific Publications, 1979.

Wilson, C. "The Effects of Time-Limited Group Counseling on the Level of Functioning of Chronic Home Dialysis Patients." *Dissertation Abstracts International*, 1973, *34* (4-A), 1633-1634.

Wilson, C., and others. "Time-Limited Group Counseling for Chronic Home Hemodialysis Patients." *Journal of Counseling Psychology*, 1974, *21*, 376-379.

Wolff, H. H. "The Psychotherapeutic Approach." In R. Hopkins and H. H. Wolff (Eds.), *Principles of Treatment of Psychosomatic Disorders*. Oxford, England: Pergamon Press, 1965.

8

E. Mansell Pattison, M.D.

❋ ❋ ❋ ❋ ❋ ❋ ❋ ❋ ❋ ❋ ❋ ❋ ❋

Chronic Lung Disease

Patients with chronic lung disease are a major challenge to bio-psychosocial health care. These are not exciting, exotic, or dramatic medical patients. Quite the contrary, the bulk of patients are drab, persons who have lived quiet, unobtrusive lives of heavy smoking and drinking. Their physical health and psychosocial adjustment have gradually deteriorated, and they suffer from emphysema, which is a rigidly fixed rib cage that impedes regular breathing and results in a chronic shortage of breath. The most severe cases require continuous hospitalization because physical activity is severely limited and intensive nursing care is needed. These patients may live for months or years in hospital or convalescent wards with little change in their clinical status. Even if not medically neglected, these patients arouse little interest. Thus it is not surprising that the psychosocial aspects of this illness have mostly been ignored. In fact, almost no psychosocial literature is published on this patient population. Consequently, the observations in this chapter are based primarily on my own experience as a consultant for three years to a convalescent unit for chronic lung disease patients.

Three major psychosocial domains must be considered with these patients: the problems of psychosocial limitation im-

190

posed by the physical illness, the problems of living in a hospital ward, and the problems of the family in adapting to the patient's chronic debilitating illness, regardless of whether the patient is an outpatient or an inpatient. We shall consider different group interventions for each domain.

Clinical Characteristics of Chronic Obstructive Pulmonary Disease

Chronic obstructive pulmonary disease (COPD) is a general medical syndrome in which breathing is impaired. The deterioration of the lung operation can be caused by an agent that irritates the thin cellular linings of the air sacs (alveoli). In normal breathing, oxygen is transferred into the bloodstream and carbon dioxide is extruded from the bloodstream into the air sac. This two-way exchange occurs through the single-cell lining of the alveolar air sac. In normal breathing, the rib cage expands and the diaphragm pulls down, producing a vacuum in the lungs that sucks oxygen-rich air into the alveoli. Oxygen transfers into the bloodstream and carbon dioxide transfers into the alveoli. Then the rib cage contracts, pushing the carbon-dioxide-rich air out of the lungs. This normal cycle occurs twenty to thirty times per minute.

The normal breathing process is regulated by a carbon-dioxide-monitoring system in the midbrain, which continuously samples the oxygen and carbon dioxide levels in the bloodstream. When the oxygen level drops or the carbon dioxide level rises, this midbrain monitor changes the rate of breathing to produce more effective oxygenation. Both rapid breathing (as occurs during excitement) and slow breathing (as occurs in a stupor) constitute ineffective breathing. Rapid breathing moves air in and out of the alveoli too fast for proper oxygen and carbon dioxide exchange. Slow breathing does not exchange enough air per minute to allow gas transfer. In either case, an oxygen debt or carbon dioxide buildup occurs.

If the midbrain signal to the lungs does not change the pattern of breathing or if the breathing capacity has reached its limit (as occurs during strenuous exercise), then the midbrain sends neural signals to the frontal cortex, which we consciously experience as the sense of "being out of breath" or "being unable to breathe." These two phrases describe an experience we call *dyspnea*. If we experience dyspnea, in a few seconds we begin to panic and feel that we will die if we do not "get our breath." In fact, we shall indeed die in a few minutes if proper breathing is not restored. Most of us have experienced having the breath knocked out of us or choking. Even that short cessation of breathing creates the sense of dyspnea. These normal everyday experiences illustrate how fragile and delicate the regulation of our breathing process is.

Now let us consider the effects of disease processes on this breathing operation. Any agent that irritates the alveolar cell lining can produce swelling of the lining and secretions that coat the alveolar lining. These effects impede the transfer of oxygen and carbon dioxide across the lining. Even if breathing rates are normal, normal gas transfer does not occur. This is seen in asthma, where there is an allergic irritation of the alveolar lining that produces the wheezing respiration of an asthmatic attack. The asthmatic experiences episodic dyspnea during acute attacks but otherwise may breathe normally. Similarly acute lung syndromes are produced by inhaling a noxious chemical, such as chlorine gas, gasoline, or glue, or a variety of other noxious fumes encountered in laboratories. Usually such acute episodes are limited and do not produce chronic lung disease.

A variety of irritative agents produce chronic lung disease. They include coal dust (which produces miner's "black lung" disease), asbestos in manufacturing plants (which produces asbestosis), plant fibers in clothing mills, and fungi (which produce various diseases of the lung, such as coccidioidomycosis). But by far the most common cause of COPD is chronic heavy smoking.

The pathophysiology of COPD is of some importance in understanding the behavior of COPD patients. Regardless of the irritative agent, the effects on the lungs and breathing processes are very similar.

Almost all patients develop COPD after smoking heavily

over a period of years. The smoke irritates the alveolar walls of the lung and bronchi, resulting in secretions that block airflow, create chronic low-grade lung infections, and ultimately lead to the breakdown of the thin alveolar walls. When this happens, the many small chambers (alveoli) deteriorate to form larger air sacs. Hence the available membrane surface for exchanging oxygen is diminished and one must breathe more frequently to obtain the same oxygen exchange. At the same time, when the elasticity of the alveolar walls is lost, the lungs lose their contractile power, the chest cage becomes rigidly fixed, and the person cannot move the lungs to exchange oxygen rapidly. Chronic secretions and infections aggravate the situation by impairing both airflow and oxygen transport across the damaged alveolar walls. Chronic coughing expels air but impairs inhalation. The eventual result is the progressive impairment of the ability to obtain oxygen. Exercise, work, play, and even simple activities like climbing stairs or walking up a slight incline become difficult because the lungs cannot exchange enough oxygen to meet the physical demands of the body.

This disease process often has a devastating impact on the life-style of COPD patients. Since males are more exposed to industrial hazards and are the heaviest smokers, the COPD population is predominantly male. Other characteristics of this population contribute to their vulnerability to COPD. Studies of their life histories (Martin, Pardee, and Dominik, 1966) reveal lifelong precarious psychosocial adjustments. Their personalities are described as sensitive, anxious, rigid, and emotionally labile. Many have socially marginal life-styles, and perhaps a majority are alcoholic (Lyons, 1982). Their disease onset is insidious. They experience a gradual loss of energy and vitality, and weakness and lethargy ensue. The ability to pursue vigorous physical activity diminishes. These effects are probably due to chronic oxygen depletion, low-grade chronic infections in the lungs, and subtle degrees of organic brain damage due to insufficient brain oxygenation. Since the process is insidious, these persons are not aware of the causes of their diminished vitality and capacity to function. They initially attempt to compensate by exerting extra effort during work and exercise. They finally seek medical attention late in the process of the COPD, often when they are in their middle fifties. By this time they are unable to work, cannot conduct routine household chores, and are dispirited, depressed, and demoralized.

The cultural emphasis placed on strength, physical activity, and a working-class life-style all contribute to a severe loss of self-identity, self-esteem, sense of masculinity, and sense of personal competency. Emotionally sensitive and labile, these patients experience intense emotional reactions, but are inarticulate and not introspective. Hence it is difficult for them to identify or verbalize their personal reactions to their deteriorating life-style. Physical coping strategies are not available to them any longer, and they have poorly developed cognitive coping abilities.

Another major problem of psychosocial adaptation for these men is a chronic sick role involving a set of paradoxes: They are sickly but not acutely sick, they have a weak body but an active mind, and they interact with people daily but are in a passive relationship to others. This chronic sick role presents the problem of an "ambiguous death prognosis." Present is a chronic, progressive illness for which there is no definitive treatment; it is possible only to ameliorate acute symptoms. The illness is fatal, but its progress, although inexorable, is slow and uncertain. At no time in the course of the disease does the patient know for certain that he will continue living or die.

In fact, the COPD population has a high morbidity rate (degree of incapacitation) because of an associated deterioration of cardiac function, the susceptibility to infections, and general poor health. The mortality rate is exceptionally high for a chronic disease: a 50 percent five-year survival rate and a 10 percent ten-year survival rate (Dudley and others, 1969). In my studies of dying trajectories for different diseases, I found that these "ambiguous dying trajectories" create the most personal anxiety and depression among the chronically ill (Pattison, 1977). It also produces the most psychosocial distress, because no definitive action can be taken by patient, family, or professional staff.

A final coping problem for this patient population is the

issue of chronic dyspnea. As we have noted, dyspnea is encountered by almost everyone at some time. In the asthmatic, dyspnea is acute and episodic. But in the COPD patient, dyspnea is a minute-to-minute fact of life. This critically affects the emotional adaptation of the patient, because respiration is so closely linked to emotional experience (Dudley and others, 1964). COPD patients continually suffer from a marginal lack of oxygen, and even the smallest amount of physical exertion may precipitate dyspnea. However, they cannot breathe more deeply or faster to acquire more oxygen because their respiration is impaired, as outlined above (Baldwin, Cournand, and Richards, 1948; Dudley, Martin, and Holmes, 1964; Turpin, Marcer, and Howell, 1979).

Patients' emotional response to breathing behavior and breathing sensations becomes critical. Patients become fixated on their breathing, and they are constantly aware of how they are breathing. If they sense that they are not breathing correctly, they immediately become intensely anxious. If they become dyspneic, panic ensues. Therefore, these patients should avoid the experience of dyspnea at all costs.

This fear is compounded by the fact that emotional responses also affect respiration (Kinsman, Dirks, and Jones, 1982). Even small emotional upsets can produce dyspnea because of the precarious balance of respiratory function in severe COPD patients. Thus emotional inhibition, as in fleeting apathy, sadness, or depression, may slow breathing and precipitate dyspnea. On the other hand, emotional arousal, as in fleeting anxiety, anger, or fear, may accelerate breathing and precipitate dyspnea. Of great clinical import, then, is the fact that the severe COPD patient can tolerate very little emotional inhibition or activation. They must maintain a flat, emotionless demeanor in order to avoid the dreaded experience of dyspnea. Thus, to exist, the COPD patient must live in an emotional straitjacket (Dudley, Holmes, and Martin, 1968).

In summary, we are presented with a disease process that progressively impairs physical activity without impairing the mind. It is a disease with a high mortality rate but an unpredictable course, and one in which the physiological processes of breathing are intimately linked with emotional experiences, leading to an emotional straitjacket style of adaptation. All of this is present in a patient population that is ill equipped in terms of life history, personality characteristics, and psychosocial coping styles to adjust to the impairments of COPD. Thus we are faced with the need for psychosocial interventions to help patients adapt to their condition, to the ward milieu, and to their families' responses.

Review of Group Treatment Interventions

The biopsychosocial nature of chronic lung disease has long been appreciated. A century ago the major chronic lung disease was tuberculosis. The severe chronic tubercular exhibited many of the clinical features of the COPD. Most patients lived for many years, weak and debilitated, following an ambiguous dying trajectory. They had severe physical limitations but active minds. There was a loss of the vocational and family roles that contribute to self-identity and self-esteem. Social deprivation was accentuated in their life in a chronic ward, where time was filled with petty complaints, intrigues with the institutional staff, and the interactions between patients with no common bonds except the fate of being passive victims.

As Roback noted in the first chapter, the American pioneer in group therapy, J. H. Pratt (1907), first instituted a type of group therapy with tubercular patients and their families. Pratt termed his method the "class method" because he used the format of didactic lectures and group discussion. He had several goals in mind: to restore self-esteem and personal integrity to the lives of the demoralized patients, to help patients and their families adjust to the chronic sickness of the patient, and to teach patients and their families how to cope with the physical aspects of the disease process.

It is noteworthy that Pratt did not intend to conduct psychotherapy in the sense of resolving neurotic conflicts or changing personality or character styles. Rather, he focused on changing behavioral life-styles so that patients could cope with the real problems resulting from the disease process. He was more behavioral than introspective, more practical than theoretical, more cognitive than affective, and more didactic than evocative. I should like to note that this class method of Pratt may have been a serendipitous discovery, because our experience supports the concept of his basic group style—a didactic, nonevocative group interaction rather than a more exploratory and psychodynamic group technique.

Psychiatrist Harry Wilmer (1952), who was himself hospitalized in a tuberculosis ward, provided further support for the didactic-behavioral approach. He wrote about his own experience as a patient and eventual therapist within his own treatment setting. He, too, observed the chronic depression, loss of identity, and demoralization of the patients. He noted the petty conflicts that developed between patients and staff and the difficulties that patients had in establishing meaningful relationships with fellow patients whom they lived with for many months or years.

Wilmer did not consider these psychosocial problems to reflect primary psychopathology in the patients but rather the coping and adaptive problems presented by the disease process and the constraints of the treatment milieu. His treatment strategy was to introduce group activities in which patients and staff could all participate with various degrees of intensity and normalizing social interactions could occur. Examples of group activities include staging musicals, playing games, taking up arts and crafts, discussing books, and learning pertinent medical facts. Note that like the Pratt method, the Wilmer method did not focus on the individual patient, on psychopathology, or on change in the person. Rather, the focus was on normative socialization and the enhancement of interpersonal relations through group activities.

The genre of group intervention was further developed by Sparer, Cockrell, and Shelton (1956) as a "psychosomatic approach to the therapeutic milieu." Their work was again in a tuberculosis ward, but they emphasized the importance of viewing the ward as a social unit where group interventions could make the social structure approximate normal social interactions of the external world, rather than the social structure of a

hospital ward for short-term patients. Again, this group of therapists eschewed a psychodynamic group therapy technique and
incorporated group activities like Wilmer's. In addition, they
conducted group discussions about the disease process, breathing behavior, and changing one's life-style to accommodate
physical limitations. They also introduced family group sessions
to reestablish family ties, promote family support, and reduce
the social alienation of the patients from their families.

These lessons from the treatment of chronic tuberculars
correspond remarkably with the group methods described for
patients with other chronic illnesses. That is, group therapy
needs to address the issues of coping with physical limitations
and changes in psychosocial status and interpersonal relations
imposed by the disease process. There appears to be a consensus that a psychodynamic group therapy focused on internal
psychodynamics and the neurotic elements of a patient's personal coping style is usually not effective (Ford, 1983; Miles,
1983; Seligman, 1982).

These conclusions do not mean that chronic illness patients do not have dysfunctional elements in their character
structure or lack neurotic conflicts or neurotic adaptations.
Rather, the key element here is that the psychodynamic conflicts or character structure did not produce the physical illness. The source of conflict is therefore not intrapsychic but
rather the external reality of an impersonal disease process and
the external reality of the social treatment milieu. How the person copes and adapts to these external realities is of course in
part determined by the patient's psychic structure and function. But it may be a mistake to assume that just because we
resolve neurotic conflicts or achieve some maturational change
in a patient, the patient's behavior or coping strategies will
change. Put simply, a psychologically mature and healthy person will likely have problems in coping with a devastating disease process. Freud himself noted that the task of psychoanalysis was to transform neurosis into common unhappiness.

We suggest that the therapeutic goal in treating patients
with chronic illness is to teach new coping strategies for dealing
with physical, psychological, and social effects of the disease.

To that end, we may assume that the patient has the psychological capacities to learn new coping styles. This goal of treatment is not to resolve intrapsychic conflict or to change personality style. Rather, the goals are to educate the patient about the disease process, to help the patient develop new skills for dealing with his (or her) condition, to help the patient comply with treatment regimes, and to modify the patient's social roles so that roles and relationships with family and friends are maintained. This orientation should not be labeled psychotherapy but rather psychoeducation or psychomaintenance. In other words, the goals of treatment are a new set of behavioral skills (Alexander, 1982; Kinsman, Dirks, and Jones, 1982). This approach to therapeutic intervention has recently been described as a "humanistic-behavioral" technique (Sobel, 1982).

Most models of group therapy have been developed from clinical experience with outpatient groups, where the goals of therapists and patients alike were changes in intrapsychic operations. Translating such models of group therapy to inpatient group therapy and particularly to patients with chronic medical illness appears inappropriate and ineffective. In an early study of inpatient group psychotherapy, Pattison, Brissenden, and Wohl (1967) evaluated a matched group of psychiatric inpatients; one group participated in weekly insight-oriented psychoanalytic group therapy, while a control group only participated in the ward milieu. Over a six-month experimental period, not only were there few differences between the two patient sets, but the behavior and clinical status of the patients in group psychotherapy actually deteriorated. Our observations led us to conclude that the attempt to focus on internal processes hindered the patients in learning better interpersonal behavior.

A similar example of the importance of group models comes from group therapy with asthmatics. Psychodynamic group psychotherapy in the outpatient treatment of asthmatic adults has been reported as quite successful in reducing asthmatic attacks and changing the personality styles of the asthmatics (Groen and Pelser, 1960; Lange-Nielsen and Retterstal, 1959). However, this group model cannot be assumed appropriate for COPD patients, even though we have respiratory disease in both instances. Asthmatic attacks are at least partly triggered by emotional states, whereas in COPD there is a continuing respiratory impairment regardless of emotional status. The asthmatic has acute intermittent episodes between periods of normal respiration; the COPD patient has no respite. The asthmatic patient has a large respiratory reserve, while the COPD patient has none. The asthmatic patient can learn to tolerate affect arousal, while the COPD patient cannot physiologically do so. Finally, the resolution of intrapsychic conflicts will improve the physical status of the asthmatic, while change in the intrapsychic operations of the COPD patient will not change the respiratory distress. These comparisons illustrate the need for group therapists to consider the effects of different disease processes when developing group treatment methods.

Recently Yalom (1983) reviewed inpatient psychotherapy and concluded that outpatient models are inappropriate for inpatients. He has proposed a model for group technique in which an active leader didactically educates the group, information is shared, and the external realities of interpersonal behavior in the ward milieu are emphasized.

This model and technique obviously relate to the concepts of group treatment proposed above. Some recent research validates these approaches. Butler and Fuhriman (1983) collected patient evaluations of the value of curative group factors. They found that outpatient group members valued self-understanding, catharsis, and personal growth through interpersonal experience. However, in inpatient groups, the patients valued none of those factors. Only one curative factor was salient: the value of belonging to a cohesive group of people! These findings suggest that the seriously ill inpatient population is not directed toward personal change; instead, they look for group experience to improve their morale.

In conclusion, group experience with chronic lung disease patients does not support a psychodynamic psychotherapy group model where the goal is personal growth. Rather, these data suggest a model of group activities that promotes group membership and social cohesion and that allows psychoeducation and psychomaintenance. Group content is not focused on the person who has the illness but on the illness itself and its consequences for the person. We could also state that group psychotherapy focuses on the unique individual, whereas group activity focuses on the common external reality.

Unsuccessful Psychodynamic Group Therapy

To highlight the particular psychophysiological constraints to be addressed in the treatment of COPD patients, I shall describe our attempts to employ standard psychodynamic group psychotherapy with a group of typical COPD patients (Dudley and Pattison, 1969; Pattison, Rhodes, and Dudley, 1971).

These studies were conducted in a COPD ward with twenty-five male patients. We were asked to work with this unit because of typical patient care problems: noncompliance with treatment regimes, irascible interpersonal behavior, depressive symptomatology with suicidal thoughts, and chronic somatizing. Twelve patients were randomly selected for group psychotherapy and were matched with twelve ward treatment controls. We assessed blood gases (oxygenation levels), ventilatory capacities, personality traits, and current social adaptation before the group met, at monthly intervals while the group met, and after termination of the group. The experimental group was to meet weekly for ninety minutes with cotherapists. All patients volunteered to participate after being informed through individual discussions and a pregroup briefing.

The group meetings were held in a large room in the COPD nursing unit. The patients were almost all in wheelchairs, since even mild ambulation produced dyspnea in them. Most had oxygen tanks and masks attached to their wheelchairs, and such equipment was available in the group meeting room as standard ward procedure.

The group was started with brief introductions about the purpose of the group (to aid in their adjustment to their illness) and group method (a nonstructured format in which anyone could introduce topics for discussion). So we commenced—mostly in silence. Desultory comments about ward trivia filled the first meetings. We were satisfied to proceed slowly, but the content of the sessions remained centered on impersonal ward events. We attempted to personalize ward events so that the group would become person focused. This met with passive resistance.

After two months, one or two patients made a few personal remarks about their lives. These reflections on personal feelings were genuine, and the patients did manifest obvious feeling. But they immediately began to experience respiratory distress and quickly returned to discussing mundane trivia. Encouraged by what we interpreted as a movement toward acknowledging their ward living problems, we more actively attempted to draw the patients out with comments about their personal thoughts and feelings. Again we met with passive resistance.

During the next six to ten weeks, patients started to drop out of the group. This usually occurred after a minor, intense emotional expression in the group, during which the patient would start to become cyanotic, stop talking, grab for the oxygen mask to suck air, and then fall silent. Group members accused us of trying to kill them by making them talk. Their fears were understandable, since several patients had died in the ward of respiratory distress during states of emotional distress.

Only five of the twelve patients completed the six-month group experience. These five had a history of effective psychosocial assets and good interpersonal relations in the ward (Pattison and Rhodes, 1974). In a word, these patients had better psychosocial abilities to cope with their emotions and responses to their environment. Although these five patients did participate effectively in the group process, positive group participation did not predict clinical outcome at a two-year follow-up. Further, since these were not problem patients, it is doubtful that the group therapy experience added much to their treatment experience. The seven group dropouts were problem patients who could not tolerate the emotional perturbations of personal exploration that we pursued in the group therapy. Thus they did not benefit from this group therapy approach.

We evaluated the two-year clinical outcomes of this group

of patients. Of interest is the fact that physiological measures (of blood gases and ventilation) were not predictive, nor were psychological trait and state measures. However, psychosocial assets (as measured by the Berle Index), current family relations, and ward interaction (as measured by the Nosie-30 scale) all predicted clinical outcomes (Pattison, 1974). Our data suggest that measured improvement in interpersonal and psychosocial functions is more relevant to clinical outcome than basic personality or basic coping styles, which showed no change and were not predictive of outcomes.

From this experience, we learned that we focused on the wrong dimensions of behavior. We attempted to change cognitive and affective styles of intrapsychic operations, which required personal experiencing that these patients could not tolerate. On the other hand, we ignored interpersonal social behavior that was predictive of clinical outcome.

Not all therapeutic strategies were useful for direct and indirect cognitive-affective exploration with these COPD patients. Obviously, the lives of the patients were filled with emotional significance. We observed in these patients emotional reactions to the myriad of daily events on the ward. In fact, the patients were sensitive and emotionally labile. But they could not tolerate the immediate, intense experiencing of emotion: Affective arousal immediately led to dyspnea. Hence they quickly learned to mobilize ego defenses to repress the experience of emotion and ward off affect arousal. The defense mechanisms most frequently used were projection, reaction formation (passive aggression), and massive denial.

This ego-defensive strategy precluded effective problem solving in the patients' everyday life in the ward because they could not examine problems without intense affect arousal. As a result, problems were repressed from consciousness as soon as issues became manifest. In terms of ego processes (Loevinger, 1976), the cognitive ego system was too tightly linked to the affective ego system. Thus, the patients could not think without feeling. We observed both the lack of cognition on problems and the lack of feelings about problems. In group therapy, we attempted to make the patients be cognitive about their personal conflicts. However, the intimate process of this style of thinking evoked the linked affective arousal. Of course, our attempts to evoke immediate affective experience were equally unsuccessful.

A more effective technique is to explore cognition indirectly, that is, to have patients consider conflicts in universal and impersonal terms. For example, we can ask patients to discuss problems that occur on the ward rather than their own specific problems. Or, we can discuss a problem as it occurred in the past but not as it exists right now. These strategies dissociate the patient from the conflict he is discussing. In a similar fashion, we can unlink the cognitive system from the affective system by asking the patient to talk about feelings rather than demanding that the patient experience feelings. To use a cliche, the strategy is to focus on the "there and then" rather than the "here and now." This strategy aims at self-evaluation from a distance, which reduces the need for defense against accurate cognition and the associated arousal of affect. Similarly, symbolic group activities can help resolve interpersonal conflicts through action activities without interpreting or explicating the personal meanings of the symbolic behavior. Elsewhere, I have described this as the therapeutic use of play (Pattison, 1969). In this case, we promote learning through doing without insight.

One might argue that failing to work through the affective dimensions of conflict leaves these patients too vulnerable. That is probably true. However, I doubt that we can achieve optimal treatment goals in a patient population that can psychophysiologically tolerate so little affect. Thus the disease process limits our therapeutic work with the affect system.

Case Illustrations of Interactive Effects

What we face is the interplay of various forces in the drama of COPD. Not every patient plays out the same role. Each patient brings a different personality and coping style to the drama, and each comes with different psychosocial resources. The disease process is variable. As a consequence, each patient can accept or reject the available psychosocial resources available in the treatment program. To illustrate this interplay, I shall present two case studies. The status of the disease in both men was very similar, but their psychosocial adaptation prior to hospitalization differed significantly. In turn, this difference affected their participation in therapy and their clinical outcome. The first man made excellent use of group therapy, while the second man dropped out of the group early.

Case 1 was a fifty-one-year-old married white male, an occasional alcoholic, with a twenty-five-year history of coughing, sputum production, and wheezing and a thirty-year history of heavy smoking, who was admitted for the first time. His chronic lung disease was diagnosed eight years before his admission. Following admission he would become short of breath after walking one level block, occasionally while at rest, and when experiencing emotional changes. The patient had been admitted to at least eight other hospitals for chronic lung problems and had had pneumonia at least fifteen times. He was married to a thirty-eight-year-old retarded woman and had no children. He had worked steadily all of his life at manual labor until forced to retire eight years before his admission. For the two years before admission, he had been on total disability and his only income was from public assistance. His wife was too retarded to care for herself and was almost totally dependent on him to transact business and do the daily chores. On the other hand, she cared for him when he was ill and was available when he needed her. He also had several relatives living nearby who were supportive and encouraging. He made it apparent early in his hospitalization that he was needed at home and wanted to leave as soon as possible. He was hospitalized a total of six months for suspected tuberculosis and inpatient treatment of his chronic lung disease.

Prior to the beginning of the group, his vital capacity (VC) was 2.1 (52 percent of normal), maximal breathing capacity (MBC) 44 (37 percent of normal), maximal expiratory flow rate (MEF) 100, pH 7.4, $PaCo_2$ 51, PaO_2 57, and SaO_2 86. He was discharged after the fourteenth of twenty-four group meetings, having attended all fourteen meetings. At the time of his discharge, his VC was 3.4 (85 percent) of normal, MBC 57 (49 percent of normal), MEF 120, pH 7.39, $PaCO_2$ 45, PaO_2 66, and SaO_2 91.

His response to the group was accepting. He participated in discussions and attempted to bring up and solve personal and ward problems.

Case 2 was a sixty-two-year-old married white male who was hospitalized for the first time with a diagnosis of chronic obstructive lung disease. The patient had a forty-year history of heavy smoking, had mild to moderate exertional dyspnea, and had had a chronic productive cough for as long as he could remember. He had been continuously hospitalized since his admission four years before the start of this study.

The patient was married for the second time thirty years before admission. His first wife had remarried, and she and the patient's son had had no further contact with him. His second wife had always been independent and self-supporting as a waitress. The patient was a chronic alcoholic until two years before admission, when he was rehabilitated. For the year before admission, he had worked as a grocery clerk and continued this occupation until five days before admission. One year before admission his physical status began to deteriorate. At that time he was able to walk on the level for miles. By three months before admission, he was limited to walking four blocks on the level; by two months, to one block. Two years before admission, he and his wife had separated, and she had been planning to divorce him. On admission he was penniless and had no source of income.

Over the four years of his hospitalization, he formed a close attachment to the hospital. When confronted with discharge one year before this study, he became very angry and subsequently developed respiratory failure. After that time, he was not threatened with discharge. When asked about going home, he said, "This is my home," and he made it clear that he was going to stay in the hospital at any cost. During his hospitalization, he was given a veterans pension and social security benefits, which amounted to $275 per month. His wife retired on $90 per month. After the change in finances, he and his wife were partially reconciled. For the first time in their marriage, she became financially dependent on him. The patient was dependent on his wife for emotional support. At the time of the study, she did not want him home and he did not want to return there. His wife was his only visitor, and he had been abandoned by all other relatives and friends.

Prior to the study, his VC was 1.6 (47 percent of normal), his MBC 1.9 (20 percent of normal), his MEF 40, pH 7.41, $PaCO_2$ 43, PaO_2 65, and SaO_2 91. He attended five of the first six meetings, became increasingly negative and angry, and then refused to continue. After attending two group meetings his pH was 7.39, $PaCO_2$ 50, PaO_2 34, and SaO_2 63. After leaving the group, his pH was 7.41, $PaCO_2$ 50, PaO_2 50, and SaO_2 81. One year after the start of the group, his pH was 7.29, $PaCO_2$ 50, PaO_2 50, and SaO_2 81.

This patient's initial positive hopeful response to the group quickly became negative and rejecting. In the group, he actively and passively tried to avoid talking of emotionally laden topics, and his comments were openly rejecting and destructive. He quit the group because "It can't do any good." At that time he appeared to be deteriorating physiologically, as reflected in the blood gas changes shown after participating in two meetings.

Both of these patients presented a long history of alcoholism and chronic lung disease. They both worked well until their chronic lung disease became severe enough to incapacitate them almost completely. Their responses to group therapy differed: Case 1 accepted the group and benefited from it, while Case 2 rejected the group and gained nothing. In their subsequent hospital course, Case 1 was discharged and returned to his accepting family, while Case 2 remained in the hospital.

Successful Group Interventions

In reviewing our failed group experience, we began a consultation program with the COPD ward staff in order to address the problem of the coping behavior of the patients. We met weekly with the medical and nursing staff to define the patients' problems and develop staff responses. The staff was unaware of the patients' psychophysiological adaptational problems and did not appreciate the severity of the emotional-straitjacket style of the patients. Further, we were able to develop neutral styles in the patient-staff interactions. As a result, patient management problems in the ward decreased.

We also discovered two other group experiences that had been conducted quite successfully in the ward unit but were not labeled group therapy.

The first was a one-hour weekly didactic class conducted by the ward physician. He drew diagrams of the cardiopulmonary anatomy and function for the patients and offered medical advice on how the patients could cope with their symptoms. All the patients on the ward were eager to attend, asked questions, and generally considered this "group" a positive experience.

The second was a "bottle-blowing" group conducted by a young female physical therapist. The patients engaged in breathing exercises, using tubes connected to water jars. Good breathing techniques produced a rise and fall of the water in the jar. This group was quite spirited. The men competed with each other, and there was good-natured ribbing and kidding. This was the most popular activity in the ward and was regularly attended by almost every patient.

These two groups reflect the same principles of "didactic group intervention" first described by Pratt. Group activities focused on impersonal but real issues relevant to each patient. Because the content of the group activities was objective and universal, affective perturbation was minimized. Personal introspection and verbalization were minimal, while real activities that these men could perform were emphasized. Again, the patients were not asked to change themselves as persons but were guided toward actions they could take in their world.

Recent reports on comprehensive biopsychosocial treatment programs for COPD patients suggest that the survival rate increases 50 percent in groups that are taught technical aspects of caring for themselves and whose families are taught how to adapt to the psychosocial constraints of the illness (Petty and others, 1979; Sahn, Nett, and Petty, 1980). In these programs it is feasible to structure group experiences that are primarily didactic and focus on the patients' acquiring new skills for coping with their illness and treatment. Theoretically, these group interventions have been described as "structured groups for life skills training" (Drum and Knott, 1977).

Recommendations for Group Interventions

In considering the whole domain of treatment for COPD patients, we shall consider three aspects of group intervention: the ward milieu, individual patient change, and family interactions.

Ward Milieu. In this context we consider the ward inpatient unit as a social system. An acute patient care model of staff function is not appropriate. Rather we must study a social organization that approximates a normalized intimate social environment. It is most desirable to have a ward administrator or consultant serve as an organizational group leader. Training and educating the staff about the special physical and psychosocial problems of the COPD patient are necessary, as is ongoing staff training. Regular staff group meetings to review patient-staff interactions are very important in making the professional staff work cohesively. Norms, rules, regulations, and informal and formal expectations of staff behavior need to be defined, reviewed, and refined. Given this foundation, the behavior of difficult patients can be understood and anticipated. Problems in patient-staff interaction can be evaluated against established norms for patient management. The administrative group leader should try to establish and maintain staff group norms, build and maintain staff morale, and resolve both intrastaff and patient-staff conflicts through the group process. These are all well-established functions of group treatment (Edelson, 1964; Moos, 1977).

A second group intervention strategy involves patient-group activities in the ward. Here the goal is to promote group cohesion, group socialization, and effective interaction among the patients. Group activities (involving music, arts and crafts, games, and so on) should be regularly scheduled with specific leaders assigned for each activity.

A third type of group intervention should be aimed at

training the patients to manage their illness. This can include didactic lectures and group discussions. Demonstrations of medical procedures can also include practice at self-administering medication, breathing exercises, physical activity, and so on. Again, regularly scheduled lectures, demonstrations, and practice sessions should be organized, with leaders assigned to each group activity.

Personal Change. More individual-oriented group intervention can be undertaken if a leader skilled in group dynamics is available. Again, a regularly scheduled group session is essential. I would recommend an open-ended group format with voluntary attendance. Since patients enter and leave a treatment unit and their clinical status can change from day to day, an open format is preferable to a closed, time-limited group.

The group should not focus on group dynamics or personalize issues, and should avoid direct personal confrontation. "Casual discussion" might best describe the group interaction. The leader should feel free to provide information, comment on ward issues, and bring up family interactions. In other words, the leader should continually introduce new information common to all members into the group discussion. Although confidentiality should be respected, the group should avoid intimate personal revelations except when patients feel free to introduce personal topics, as they might in any social conversation. This avoids making patients defensive about sensitive issues that might be inappropriate to share.

If possible, the group leader should be at least a part-time member of the professional staff so that group discussion can be oriented toward events in the everyday life of the ward. In this sense, the group discussion becomes an arena for review, evaluation, and coping decisions related to the realities of life in the ward. Thus, the format of group therapy is not isolated from ward life but integrated into it. The group therapy should catalyze the acquisition of more effective life-coping skills.

In this type of group format, focusing on specific phase developments of group dynamics is inappropriate. More likely, group dynamics typical of early group formation will continuously reappear as patients move in and out of the group discussion every week.

The leader should not focus attention on himself or herself. Frankness, personal openness, and personal empathy are desirable qualities in a group leader. The leader should possess considerable technical knowledge (not medical expertise) about the medical aspects of COPD and be able to reinforce appropriate information and management skills presented in other group activities in which the patients participate.

Family Interventions. Thus far we have focused mostly upon inpatient group interventions. Almost all of the group strategies outlined above can also be conducted on an outpatient basis with modified schedules. For outpatients, several related group activities scheduled on a half-day are probably better than requiring patients to make several visits every week. The most important aspect of outpatient management is to prepare the family to receive a patient back in the home environment and to continue work with the family on an outpatient basis (Bennett, 1979). Family systems can impede or impair patient adjustment or they can help the chronically ill person to adapt. However, the family system will not operate effectively if it does not accommodate the chronically ill patient member (Pattison and Anderson, 1978).

The same general principles of group intervention obtain in family treatment interventions. That is, the focus is not on family therapy for family pathology but rather on family education and restructuring the roles and functions of the family to adapt to the chronically ill member. We can include social network interventions with the patient's extended family, friends, and acquaintances. Recruiting such persons to assist in patient care, transportation, and household tasks can be a source of both emotional and material support (Pattison, 1982). A related group intervention to be considered is the organization of self-help groups of COPD patients who can offer ongoing assistance to each other outside the formal health care system (Politser and Pattison, 1979, 1980). Here the group leader can serve effectively as a group advisor and consultant.

In sum, the COPD patient population presents a unique set of biopsychosocial problems. The patients themselves are a high-risk population with marginal life histories and problematic psychosocial coping skills. The disease process of the res-

piratory system creates an ambiguous chronic dying state that
can promote anxiety and depression. Further, the intimate link-
age between respiration and emotions progressively limits the
degree of affective arousal that these patients can physiologically tolerate. As a result, they become confined to an emotional straitjacket.

Psychotherapeutic intervention must avoid direct and
personalized cognitive-affective styles of treatment. Technical
distancing maneuvers must be used to achieve cognitive and affective exploration and adaptation. Thus therapy must be
through indirect routes.

Group intervention strategies can be considered in three
domains: in the ward milieu, in individual change, and in family intervention. A variety of group methods and formats can be
prescribed to encompass each of these domains for intervention.

References

Alexander, A. B. "Behavioral Medicine in Asthma." In R. B.
    Stuart (Ed.), *Adherence, Compliance, and Generalization in
    Behavioral Medicine.* New York: Brunner/Mazel, 1982.
Baldwin, E. D., Cournand, A., and Richards, D. W., Jr. "Pul-
    monary Insufficiency. I. Physiological Classification, Clinical
    Methods of Analysis, Standard Values in Normal Subjects."
    Medicine, 1948, *27,* 243-278.
Bennett, L. "Group Services for COPD Out-Patients." *Social
    Work with Groups,* 1979, *2,* 145-160.
Butler, T., and Fuhriman, A. "Curative Factors in Group Ther-
    apy." *Small Group Behavior,* 1983, *14,* 131-142.
Drum, D. J., and Knott, J. E. *Structured Groups for Facilitat-
    ing Development.* New York: Human Sciences Press, 1977.
Dudley, D. L., Holmes, T. H., and Martin, C. J. "Dyspnea: Psy-
    chological and Physiological Observations." *Journal of Psy-
    chosomatic Research,* 1968, *11,* 325-339.
Dudley, D. L., Martin, C. J., and Holmes, T. H. "Psychophysio-
    logic Studies of Pulmonary Ventilation." *Psychosomatic
    Medicine,* 1964, *26,* 645-660.
Dudley, D. L., and Pattison, E. M. "Group Psychotherapy in Pa-

tients with Severe Diffuse Obstructive Pulmonary Syndrome." *American Review of Respiratory Disease,* 1969, *100,* 575-576.

Dudley, D. L., and others. "Changes in Respiration Associated with Hypnotically Induced Emotion, Pain, and Exercise." *Psychosomatic Medicine,* 1964, *26,* 46-57.

Dudley, D. L., and others. "Long-Term Adjustment, Prognosis, and Death in Irreversible Diffuse Obstructive Pulmonary Syndrome." *Psychosomatic Medicine,* 1969, *31,* 310-325.

Edelson, M. *Ego Psychology, Group Dynamics, and the Therapeutic Community.* New York: Grune & Stratton, 1964.

Ford, C. V. "Group Psychotherapy with Psychosomatic Patients." In M. Grotjahn, F. M. Kline, and C. T. H. Friedman (Eds.), *Handbook of Group Therapy.* New York: Van Nostrand Reinhold, 1983.

Groen, J. J., and Pelser, H. E. "Experience with, and Results of, Group Therapy with Patients with Bronchial Asthma." *Journal of Psychosomatic Research,* 1960, *4,* 191-205.

Kinsman, R. A., Dirks, J. F., and Jones, N. F. "Psycho-Maintenance of Chronic Physical Illness: Clinical Assessment of Personal Styles Affecting Medical Management." In T. Millon, C. Green, and R. Meagher (Eds.), *Handbook of Clinical Health Psychology.* New York: Plenum, 1982.

Lange-Nielsen, F., and Retterstal, N. "Group Psychotherapy in Bronchial Asthma." *Acta Psychiatrica Scandinavia,* 1959, *34,* 187-204.

Loevinger, J. *Ego Development.* San Francisco: Jossey-Bass, 1976.

Lyons, H. A. "The Respiratory System and Specifics of Alcoholism." In E. M. Pattison and E. Kaufman (Eds.), *Encyclopedic Handbook of Alcoholism.* New York: Gardner Press, 1982.

Martin, C. J., Pardee, N., and Dominik, J. "The Diffuse Obstructive Pulmonary Syndrome: I. Natural History." *American Review of Respiratory Diseases,* 1966, *93,* 383-389.

Miles, S. "Group Therapy in Medical Illness." In M. Grotjahn, F. M. Kline, and C. T. H. Friedman (Eds.), *Handbook of Group Therapy.* New York: Van Nostrand Reinhold, 1983.

Moos, R. H. (Ed.). *Coping with Physical Illness.* New York: Plenum, 1977.

Pattison, E. M. "The Relationship of Adjunctive and Therapeutic Recreation Services to Community Mental Health Programs." *Therapeutic Recreation Journal,* 1969, *3,* 16-25.

Pattison, E. M. "Psychosocial Predictors of Death Prognosis." *Omega,* 1974, *5,* 145-160.

Pattison, E. M. *The Experience of Dying.* Englewood Cliffs, N.J.: Prentice-Hall, 1977.

Pattison, E. M. (Ed.). *Clinical Applications of Social Network Theory.* New York: Human Sciences Press, 1982.

Pattison, E. M., and Anderson, R. C. "Family Health Care." *International Public Health Review,* 1978, *7,* 83-134.

Pattison, E. M., Brissenden, A., and Wohl, T. "Assessing Specific Effects of Inpatient Group Psychotherapy." *International Journal of Group Psychotherapy,* 1967, *17,* 283-297.

Pattison, E. M., and Rhodes, R. J. "Clinical Prediction with the Nosie-30 Scale." *Journal of Clinical Psychology,* 1974, *30,* 200-201.

Pattison, E. M., Rhodes, R. J., and Dudley, D. L. "Response to Group Treatment in Patients with Severe Chronic Lung Disease." *International Journal of Group Psychotherapy,* 1971, *21,* 214-225.

Petty, T. L., and others. "Outpatient Oxygen Therapy in Chronic Obstructive Pulmonary Disease: A Review of Thirteen Years Experience and an Evaluation of Modes of Therapy." *Archives of Internal Medicine,* 1979, *139,* 28-32.

Politser, P. E., and Pattison, E. M. "Mental Health Functions of Community Groups." *Group,* 1979, *10,* 19-26.

Politser, P. E., and Pattison, E. M. "Social Climates in Community Groups: Toward a Taxonomy." *Community Mental Health Journal,* 1980, *16,* 187-200.

Pratt, J. H. "The Class Method of Treating Consumption in the Homes of the Poor." *Journal of the American Medical Association,* 1907, *49,* 755-759.

Sahn, S. A., Nett, L. M., and Petty, T. L. "Ten-Year Follow-Up of a Comprehensive Rehabilitation Program for Severe COPD." *Chest,* 1980, *77,* 311-314.

Seligman, M. (Ed.). *Group Psychotherapy and Counseling with Special Populations*. Baltimore, Md.: University Park Press, 1982.

Sobel, E. (Ed.). *Behavioral Thanatology*. Baltimore, Md.: Williams & Wilkins, 1982.

Sparer, P. J., Cockrell, B. A., and Shelton, N. W. "Psychosomatic Program of a Comprehensive Service to Hospitalized Tuberculosis Patients." In P. J. Sparer (Ed.), *Personality, Stress, and Tuberculosis*. New York: International Universities Press, 1956.

Turpin, G., Marcer, D., and Howell, J. B. L. "Psychological Approaches to the Study of Breathlessness and Other Respiratory Sensations." In D. J. Oborne, M. M. Gruneberg, and J. R. Elser (Eds.), *Research in Psychology and Medicine*. Vol. 1. New York: Academic Press, 1979.

Wilmer, H. A. *This Is Your World*. Springfield, Ill.: Thomas, 1952.

Yalom, I. D. *Inpatient Group Psychotherapy*. New York: Basic Books, 1983.

9

Andrew M. Razin, Ph.D., M.D.

▦ ▦ ▦ ▦ ▦ ▦ ▦ ▦ ▦ ▦ ▦ ▦ ▦

Coronary Artery Disease

For many years, coronary artery disease (CAD) has been the leading cause of death in this country in adults over forty years of age. Its severity is even greater when we consider the incidence of nonfatal CAD events. Although CAD incidence and mortality have been declining over the last few years (presumably because of improved acute care facilities and increased national attention to reducing risk factors), CAD has nonetheless retained its position as the leading cause of death.

What exactly is CAD? It is a broad, generic term including both atherosclerotic and nonatherosclerotic disease of the coronary (heart) arteries, as well as the resultant disease of the heart itself. Like all other muscle tissue, the myocardium (the muscle that comprises virtually all of the functioning pumping

This work was supported in part by a fellowship from Biological Sciences Training Grant MH-14612. This fellowship was approved and administered by the Research Fellowship Program of the Department of Psychiatry at Montefiore Hospital, Bronx, New York.

heart) requires oxygen in amounts that vary with the effort (rate and contractile force) with which the heart is pumping. The coronary arteries (which take their name from the crown-shaped arrangement that they form around the upper portion of the heart) branch out to provide the heart itself with oxygenated blood. When the supply of oxygen is insufficient for the momentary demand, ischemia is said to occur. Often, though not always, such ischemia is experienced as chest pain. When ischemia is sufficiently prolonged or severe, myocardial tissue dies, and the patient is said to have suffered a myocardial infarction, or heart attack. The amount and location of infarcted tissue determine the severity of the myocardial infarction (MI). A massive MI, involving large portions of the left ventricle (the primary pumping chamber for the entire body), may kill its victim, while a mild MI involving only a small area of hemodynamically less significant tissue might leave its victim able to resume a fully active, long life. Because the conductive (electrical) activity of the heart typically changes in characteristic ways during and after MI, electrocardiograms (ECGs) will usually be diagnostic. In addition, with the death of muscle tissue, certain enzymes are released from within muscle cells into the bloodstream; these "cardiac enzymes" will therefore appear in greater concentration in the blood, and such elevations are also diagnostic of MI.

The coronary arteries may allow insufficient blood flow for several reasons. Most commonly, as we age, lipids such as cholesterol deposit themselves as plaques (or atheromata) on the inner walls of coronary (and other) arteries, progressively reducing the inner cross-sectional area (lumen) of the artery and thus reducing blood flow. In addition to reducing luminal size, these plaques also eventually "harden" the arteries, that is, reduce the arteries' elastic ability to distend and thus increase blood flow. This latter process is arteriosclerosis or atherosclerosis, and it is accepted as the most common cause of CAD and MI. Additionally, a blood clot, or thrombosis, may form in or find its way into the coronary arteries. Either alone or, more especially, in combination with atherosclerosis, such a clot may occlude an artery or its branches, forming a coronary thrombosis, a term that has often been loosely used as a synonym for MI. Finally, the rings of smooth muscle, which comprise a significant part of the coronary artery walls, may spasm, constricting the arteries and reducing the blood flow. Thus, coronary spasm alone or in combination with the above mechanisms may also cause an MI. There are additional, less common causes of coronary artery insufficiency, which are well described in the cardiology text of Hurst and others (1978).

When the ischemia remits promptly enough, no permanent myocardial damage results, though the victim typically feels (transient) chest pain. Such transient, noninfarcting ischemia is recognized as angina pectoris—a characteristic syndrome of chest pain, usually precipitated by physical exertion or psychological stress and relieved by rest or medications (such as nitroglycerin) that dilate the coronary arteries. Patients may have angina that remains stable and never worsens to become a frank MI, or they may have progressively worsening "crescendo" angina, or they may suffer MI without any antecedent angina, or they may suffer a "silent" (asymptomatic) MI that is recognized only subsequently. CAD is thus a very heterogeneous group of phenomena etiologically, prognostically, and phenomenologically.

Over the past several decades, literally dozens of factors —physiological, anatomical, behavioral, social, metabolic, and so on—have been proposed as CAD risk factors. Of these, a handful have been found by careful research to contribute in some way to increased CAD risk. Hypertension, cigarette smoking, and serum cholesterol levels seem to be the three factors that can increase risk the most, while sex, age, a family history of CAD, the presence of diabetes mellitus, a sedentary life-style, and obesity each pose additional risks.

Psychosocial Precursors and Sequelae

For many centuries, practicing physicians and laypersons alike have believed that a variety of psychological factors—stress, anxiety, depression, and so on—could also predispose to or precipitate CAD events. But until the 1960s, there was very little empirical evidence that was rigorously derived to support this widespread belief. Beginning around that time, research evidence of acceptable quality began to accumulate that clearly indicates associations, some of which appear to be causal, between several psychosocial factors and CAD. An examination of the excellent reviews by Jenkins (1971, 1976) and others (Blackburn, 1974; Roskies, 1979; Russek and Russek, 1976) yields the following conclusions concerning these associations:

1. There are clearly positive associations of some kind between psychosocial factors and CAD development.
2. The strength of these associations, however, varies across different psychosocial factors. Life-stress events, anxiety, depression, and Type A behavior, for example, show relatively consistent associations, while demographic indicators, socioeconomic status, socioeconomic mobility, and socioeconomic incongruity show weak or inconsistent associations.

   The Type A behavior pattern (TABP) has been the single most extensively studied psychosocial factor and is probably the one most strongly associated with CAD. In our view, research on the TABP over the past two decades has largely been responsible for the increased interest in and acceptance of psychosocial CAD risk factors. As a primary focus of our group interventions, the TABP will be discussed in detail below.
3. The specificity of these associations varies. Life-stress events and neuroticism, for example, seem linked to general morbidity, while anxiety, depression, and life dissatisfaction may be more specifically linked to angina.
4. Even among the strongest of these associations, the precise causal nature or mechanism of each association has yet to be clearly demonstrated.
5. The highly complex interplay of social, economic, cultural, psychosocial, psychobiological, genetic, physiological, endocrinological, and other factors will undoubtedly continue to make research in this area extraordinarily difficult.
6. Thus, a definitive understanding of the relationships be-

tween psychosocial factors and CAD development, while brought closer by recent research, still eludes us.

Given the heterogeneity of prognoses and the severity described above, it should not be surprising that the impact of CAD is also quite variable, and it is thus difficult to make general statements about CAD's impact. By focusing specifically on MI, however, we can delineate factors that are associated with differential short- and long-term patient reactions to MI. Our own clinical experience and the existent literature on post-MI recovery (well reviewed by Croog, Levine, and Lurie, 1968, and by Doehrman, 1977) provide us with the following conclusions:

1. Beyond the temporary disruptive psychosocial functioning that one would expect with acute CAD, one finds long-lasting emotional distress, family turmoil, and occupational problems in a significant minority (perhaps 25 percent) of patients.

2. Coronary care unit (CCU) patients typically do *not* experience short- or long-term emotional disturbances as a result of CCU events and procedures (including witnessing cardiac arrests, being connected to cardiac monitors, and so on).

3. Emotional distress, particularly depression, tends to peak *after* hospital discharge. Family tensions are common during convalescence. Patients seek and receive most of their social support from relatives, friends, and their doctor rather than from institutional or professional services.

4. As one might expect, problems in occupational adjustment are greater among blue-collar workers, less-educated patients, those with lasting emotional distress, and those with more serious medical problems.

5. Most patients do *not* return to previous levels of sexual activity; this failure is due more often to reported psychological concerns than to physical consequences of their illness.

6. High socioeconomic status and marital stability seem to be associated with a good prognosis. The long-term psychological and physiological benefits of physical exercise have not been well demonstrated.

7.   The short- and long-term importance of denial is intriguing, though unclear. A significant proportion of patients tend to minimize or even totally deny the occurrence or (affective) significance of their MI. There is some evidence that those who do so in the acute and immediate postacute phases may do better in terms of CAD prognosis than nondeniers. Over the longer run, though, this association is less clear. Many methodological problems, however, make clear conclusions on this issue impossible.

8.   At the other end of the spectrum of reactions, "cardiac invalidism" seems to be a common, frequently refractory problem once it develops, but one that may be prevented by appropriate, early psychosocial and medical intervention.

Group Interventions in CAD

Reports of both individual and group post-MI psychotherapies have been appearing for well over a decade and are critically reviewed in detail by Razin (1982). Examination of the (six) individual therapy reports indicates that while all show generally positive outcomes, there are serious methodological or reporting problems: Only three studies had any controls and two were purely anecdotal; *treatment* is often not well defined; many of the positive outcome data are of debatable clinical significance; and some data are internally inconsistent. Thus, a favorable impact is suggested, but the clear clinical, particularly physiological, significance of individual post-MI psychotherapy remains to be demonstrated in a methodologically sound manner. Furthermore, although the types of therapy that seem successful are nonexploratory (that is, didactic, behavioral, and reality oriented), there are no definitive comparative data on which to base this conclusion.

The group therapy literature is somewhat more substantial, both quantitatively and qualitatively. There are at least six uncontrolled reports and six controlled studies, which we shall summarize.

Uncontrolled Studies. Mone (1970), a social worker working without a medical cotherapist, treated fourteen men and two women in ten consecutive weekly sessions. Patients (at least eleven CAD and three cardiac-surgical) were carefully selected as appropriate for group therapy (after being interviewed by Mone), as having actual or anticipated (by the referring physicians) adjustment problems, and as not functioning in their usual roles. Therapeutic emphases were similar to Adsett and Bruhn's (1968; see the discussion later in this chapter). Although there are no controls for comparison, the results seem generally favorable: All fourteen regained at least some of their usual functioning; nine of the thirteen who had been unemployed at the start of the treatment became employed; self-reported anxiety, depression, and hypochondriasis decreased, while independence and realistic attitudes reportedly increased; on the MMPI, significant improvements occurred on Dependency, Denial, and Ego Strength. Mone feels that the decreases in depression and hypochondriasis are particularly important in cardiac rehabilitation and that the group format is particularly useful for working on hypochondriasis and denial.

Bilodeau and Hackett (1971) described an uncontrolled trial of group therapy in which the former, a nurse, conducted ten weekly sessions with five male first-MI patients (ten were randomly selected, of whom five reportedly could not attend). Significantly, she met with each individual five times during hospitalization to orient them and establish rapport, and she maintained weekly phone contact with each patient's wife during treatment. Bilodeau's role was apparently didactic, noninterpretive, supportive, and facilitative of open-group interaction. The report, which by design focuses on the various issues and themes raised in sessions, provides no systematic outcome data other than the absence of cardiac symptoms during the treatment period, a uniform decrease in smoking, good return-to-work data, and members' very favorable response to the group. (At their request, it was extended at least twelve weeks.) Additionally, the degree of patient uncertainty about diagnosis and treatment (due to physicians' failure to inform and patients' failure to remember) was striking in this group.

Similarly, Weiner, Akabas, and Sommer (1973) and

Golden (cited by Hackett, 1978) provide additional favorable but uncontrolled reports of group therapy effectiveness. In both these studies, spouses were (at least in most cases) involved, the emphasis was didactic and supportive, and the treatment was brief (six to ten sessions). In both reports, outcome was assessed only informally and was similar: a positive response to the group experience, as well as self-reported improvements in hypochondriasis, sleep, appetite, and returning to work.

Frank, Heller, and Kornfeld (1979) describe an unpublished study of Millman, Penick, and Case in which group therapy began while patients were still in the CCU and continued twice per week until discharge (totaling six to eight sessions). The study is primarily descriptive, reporting the defenses, concerns, and interventions emphasized in the groups (see also the work of Rahe and others, 1973, 1975, described later). The only findings reported were the absence of coronary symptoms during the sessions, decreased denial, readiness for the transition to home, and fewer CCU requests for psychiatric consultation.

Finally, Soloff (1979) compared medically treated post-MI patients to surgical post-coronary-bypass patients. Prior to a six-week tripartite rehabilitation program of aerobic conditioning, didactic coronary education, and supportive group therapy, the medical patients showed greater mood disturbance. With the rehabilitation program, their mood disturbance abated to approximately that of the surgical patients. Soloff feels that this improvement was not attributable to an improvement in exercise tolerance or to the passage of time alone.

Controlled Studies. Adsett and Bruhn (1968), a psychiatrist and a sociologist, respectively, cotreated six male post-MI patients in ten sessions of group therapy while simultaneously treating their wives in a separate group. Patient selection was based in part on patients' being identified as having high drives, intense frustration, and unusual psychological post-MI problems. They were matched on sex, age, and race with six no-treatment ("no-psychological-problem") controls. Unlike the later studies, the therapeutic emphasis here was apparently somewhat more exploratory and psychodynamic than directive and didactic, though the interventions were nevertheless focal, supportive, and oriented to current problems and solutions. Results showed a very high acceptance (of therapy) rate and "improved psychosocial adaptation" among both patients and wives (though this seems to represent the authors' judgment rather than any systematic data). No experimental-control differences were found (either during therapy or at a six-month follow-up) in blood pressure, anxiety, depression, ECGs, or reinfarctions or rehospitalization (none in either group). In fact, treated subjects had significantly higher cholesterol and uric acid levels after therapy. Among the four patients who refused participation, there was a subsequent fatal MI and a mild stroke. Although the authors do not provide substantial follow-up data, they do give detailed descriptions of the process and themes of their sessions, as well as husband-wife group comparisons. A later report (Bruhn, Wolf, and Philips, 1971) followed the treated subjects and a different no-treatment "control" group (more accurately, a comparison group) over nine years. Neither MMPI changes (over time) among treated subjects nor MMPI differences between the treatment and the control groups were noted over this period. The treated groups seem to have had much better long-term survival, but the form of data presentation does not easily permit such a conclusion.

Ibrahim and others (1974) conducted a large-scale study of post-MI group therapy, randomly assigning fifty postdischarge patients to treatment groups and sixty more to receive no treatment. Weekly sessions were conducted by clinical psychologists for a year, with assessments made at six, twelve, and eighteen months. Early on, the therapists attempted an exploratory, nondidactic emphasis, but they quickly found patients very reluctant to work in a psychodynamic, exploratory manner, and the therapists thereafter shifted the focus to practical daily concerns and employed a different technique. Results indicated high degrees of patient and physician acceptance (that is, favorable attitude and attendance) of and patient adherence to the treatment. Also found were less social alienation, cynicism, and competitiveness in treated patients (though competitiveness resumed its pretreatment level six months after treatment). Both groups seemed to decrease job involvement and impulsive behavior over time, and no changes appeared in either group on several self-report personality measures or in smoking habits, employment status, or marital harmony. A similar proportion of each group was rehospitalized, but treated subjects had shorter stays. There were no significant differences between the treatment and the control groups at follow-up in measures of blood pressure, heart rate, relative body mass, serum cholesterol, triglycerides, glucose, or uric acid. Treated subjects, however, especially those most severely ill, did enjoy a better survival rate that approached statistical significance. The authors interpret the CAD-prognostic significance of their findings very cautiously.

In a widely cited longitudinal study of post-MI group therapy, Rahe and his colleagues (Rahe, Ward, and Hayes, 1979; Rahe and others, 1973, 1975) followed two treatment groups (one with twenty-two and one with seventeen subjects) and one control group (receiving routine post-MI medical follow-up) with twenty-two patients over three to four years. Patients were all first-MI hospital outpatients, randomly assigned, and nearly all male. Four to six biweekly, ninety-minute group sessions were coled by Rahe himself (who was trained in psychiatry as well as internal medicine) and one or two other medical staff members over three months.

The authors' first report (1973) is descriptive, reporting their didactic, practical emphasis and the patients' surprising readiness to examine previous life experiences (particularly life-stress events) and TABP. Also described are the expected denial, post-MI depression, frequent Type A behavior, and post-MI family adjustment problems. The second report (1975) indicated that at (up to) eighteen months post-MI, treated subjects had significantly fewer severe CAD events (coronary insufficiency, bypass surgery, reinfarction, or CAD-related death). Furthermore, on written tests, treated subjects demonstrated greater knowledge of CAD (its physiology, treatment, risk factors, and so on).

The authors note a few methodological problems. Control patients could not be kept "naive" and apparently felt they were receiving less care or a less favorable prognosis. There were, therefore, a substantial number of control-group dropouts and a poorer questionnaire return rate among controls. The authors (Rahe, Ward, and Hayes, 1979) nonetheless managed to secure a very commendable 95 percent follow-up rate after three to four years and found fewer reinfarctions and coronary deaths, through differences in coronary insufficiency and by-pass surgery were nonsignificant. "Mild-to-moderate" CAD morbidity data included no differences in the incidences of mild congestive heart failure or arrhythmias but a significant favorable difference in the incidence of angina. Treated subjects also showed significantly better return-to-work records and a greater improvement on overwork and time urgency (rated via interview). No differences were observed in depression, anxiety, sexual functioning, knowledge of CAD, life dissatisfaction, reduction of weight, smoking, or serum cholesterol.

It should be noted that the authors accept a 0.15 probability level (instead of the usual 0.05) as significant. This level is especially problematical given the large number of data comparisons made. Nonetheless, the methodology of this work is impressive, the clinical value of the intervention is quite convincing, and the authors offer several useful guidelines based on their work. They feel that the group leader's focusing on the relationship between psychological-behavioral patterns and compliance problems was particularly useful in the group context and that patients were then able to "recognize themselves" in each other and thus to reduce their Type A behavior. They also felt that the rehearsal of anticipated stresses, the felt "emotional support" derived from group membership, and the resulting ability to modify Type A behavior were all important factors. Noting treated subjects' loss of earlier CAD-"educational" superiority, the authors stress the need for periodic educational "reinforcement." Finally, they note that the improved TABP and morbidity-mortality findings with no apparent improvement in weight or diet, smoking habits, or cholesterol level provide support for the independence of the TABP as a risk factor.

In addition to these three controlled studies, there are three others that focused specifically on group interventions aimed at TABP reduction in CAD patients. (The reader interested in studies of TABP reduction in non-CAD as well as CAD subjects should consult the comprehensive reviews of Razin, 1982, forthcoming, and Suinn, 1982.)

As part of a thorough recruitment plan, Roskies and others (1978) used the TABP structured interview developed by Rosenman and Friedman to select thirty volunteer extreme A's, all male Canadians, all in professional-executive positions, all free of known CAD, and aged between thirty-nine and fifty-nine. A battery of measures included nearly all the traditional risk factors, state and trait anxiety, several sociodemographic and work-related measures, and so on. The sample as a whole seemed more health conscious and at lower risk than a comparable sample of Canadian managers. The subjects were randomly assigned to group psychotherapy or group behavior therapy. The former was apparently exploratory and insight oriented, aiming to provide a "corrective emotional experience." The behavior therapy program stressed Jacobsonian muscle relaxation and record keeping (of tension levels and situations of stress); the aim was to increase awareness of and control over felt stress. Both groups met weekly for fourteen sessions.

All subjects were instructed not to make changes in diet, exercise, smoking, work conditions, and so on, during treatment, and apparently both groups complied with this prescription well. However, both groups did show significant changes on nearly all psychological and physiological variables: cholesterol level, systolic blood pressure, number of psychological symptoms, life satisfaction, and sense of time pressure. Diastolic blood pressure and triglycerides showed nonsignificant favorable changes. Behavior therapy seemed slightly (nonsignificantly) superior to psychotherapy in cholesterol reduction, with behavior therapy showing a greater mean decrease (46 versus 16 mg %), more subjects decreasing, and more subjects changing their levels from high-risk categories.

The six-month follow-up of these subjects (Roskies and others, 1979) indicated that both groups continued to improve on diastolic and systolic blood pressure. But the slight superiority of behavior therapy seen immediately after treatment became more substantial over the follow-up period: Cholesterol, number of psychological symptoms, and life satisfaction data all showed greater improvement with behavior therapy. The authors suggest that the daily practice of tension reduction, seen in behavior therapy but not psychotherapy, may be responsible for behavior therapy's superiority. In this second report, moreover, the authors also describe their application of the identical behavior therapy regimen to an additional, "clinical" group (whose six subjects' ECG stress tests indicated CAD). These subjects achieved even better results posttreatment and at follow-up than the nonclinical behavior therapy group.

Jenni and Wollersheim (1979) also attempted to change the Type A pattern in a quite heterogeneous sample of forty-two subjects recruited through physicians and through advertisements that called for people experiencing time pressure, job stress, and so on. Fifty-one applicants were interviewed with the structured interview, and the nine subjects thereby designated as type B's were eliminated. Twenty-seven of the remaining subjects were men, of whom seven had had MIs; none of the fifteen women had. All the occupations held involved initiative, responsibility, or managerial status. The subjects were assigned quasi-randomly (that is, groups were matched for sex and number of subjects designated as extreme A's) (1) to a cognitive therapy group, which used a variant of Ellis's (1973) rational-emotive therapy (emphasizing the recognition of tension, which precipitates events, beliefs, and interpretations; the critical evaluation of beliefs; and the substitution of more reasonable beliefs), (2) to a stress management training group, which used Suinn's (1974) cognitive stress management training (CSMT; relaxation plus guided imagery), or (3) to a waiting-list control group. In neither treatment were subjects urged to slow down, restrict activities, or become less achievement oriented.

Type A behavior, measured pre- and posttreatment via the Bortner Self-Rating Scale, was reduced significantly for the five extreme A's in cognitive therapy, though not for the five CSMT group members or six control extreme A's. Self-reported state anxiety decreased in both treatment groups (not in controls) but returned to pretreatment levels at the six-week follow-up. Trait anxiety similarly decreased in both treatment groups and remained low at follow-up. The authors view the last findings as long-term positive effects. Changes in cholesterol and systolic and diastolic blood pressure were nonsignificant except for a significant increase in CSMT group cholesterol. Subjects in both groups rated the treatment very positively. Subsequent treatment of controls with cognitive therapy produced a similar reduction of self-reported Type A behavior.

Most recently, Friedman and others (1982) published a preliminary report on the only large-scale longitudinal study of TABP reduction and the impact of such reduction on subsequent CAD. They randomly assigned 900 post-MI patients to either traditional-risk-factor-oriented cardiological-counseling groups ($n = 300$) or to groups that, in addition, provided a variety of didactic and cognitive-behavioral techniques (for example, behavioral self-assessment and self-reinforcement, and role playing) aimed at TABP reduction ($n = 600$). One hundred and thirty-five additional subjects volunteered to serve as no-counseling controls, undergoing only annual examinations and interviews. The cardiological-counseling-only groups were staffed by cardiologists, comprised about twelve patients per group, and met on a tapering frequency (biweekly, then monthly, and then every three months for a variable total number of sessions) over the five years of the study. (Only the first year's results were available for this report.) The TABP-counseling groups were staffed by psychiatrists, psychologists, and two cardiologists familiar with TABP counseling; each group had about ten members and met on a tapering, but more frequent, basis (weekly, then biweekly, and then monthly).

Results indicate that the three treatment conditions were well balanced on sociodemographic and medical measures and that all treatment conditions included approximately equal, and very high, proportions (about 97 percent) of Type A subjects. The rates of reinfarction and cardiovascular death were lower among TABP-counseling subjects than among untreated controls; the rate of nonfatal infarction was lower among TABP-counseling subjects than among cardiological-counseling-only subjects and among untreated controls.

Research Implications. Review of all these controlled studies and the uncontrolled studies leads to two primary conclusions. First, and probably most important, the weight of the evidence indicates that group treatment is beneficial: There are consistent, moderate psychological gains and less consistent, but clinically significant, physiological CAD-prognostic gains from such treatment. Second, we are at a point where conceptual and methodological clarification is feasible and called for. As Hackett (1978) and Frank, Heller, and Kornfeld (1979) point out, we must at this point apply much more precise, rigorous scientific methodology. Post-MI groups, which are now clearly much more common than this small number of studies might suggest (Hackett, 1978), must be studied more systematically, with attention to self-report, pre- and posttreatment, and correlative physiological data. The Friedman and others (1982) and Rahe and others (1973, 1975; Rahe, Ward, and Hayes, 1979) studies represent commendable examples of the quality of research that can be done in this area.

Given that group interventions do seem to exert a beneficial influence, there is currently enough data to allow us to hypothesize and test more refined, specific ideas about group intervention. For example, the success of such treatment seems to hinge in large part on its *not* using usual (exploratory, character-analytic or transference-analytic) psychodynamic methods. Rather, supportive techniques (for example, catharsis, advice, and defense strengthening), teaching, exploration only in carefully focused areas, and so on seem to be much more acceptable to patients. However, Hackett (1978) suggests that for patients with clinically significant psychological problems, a more usual psychotherapy might be more useful than supportive-didactic intervention. But two studies (Adsett and Bruhn, 1968; Mone, 1970) apparently did enlist more "disturbed" patients, so that the current data are inconclusive on patient selection criteria. Clinical experience suggests that the severely disturbed patient is all the more unlikely to benefit from exploratory psychodynamic intervention and all the more in need of supportive, reality-oriented intervention. Thus, there may be a nonlinear (inverted U) relationship between the severity of psychological disturbance and the utility of an exploratory psychodynamic approach. Thus, research helping to specify which patients can benefit from which (if any) type of intervention would be quite valuable.

To our knowledge, there is not a single study comparing group and individual interventions in CAD or similar populations. Moreover, other treatments such as family therapy and behavioral, autoregulatory, and relaxation techniques also warrant systematic comparative study. Another issue is the timing of psychological interventions: Early ones clearly seem better (Frank, Heller, and Kornfeld, 1979) and easier than later ones; there may well be a critical period for such interventions in preventing cardiac invalidism, at least in certain susceptible patients, so that a sequence of early individual treatment followed by later group treatment might be optimal, as the work of Bilodeau and Hackett (1971) and Gruen (1975) suggests.

Several findings suggest the importance of including spouses; the particular value of treating spouses separately (for example, by phone or in a group meeting), though recommended by Hackett and others, is unclear. The best choice of discipline and gender of the therapist or leader is also unclear. All studies, of course, emphasize the necessity of ongoing medical care and providing information, but some have utilized nonmedical group therapists and respected the existing doctor-patient relationships, while others (such as Rahe) have emphasized medical content within group sessions. One can infer from the Bilodeau and Hackett (1971) study that a nurse or physician's assistant might be an ideal leader, enjoying enough status and recognition by being medically knowledgeable and yet not so intimidating as to stifle "foolish" questions and other embarrassing concerns. Apparently, men could and did discuss sex with a female group leader, but comparative data would be more conclusive.

In any case, group leaders are apparently subject to the same worries as patients' families concerning the psychogenic precipitation of coronary events (Adsett and Bruhn, 1968; Mone, 1970), and Hackett (1978) wisely counsels that all leaders should have access to, or familiarity with, emergency care (including cardiopulmonary resuscitation), even if primarily for their own comfort, since no study reports a single coronary event in any group session. Equally important is the need for leaders to be trained in group process; as Hackett (1978) points out, the recommended omission of explicit analysis of group process does not mean that group process is ignored. On the contrary, leaders must be able to perceive and intervene with unconscious and preconscious individual and group dynamics.

The reported response of internists seems puzzling. They generally seem enthusiastic, and yet there are problems in eliciting referrals (Mone, 1970; Hackett, 1978) and collecting medical after-care data (Rahe, Ward, and Hayes, 1979). Whether more interdisciplinary consciousness-raising would suffice to resolve such problems or whether there are some less obvious, more problematical reasons for this apparent resistance is unclear. Perhaps the dramatic results of the Friedman and others (1982) study may exert a substantial impact. The complexities of interdisciplinary interaction, however, especially in liaison psychiatry, are themselves in need of careful study both to advance knowledge in the sociology and social psychology of medicine and, more specifically and practically, to help psychiatrists and their consultees in their frequently difficult or ambivalent relationships.

A comprehensive review of studies focusing specifically on TABP reduction involves many issues and would greatly exceed the space limitations here. The interested reader should consult Razin's (1982) discussion of work in this area. Nonetheless, we can summarily note that nearly all such studies are positive in suggesting diminution of at least some aspect of the TABP, that major methodological and conceptual issues in this research remain, and that the physiological outcome data are conflicting and unclear. To be sure, the recently published, very dramatic, and methodologically sound results of the Friedman and others (1982) study have addressed and to some extent resolved some of these problems, and as such it is a most encouraging development. These last findings may provide a solid base for resolving the several remaining TABP-reduction issues.

Given that no studies compare group with individual (or

family, or other) therapy modalities for CAD patients, and given that there is at least suggestive evidence that individual interventions may be effective (Razin, 1982), the possible advantages of group intervention must be delineated only by sifting through virtually all the above literature and somehow integrating these findings with our own and others' actual clinical experience with each modality. Our attempt to do so yields the following conclusions:

1. Repeatedly one finds in the literature conclusions or admonitions that the CAD patient is uninterested in, if not actively hostile to, psychotherapy, self-exploration, and the notion that it might be useful for him or her to see a psychotherapist. Though there has been no comparative study across diseases, our impression is that this is truer for CAD patients than for those with other diseases. While individual (or family) interventions have been implemented that circumvent such reluctance (for example, Gruen, 1975), the far greater number of (reported and unreported) group interventions indicates that the group format more easily lends itself to deemphasizing in-depth self-exploration.

2. The greater ease with which a (social) "club" or (didactic) "class" atmosphere can be encouraged is clear. This, understandably, also lessens felt stigma, which may be substantial in these patients.

3. Camaraderie, universality of experience, mutual support, cohesiveness, interpersonal learning, availability of multiple positive models for identification, and other factors that Yalom (1970) and others have identified as curative in psychotherapy groups clearly seem to operate in CAD groups as well as traditional therapy groups, and probably to a much greater extent than in individual interventions.

4. Finally, the possibility of increasing or strengthening support systems is probably much greater in groups for at least two reasons. First, new therapeutic relationships are formed that can exert their supportive influence both within the group and outside the group, as members often meet and develop extragroup relationships. Second, the involvement

of spouses, either within the primary group or in a separate group, serves both to increase the support that spouses give to CAD patients and to increase the support that these spouses receive by creating an additional support system of spouses.

The Cardiac Stress Management Program

The above literature and our own clinical experience led us to believe that a program aimed primarily at modifying the TABP and more broadly at post-MI psychosocial rehabilitation ought to incorporate several characteristics: a group format; a didactic-supportive-behavioral orientation with an emphasis on specific, delimited goals; meaningful spouse involvement; relatively brief duration; therapeutic techniques that would facilitate development of the curative factors of therapeutic groups; deemphasis on psychopathology, unconscious dynamic processes, exploration, and other phenomena that would encourage viewing the program as psychotherapy or the participants as being mentally ill; and detailed pre- and posttreatment assessment of each participant (CAD patient and spouse as well) on medical, general psychological, and specific TABP dimensions, so that treatment could be tailored somewhat for each individual and the efficacy of treatment could be assessed meaningfully.

The content of the Cardiac Stress Management Training (CSMT) program has evolved with each administration of it. What follows is a detailed description of the program in its most recent form.

Recruitment, Screening, and Pretreatment Assessment. To date, most of our patients have been solicited through the Montefiore Hospital Cardiac Rehabilitation Exercise Laboratory. Located in a large, private general hospital, this service has in place several supervised exercise programs for post-MI patients. Because of the interest of the laboratory's director in the psychosocial aspects of post-MI recovery, the laboratory sent out mail brochures, which we composed, to virtually all active members in its exercise programs. The brochures are didactic, describing CSMT as a course, and explicitly disclaim offering psychotherapy. The emphasis is on stress reduction and teaching relaxation and coping skills. Spouse participation is strongly urged and facilitated by a reduction in the already modest fee ($100 for individuals and $150 for couples). A copy of a *New York Times* article is attached that describes the results of the Friedman and others (1982) study, stating that recurrent MIs were reduced as a result of TABP reduction. Recruitment for each offering ends after twelve to fifteen participants have been enrolled.

Patients who respond are then contacted to arrange a two-part screening-pretreatment assessment session. In the first session, a couple is jointly interviewed by the author; a general medical history and detailed cardiac history are taken with particular attention to the physical and psychosocial circumstances before, during, and after the MI(s). A brief, general psychiatric assessment is also made, and the couple is oriented to the concept of TABP. Except for cardiac history, the identical inquiry is made of the (non-CAD) spouse, with the intent of communicating at the outset that spouses are to be full participants. Our intention was to exclude psychiatrically only those with severe functional (schizophrenia, affective disorder, or severe character disorder) or organic conditions, and in fact, we excluded only one such person in two years. This interview also serves to orient participants: They are given brief course outlines, general explanations of the CSMT, and individual self-report questionnaires to be completed and turned in by the first course session.

Immediately after this interview, patients are directed to a separate interview area for pretreatment behavioral and physiological assessment. This consists of the structured interview (SI) developed by the Rosenman-Friedman group to assess the TABP. It is a mildly stressful interview, clearly the most valid TABP measure, and requires special training to conduct and rate. Charles Swencionis, a trained SI interviewer-rater, conducted these interview-assessments. As the SI requires for proper administration, interviewees (patients) are kept waiting for perhaps ten to thirty minutes beyond the appointed time, and

the interviews are begun without explanation or apology. After
their unexplained wait, patients are fitted with a blood pressure
and heart rate recording cuff on their nondominant arm. This
cuff is attached to a device that self-inflates and deflates, giving
systolic blood pressure (SBP), diastolic blood pressure (DBP),
and heart rate readings every ninety seconds. Patients are given
reading material and asked to sit comfortably until their blood
pressure and heart rate readings come to baseline, which we defined as that point at which there are two consecutive SBP,
DBP, and heart rate readings within 5 mm Hg (for blood pressure) and five beats per minute (for heart rate). When baseline is
reached, the SI proper begins, which requires about twelve to fifteen minutes. SBP, DBP, and heart rate are recorded throughout, and the entire interview session is videotaped as well.

At the end of the SI, the interviewer proceeds through
two additional tasks, a brief but difficult history quiz and a
mental arithmetic quiz. For the latter, the interviewer sets a
loudly ticking timer and prods the patient to work faster or better at the task of subtracting 17 from a four-digit number repeatedly. Each of these tasks requires two to five minutes; they
were selected for their proven efficacy in raising the blood pressure and heart rate from baseline. As we shall discuss below,
physiological hyperreactivity, that is, lability of the blood pressure, heart rate, and other measures in response to stressors may
be a key CAD-pathogenic characteristic of TABP and thus one
that we feel is crucial to target.

The CSMT Course. The course proper consists of ten one-
and-a-half-hour weekly group sessions, held on weekday eve-
nings, in the Cardiac Rehabilitation Exercise Laboratory's gymnasium. Eight to twelve patients comprise a group. The author
has conducted all sessions.

In the first session, participants (CAD patients or their
spouses) introduce themselves and describe their (or their
spouse's) cardiac events. Using chalk and blackboard, the author asks the group members to generate their own list of CAD
risk factors. The risk factors are then discussed in some detail
(for example, the magnitude of risk posed by each factor and
the modifiability of each) with stress or emotional factors left

for last as the main focus of the course. Stress is then defined and discussed, and participants are encouraged to discuss the stressors in their life in general and around the time of each of their MIs in particular. Following this discussion, participants undergo their first session of Jacobsonian progressive relaxation. This experience is then discussed; finally, homework is assigned, consisting of twice daily practice of the relaxation exercise. Members are also asked to bring a tape recorder to the next session to record subsequent relaxation instructions.

Spouses discuss reactions, undergo relaxation training, do homework, and perform all other course activities as fully as their CAD spouses. Also, the gymnasium was selected to keep the course on familiar, medical, nonpsychiatric grounds. Generation of the risk factor list emphasizes the course's didactic approach; equally important, because this task involves all members, the group begins to develop group cohesion. Homework is especially emphasized to maximize involvement and actual practice.

In the second session, homework is reviewed; difficulties with relaxation are discussed; the experience of relaxation is described, and any other problems and questions are discussed. Stress remains the focus of discussion, and the group examines in detail the cognitive and affective experiences of stressful events. This work closely follows the cognitive-behavioral approaches delineated by Meichenbaum (1977), Novaco (1975), and others. Evaluative, expectational, perceptual, and interpretive aspects of cognition are emphasized as major mediators of the stress created by internal or external precipitating events (stressors). As such, "self-talk" is greatly emphasized as the most available means of recognizing one's own cognition. Similarly, affective and behavioral mediating factors are discussed. Concretely, this work takes the form of teaching participants to become increasingly sensitive to and comfortable in reporting what they think, feel, and do in anticipation of, in the face of, and in the wake of exposure to stressors. In this session, they are given notebooks in which to begin keeping "stress diaries." Each entry consists of a stressful event and the cognitive (self-talk), affective (feelings), physiological (physical sensations), and behavioral concomitants of the events. This is not a task that the participants master easily despite adequate intelligence. It requires repeated encouragement, instruction, mutual support, and raising patients' awareness of internal events and states. This work is also conducted to some degree throughout the rest of the course. Toward the end of the second session, relaxation training is repeated, this time with tape-recorded instructions. Homework consists of twice daily relaxation plus maintaining the stress diary.

In the third session, individual diaries are reviewed, again with attention to sharpening participants' ability to note cognitive, affective, and physiological precursors and mediators of stress. Also in this session, the concept of Type A behavior is discussed in some detail with reference to its importance as a risk factor. It is emphasized that Type A's are more likely to create stress for themselves, and participants' own examples are elicited. Finally, a somewhat briefer relaxation exercise (omitting the muscle tensing of the original exercise) is taught and taped, so that participants can progress to a briefer exercise as they practice at home. Homework is identical to that of the previous session.

In the fourth and fifth sessions, selections from videotapes of individual members' pretreatment SIs are played back. (Shortly after pretreatment assessment, Razin and Swencionis review the tapes and accompanying physiological [blood pressure and heart rate] data. Swencionis rates the tapes for overall TABP and component parts, and segments are selected for this viewing.) Any participant may decline to have his tape shown, but to date none have declined despite some initial hesitation.

The tape viewing is freely interrupted as needed by either participants or course leaders. The group becomes actively yet coherently and supportively involved in noticing Type A and Type B behaviors on the tapes. Physiological data are also fed back, frequently documenting the physiological concomitants of the TABP. Thus, the graphic, undeniable visual feedback data, the correlated physiological data, and the atmosphere of mutual support in which to perceive the data combine to make these two sessions quite remarkable for their dramatic impact, camaraderie, generally good humor, and cohesiveness. We carefully planned the stage at which this feedback occurs in the course: late enough to allow time for some group cohesiveness to have developed before unleashing such potent, and often far from positive, feedback, yet with enough time left in the course for participants to integrate what they experienced.

Most of the next four to five sessions is concerned with "anger management." This is a specific application, or redefinition, of cognitive-behavioral stress management. As such, it is adapted from Novaco's (1975) work in this area, which in turn is adapted from Meichenbaum (1977). Thus, for those individuals for whom chronic hostility, explosiveness, or irritability are identified as problems by self-report or videotape viewing, the principles and techniques described above for stress management are specifically applied to anger management. Thus, again, the focus is on cognitive, affective, physiological, and behavioral precursors, mediators, and sequelae. Anger is differentiated from aggression and assertiveness; its positive as well as negative functions are emphasized; effort is made to identify, within a provocative situation, the very earliest cues of anger; and diary keeping of events that provoke anger becomes a principal part of home practice.

Relaxation training, which has by now been well learned, forms the basis for "stress inoculation," an intervention developed by Meichenbaum (1977) and resembling systematic desensitization. That is, progressively stressful situations are imagined while the group member is in a relaxed state, just as anxiety-laden situations are imagined in desensitization. In our course, recurrent angering situations are used. This calls for homework in which such situations are identified and ordered into a hierarchy. Again, this is not an easy task for many participants, and they must be carefully assisted. For example, the recurrent, predictable situations to be used in stress inoculation and the daily, often unique, unpredictable situations to be entered in the diary often overlap and therefore cause confusion. We therefore use index cards for the former, especially since these items are repeatedly used and rearranged in practice. In the course, more relaxation sessions take place with a provoking scene now added at the end of each exercise.

Role playing of angering situations selected from diaries

or hierarchies occurs in the last session or two; overly submissive, overly aggressive, and appropriately assertive scenarios are enacted. Group members can become quite involved in these exercises, and they both support and contribute to others' efforts, as well as vicariously benefiting themselves.

To be sure, not all participants have anger management problems. Thus, this latter half of the course must be tailored to the individuals. With some participants, the very same cognitive-behavioral techniques can be applied to other TABP components: impatience and time urgency or excessive drive and competitiveness. Furthermore, for many participants, especially women, excessive hostility, explosive anger, or aggressiveness is not the problem; submissiveness and a lack of assertiveness are. For them, virtually the same anger management techniques can be used and appropriately renamed assertiveness training. Significantly, where a husband displays aggressiveness and chronic hostility and his wife is insufficiently assertive, couple interventions can be very useful, although care must be taken in this time-limited, didactic-supportive context to choose the right couples, the right timing, and the right interventions.

The last half-session is a group wrap-up. Participants review what problems and strengths they brought to the course, what progress they feel they have made, what problems remain, and what further (self- or professional) help they might wish, and comment on the course. They are again given self-report questionnaires (posttreatment assessment), which are turned in at their final individual wrap-up sessions (described just below).

Posttreatment Assessment. This very last session with Razin follows the posttreatment behavioral and physiological assessment, again conducted by Swencionis, using equivalent questions and the identical format (monitoring of blood pressure and heart rate, videotaping, and so on) used in the pretreatment behavioral and physiological assessment. The pre- and posttreatment self-report and behavioral and physiological data are collected for formal statistical analysis.

Group Process and Dynamics. One major consequence, perhaps unfavorable, of the distinctly didactic-behavioral approach is that the groups tend to be leader centered. Member-

member interaction is not minimal, but it is less frequent and affectively less intense than it might be in exploratory group psychotherapy. This observation echoes that of Hackett (1978) and others who have done group therapy with CAD patients even without a distinctly didactic or behavioral emphasis. That is, there is an ethos of conformity, a denial of psychopathology, a kid-gloves quality to relations between patients and, of course, a resistance to self-exploration. We believe that CAD groups manifest this ethos more than other medically ill groups, but the findings reported in the other chapters of this volume should prove enlightening in this regard. In any case, it is not necessarily an unexpected development, given our goals and emphases.

Consistent with this ethos is the characteristic transference stance among both men and women: the respectful, somewhat supplicant student-patient of the teacher-healer. Surprisingly few were macho or overtly competitive transferences. Very likely, the decision to enter our program indicates either an absence of or a willingness to reduce the use of such a defensive stance. Nevertheless, denial and minimization were more common among men.

Group Phases. We can delineate a first phase of *anxious curiosity,* during which members are eager to learn new material and skills, perhaps hoping to acquire some magical cure. Mixed with this, however, is a degree of *resistance,* which increases through the third session and which frequently takes the form of minimization and denial, an apparent ignorance of cognitive and affective events and states, and noncompliance with homework assignments.

The dramatic impact of videotapes in the fourth and fifth sessions carries through to at least one more session. Clearly one effect of this period of intense, involuntary self-revelation is sharply increased group cohesiveness; therefore, we might label this an *integration* phase. In the remaining sessions, despite the focus on individual problems and individualized techniques, members are increasingly willing to offer feedback, advice, suggestions for alternative behavior, and so on, to each other. There is a *mutual-aid-society* atmosphere, which endures until the course ends. Interestingly, some members indicate in follow-up sessions that they would have preferred a more exploratory emphasis during this phase, perhaps even a couples therapy group, with content unrelated to TABP or CAD. Others, however, clearly did not want this.

Therapeutic Factors. Across all stages, the three elements that seem to us most powerfully therapeutic are the teaching of specific behavioral skills, the use of videotape feedback, and the active participation of spouses. As the first two of these have been discussed above, I shall focus here on spouses' involvement.

In all cases but one, the spouse was the wife of a CAD male. Because we increasingly emphasized spouse involvement, our last two groups have been largely couples groups. Interestingly, those who participated without spouses in these latter groups did relatively poorly in terms of compliance, attendance, and felt satisfaction. Of course, their failure to involve their own spouses may have indicated other problems that would rather predispose to a poor outcome than cause one, but in any case the failure to involve an existent spouse clearly bodes ill in our experience.

The presence of spouses added in several ways to the group experience: additional significant behavioral data (often minimized or denied by men) were provided; the impact of one's TABP on others could be assessed; alternative perceptions, behavior, and defensive and coping skills emerged; and so on. One possible cost of this format was the absence of camaraderie that all-male groups often manifest, but in our judgment the benefits of increased support far outweigh this loss.

Results

Participants, Attrition, and Compliance. Our participants, as we indicated, were solicited by mailed brochures. Because the same overall population (of Cardiac Rehabilitation Exercise Laboratory patients) was repeatedly approached in this way, there are no meaningful data on the percent response to be developed. Qualitatively, participants ranged from lower-middle to upper-middle class and varied quite widely in educational level, psychological mindedness, and CAD severity. About 10 percent of our participants had no known CAD but were accepted because of their high CAD risk on one or more factors, including self-reported stress. Nearly all CAD patients were male, primarily in their late forties to early sixties. Psychologically, they seemed as a group to resemble closely the CAD patients described in other group therapy reports. Virtually all members, including women, were rated Type A on both behavioral (SI) and self-report (Jenkins) measures of TABP. Attrition from the time of screening to the course ending was minimal (about 7 percent). Compliance with specific home assignments varied. Relaxation seemed to elicit very good compliance (perhaps 80 to 90 percent); diary keeping about 75 percent; hierarchy construction about 60 to 70 percent.

Treatment Outcome. We began keeping systematic self-report data in the last three courses (thirty-three group members altogether), behavioral data in the last two courses (twenty-three members), and physiological data in the last course (twelve members). Formal statistical analyses were being prepared as this chapter was written and will be presented in a later report. Here, however, we can offer preliminary results (subject to possible change). We assessed participants on three types of measures: behavioral, physiological, and self-report affective-cognitive. The behavioral indexes were interview-rated overall Type A behavior, and our behavioral outcome measures consisted of pre- to posttreatment changes in two overall TABP ratings (the global typing of subjects into one of five TABP categories, ranging from extreme A to extreme B, and a total TABP score) and five behavioral TABP components (response latency, hostility, competitiveness, loud-explosive speech, and rapid-accelerated speech).

The physiological indexes require brief explanation. Resting (static) measures of blood pressure and heart rate do not differentiate A's and B's. If, however, A and B subjects are stressed or provoked, blood pressure and heart rate will reactively and transiently rise. This stress-induced rise, or physiological reactivity as we call it, is typically greater among A's than B's on SBP,

244   Group Treatments for Specific Medical Problems

DBP, heart rate, and serum catecholamine levels, and perhaps other parameters (Razin, 1982) that have putative CAD-pathogenic significance. By monitoring heart rate, SBP, and DBP under stress, that is, during the SI, history quiz, and mental arithmetic quiz, both before and after treatment, we can assess the modifiability of this physiological hyperreactivity. Other TABP modification programs and studies have either not examined physiological concomitants of the TABP or have assessed only static levels of these dimensions. To our knowledge, our program is unique in this regard. Our physiological measures thus consisted of pre- to posttreatment changes in heart rate reactivity (change from baseline) during the SI, during the history quiz, and during the mental arithmetic quiz; SBP reactivity during the same three events, and DBP reactivity during those events.

Our self-report (affective-cognitive) measures covered not only TABP but also overall psychological well-being and symptomatology. Our outcome measures thus consisted of pre- to posttreatment changes in the Jenkins Activity Survey (JAS) ratings of overall TABP, speed impatience, job involvement, and hard-driving; Novaco Anger Scale ratings; Spielberger state and trait anxiety; Spielberger state and trait anger; Hopkins Symptom Checklist (HSCL-58) ratings of depression, anxiety, obsessive-compulsiveness, interpersonal sensitivity, and somatization; and Beck Depression Inventory ratings.

The psychometric and other characteristics of all these behavioral, physiological, and self-report measures will be discussed in detail in the forthcoming research report of this study. The results on all three (behavioral, physiological, and self-rating) parameters are summarized in Table 1.

Observations and Reflections

As can be seen in Table 1, results are generally quite favorable across all three classes of measurement. Furthermore, the fact that self-report changes seem most substantially and uniformly favorable is consistent with informal observations, for example, of unsolicited testimonials, requests for refresher courses, and so forth.

Table 1. Summary of Outcome Data on Cardiac Stress
Management Training Patients.

Measure	N	p-value
Behavioral Measures[a]		
(Global) TABP "Type" Rating	23	0.004
(Global) Sum of TABP Components	23	0.003
Response Latency Component	23	0.005
Hostility Component	23	0.05
Competitiveness Component	23	0.08
Loud-Explosive Speech Component	23	N.S.
Rapid-Accelerated Speech Component	23	N.S.
Physiological Measures[b]		
HR Reactivity During SI	12	N.S.
HR Reactivity During HQ	12	N.S.
HR Reactivity During MAQ	12	N.S.
SBP Reactivity During SI	12	N.S.
SBP Reactivity During HQ	12	0.05
SBP Reactivity During MAQ	12	0.07
DBP Reactivity During SI	12	N.S.
DBP Reactivity During HQ	12	N.S.
DBP Reactivity During MAQ	12	N.S.
Self-Report Measures[a]		
Jenkins (JAS) TABP	30	0.002
JAS Speed-Impatience	30	0.03
JAS Job Involvement	30	N.S.
JAS Hard-Driving	30	N.S.
Novaco Anger Rating	30	0.05
Spielberger State Anxiety	33	N.S.
Spielberger Trait Anxiety	33	N.S.
Spielberger State Anger	33	N.S.
Spielberger Trait Anger	33	N.S.
HSCL Depression	33	0.01
HSCL Anxiety	33	0.005
HSCL Obsessive-Compulsiveness Scale	33	0.01
HSCL Interpersonal Sensitivity Scale	33	0.01
HSCL Somatization Scale	33	0.006
Beck Depression Inventory	33	0.08

Notes: Outcome data are in the form of pre- to posttreatment changes. All
changes were in a favorable (less pathological) direction.

TABP = Type A behavioral pattern; HR = heart rate; SI = structured interview; HQ = history quiz; MAQ = mental arithmetic quiz; JAS = Jenkins Activity Survey.

[a]p-values derived from dependent t-tests.

[b]p-values derived from analyses of covariance, with baseline value of each
physiological measure being covaried.

A few cautions must be kept in mind, however, in viewing the data. First, the study was totally uncontrolled. Without a control or comparison group, there is little reason to dismiss Hawthorne or placebo effects (in obviously highly motivated subjects) as responsible for part, or even all, of these very short-term results, especially the self-report data. Furthermore, without follow-up assessment, we cannot make any claims concerning the durability of any of these changes. In addition, the behavioral ratings, though made with strict adherence to established criteria, were all done by one rater-interviewer who was, of therapeutic necessity, quite aware (during ratings) of which interviews were pretreatment and which were posttreatment. Finally, it is quite probable that habituation (that is, reduction over time in the magnitude of a provoked response simply by virtue of repeated exposure to the same provoking stimulus) played at least some role in the apparent reduction of physiological hyperreactivity. Habituation is a very common phenomenon in psychophysiological research, and we should expect that even with our use of alternate equivalent questions (in the posttreatment stress interview, history quiz, and mental arithmetic quiz), some degree of habituation would occur.

Even with these qualifications or difficulties, however, we view our data as quite positive and promising. Certainly, they are consistent with the overall positive trend of TABP modification studies. In subsequent data analyses, we shall examine the comparative treatment outcomes of A's versus B's, men versus women, and CAD versus non-CAD participants.

Clearly, at least some of the above difficulties result from our attempt to conduct both an ongoing clinical program and a research project in the same single endeavor. It is apparent that these two types of endeavor present conflicting priorities: the need for patient homogeneity for research purposes versus patient heterogeneity to maximize appeal to, and therapeutic involvement of, patients; the research need for uniformity of treatment offered versus the clinical need to modify and tailor interventions according to individual needs; the obvious research need for a control group versus the clinical need to offer real, effective treatment; and so on. In our view, though, despite these inevitable, thorny problems, such clinical research, with emphasis on improving both clinical and research aspects, is possible, warranted, and desirable.

From clinical and research standpoints, refinements in our program should include: the development of follow-up (booster) sessions (perhaps at three, six, and twelve months), which would serve both to reinforce changes and skills integrated earlier *and* to permit follow-up assessment of the durability of the outcome. Second, we could become even more individualized in targeting patient-specific TABP problem areas in the second half of the course; for example, "thought stopping" or other techniques could be utilized around speed-impatience. "Target problem" outcome assessment would thus have to be adopted. Third, it should be possible to assess comparison, if not control, groups; unstructured supportive group and individual therapy, as well as an individual CSMT, might be systematically compared with our group CSMT program. In addition, blind ratings might be made for pure research purposes in addition to the nonblind ratings needed for the clinical intervention; long-term (three-to-five-year) follow-up of participants' CAD-medical status clearly should be done once a suitable control or comparison group is in place (such a study could usefully replicate and elaborate on the large-scale project by Friedman and others, 1982).

Group therapy is a highly desirable modality of treatment for general post-MI psychosocial recovery. A didactic, supportive cognitive-behavioral approach may be particularly useful for modifying TABP in such patients. The tasks of conducting such a program and assessing its efficacy systematically are complex but gratifying to the therapist and generally very well received by patients. We therefore strongly encourage that such programs be adopted and refined.

References

Adsett, C. A., and Bruhn, J. G. "Short-Term Group Psychotherapy for Post-Myocardial Infarction Patients and Their Wives." *Canadian Medical Association Journal*, 1968, *99*, 577-584.

Bilodeau, C. B., and Hackett, T. P. "Issues Raised in a Group Setting by Patients Recovering from Myocardial Infarction." *American Journal of Psychiatry,* 1971, *128,* 73-78.

Blackburn, H. "Progress in the Epidemiology and Prevention of Coronary Heart Disease." In P. N. Yu and J. F. Goodwin (Eds.), *Progress in Cardiology.* Philadelphia: Lea & Febiger, 1974.

Bruhn, J. G., Wolf, S., and Philips, B. U. "A Psycho-Social Study of Surviving Male Coronary Patients and Controls Followed over Nine Years." *Journal of Psychosomatic Research,* 1971, *15,* 305-313.

Croog, S. M., Levine, S., and Lurie, Z. "The Heart Patient and the Recovery Process: A Review of the Literature on Social and Psychological Factors." *Social Science and Medicine,* 1968, *2,* 111-164.

Doehrman, S. R. "Psycho-Social Aspects of Recovery from Coronary Heart Disease: A Review." *Social Science and Medicine,* 1977, *11,* 199-218.

Ellis, A. *Humanistic Psychotherapy.* New York: Julian Press, 1973.

Frank, K. A., Heller, S. S., and Kornfeld, D. S. "Psychological Intervention in Coronary Heart Disease." *General Hospital Psychiatry,* 1979, *1,* 18-23.

Friedman, M., and others. "Feasibility of Altering Type A Behavior Pattern After Myocardial Infarction." *Circulation,* 1982, *66,* 83-92.

Glass, D. "Stress, Behavior Patterns, and Coronary Disease." *American Scientist,* 1977, *65,* 177-187.

Gruen, W. "Effects of Brief Psychotherapy During the Hospitalization Period or the Recovery Process in Heart Attacks." *Journal of Consulting and Clinical Psychology,* 1975, *43,* 223-232.

Hackett, T. P. "The Use of Groups in the Rehabilitation of the Postcoronary Patient." *Advances in Cardiology,* 1978, *24,* 127-135.

Hurst, J. W., Logue, R. B., and Walter, P. F. "The Clinical Recognition and Management of Coronary Atherosclerotic Heart Disease." In J. W. Hurst and others (Eds.), *The Heart.* (4th ed.) New York: McGraw-Hill, 1978.

Hurst, J. W., and others. *The Heart*. (4th ed.) New York: McGraw-Hill, 1978.

Ibrahim, M. A., and others. "Management After Myocardial Infarction: A Controlled Trial of the Effect of Group Psychotherapy." *International Journal of Psychiatry in Medicine*, 1974, *5*, 253-268.

Jenkins, C. D. "Psychologic and Social Precursors of Coronary Disease." *New England Journal of Medicine*, 1971, *284*, 244-255, 307-317.

Jenkins, C. D. "Recent Evidence Supporting Psychologic and Social Risk Factors for Coronary Disease." *New England Journal of Medicine*, 1976, *294*, 987-997, 1033-1038.

Jenni, M. A., and Wollersheim, J. P. "Cognitive Therapy, Stress Management Training and Type A Behavior Pattern." *Cognitive Therapy and Research*, 1979, *3*, 61-73.

Meichenbaum, D. *Cognitive-Behavior Modification: An Integrative Approach*. New York: Plenum, 1977.

Minc, S. "Psychological Factors in Coronary Heart Disease." *Geriatrics*, 1965, *20*, 747-755.

Mone, L. C. "Short-Term Psychotherapy with Postcardiac Patients." *International Journal of Group Psychotherapy*, 1970, *20*, 99-108.

Novaco, R. W. *Anger Control: The Development and Evaluation of an Experimental Treatment*. Lexington, Mass.: Lexington Books, 1975.

Rahe, R. M., Ward, H. W., and Hayes, V. "Brief Group Therapy in Myocardial Infarction Rehabilitation: Three to Four Year Follow-up of a Controlled Trial." *Psychosomatic Medicine*, 1979, *41*, 229-242.

Rahe, R. H., and others. "Group Therapy in the Out-Patient Management of Post-Myocardial Infarction Patients." *Psychiatry in Medicine*, 1973, *4*, 77-88.

Rahe, R. H., and others. "Brief Group Therapy Following Myocardial Infarction: Eighteen Months Follow-Up of a Controlled Trial." *International Journal of Psychiatry in Medicine*, 1975, *6*, 349-358.

Razin, A. M. "Psychosocial Intervention in Coronary Artery Disease: A Review." *Psychosomatic Medicine*, 1982, *44*, 363-387.

Razin, A. M. "Type A Behavior: Can It Be Modified?" In L. Zohman and R. Kohn (Eds.), *Progress in Cardiac Rehabilitation*. New York: Thieme-Stratton, forthcoming.

Roskies, E. "Considerations in Developing a Treatment Program for the Coronary-Prone (Type A) Behavior Pattern." In P. Davidson (Ed.), *Behavioral Medicine: Changing Health Life Style*. New York: Brunner/Mazel, 1979.

Roskies, E., and others. "Changing the Coronary-Prone (Type A) Behavior Pattern in a Non-Clinical Population." *Journal of Behavioral Medicine*, 1978, *1*, 201-216.

Roskies, E., and others. "Generalizability and Durability of Treatment Effects in an Intervention Program for Coronary-Prone (Type A) Managers." *Journal of Behavioral Medicine*, 1979, *2*, 195-207.

Russek, H. I., and Russek, L. G. "Is Emotional Stress an Etiologic Factor in Coronary Heart Disease?" *Psychosomatic Medicine*, 1976, *17*, 63-67.

Soloff, P. M. "Medically and Surgically Treated Coronary Patients in Cardiovascular Rehabilitation: A Comparative Study." *International Journal of Psychiatry in Medicine*, 1979, *9*, 93-106.

Suinn, R. M. "Behavior Therapy for Cardiac Patients." *Behavior Therapy*, 1974, *5*, 569-571.

Suinn, R. M. "Intervention with Type A Behaviors." *Journal of Consulting and Clinical Psychology*, 1982, *50*, 933-949.

Weiner, H. J., Akabas, S. H., and Sommer, J. J. *Mental Health Care in the World of Work*. New York: Association Press, 1973.

Yalom, I. *The Theory and Practice of Group Psychotherapy*. New York: Basic Books, 1970.

Mary A. Jerse, M.D.
Helen H. Whitman, R.N.
James P. Gustafson, M.D.

10

Cancer
in Adults

Cancer is a disease long characterized by misleading myth and painful reality. The diagnosis brings out fears unmatched by those elicited by other catastrophic illnesses. Clearly, the effects of this disease are profoundly felt by patients, families, and care givers alike. It is apparent that there is a need for a forum where the many feelings aroused by cancer can be faced. This chapter demonstrates that supportive group therapy meetings are an important means toward that end.

The myths that surround cancer create a horrific atmosphere. The diagnosis of cancer is often heard as a death knell. Many feel that no one can survive it or its ravages. In addition, many believe cancer to be contagious, which fuels fears of rejection, abandonment, and isolation as well as feelings of contamination. Another myth is that suffering and pain are inevitable. Indeed, many fear the process of dying more than death itself. Further, the belief that cancer spreads like wildfire leads to feelings of helplessness and impotence in the face of an overwhelming force.

Truly, the realities of cancer are difficult. Its course is

often lengthy and undulant, with cycles of remission and recurrence, hope and despair. The need to face death is dictated by
both personal and pragmatic needs concerning employment, the
ability to participate in leisure activities, and one's role in the
family and the community. All of the above affect self-concept
and self-expectations. Change is inevitable and significant, with
the needs of the individuals involved often varied and conflicting.

In this chapter, we first explore some of the literature on
cancer patients and groups for cancer patients. Rationales for
group approaches with this population are explained. Next
there is an in-depth analysis of the ongoing cancer patients'
group at the University of Wisconsin. This experience has led to
a number of new theories and possibilities for this type of group
therapy. These include specific technical interventions at the individual, family, group, and oncology ward levels of the project.

The Phenomenology of Cancer Patients

A number of authors have studied cancer patients in an
effort to understand their experience more clearly. Some have
attempted to describe developmental stages. This approach is
useful in helping to understand the flood of emotions and reactions that cancer patients and their families experience. Making
some sense of it all is a necessary step toward finding better
ways to help. Identifying stages, however, can also be a way of
defending against the pain and chaos that cancer patients must
often endure. The course of this illness is marked by dramatic
swings of emotion. When presented with uncomfortable affects,
health professionals may try to ward them off in the manner
they know best. A clear intellectualizing style places the problem at a rational arm's length, as does categorizing people's
reactions to their cancer. It is easier to remove oneself from a patient's powerful anger if it can be rationalized as "a stage he's
going through."

Several authors take pains to point out that the categories may overlap or be missing entirely. With this caution in
mind, the phenomenology and dynamics of these patients are
described within the framework of developmental stages de-

scribed by Kubler-Ross (1969), Abrams (1966), and Cassem (1976).

Kubler-Ross (1969), in her classic study, explores the thoughts, feelings, and reactions of terminally ill patients gleaned from interviews of some two hundred persons. The belief that the dying are our best teachers on that subject, although seemingly obvious, is something Kubler-Ross emphasizes repeatedly. She has formulated five basic stages through which patients usually pass when dying. The first stage is *denial,* characterized by total disbelief and numbness. The second stage is *anger,* which may abate, but which often returns in differing forms as death becomes imminent. *Bargaining* is the third stage, followed by *depression,* when a patient carefully drops defenses and faces directly the sadness and pain of impending death. Finally, there is *acceptance,* which occurs toward the end of life when a patient is actually ready for death.

Abrams (1966) explores varying modes or patterns of communication that cancer patients use at different points in their illness. She draws her data from observations of a large number of cancer patients who came through an outpatient oncology clinic. She makes the point that we can gain much insight into a patient's state of mind and personal experience by closely observing his or her verbal and nonverbal cues.

Abrams notes three prominent styles of communication that a patient exhibits during the course of a terminal illness. The first of these is correlated with the *initial stage,* in which the diagnosis is ascertained and the goal is to eradicate or control the cancer. This time is marked by hopefulness, relatively low anxiety, and a desire for truthful communication. The *advancing stage* is the time after relapse and is considered to be the most difficult. Fear of abandonment, particularly by the primary physician, becomes an overriding concern. The offer of comfort and assurances of continued involvement and care are essential to patients in this stage. In the *terminal stage,* the disease has gotten out of control and only palliative measures can be offered. Patients respond to this stage in a myriad of ways. Some withdraw; some become increasingly dependent; some become rejecting. Care givers can best help by trying to interpret the patient's messages and by providing an environment that offers the most comfort and warmth.

Cassem (1976) also addresses the phenomenology and needs of cancer patients. He reviews a number of studies on the problems of the terminally ill. He recommends *truth telling* as a most appropriate and desirable beginning. For both the family and the patient who must bear the burden of treatment (successful or not), it is essential to start off honestly with accurate information and as true a picture of the situation as possible.

From his observations, Cassem has described eight features of care that he considers to be essential. These include competence in the care-giving personnel, concern and compassion, attention to physical comfort, adequate communication, the presence of children, family cohesion and integration, cheerfulness, and perseverence to the end.

Many other workers in the field of death and dying have various emphases and employ different methods (Cassell, 1982; Cohen, 1976; Leiber and others, 1976; Parkes, 1975; Surawicz and others, 1976). The above three authors provide a broad base of knowledge concerning the phenomenology of dying patients.

Psychiatric Symptomatology in Cancer Patients

When we consider the difficult experiences of cancer patients, we want to keep our attention to the problem of how to help them best. To this end, it is important to clarify which kinds of coping are functional and which are dysfunctional, not only for the patient but also for the family. This surely has ramifications on how care givers in general and therapists in particular should use their skills to facilitate the patient's comfort, psychological as well as physical. Several groups have addressed this issue by describing the correlation between cancer patients' psychiatric symptomatology and its effect on survival time.

In one study, Derogatis (Derogatis, Abeloff, and McBeth, 1976) addresses the issue of how accurately physicians perceive psychological distress in their cancer patients. Testing twenty-three patients and their staff physicians, he noted that physicians and patients varied significantly in their assessments of specific areas of distress when physicians rated the overall stress level as high. In fact, physicians rated anxiety and interpersonal stress as significantly greater than these fears were rated by patients themselves. On the other hand, physicians rated the presence of depression as significantly less prevalent than did patients. These data can be mitigated by various considerations, such as patient hesitancy to report anxiety or the patient being more aware of depression than able to express it. Nevertheless, this study calls into question our ability as observers to draw meaningful conclusions about cancer patients' psychiatric distress.

In another interesting study, Derogatis (Derogatis, Abeloff, and Melisaratos, 1979) analyzed data from baseline psychological tests given to thirty-five women with metastatic breast carcinoma, with respect to the patients' subsequent survival time. There were no significant differences between short-term (less than one year) and long-term (greater than one year) survivors regarding several demographic characteristics and medical factors considered to influence survival time. There were differences in psychological distress, however. Specifically, long-term survivors showed significantly higher levels of anxiety, psychosis, hostility, and general severity of psychiatric symptoms. In addition, oncologists rated these long-term survivors as significantly less well adjusted to their disease than the short-term survivors.

It is important to remember that the data from the above two studies are correlational and not conclusive. Generally, though, they lead to the hypothesis that there is a relationship between the long-term survival of cancer patients and their ability to express negative affects.

Greer and associates (Greer, Morris, and Pettingale, 1979) prospectively studied sixty-nine women with metastatic breast carcinoma who all had the same Manchester staging (extensiveness of tumor spread) at diagnosis. Psychological assessments were done at diagnosis and after three months, twelve months, and five years. They found that there was a statistical difference in five-year survival that related to the patient's psychological attitude toward the disease at three months. Those patients who fell into the categories of *denial* or *fighting spirit* had a significantly better outcome than those who were in the categories of *stoic acceptance* or *helplessness/hopelessness*. Again, this is correlational data, but one speculation is that psychological attitude affects outcome.

It is difficult to say how these categories of distress match or overlap those traits described by Derogatis. There is an apparent contradiction between the two groups of long-term survivors. Derogatis's group expressed negative affect openly, while Greer's group was strong in denial and fighting spirit. Perhaps the fighting-spirit aspect is the common denominator here. In any case, further studies are necessary to clarify the effect of psychological distress and coping styles on disease process and outcome.

Rationales for Group Therapy

A number of workers use group therapy as a therapeutic modality for helping cancer patients. A review of the major contributions in this area is included here.

Yalom and associates describe their experience with an ongoing support group for patients with metastatic breast carcinoma (Spiegel and Yalom, 1978; Yalom and Greaves, 1977). They emphasize what they consider to be curative mechanisms for change (Yalom, 1970). Within this group, they observed *altruism,* or the ability to help the other members, as a beneficial force. It seemed to reduce the tendency for "self-absorption" and to provide feelings of "fulfillment." The group provided a forum for *catharsis.* Painful feelings patients experienced but kept from everyone else were shared in the group. *Group cohesiveness* was noted to be an important factor in dealing with feelings of abandonment or isolation. Members felt an identity among themselves that could not have been shared by other care givers or family members. The *universality* of experiences shared and feelings expressed also provided relief. Finally, they found that *existential factors* surrounding death and dying of cancer gave group members a common territory to explore.

In their most recent paper, Spiegel, Bloom, and Yalom (1981) reported results from randomized prospective research of a cancer group. Theirs is one of the first systematic studies of what support groups actually provide for the cancer patient. Women with metastatic breast carcinoma were accepted into the study and then randomized into a treatment group or a control group. The randomization is very important here, since most of the cancer groups described in the literature and the observations based on them are colored by self-selection. Baseline psychological testing was done at the outset and at four-month intervals for the year during which the group met. Statistically significant differences were found between control and treatment groups but did not show until the one-year mark. Treatment-group members showed significant improvements with respect to Tension-Anxiety, Vigor, Fatigue, and Confusion. Insignificant improvement was seen on the Depression scales. No change was seen in ratings for Anger, Denial, Self-Esteem, or Sense of Control. The treatment group also showed decreases in feelings of fearfulness and responses considered to be maladaptive. These results support the argument that members of ongoing cancer support groups make meaningful changes. An important question not addressed by this study is whether these changes persist after patients leave treatment.

Vachon and associates (Vachon and Lyall, 1976; Vachon and others, 1979) have also published data about the use of group therapy with cancer patients and their families. These researchers are involved in a longitudinal study of groups for cancer patients. The groups under study consist of patients who stayed in a residential lodge affiliated with a nearby hospital where cancer treatment was received. These groups focused particularly on coping skills and information gathering. They did address feeling states and issues of death and dying as members initiated these topics but did not focus on them. The group participants are compared with a control group of matched outpatients. Psychological parameters were evaluated at baseline and at six, twelve, and twenty-four months after diagnosis. Vachon found significant lowering of the psychological distress level and improvement in the level of satisfaction among group participants but found that these improvements did not persist once a patient left the group.

Wellisch and associates (Wellisch, Mosher, and Van Scoy, 1978) describe their experience with groups that combine both family members and cancer patients. They note that their initial fear that patients could not tolerate such groups was unfounded. For the first seven months, only family members participated. However, when patients were finally asked to join, attendance, openness, and felt support were all markedly increased. Their observations of families affected by cancer support the idea that the structure and interpersonal dynamics within a family change when this diagnosis is given to a member. In addition, old dysfunctional patterns are often exacerbated. The group provides a forum in which to express the powerful feelings that arise and to work through problematic interactions.

The above studies and reports present convincing evidence that the use of groups as a therapeutic modality for cancer patients and their families promotes functional adjustment and mitigates psychological distress. Theories about the impact of group meetings on cancer survival rates of cancer patients and on overall dynamic changes within individuals or family members warrant further testing.

There are additional rationales for using group approaches. Cancer is indeed a group illness. Teams of health care providers are involved in dealing with it, including oncologists, nurses, social workers, researchers, consultants, and other paraprofessionals. The illness is treated intermittently in tertiary care centers. Patients leave the familiarity of their primary physician to be cared for by many changing personnel. Also, the ramifications of cancer are felt by the patient's entire social support system. Family, friends, neighbors, and work colleagues must react, adjust, and readjust. The psychosocial structure surrounding a cancer patient is rearranged constantly throughout the course of the illness. For the patient the feeling of isolation caused by being the victim within this network is only intensified as the subtle and not so subtle shifting goes on around him or her. An approach to this situation in which as many members of the system as possible are involved and affected makes very good sense.

Cancer is a stressful illness for all involved. Observations to date indicate that the stresses and shock of cancer and an individual's responses to them are often similar to those described in posttraumatic stress syndrome. Criteria of this syndrome (American Psychiatric Association, 1980) are met by cancer patients at various points in the course of the disease. One of the most helpful modalities of treatment for this syndrome is group therapy. Specifically, it addresses the phenomenon of "no one really knows what it's like." Groups gather together people who are experiencing the same catastrophic situation in an effort to find some mutually helpful solutions and relief.

The group, via both its members and its leaders, provides care givers generalized (and at times specific) feedback that might otherwise not take place. It provides a vehicle to enhance staff awareness of and sensitivity to the difficult issues faced by patients with cancer. Again, listening to patients is the best way to learn about them, and group meetings provide a cohesive, centralized forum within which to gather the data needed to facilitate this process.

In addition, few cancer patients ever present to psychotherapy clinics, and a group setting offers a means to screen this at-risk patient population for those who might benefit from further intervention. Particularly troubled individuals or families often display their distress within the group setting. Here, patients and family members are observed by psychiatrically minded leaders who view psychosocial stress against the background of physical illness. This provides the most efficient way to identify those who might benefit from further psychological help.

The University of Wisconsin Group

The Structure. The cancer patients' group at the University of Wisconsin Hospitals and Clinics has an eight-year history and has been described elsewhere in the literature (Gustafson and Whitman, 1978; Gustafson and others, 1978; Ringler and others, 1981; Whitman, Gustafson, and Coleman, 1979). A brief description is appropriate here. The group is conducted on one of the inpatient oncology wards at the hospital. The head nurse, who has been involved since the group's inception, and a psychiatry resident or psychology fellow function as coleaders. The trainee's stay lasts from eight months to a year. A staff psychiatrist, who has also been involved with the group from the start, provides weekly supervision and consultation to the coleaders. All inpatients present at a given time are invited to join the group meeting, which occurs weekly. In addition, any family members or friends who are available and interested are invited to participate. Attendance is variable, ranging from four to more than twenty participants. Patients vary widely in age, background, and type and stage of their cancer. It is not unusual to have patients who are at the very end of their disease course together with newly diagnosed patients, as well as patients at all stages in between. Although the group does not have a constant membership, it is not uncommon for persons who frequently return to the hospital to attend fairly regularly and become veteran members. The focus of the group is on feelings rather than information gathering about the disease and its treatment.

The Development. The stages of development through which the group has gone are well noted in a previous paper (Ringler and others, 1981). We shall briefly review this history here. At the start, when considering whether to form such a group, staff fears about patients' emotional fragility and willingness to address painful material were prominent. With time and group experience, these fears decreased. Patients and families came to the group regularly. However, at first, members tended to avoid affect-laden material and to concentrate on information gathering or to spend time relating individual "war stories" about the diagnosis and treatment of their cancers.

After this first phase, leaders and staff members were quite frustrated. While the anticipated flood of raw emotion had not materialized, neither did there appear to be progress in getting around the defense mechanisms blocking the expression of affect. However, members eventually began to express their fears and suffering more frankly, and gradually the quality of the group experience changed considerably. What had happened?

One of the first elements of the change we examined was what effect group leaders had on the transient nature of group membership. Several things are noteworthy. It must be remembered that group leaders (as well as group members) have difficulties with resistance and countertransference. As these problems became less frightening, more technical advances were made. More technical skill also made the fears more bearable. The belief that group members were too vulnerable to face painful material was found to be a projection by group leaders. This could be seen in the way that invitations to the group were made and the tone of the opening remarks at the meeting. In the beginning, the group was described as a casual get-together with a light-hearted ambience. The group was begun with the suggestion that group members ask fact-finding questions. Leaders gradually changed the introduction to indicate that the focus was to work on the difficult feelings that go with having cancer.

Another major change was in the way leaders viewed and conducted their role in the group process. It became clear that because the membership of the group changed each week, some interventions were necessary to help facilitate the work. If members are to join together and learn from each other about painful and well-defended feelings, an atmosphere of safety is needed. This can be accomplished through leader interventions that let people know that their feelings and experiences are valued and worth expressing. Inviting silent members to participate is often helpful. Reflective and encouraging comments, which can serve to keep a member going when he or she might otherwise stop talking, are welcome. It is also important to protect members from injuring one another; supporting and balancing opposing viewpoints allows different members to express fully the wide range of feelings they experience.

Leaders also improved their ability to let difficult affects unfold to their fullest without intervention as they realized that group members could handle painful subjects and recover on their own. Leaders did not have to rush to their aid. Finally, leaders came to recognize that group members' projections onto group leaders had to be dealt with. Members had to be certain that the leaders could take whatever they had to give out. This was important because one of the group leaders was the head nurse of the unit and the other group leader was often a physician. If the patients feared retaliation, clearly the work of the group would be stunted.

The Working Hypotheses. With this developmental history in mind, the working hypotheses of this group need to be stated. The supportive nature of the group provides a safe place to deal with emotional issues in an understanding, receptive environment. Many patients and family members have no opportunity for expressing and working through the flood of feelings, changing family dynamics, and painful experiences that having cancer induces, and they often find that their existing support network cannot handle the situation. Parents, spouses, and children are caught in webs of miscommunication, trying to help but unable to do so successfully. Physicians are concerned with medical management and often are unavailable, since procedures and treatments that they must administer are urgent and take precedence. The group offers a place to gather and discuss mutual problems and feelings with persons in a similar situation.

The group also allows patients and their families to learn more about the complex emotional issues they face. When people lack the opportunity to verbalize their feelings, it is difficult to know what is bothering them. Exploring interpersonal interactions that help or hinder various parties in getting their needs met is an important function of the group, because it increases the ability of group members to help themselves and each other.

The safety of a particular group session for a particular group member is affected by who actually attends. At times a patient is present with his or her family, at times no family is present, and at times the family is present without the patient. The first combination makes self-disclosure the riskiest for both the patient and the family. We have observed a family crossover phenomenon, which occurs when a patient interacts with another patient's family. This can be a time for both parties to explore loaded issues directly without fearing adverse reactions from their own family members. For example, a patient can more openly express grief and pain and then explore the reactions of another patient's family to such a self-disclosure. Likewise, a family may deal with feelings of deprivation, anger, and guilt while monitoring and learning from the reactions of an unrelated patient. This membership combination offers a good opportunity to explore important feelings that have been kept below the surface within a family. Such communication encourages members to pursue issues within their own families both inside and outside the group.

The group also has the important function of opening lines of communication between members and primary care givers. The group takes place in an oncology ward, and its members are directly affected by the ward personnel. Any feedback to staff makes immediate improvements in care possible. It also has indirect value for future interactions with other cancer patients and families. Increasingly, the group leaders have noticed members who need further individual or family therapy and have referred them to appropriate sources.

This ongoing experience continues to play an important role in research for the group leaders. Within this context, leaders hope to increase their knowledge about the dynamics of cancer patients and their families in an effort to help them more effectively.

Finally, and most importantly, the existence of this group counteracts the process of selective inattention (looking the other way) described by Sullivan ([1956], 1973). This process is prominent in the medical profession, especially in oncology, and in all human interaction that is loaded with great existential and moral conflicts. A particularly vivid example of selective inattention is documented by Bourne (1968) in his study of physicians' reactions to stillbirth. He compared one hundred cases of stillbirth with one hundred cases of live births and found a significant tendency among doctors not to "know, notice, or remember anything about the patient who has had a stillbirth" (p. 103). Bourne suspects this unexpectedly large "professional blindspot" (p. 111) arises out of painful and overwhelming feelings in the physician. The consequence is that the doctor "cannot now be fully alive to his patient's needs and that his relationship with her has suffered" (p. 109).

Selective inattention also obscures the ethical and pragmatic problems specific to the field of oncology, which are immense. Pain management, protocol choices, the termination of extraordinary medical measures, and consideration of the ravages of ordinary treatments are only a few of the moral issues faced by patients, families, and physicians. These, as well as the internal chaos felt by patients and families, create quite a large burden. It is superficially relieving not to look too closely, but for the patient, the family, and the doctor, this means concealed pain and uninformed, suboptimal interactions and decision making.

New Theories and Techniques

Recently some new theories and techniques have evolved from our group experience. These ideas reflect the earlier hypotheses already discussed. They extend from there, though, and add new dimensions to our ideas about group therapy with cancer patients. Several tasks, of increasing difficulty and requiring increasing technical skill, have become evident.

Beginning. The first task of each group session is to begin. This involves several discrete events. First, the leaders must give an invitation to attend. In the University of Wisconsin group, the nursing staff invites each patient and family a day or two before the meeting. As noted above, the stated purpose of the group is to discuss the feelings that go along with having cancer. Then the patients and family must decide whether to attend. Thus, the group membership is self-selected at this point. Undoubtedly, complex internal and external conditions affect this decision; these have not been well studied, and such a study would surely provide interesting data. The group itself begins with the introduction by the head nurse. We have found that how this is done can set the tenor for the entire session. Here the emphasis is on exploring feelings and finding new coping methods.

Recognizing Snags. The second task, somewhat more difficult and requiring greater technical ability on the part of group leaders, is to recognize the inevitable snags or blocks that arise once the group is under way. We have noticed several recurrently.

1. One problem is that the first person to speak may determine the atmosphere and substance of the discussion.
   Though not inherently bad, this can prevent other members
   from speaking. With many people present and many different preoccupations, diverse questions must be aired. Sometimes the initial theme is pertinent to many participants,
   but at other times it can either sidetrack the group from
   considering more important subjects or be completely irrelevant to other members' concerns. This is an important
   problem to recognize and address.
2. Another problem occurs when different subgroups have different viewpoints that bring the subgroups into conflict.
   This can happen when strongly stated opinions are opposed
   by other strongly stated opinions, and members are at a
   loss to move on from there. It can also happen when a subgroup states a point of view that is unopposed openly but
   is nevertheless unshared by a silent subgroup. This situation
   leaves the silent group without empathy from the other
   members and concerned about the acceptability of their
   feelings to the others. Group members are not always
   equipped to handle such differences productively. When
   they are not, it is the responsibility of the group leaders to
   appreciate the problem and to intervene.
3. The problem of the monopolist or "war story" teller is not
   uncommon. A group member may decide to tell his or her
   particular story in the finest detail. Although relating experiences has its place, the monopolist goes far beyond this.
   Other members listen attentively at the start, then begin to
   shift uneasily as time goes on. Many agendas are left un-
   completed when this behavior is allowed to continue. This
   can happen at any time during a session and starts for different reasons. Leaders and members alike may feel reluctant to intervene, fearing the monopolist would be offended, but intervention is mandatory if the group is to
   progress.
4. Occasionally there is the problem of the group in which
   nothing happens. This is not correlated to group size. After
   the introductory remarks, most groups get going, but members of an inert group never engage on any level of their

own accord. There is a clear need to expedite group involvement when the groups cannot do this for themselves.
5. Finally, there is the problem of several factions suddenly
breaking off and beginning separate dialogues, usually of a
noncontributory nature. Our group has seen three members
suddenly talking about the weather, two members about
the farming season, and yet another subgroup about insurance plans. This happens most frequently in mid-session,
when emotions are running high about a particularly difficult issue. Members use it to divert themselves and to get
some space from their own pain. Sessions often take an up-
and-down course, alternating between painful material and
light-hearted anecdotes. This becomes problematic only if
it derails the group from its work. Members can return
themselves to the work and often do, but this does not invariably happen; leaders may need to remind group members where they got off the track.

Recognizing the snags noted above is particularly important for our type of group, since there is no second chance for
many patients and only one hour to complete their business.
Leaders are responsible for helping group members create the
optimal group environment for the hour they have together so
that they can maximize the benefit of their shared work. It is
imperative, therefore, that leaders be able to recognize stum-
bling blocks along the way and to intercede appropriately and
in a timely fashion.

Intervening Effectively. The third task, after recognizing
these snags, is to deal with them effectively. This task is closely
related to the second but requires more sophisticated skill on
the part of leaders. The leaders may know where the group got
waylaid, but not know how to help them become reinvolved.
Our experience has shown the following strategies to be especially helpful.

One clear requirement for the leaders is readiness for activity. This may involve inviting silent members to talk. This
move was once feared as overly intrusive and controlling, but
we have found that silent members are often brimming with

material that they wish to express and work on. They are thankful for the invitation to participate, and groups have been invigorated by what they have to offer. The structure of our group does not allow for lengthy character analyses of individual defense styles. In this type of setting, it is both appropriate and efficient to invite timid members into the discussion. The risk is negligible, and truly reticent members are free to decline the invitation (and often do).

The other side of this technique is the intervention required to silence an overly raucous member. This can involve a clearly obnoxious person, a monopolist, or a particularly loud subgroup. Group members do not consider it rude when they are gently redirected. Monopolists can be quieted quite easily with a simple comment such as "I think we're getting a bit off the track from feelings." Inert groups can also be moved along by the active intervention of a leader, as previously described. Many lethargic sessions have gotten off the ground after the comment "There are lots of hard feelings that go along with having cancer." Groups splintered by subgrouping can be handled in the same way. A reflection on what has happened often returns members to the original topic with renewed enthusiasm. None of these interventions need be elaborate, and ordinarily interventions are best when they are as infrequent and concise as possible.

Although group leaders need to be ready with interventions to keep the group on course, it is important that they not be overly active and directive. If the group members do something themselves, any resulting insight is more valid and credible. For example, a good group can quickly handle an opening statement that is not in keeping with the underlying emotional tone of the group with an appropriate counter. This often happens in a strong collaborative group that can keep to the task at hand with little intervention by group leaders. Such groups can skillfully right things when they find themselves listing too far to one side.

A technique found to be important with our group is that of balancing, as described by Gustafson and associates (Gustafson and others, 1981a, 1981b). When two sides of an issue emerge, the group leader acknowledges the value of both sides and suggests that they are not mutually exclusive and that it is worthwhile to express both points of view. This technique, requiring greater control on the part of leaders, applies particularly well to the problem of warring subgroups. Balancing provides a safe environment for group participants and allows deadlocked groups to explore the valuable aspects of each person's or subgroup's ideas. The constant optimist is directed to the obvious pain of the depressed, terminally ill patient and given the opportunity to share some of his own pain, which may have similar roots. The despondent patient can be comforted by the acceptance of his or her misery by those who previously had not allowed it. All members benefit once the need to ascertain right and wrong has been allayed and adversarial roles have been dropped. This technique is helpful whenever conflicting messages arise during a group meeting.

Finally, there is the introduction of the warded-off feeling as described by Skynner (1979, 1981, 1982). When the leaders notice intense feeling building up in themselves that is excluded from the discussion of the entire group, they must carefully consider whether this feeling belongs to the group but is unacknowledged. If they conclude that it is, they must carefully consider how to introduce this volatile material while showing the group how to defuse the dangerous emotion. This is a considerably more difficult maneuver, requiring a high level of technical proficiency on the part of group leaders.

At times, balancing may not keep members and leaders from missing the strongest feeling seeking expression. For example, during one group meeting, certain members were strongly stating that no one except immediate family members should be informed about their illness. They argued that when other people knew the cancer diagnosis, those people exhibited fear, loathing, and outright prejudice toward the patient. Others in the group strongly countered that idea, claiming that they had gotten nothing but support, warmth, and empathic responses from friends, neighbors, and colleagues. The group leaders attempted to balance the situation, and only several days after the session did leaders become aware of one individual's response to that process. This patient told a staff nurse, "I don't understand what good it does to constantly look at the other side of the coin. If there are bad feelings about one thing or another, they need to come out." It became clear that our balancing had actually thwarted the efforts of either subgroup to express their fears and feelings fully on the subjects of rejection and isolation. In other words, balancing can be motivated by the intellectual argument that everyone has a right to an opinion or feeling, but it can miss the core issue, the feeling.

To introduce warded-off feelings, the group leader must first recognize such feelings in himself. The leader then expresses this self-owned feeling in a matter-of-fact manner to the group and suggests that the group can deal with it. If anger over rejection is prevalent, as above, the group leader might suggest, "I am feeling anger right now, and yet I am not one of those being rejected. Perhaps this anger belongs to some of you. Perhaps it can be alarming how anger is passed from one person to another." The leader thus acknowledges the group's tension and offers an opening to discuss it. This technique offers important advantages in facilitating the work of the cancer support group. Patients seek in varying degrees the full exposition of some of the more difficult feelings that go with cancer, and this technique encourages that exposition.

In the previous example, the angry subgroup might well say they are angry at being force-fed the pain from the other subgroup. In any event, this technique offers the advantage of opening up the fight instead of squelching it. Disadvantages might include the feeling of group members that the leader's self-owned feelings are invalid. After all, leaders are not cancer victims. Another risk is that this technique forces issues that individuals or the group as a whole would rather not address. After all, therapists' zeal to "get at the pain" is not desirable in all cases. There are those patients and family members whose suffering and pain are well defended for good reason.

Timing and "dosage" in using any of these techniques are crucial. Striking the most effective balance between activity and inactivity requires experience and skill with groups in general and with cancer patients in particular. Staying with members in a fast-flowing, high-pitched group session is a challenge. Only by carefully following the group and appropriately intervening can leaders help patients maximize their group experience.

Transcript of an Autopilot Group

We have described how difficult supportive groups may be and how much technical skill is needed from the leaders. We would like to remind the reader of another truth: These patients and family members can be very capable on their own, with very little help from the leaders. We call such groups "autopilot" groups, since they seem able to pilot themselves through serious differences to reach great emotional depths. The first five minutes of the group meeting is critical. Either the members can take care of themselves, or they need direction to steer them on a safe but deepening course. The outcome of the hour seems to be determined in these unconscious negotiations of the first five minutes. However, this clinical impression has not yet been confirmed by a formal study. The following transcript (minimally edited for clarity) shows a group that moves very rapidly, deeply, and securely on its own, with a minimum of help from the leaders:

Head Nurse: For those of you who are new to these meetings, I would like to explain that the purpose of the group is for people with cancer and those who care about them to come together to get some new ideas and share some mutual concerns and worries. By sharing you will realize that you are not alone in your situation. You will also learn some new ways of coping with cancer. We will end at five o'clock and start with introductions: I am Mrs. W., the head nurse here. [Everyone introduces him or herself, going around the circle.] So, the meeting is open to discuss whatever is on your minds. [Pause.] And, there is a lot on everybody's mind, right? Everybody here is concerned in one way or another.

Wife, Family 1: My husband has cancer of the lung. We were discussing Mrs. A., a friend who has cancer. Her family told us she has cancer of the liver and they can't do much more for her.

My daughter wanted to tell my husband about her, you know, but I didn't think he should know that she has cancer at this point.

Daughter, Family 1:   I started to say something and dad says, "Well she still has hope doesn't she even if she is seventy-six?" and mother said, "Well, sure."

Wife, Family 1:   The whole family has been here two days— but I still don't think they should tell him everything at this point in time.

Head Nurse: It's all very new to him and it's all very hard to talk about in the beginning. You have to be alert to the clues that people put forth. He is no fool, he knows what's going on.

Daughter, Family 1:   But isn't it worse when, I mean, when we're sitting there talking and I'm blurting it out about the lady with cancer and mother says, "Oh sure, she needs a lot of hope." He knows, I'm sure he knows what I was about to say.

Wife, Family 1:   No, I don't think so.

Head Nurse: Has he met the lady?

Wife, Family 1:   No, just Mr. A. I guess I probably just want to protect him.

Doctor: So your feeling would be to protect him, then, and not to tell him. I wonder if other people would feel the same way or differently?

Sister, Family 2:   My sister feels that way about my father.

Doctor: That she would want to protect him?

Sister, Family 2:   Yes, she's been protecting him for seven years now, ever since she found out that she had cancer.

Head Nurse: I understand your father is ninety-one years old.

Sister, Family 2:   She said, "Don't tell him I have cancer." But I didn't follow her advice, I told him what she had.

Patient, Family 2:   I thought that he'd go into a tailspin.

Head Nurse: But he didn't, right?

Patient and Sister: Right.

Head Nurse: You are saying that he's stronger than either of you thought. Don't you think by the time you have lived ninety years that few things will shock you, or surprise you?

Sister: Yes.

Patient: I was surprised that he knew all along. We were each trying to protect the other.

Wife, Family 1: Well, see, my husband had a heart attack twenty years ago, and I think ever since then, when anything happens to the children or anything happens to anybody, that worries him. I tell him things in my own way and in my own time, when I think he can take it, rather than blurt it out. But maybe that's the way I am, I don't know if it's good for him or not.

Head Nurse: Well, for twenty years it's been OK, right?

Wife, Family 1: Yes. We knew yesterday that it was cancer. He still had hope after the bronchoscopy that it wasn't cancer. He was hoping some miracle would happen. Well, I didn't want to spoil his sleep you know. It was five o'clock when I found out and I thought, "Why tell him now? I'll break it to him to-morrow some way." I would have preferred that the doctor would tell him, which would maybe be harder, but I told him this morning before the doctor came. I said, "You know, you were 99 percent sure of the diagnosis when you came here. Dr. A. said he was 99 percent sure that it was malignant." I said, "So you kinda know what's coming. So no matter what the doctor says, it isn't going to be too much of a shock for you is it?" So I mean, I kind of prepared him a little, so that when Dr. B. came in and told him, I don't think he was surprised. But he knew that when we came here, we all knew that there was little hope that it was going to be benign.

Doctor: It's still hard to hear it, though.

Wife, Family 1: Oh, yes. That's why I didn't tell him yesterday.

Head Nurse: It's difficult for anybody to tell somebody they love that they have cancer.

Wife, Family 1: Oh, yes. That's why I preferred for the doctor to tell him. I didn't want to be the bearer of bad news.

Head Nurse: You're shaking your head, Mr. B. Don't you agree?

Husband, Family 3: The patient should know. Like my wife, she's known it all the time that she's had it. My wife has had cancer for twenty-three years this May, and she's loaded from head to foot you know. Like I say, she knew it, but she's still fighting, she still has hope. It gives you a better chance to beat it.

Wife, Family 1: But to me, I think men are much more vulnerable. I look at my husband and I want to cry.

Husband, Family 3: She knows it and I know it, everything that's wrong.

Patient, Family 3: Hard as it is, it's easier if everything is out in the open.

Wife, Family 1: It's harder, I think, for men to accept things than women. I think women are much stronger. Although he surprised us, because I didn't think he would want any treatment, and now he's talking about chemotherapy here. It's a great thing, and I thought we were going to have a battle. I wasn't even going to insist on it. I thought, "Let him make up his own mind what he wants to do."

Head Nurse: Did that surprise you?

Wife, Family 1: Yes, before he came here, he said, "If they find it, forget it."

Head Nurse: How do you explain this?

Wife, Family 1: He's getting hope from being here.

Head Nurse: That's one of the hardest things. How do you keep everybody's hope up? I mean, including his, when you keep thinking the worst.

Wife, Family 1: That's what I'm going to have trouble with; how to keep his spirits up.

Head Nurse: How do you think you can do this?

Wife, Family 1: Well, my husband still doesn't want to talk about his situation—even though he told me "You knew when I came in what I had. They said that I had only about two weeks to live." But, I don't know, I uh, I still don't think one ever loses hope. We're not going to give up without a tussle. And it's like the gentleman there says, it gives us a better chance. They told him right off, "You've got the oat cell and it's incurable," but my husband still doesn't want to talk about it. But it doesn't mean that he don't talk about it with me, because we are one person, in this thing together. If he gives up entirely, well, I'm afraid that might influence my whatever you call it, fight, or whatever it is, that you have for this thing. I really believe the patient has the right to know.

Head Nurse: And to share his fears with others. In other words you are saying that sharing is what matters.

Wife, Family 1: That is what my husband said. He said, "You have to know what is going on too." And I told him, "Whatever happens to you, I'm with you 100 percent." I think women are stronger than men. I mean for illness, stuff like that. I don't know why, but it seems to me they are. He's probably cried over his situation more than I have. Not in front of me, no, but he's been pretty choked up.

Head Nurse: Is that good or bad? I mean, would it bother you if he cried in front of you?

Wife, Family 1: No, I've been with him too long and we share everything together, and if this was me in the same situation he would be the same way. I don't say that I am standing here and being big and heroic about it. I'm not heroic about it, but I've got no choice but to accept the truth or to just fall down and go boom.

Daughter, Family 4: I guess I can't see keeping everything inside because my father-in-law died from cancer, and that was such a terrible struggle 'cause nobody talked at all. When we first found out about daddy we said, "Let's not put it under the carpet, let's talk about it." So we did, all the kids. Yeah, it was uncomfortable to talk about, you know. We had all the kids over. They all have been fighting for two weeks about which hospital to go to. I thought to come here would be very hard on him, he's a very private person. But who's private when they have cancer? At St. Ann's hospital, they have a doctor on oncology now. We thought coming to Madison for treatments is a long distance to go. I thought it would be hard on him, his energy, but the kids all wanted him to come up here, and the kids won out, and here we are. Now we are beginning to realize that it's OK, you know. After all he's young, he is only sixty-seven.

Patient 4:   I'm sixty-six, so wait—I've got another month before I'm sixty-seven.

Head Nurse: You've got a lot of living to do yet.

Patient 4:   Yeah, you bet.

Head Nurse: Well, talk about somebody with a lot of living to do, how is it for the mother of somebody so young?

Mother, Family 5:   Terrible. . . . However, they have given us so much hope, with the cancer that my daughter has and I have faith that she'll be fine. When we first found out that she had Hodgkin's disease, Sarah was only twenty-four, she had only been married ten months. When the doctor said Hodgkin's to her, she almost fell off the chair. She's afraid of everything, she's always been a very squeamish person, covers her eyes at the sight of blood. When they told her what she had to go through, I was waiting for her to say, "Mom, I won't do it." Then he told her about the cure rate and some of the different stages and what would have to be done, and what she would have to go through. When we came home that night—she and I were alone and we hugged each other and we started to cry and I cried right in front of her and I said, "We'll go to the ends of the world for you, I want to kiss you and hold you." And then I apologized later for having broken down. And you know what her answer was? and that's why I'm saying this—her answer was "Mom, it helped me, it really helped me. If you had sat there and, you know, just voiced something like 'You're going to be fine, Sarah, nothing to it,' I wouldn't have believed you. Now that you told me that, we are both going to fight. I feel stronger." You know, I felt really bad about crying in front of her, but she didn't mind.

Head Nurse: Not only that, but she knew that you cared about her.

Mother, Family 5:   And at the bone marrow the other day when I came into her room and she was crying, I cried right along with her. It hurts, it hurts very much to have somebody you love lying there in pain.

Doctor: That must have been hard.

Mother, Family 5:   Especially your own child. And yet, the young guy in the room next to her said, "Gee, I wish I had what Sarah had."

Head Nurse: That was a very poignant comment . . .

Mother, Family 5:   Well, I thought I'm almost afraid to tell anybody that she had Hodgkin's and there's an 80 percent cure rate and this little guy the same age has lymphoma. It makes you feel that you're lucky and somebody else isn't.

The reader will notice that the group leaders make twenty-three interventions in this initial group session. The head nurse offers the purpose of the meeting: "To get some new ideas and share some mutual concerns and worries. By sharing, you will realize that you are not alone in your situation. You will also learn some new ways of coping with cancer." The doctor poses the first problem, brought up in the group by several members, to the group as a whole: "So your feeling would be to protect him, then, and not to tell him. I wonder if other people would feel the same way or differently?" When a very difficult and poignant dilemma about this protecting and telling is told by a family, the doctor is there with them, saying very simply: "It's still hard to hear it, though." The head nurse notes Mr. B. shaking his head at this and invites his disagreement, giving room for an important difference of opinion. The doctor later acknowledges another rough passage. The majority of brief remarks by the head nurse are transitional comments inviting participation, which become somewhat less frequent as the group gets under way.

These interventions sufficed because of the very able membership of this particular group. When one considers how much skill may be needed for the most difficult groups, one may take comfort from the fact that a modest technique can do

much. These five interventions are typical of the minimum help
needed from the group leaders: (1) a simple, encouraging introduction of the purpose of the group; (2) commenting and asking questions until the group takes up their job; (3) posing of
the problems that are offered by the first speakers to the whole
group; (4) allowing for and noticing serious differences; and (5)
being there with the group, with their situations and feelings.

What happens then in this particular group? The problem
posed is how to protect people from terrible news. What comes
out are several moving stories of how this protection can be
given in very different ways: by not telling the husband until
tomorrow, but preparing him a little beforehand; by being
close, by being as one person (the husband and wife), and by
fighting together; by crying along with the daughter.

Using such a modest technique, we find that many of
the groups are as moving as this one, while others stumble along
and we only realize later in supervision what they needed. When
the groups go well, an hour is enough time. When they stumble,
more time does not help, since it is the beginning of the hour
that seems to make the most difference. The returning members often help a lot, but new members can give just as much.
When the nursing staff makes rounds after the group and asks
how the group has been, the reactions always cover a wide
range. Some do not want to come again because it is too depressing. Some learn a lot. Some feel a lot of support. Most say
it was very interesting and they would like to come again.

We have been giving more attention to these follow-up
conversations, which are fitted into other nursing rounds and
duties, and they have become ever more meaningful, emotional, and thoughtful occasions to reexperience the group. Like
Redl's "closet interviews" with individual children in his activity groups, these inquiries after the group can give something that may be needed as much as the group itself. Perhaps
even more important are the conversations begun among group
members, which often continue for days after the group meeting. Where the therapeutic effect is most powerful we do not
yet know. Probably it lies in different aspects of the situation
for different members.

Supervision, Monitoring, and Follow-up

An important part of the cancer group at the University of Wisconsin has been the ongoing supervision process, which started primarily to assist the trainee. Initially, the trainee and the staff psychiatrist (who typically does not attend group sessions) would discuss the group without the ideas of the cotherapist (the head nurse) or the feedback of group members. (The trainee acted as a consultant-in-training to the head nurse.) We now operate supervisory sessions with both the head nurse and another staff nurse who has made an effort to elicit group members' reactions to a particular group meeting. In addition, a ten-minute segment of audiotape is played each time.

This added input helps bring the group dynamics into clearer relief. Selective inattention to vital areas (which is rampant when material is presented in an anecdotal manner) is greatly reduced, and cotherapist conflicts must be faced more directly. Shortcomings of technique must be assessed, and positive and negative reactions of group members are reviewed. Finally, the feelings in each group, which are often painful and poignant, come through much more clearly. Time seems to temper our need to look away, which is a hurdle that must be continually overcome by anyone working with cancer patients. Their suffering, their heroism, and their triumphs are powerful and difficult to address without experiencing strong feelings of one's own.

By looking closely, we have noted some areas that need improvement and have made steps in that direction. A better understanding of cancer patients' needs and anxieties has been influential. There is now in operation an ongoing series of ethics meetings involving nurses, physicians, and consultants that provides a link between the group and primary care givers. Both general and case-specific ethical problems are addressed at these meetings. Concerns of patients voiced in a particular group session regarding euthanasia, human experimentation, decisions about treatment, informal consent, and the quality of life with cancer are often passed to the ethics meeting (Whitman, 1980).

Part of our intent is to use the groups for screening patients and families who might benefit from more intense intervention. Family conferences have become a regular event at which a staff psychiatrist specializing in family therapy is available for consultation sessions and for ongoing therapy. There is also access to individual therapy if it is indicated. We would like to offer outpatient, ongoing group therapy as well, but this has been difficult to arrange in our university hospital, which has many other political and medical interests and serves a large geographical area.

One of the most pressing needs in this field is for follow-up studies to determine the efficacy of this treatment modality. We are beginning to plan studies of the University of Wisconsin cancer group. Presently there are very few data on cancer group follow-up (Cunningham, Strassberg, and Roback, 1978). It is clear that group leaders' tasks are complex and change throughout the course of a particular group session. There is a need to be sensitive to and knowledgeable about patients' defenses and individual limitations as expressed during the brief duration of the group. Timing and frequency of interventions as well as the choice of technique will vary and are extremely important.

It is particularly incumbent upon leaders to be mindful of the hypothesis that group therapies are not harmless for all individuals (Lieberman, Yalom, and Miles, 1973, chap. 5). We have yet to locate a single casualty from our group project in the last eight years; however, we have only begun in the last year to interview all participants, and we have no long-term follow-up. Follow-up studies would have implications for both the development of screening procedures for prospective group participants as well as for the development of technical interventions useful in group therapies for cancer patients. Optimizing the group experience for cancer patients and their families is vital, and improving the quality of their lives is a challenging and worthy goal.

Afterword: In Memoriam

Mary Jerse was murdered by one of her patients on January 31, 1983. It is impossible to describe what this has meant to us who have known her, but it is possible to say at the conclu-

sion of this chapter what Mary stood for in psychiatry. I can never forget her spirit, which she conveyed to me in her favorite word in our discussions—science. "Yes, Dr. Gustafson," she would say, "we know what the theories say and what the group leaders think, but didn't Yalom's research show that this might have very little to do with what actually happened in the group? Isn't it true that the group leaders were unable to predict the members who became casualties? Don't we have to ask the group members what actually happened from their perspective?"

Of course, she was right. The theory and thoughts of group leaders can have little to do with what actually happens in their groups. Mary wanted us to come to terms with what actually happened. Given her spirit, her logic, and the rightness of her argument, we moved very much in the directions she wanted. Instead of having only the trainee and myself for supervision, the head nurse came, too. Instead of having only anecdotal reports, we also listened to the first ten minutes of the group on audiotape. Instead of surmising the outcome, we held follow-up interviews of all the group members; these were reported in supervision by one of the nursing staff. If we could not yet get a long-term, systematic follow-up, we could at least correct our theories and thinking by coming closer to the actual experiences of the group members and leaders.

When Mary tried one of my favorite technical ideas in a group, she was most delighted to show me how the follow-up failed to indicate how helpful it actually was. I, of course, would reply that she hadn't carried out the maneuver I had in mind, and so our debate would go on in a spirited duel between theory and empirical findings.

It was invigorating to work with her. Science was serious and it was fun. When I suggested that she could write this chapter on our behalf, she soon provided us with a provisional outline for our discussion, and her drafts of the chapter followed soon after. Our criticisms were soon incorporated into a revised manuscript. I was beginning to think of her as a young professor, as she had the vitality, the dash, the critical mind, and the readiness to improve her thinking at every turn. I had given her P. B. Medawar's (1979) "Advice to a Young Scientist" with some comments on the last draft of her chapter. We never got a chance to discuss it. She was suddenly killed soon after. We shall miss her dearly. All we can do here is to commend to the world all that she gave to us.

James P. Gustafson, M.D.

References

"The Abhorrence of Stillbirth." *Lancet,* 1977, *1* (8023), 1188-1190.

Abrams, R. D. "The Patient with Cancer—His Changing Pattern of Communication." *New England Journal of Medicine,* 1966, *274* (6), 317-322.

American Psychiatric Association. *Diagnostic and Statistical Manual of Mental Disorders.* (3rd ed.) Washington, D.C.: American Psychiatric Association, 1980.

Bourne, S. "The Psychological Effects of Stillbirths on Women and Their Doctors." *Journal of the Royal College of General Practitioners,* 1968, *103* (16), 103-112.

Cassell, E. J. "The Nature of Suffering and the Goals of Medicine." *New England Journal of Medicine,* 1982, *306* (11), 639-645.

Cassem, H. H., and Stewart, R. S. "Management and Care of the Dying Patient." *International Journal of Psychiatry in Medicine,* 1976, *6* (1/2), 3293-3304.

Cohen, R. J. "Is Dying Being Worked to Death?" *American Journal of Psychiatry,* 1976, *133* (5), 575-577.

Cunningham, J., Strassberg, D., and Roback, H. "Group Psychotherapy for Medical Patients." *Comprehensive Psychiatry,* 1978, *19* (2), 135-140.

Derogatis, L. R., Abeloff, M. D., and McBeth, C. D. "Cancer Patients and Their Physicians in the Perception of Psychological Symptoms." *Psychosomatics,* 1976, *17,* 197-201.

Derogatis, L. R., Abeloff, M. D., and Melisaratos, N. "Psychological Coping Mechanisms and Survival Time in Metastatic

Breast Cancer." *Journal of the American Medical Association*, 1979, *242* (14), 1504-1508.

Greer, S., Morris, T., and Pettingale, K. W. "Psychological Response to Breast Cancer: Effect on Outcome." *Lancet*, 1979, *II* (8146), 785-787.

Gustafson, J. P., and Whitman, H. H. "Towards a Balanced Social Environment on the Oncology Service: The Cancer Patients' Group." *Social Psychiatry*, 1978, *13*, 147-152.

Gustafson, J. P., and others. "A Cancer Patients' Group—The Problem of Containment." *Journal of Personality and Social Systems*, 1978, *1* (3), 6-18.

Gustafson, J. P., and others. "Cooperative and Clashing Interests in Small Groups. Part I: Theory." *Human Relations*, 1981a, *34* (4), 315-339.

Gustafson, J. P., and others. "Cooperative and Clashing Interests in Small Groups. Part II: Group Narratives." *Human Relations*, 1981b, *34* (5), 367-377.

Krant, M. J., and others. "The Role of a Hospital-Based Psychosocial Unit in Terminal Cancer Illness and Bereavement." *Journal of Chronic Disease*, 1976, *29*, 115-127.

Kubler-Ross, E. *On Death and Dying*. New York: Macmillan, 1969.

Kubler-Ross, E. *Death, the Final Stage of Growth*. Englewood Cliffs, N.J.: Prentice-Hall, 1975.

Leiber, L., and others. "The Communication of Affection Between Cancer Patients and Their Spouses." *Psychosomatic Medicine*, 1976, *38* (6), 379-389.

Lieberman, M. A., Yalom, I. D., and Miles, M. B. *Encounter Groups: First Facts*. New York: Basic Books, 1973.

Medawar, P. B. "Advice to a Young Scientist." *Harper's*, September 1979.

Parkes, C. M. "The Emotional Impact of Cancer of Ear, Nose and Throat on Patients and Their Families." *Journal of Laryngology and Otology*, 1975, *89* (12), 1271-1279.

Ringler, K. E., and others. "Technical Advances in Leading a Cancer Patient Group." *International Journal of Group Psychotherapy*, 1981, *31* (3), 329-343.

Skynner, A. C. R. "Reflections on the Family Therapist as

Family Scapegoat." *Journal of Family Therapy,* 1979, *1,* 7-22.

Skynner, A. C. R. "An Open-Systems, Group-Analytic Approach to Family Therapy." In A. S. Gurman and D. Kniskern (Eds.), *The Handbook of Family Therapy.* New York: Brunner/Mazel, 1981.

Skynner, A. C. R. "Group Analysis and Family Therapy." Paper presented at the Symposium in Group Analysis at the American Group Psychotherapy Association Conference, New York, February 1982.

Spiegel, D., Bloom, J. R., and Yalom, I. "Group Support for Patients with Metastatic Cancer: A Randomized Prospective Outcome Study." *Archives of General Psychiatry,* 1981, *38,* 527-533.

Spiegel, D., and Yalom, I. D. "A Support Group for Dying Patients." *International Journal of Group Psychotherapy,* 1978, *28,* 233-245.

Sullivan, H. S. *Clinical Studies in Psychiatry.* New York: Norton, 1973. (Originally published 1956.)

Surawicz, F. G., and others. "Cancer, Emotions, and Mental Illness: The Present State of Understanding." *American Journal of Psychiatry,* 1976, *133* (11), 1306-1309.

Vachon, M. L., and Lyall, W. A. "Applying Psychiatric Techniques to Patients with Cancer." *Hospital and Community Psychiatry,* 1976, *27* (8), 582-584.

Vachon, M. L., and others. "The Use of Group Meetings with Cancer Patients and Their Families." In J. Tache, H. Selye, and S. B. Day (Eds.), *Cancer, Stress, and Death.* New York: Plenum, 1979.

Wellisch, D. K., Mosher, M. B., and Van Scoy, C. "Management of Family Emotional Stress; Family Group Therapy in a Private Oncology Practice." *International Journal of Group Psychotherapy,* 1978, *28* (2), 225-231.

Whitman, H. H. "Ethical Issues in Cancer Nursing." *Oncology Nursing Forum,* 1980, *7* (4), 37-40.

Whitman, H. H., Gustafson, J. P., and Coleman, F. W. "Group Approaches for Cancer Patients: Leaders and Members." *American Journal of Nursing,* 1979, *79* (5), 910-913.

Yalom, I. D. *The Theory and Practice of Group Psychotherapy.*
New York: Basic Books, 1970.

Yalom, I. D., and Greaves, C. "Group Therapy with the Terminally Ill." *American Journal of Psychiatry,* 1977, *134* (4), 396-400.

11

Susan Lewis, Ph.D.

❖ ❖ ❖ ❖ ❖ ❖ ❖ ❖ ❖ ❖ ❖ ❖ ❖

Cancer
in Adolescents

To be a teenager is to enter the prime of one's life: Everything is possible, especially physical and sexual fulfillment. Confrontation with a life-threatening illness, such as cancer, seems to contradict all that adolescence implies and is clearly a major impediment to accomplishing age-appropriate developmental tasks. Because of the importance of peer relationships to adolescents, a group approach is especially well suited to helping them cope with the impact of cancer. Following a description of those adolescent developmental tasks that are complicated by the disease and its treatment, I will describe the methods adolescents characteristically use to cope with life-threatening illness. This chapter will then review the literature on group interventions with chronically ill teenagers and finally report on a group approach used with teenagers having cancer at the Vanderbilt University Medical Center.

Of the several types of cancer found in the adolescent age group, the two most common are acute leukemia and Hodgkin's disease. Acute leukemia is a malignant process involving the growth of abnormal white blood cells. This malignant process

285

causes anemia, bleeding, and infection and can involve various body organs. Hodgkin's disease is a malignancy of the lymphoid tissue, resulting in painless enlarged nodes at various sites in the body. Other types of cancer often found in this age group include Ewing's sarcoma, osteogenic sarcoma, brain tumor, and small-cell sarcoma. Depending on the specific nature and location of the cancer and the treatment and course of the disease, there is a great diversity of physical side effects as well as prognoses. Teenagers are usually hospitalized at the time of diagnosis for further medical evaluation or the initiation of treatment. Subsequently, much of the treatment can be performed on an outpatient basis, and teenagers come in to the Pediatric Hematology–Oncology Clinic for that purpose. Clinic visits may be conducted over several consecutive days or spaced a month apart, depending on the treatment protocol. Some teenagers have to be rehospitalized after their initial stay to receive chemotherapy, radiation, or intravenous antibiotics to combat infection.

When teenagers are first diagnosed as having cancer, most think of the possibility of death. While recent progress has made death increasingly unlikely, the diagnosis and the treatment process involve many potentially painful and intrusive procedures, including venipunctures, lumbar punctures, and bone marrow aspirations. Common side effects of the disease itself are weakness, fatigue, pain, and weight loss. The treatment process has its own set of side effects, which may include disfigurement in the case of amputations, nausea, alopecia (hair loss), weight gain, and further weakness. The long-term consequences of some treatments can involve neurological problems if treatment is started at an early age, interference with the reproductive capacities, and increased chance of second malignancies.

Major Developmental Tasks

Although cancer is psychologically devastating to anyone, it is particularly so for the adolescent. Both the disease and many forms of treatment, including chemotherapy, radiation, and mutilative surgery, affect major developmental tasks, such as the assertion of independence and planning for the future. Schowalter (1977), drawing from clinical observations and theory, illustrated the extent to which physical illness during adolescence puts the patient at risk in terms of the various physical and psychological transitions characterizing this stage of development. He maintained that the usual adolescent conflicts between dependence and independence and between regressive and progressive forces are further complicated by the bodily effects of the illness and its treatment. At a time when control over one's life is of the utmost importance, the teenager with cancer feels that his or her body is out of control. The physical changes accompanying serious illness and its treatment arouse shame and embarrassment at any age, but this is especially true during adolescence, when body, health, strength, and looks are so important for developing a sense of personal adequacy.

Kellerman and Katz (1977) organized the major developmental tasks facing adolescents into three conceptual categories: the establishment of autonomy, psychosexual-psychosocial development, and future orientation. The adolescent with cancer experiences a loss of control in each of these areas (Berman, 1980). Using these three categories as a guide, this chapter discusses in detail how each of these tasks is made more difficult by cancer and its treatment process. While each of these tasks can be conceptualized separately, they actually overlap and interact with one another to a significant degree.

The Development of Autonomy. The teenager's development of autonomy involves becoming both emotionally and economically independent of the parents. Erikson (1968) spelled out the major task of adolescence as the need to gain an ego identity, an identity in his or her own right and not simply that of being a son or daughter. The role of the patient, especially one with a life-threatening illness, involves an enforced passivity and regression, which are counter to the teenager's move toward independence. Specifically, hospitalization transfers control of the teenager's life from the adolescent to the hospital staff and parents. Once again, the teenager has to depend on parents for transportation and financial support. Overprotectiveness, infantilization, and overpermissiveness are typical and understandable parental responses to the diagnosis of cancer in their child, but they undermine the child's thrust toward independence. As a result of the weakness produced by the physical side effects of the disease and its treatment, adolescents' symptoms become a legitimate way to ask for and obtain caring and attention, especially from parents. The resulting intensified dependency is highly threatening to the self-esteem of adolescents, who are developmentally feeling pressure to take care of themselves.

The following case example illustrates the threat to autonomy that the diagnosis of cancer brings. Charles was a healthy teenager and a good student who was active in extracurricular activities until he was diagnosed with lymphoma at age sixteen. During his initial hospitalization and chemotherapy treatment, he became a whining, demanding, and childish person, while his mother, a nurse, attended diligently to his every need. He lost interest in his schoolwork and consequently fell behind, and he was not willing to visit with his peers. When he left the hospital, he managed to get a homebound teacher and a private-duty nurse, which further removed him from his peer group and normal teenage activities. This extended regression at least temporarily disrupted his movement toward separation and greater autonomy by increasing his dependence on adults and removing his sources of independent achievement, such as academic performance and positive peer interactions. Timely intervention by the hematology team was necessary to prevent a more prolonged regressive period, perhaps resulting in the refusal to attend school and the total withdrawal from his peers.

Psychosocial-Psychosexual Development. Two separate yet closely related tasks in this category are the mastery of body image and the development of peer relationships. For adolescents, body image and self-esteem are closely intertwined (Schowalter, 1977). Little (1960) pointed out that establishing an identity is intimately connected with feelings and sensations that the teenager has about his or her character and external appearance. During adolescence, due to hormonal and physical changes, there is a heightened awareness of and attention to one's body. Comparing body size and shape is a common activity for teenagers of the same sex, and relating to the opposite sex is often linked to physical appearance. Teenagers hospitalized with a life-threatening illness and subsequently cared for by protective parents have little sense of privacy for exploring their bodies as they adjust to the normal anxieties provoked by physical changes.

Further, the perception of having a damaged and diseased body during this time can in itself lower self-esteem. As Plumb and Holland (1974) stated, adolescent patients focus their feelings about their cancer on the specific symptoms they are experiencing. Although the fear of death is inevitable when the diagnosis is made, an adolescent's concerns shift quickly from this to a keen sense of being different from his or her former self as well as from peers. Certainly in the case of alopecia or amputation, the changes are vivid. But even less visible changes, such as weakness, fatigue, and weight loss, can be humiliating to a teenager. The physical side effects of the disease and treatment often lessen physical attractiveness and athletic ability when the value of physical appearance, athletic performance, and peer acceptance are most important (Koocher and O'Malley, 1981). The premium put on conformity during adolescence highlights these teenagers' feelings of being different (Moore, Holton, and Marten, 1969). The sense of oneself as sexually attractive, an important achievement of adolescence, can be undermined by these same changes in physical appearance and ability.

The development of meaningful peer relationships is a critical step in the transition between childhood and adulthood. Many aspects of having cancer disrupt normal peer relationships. First, hospitalization causes a separation from peers. Second, the inability to participate in teenage activities or school can lead to further isolation from peers and a loss of self-esteem. In addition, a patient's peers often have difficulty relating to the teenager with cancer. They may prefer to avoid the teenager because they do not know what to say, feel embarrassed, and even fear that the cancer is contagious.

The following case example demonstrates the difficulties

a teenager with cancer faces in the areas just described. Tara was diagnosed as having leukemia at age thirteen. At age sixteen, just when the doctors were ready to discontinue her chemotherapy due to her continuous remission, her leukemia recurred. She was referred to me because of her depression, which seemed an appropriate response to her situation. I felt certain that she would be worried about dying, although she quickly let me know that that was not her major concern. Rather, her immediate worry was her physical appearance. Bloated and with thinning hair from her chemotherapy, she said she "felt like wearing a bag over her head." Additionally, she felt tired and sick and was unable to participate in her favorite activities with peers, which led to further feelings of isolation. She was spending all of her time at home on the couch being cared for by, and becoming increasingly dependent on, her mother, with whom she was already engaged in a fierce struggle for independence. Her boyfriend, whom she had earlier been able to count on for support, was also having difficulty with the visible reminders of her illness and was seeing her less often.

Future Orientation. Adolescence is a time of planning for and working toward the future. Related activities include developing necessary intellectual skills and concepts, choosing and preparing for an occupation, and preparing for marriage and family life (Kellerman and Katz, 1977). The philosophy often adopted by persons with cancer is to "live one day at a time," an attitude that is ostensibly adaptive but that works against reaching one's intellectual and social potential. At least initially, the adjustment to the cancer diagnosis and treatment focuses all the energy and attention on the immediate future of the teenage patient, rather than on the more ordinary and long-term vocational and educational pursuits.

Most living skills are learned in school. A prolonged absence from school caused by illness and the reluctance to attend school because of changes in physical appearance can lead to a deterioration in school performance and hence another assault on self-esteem. Tom, age fifteen when his cancer recurred, was already behind in school and had never been a good student. At the time of his recurrence, he was reluctant to go back to school, and he was also unwilling to pursue vocational training. His comment to me was "Why should I go back to school? I might as well live it up for the time that I have left."

Choosing and planning for a future occupation and thinking about starting one's own family both have to be reconsidered in light of the consequences and implications of cancer and its treatment. For teenagers whose occupational goals are heavily dependent on physical activity, the impact of cancer is greatest. The potential reproductive problems related to chemotherapy or radiation certainly must be considered as the teenager faces the prospects of marriage and family life.

Coping Mechanisms of Adolescents with Cancer

The major defense mechanism used by teenagers with cancer is denial (Karon, 1973; Kellerman and Katz, 1977; and Zeltzer, 1980). Roback discusses the overuse of denial in Chapter One, so I will only reiterate that some types of denial are adaptive. For instance, Lazarus (1981) states that denial of "implication," that is, shutting the prognosis out of one's mind and continuing to hope one will get well despite obvious setbacks, is a healthy way of coping with a life-threatening illness. Geist (1979) discussed what he termed the chronically ill youngster's "denial in the service of hope," which permits the patient to lead a fairly normal life while accepting the need for medical interventions.

A typical conversation with a teenager follows that illustrates how she uses denial in discussing her cancer. Despite her own admission that she had occasionally worried about dying from her leukemia, Melinda, age twelve, insisted that this hardly ever bothered her. This teenager, who also had a good understanding of her disease, explained to me, "It is sort of like cancer. Well, . . . it is cancer," and then went on to deny that it was difficult for her to acknowledge this fact. Most practitioners encourage support of a teenager's use of denial as a defense mechanism. To be future oriented, one has to have this kind of hope. Thus, it allows teenagers to stay involved in this developmentally appropriate activity.

A second coping mechanism used by teenagers with cancer is overcompensation in activities (Moore, Holton, and Marten, 1969). When teenagers have no side effects that restrict activity, they may become excessively involved in peer groups or sports to make up for lost time and to counteract feelings of passivity engendered by their cancer. Within limits, this coping mechanism can be adaptive. For example, such activity allows for continued peer contact and possible achievements enhancing self-esteem. This can aid in the process of developing a sense of adequacy and autonomy in the face of debilitating illness. However, some teenagers overdo such activities, thereby excluding other essential responsibilities, such as obtaining continued medical care. Following his cancer diagnosis and initial treatment, one fourteen-year-old, a former football player, became manager of the team. Whereas this new position helped ease his loss of playing on the team, he began to miss necessary appointments at the hematology clinic, claiming that his football schedule did not allow him time.

Emphasizing the adolescents' actual or perceived control over their treatment is one means of counteracting the inevitable feelings of helplessness elicited by the diagnosis of cancer (Berman, 1980; Kellerman and Katz, 1977). This approach involves giving adolescent cancer patients enough information about their disease and their treatment so that they can make informed choices. It is important for a physician to have a relationship with a teenager that is based on trust and open communication. This allows teenagers to feel they can ask questions about their illness and that they can expect an honest answer. Encouraging such active involvement of the teenager in his or her own medical care is vital, as illustrated in the following case example.

Fred was first diagnosed with leukemia at age five. At the time there was little discussion with Fred about the disease or the treatment process. He did well for the next few years, discontinuing his chemotherapy at age nine. At age fourteen, Fred had a relapse. He was referred to me when the doctors had to discontinue his lumbar punctures, a necessary part of his treatment, because Fred's lack of cooperation and defiant behavior in the treatment room made it impossible to perform the procedure. In talking with Fred, it quickly became apparent that he had minimal knowledge of his illness and no understanding of the treatment process. Providing Fred with accurate information about the purpose of lumbar punctures and giving him control over when treatments would be reestablished allowed him to accept the recommended medical regime.

Schowalter (1977) suggested another technique for strengthening chronically ill teenagers' self-esteem, namely, providing a newly diagnosed teenager with a peer role model who has successfully coped with the same disease. Simply seeing and talking with someone comparable in age who has already gone through what the teenager is experiencing relieves feelings of isolation and gives the newly diagnosed teenager a sense of hope. This is in addition to whatever advice one teenager may give another about how to handle a specific disease-related issue. For example, Karen, when diagnosed with leukemia at age thirteen, believed that her life was over. She felt cut off from her former activities and friends, and the prospect of losing her hair made her feel she could never return to school or her former social activities. During Karen's initial hospitalization, the hematology-oncology nurse arranged to have a slightly older female patient visit her who had the same diagnosis and was in the hospital for a course of chemotherapy. The two teenagers visited together several times, during which time Karen was shown and told all about wigs and how to handle questions and teasing from peers. She felt much less isolated and better prepared for the transition back home after her meetings with the older patient.

Rationale for Group Work with Teenage Cancer Patients

According to Karon (1973), emotional support for adolescents with cancer involves establishing an atmosphere in which they can feel free to discuss their concerns and receive direct and honest information. It has been well documented by Spinetta (1982) and others that a child's adjustment to cancer is more positive when that child has the opportunity to communicate openly his or her disease-related feelings to significant persons.

Because of the special difficulties that teenagers with cancer face in maintaining relationships with peers and the previously discussed importance of these relationships developmentally, providing a peer group with whom they can identify and from whom they will not be rejected for their illness can be beneficial. Such positive and meaningful interactions and subsequent identifications with peers can counteract disease-induced regressive forces that threaten the teenagers' autonomous functioning. Group meetings that encourage expressing and working through the stages of grief and mourning normally accompanying the diagnosis of cancer will help the teenagers to accept their illness. This acceptance will lead to a restoration of their self-esteem, which is so necessary to adequate psychosocial development. Additionally, for newly diagnosed patients to have contact with longer-term patients can encourage planning for the future. It is clear that group interventions can offer teenagers the opportunity to work through the developmental tasks interfered with by their cancer.

Cunningham, Strassberg, and Roback (1978) reviewed recent studies of group psychotherapy for medical patients. They listed therapeutic factors, many of which are especially relevant to the teenager who is chronically ill. The hope instilled from meeting others who have coped well with the same disease has already been discussed. The universality experienced when teenagers recognize that they are not alone in their problems is valuable in itself. The imparting of information by a medically knowledgeable person in an open and honest fashion can correct misconceptions and relieve anxiety. Teenagers, whose self-esteem has been assaulted by the consequences of their disease and its treatment, can profit from sharing solutions to problems with other teenagers, which enhances their sense of being worthwhile. Finally, sharing with one another ways to relate to well peers, who may also have difficulty with both the life-threatening aspects of the disease and the physical side effects, is especially useful to teenagers.

Group Treatment Approaches for Teenagers with Cancer

While group interventions are widely recommended for teenagers with cancer, there are few reports in the literature of established group therapy programs of this type. To encourage the basic developmental task of improving peer relationships, both Nir and Maslin (1981) and Spinetta (1982) recommended group therapy as the treatment of choice for teenagers with cancer. Kagen-Goodheart (1977) suggested that group therapy for outpatient teenagers with cancer is valuable in their making the transition from the hospital back to the home and school. She pointed out that such meetings could be helpful in allowing teenagers to share common concerns, thereby reducing feelings of isolation, enhancing self-confidence, and helping relationships with outside peers. Gardner (1977) proposed weekly group therapy sessions for teenagers with cancer, who could be directly helped to relate to well peers by bringing their friends with them. She suggested that the meetings be didactic at first to give accurate information and teach problem-solving skills. Subsequent meetings would be more dynamically oriented, with the teenagers sharing their feelings with one another.

Thomas (1980) suggested that group meetings for hospitalized adolescent cancer patients could help patients cope with their illness, increase their social functioning, and provide them with some control over their environment. He completed a phone survey of eight cancer centers, which revealed that discussion or "rap" groups for teenagers were considered desirable and already under way or being developed. Questions regarding how to best structure these groups included whether to mix patients having various cancer diagnoses, whether to include medical staff as participants, and what the best setting and time were for the group meetings.

He concluded by proposing a structure that combined the successful group elements described by the centers he consulted. This prototype consisted of a four-session, short-term group meeting once or twice a month. These meetings would be for teenagers with mixed diagnoses and would be coled by a social worker and a clinical nurse specialist. The atmosphere would be relaxed, and topics could be initiated by patients or the staff. Group meetings would also include teenagers at different stages of their disease.

Heffron (1975) described intermittent "mini-marathon sessions" of four hours each for teenagers with various cancers. His group consisted of six staff persons and thirteen teenagers. The intensity of the meetings created a strong group identity among the members. Interestingly, the teenagers insisted that only members of their "sick world," including the health care team, immediate family, and close friends, be allowed to attend the meetings. Friends and relatives who were more distant were excluded because the teenagers did not want those people exposed to their feelings or even to the physical symptoms they experienced.

This phenomenon raises the problem of overcohesiveness referred to in Chapter One. More specifically, one should consider the risk that group involvement poses for teenagers who may stop relating to well peers and only relate to their sick friends. The teenagers in Heffron's group talked openly of family members' and friends' positive and negative reactions to them, and they also actively discussed ways of preventing their disease from interfering with future vocational and family plans. This group of teenagers also formed a "buddy system," in which subgroups of two or three members became better acquainted and made themselves available to each other in times of need.

Sachs (1980) observed common patterns in group meetings of cancer patients. The group spent time initially mourning their losses and redefining their individual roles as cancer patients. She noted that group members tired of complaining and talking about problems and wanted to take some action as a group.

She illustrated this pattern with an anecdote from her adolescent group of eight members, which had been meeting weekly for over a year. The teenagers complained about sharing a radiation waiting room with debilitated adult patients, saying that this increased their fears of radiation and advanced disease.

They decided to ask the chief radiologist for a separate waiting room. So, the group sessions served the purpose of sharing feelings with one another as well as taking some action to combat fears and feelings of passivity and helplessness. Much of what came up for discussion was related to symptoms. For example, hair loss and reentry into school while wearing wigs was a major topic. For most group members, the meetings served to resolve common problems through discussion.

In summary, these articles on groups for teenagers with cancer are primarily clinical and impressionistic. The reports of benefits to the teenage group members are taken largely from case examples and comments made by teenagers themselves; no long-term follow-up reports of the teenagers' adjustment were available. There were no empirical studies of treatment effectiveness, and there are few proven methods for ensuring success when planning a group for teenagers with cancer. However, it is noteworthy that the reports from group leaders, teenagers, and their care givers do indicate positive outcomes of such group interventions.

Vanderbilt Teenagers' Group

The suggestion to establish a group for teenagers with cancer at our center came from one of our female adolescent patients. Involving a teenager from the start, rather than having the group initiated and planned solely by professionals, was an important factor in the group's success. This teenager had learned of a group of children with cancer who had benefited from regular group meetings with one another. She and her mother approached me about forming a similar group. I was known to them as a psychologist who worked with the hematology-oncology team as a resource person for families and staff members.

In my previous clinical experience with groups for parents of handicapped children, group members demonstrated a support for one another that others who had not shared the experience probably could not have provided. Through interviews, parents of children with cancer revealed their unanimous desire to meet other parents in the same situation, because they felt that they were so alone and that none of their friends and relatives or the medical staff could fully understand their feelings. Thus, I agreed that providing an opportunity for teenagers with cancer to meet one another could have similar benefits, both in the group meetings and in the establishment of relationships that could be sustained beyond the meetings.

Structure. Several teenagers and I met to plan the first group meeting. Since our goal was to allow teenagers to get acquainted with others having similar problems, we invited all adolescent patients who shared a similar disease, leukemia. Despite the possibility that teenagers in an advanced stage of the disease might be threatening to newly diagnosed teenagers, invitations went out to all teenagers currently being treated for leukemia, regardless of the stage. We anticipated that teenagers who were very ill or hospitalized at the time could not attend the first meeting but that they might feel well enough to attend subsequent meetings. To encourage attendance, we scheduled our first meeting on a Saturday and offered lunch during the meeting. The teenagers and I did not plan beyond the initial meeting, deciding to let the group members themselves plan what they wanted the group to be and how frequently it should meet.

Group Meetings and Benefits. Out of approximately thirty teenagers who were sent invitations, twelve attended our first meeting. There were seven females and five males. The teenagers who came to the meeting included a fifteen-year-old female who had been diagnosed with leukemia at age five and who had been off treatment for a number of years. All of the other teenagers who came were between the ages of twelve and fourteen and had been diagnosed within the past few years. Despite the large number of teenagers relative to the ideal group size of six to eight persons (H. Roback, personal communication, 1982), every teenager had something to say and no one was overlooked or left out. Teenagers are known to be difficult to engage in psychotherapy, whether individual or group (Meeks, 1971). These teenagers were fairly typical in their initial response to the group meeting. They seemed uncomfortable with one another, directing their comments primarily to me and talking superficially about many things only indirectly related to their illness. Shortly, perhaps reflecting the fact that their illness was the clearest common concern, the teenagers began to engage in serious discussions about many facets of their disease and the problems they shared. Several important topics were covered during the meeting.

The teenagers' first illness-related topic was the different members of the treatment team. Talk of who preferred which physician or nurse to see them in the clinic seemed to bond the group members. Teenagers' developmental need to have adults other than their parents as role models was played out as they selected a particular member of the treatment team as their favorite. Their preferences were based on the personalities and interpersonal styles of the different care givers. The teenagers were more interested in the relationship aspects of the care giver-patient interaction than in the medical aspects. It seemed easier for the teenagers to talk initially about the people taking care of them than about the actual disease or treatment process, which was consistent with their normal use of denial as a coping mechanism. This topic also allowed them to experience the supportive responses of peers and the group leader to the expression of their feelings, whether positive or negative, about the members of the treatment team. This discussion parallels Armstrong's observation, cited in Chapter Seven, that his adolescent end-stage renal disease patients all denied the impact of chronic hemodialyses by attributing blame for their hurt to the nursing staff and clinic procedures.

Treatment procedures such as venipunctures for blood drawing or chemotherapy, lumbar punctures, and bone marrow aspirations were the next topic discussed. The relative painfulness of each procedure was discussed, and the teenagers seemed visibly relieved as they openly admitted to one another the fears and discomforts associated with each procedure. Again, their feelings about treatments were easier for them to focus on than their sad and angry feelings about having leukemia. The role of their parents during the procedures was discussed, such as how supportive they were and whether one parent was more able to

be helpful than the other. Their own sensitivity to the difficulties one or both of their parents had in adjusting to their illness
and treatment was apparent, despite parents' efforts to keep
these feelings hidden. In general, despite their developmental
need for independence, the teenagers preferred having their parents with them for the lumbar punctures and bone marrow aspirations. It seemed to be helpful for the teenagers to share
these needs for adult security with one another without experiencing peer disapproval.

The next and lengthiest topic discussed was the side effects of their disease and treatment. This discussion most clearly illustrated the teenagers' adaptive use of denial of implication, which led them to focus on day-to-day issues rather than
on the long-term implications of their disease. The loss of hair
associated with chemotherapy and radiation treatment generated a comment from practically every teenager. For most of
them, this was the most visible sign of their illness and their differentness, to themselves as well as to their peers. As one female
teenager said about her baldness, "It was like not wearing a top.
Everyone stares at you and says, what is wrong with that kid?"

All of the teenagers said that they wished that their peers
would treat them normally and not as if they had a dreaded disease. Many felt that their peers treated them as if they were fragile; one teenager said she felt people were nice to her because
they felt sorry for her. In fact, they had elected her president of
her class, and she wondered if this was because she had leukemia. Another teenager said peers treated her as though she was
going to die and were really surprised to see her when she came
back to school; one schoolmate asked her if she was going to
die. This elicited some limited discussion about the group members' own fears of dying. Several teenagers acknowledged that
early in their illness they were afraid they might die, whereas
others maintained that death was not something they had
thought about or talked about and did not like to think about
even now.

During this first group meeting, the teenagers brought up
many common problems for discussion, which seemed to comfort them despite their being unable to solve these problems.

Clearly, the most therapeutic factor operating was universality, the teenagers' realization that their problems were not unique. Several of them said it was important to have the opportunity to meet other teenagers, just so they would know somebody in the clinic instead of always wondering "who that other person was." They felt that the informal contacts would be valuable to them. Several others said that even though they were shy and did not expect to like the group meeting, they benefited from coming and talking about the problems they had in common because it made them feel less isolated and lessened their sense of differentness from their peers. Having someone really understand what they had and were going through was the most frequently expressed benefit. Most members were enthusiastic about meeting again. They decided that the next meeting should be eight weeks hence to give other teenagers plenty of time to plan to attend.

Selecting a name for the group in the first meeting provided an example of a group phenomenon described by Jerse, Whitman, and Gustafson in Chapter Ten. I obviously experienced some fear of group member fragility, since I felt that we needed to exclude from the group name any reference to illness, much less to cancer. One of the group members, whose humor lightened all of our discussions, suggested that we call ourselves the "Sick Teenagers Group." The name we decided on was Vanderbilt Teenagers' Group, and in our early invitations the word *leukemia,* but not cancer, was included in the description of the group's purpose.

Since the stated purpose of our group meeting was for teenagers to share common problems through discussion, the initial meeting certainly fulfilled our goal. The teenagers' ability and willingness to express themselves and share their fears and experiences were impressive. As the group leader, my role was largely one of promoting group interaction, providing acceptance and encouraging support among group members, and serving as a resource person for organizational purposes. My clinical skills of empathic listening and accurate rephrasing and my understanding of group dynamics were valuable in providing group leadership.

Certain features of a more traditional group psychotherapy session did not emerge during our initial meeting. For example, no teenager took on a leadership role. The group members continued to look to me for direction and guidance, perhaps because of the large attendance. In my desire to have the teenagers themselves decide what they wanted the group to be, I did not provide as much structure as I would have in a typical initial session of group therapy.

By the second group meeting, it was clear that the teenagers' agenda was different from mine. There was less talk of problems and more socializing. This observation is consistent with a fairly typical phenomenon of children and teenagers in therapy, in which the session immediately following a particularly meaningful and open one is much more neutral in content. In planning future meetings, they wanted to enjoy activities together and to have fun, which did not include continued discussions of problems related to leukemia and its treatment. This avoidance could also have been related to anxiety generated by topics raised in our previous session, particularly the brief discussion about death. However, their preference for recreational group meetings is consistent with the teenagers' expressed interest in being "normal," like their well peers.

Our third meeting, again held approximately eight weeks later, was a picnic where the teenagers cooked, ate, played softball, and could not easily be distinguished from a group of healthy teenagers. For our fourth meeting, we again had a picnic. This time we decided to invite the entire group of teenagers with cancer. Since the intent of the group members was to have a good time, the primary diagnosis became less important. Siblings and parents were also invited to this picnic, and one teenager brought her best friend. By the end of the fourth group meeting, however, I no longer felt my clinical skills were being used to facilitate group meetings; instead, I felt like a camp counselor. After some discussion, the teenagers and I decided to alternate the purposes of our future meetings, with every other meeting a "fun activity" and the other meetings consisting of lunch and a discussion session.

With the teenagers' consent, I asked a pediatric hematology-oncology nurse to join me as coleader of the group. Several times during our meetings questions came up regarding the disease or treatment that I could not answer. This need for a medically knowledgeable person, plus my desire to share responsibility for the group, prompted me to ask a nurse to join us on a regular basis.

In the last two years, the Vanderbilt Teenagers' Group has continued to meet every six to eight weeks. Our discussion meetings have alternated with bowling sessions, picnics, and even an all-day trip to a local amusement park. Because of this dual nature of the group meetings, both the coleaders and the teenagers have felt that the time spent with the group is valuable and utilizes our particular skills and resources. We have continued to have a core group of four or five teenagers who attend meetings regularly. In order to give the teenagers more responsibility for the group, we elected a slate of officers.

In addition to our regular long-term members, we have teenagers who come to several successive meetings early in their treatment and then never return. There are two likely reasons for group dropouts. One, as teenagers enter remission, they become less intensely involved with their illness and medical treatment and more involved in teenage activities with well peers. Perhaps, also, the topics raised in our group discussions generate anxiety in teenagers who prefer not to talk about their disease. Regular group members have frequently been concerned that we seem to attract so few teenagers to our meetings, but that fact does not seem to detract from the meaningfulness of the group interaction. So far, no one who has attended a group meeting has died, so that the group has not had to cope with this type of loss.

A further benefit of our group is the availability of teenagers who regularly attend meetings to newly diagnosed teens; the "veteran" teens may visit new patients in the hospital, call them on the telephone, or introduce themselves during clinic visits. A recent project undertaken by our teenagers was the preparation of a pamphlet for newly diagnosed teens. The pamphlet contains fifteen teenagers' answers to questions posed by the group members themselves when they first diagnosed.

The pamphlet is designed to alleviate the feelings of aloneness and helplessness prevalent among newly diagnosed teenagers. This project has provided a focus for discussing common problems and sharing solutions to these problems among group members at our meetings. For example, in a recent group meeting, the teenagers were discussing how to illustrate the pamphlet. To illustrate the question about initial reactions to the diagnosis, one teenager said, "A picture of a casket. I know that isn't funny, but it is realistic." Other teenagers were then able to acknowledge that the fear of dying was a common early response to learning that they had cancer.

In addition to universality, the meetings have offered a number of other therapeutic benefits. For newly diagnosed teens, contact with a teenager who has successfully survived the same or a similar disease and treatment regimen instills hope and optimism. Sharing solutions to common problems enhances self-esteem in several ways. Those teenagers who have mastered problems and can share their solutions feel they have been of help to others and hence feel worthwhile. Those teenagers who are listening to solutions to problems now have a new means to master difficult situations and feel more self-confident. Feeling a sense of group membership, so important to teenagers, is another benefit of attending group meetings.

Group Effectiveness. To obtain feedback from the teenagers about the group's effectiveness, a research assistant recently conducted a phone survey and talked with twelve teenagers, seven females and five males, being treated by our hematology team. Of these twelve, ten had attended one or more group meetings and two had attended none. The reasons given for never attending were similar to those given for dropping out—transportation problems, too many other conflicting activities, and a negative response to being reminded of their illness by associating with other teenagers with cancer. One teenager said she saw the group as an extension of the hospital, from which she wanted to get away.

Having fun at the activity-oriented meetings was frequently cited as a benefit. The other major benefit was related to universality. Such responses as "Knowing you're not alone,"

"Feeling accepted, whether you're bald or not feeling well," "Sensing that people know how you feel," and "Talking with others in the same situation" were representative responses. All of these responses attest to the significance of meaningful peer relationships to teenagers. Suggestions for improving the group included finding ways to involve more teenagers, especially newly diagnosed ones, meeting more frequently, and having more activities.

The following examples illustrate how teenagers have benefited from participating in our group. Charles is a fourteen-year-old with lymphoma, which had recurred several times. He was refusing to go back to school because his hair was falling out, and he preferred to wear a wig plus a hat to ensure that the wig would not fall off. A school rule prohibited wearing hats, and the principal was reluctant to change the rule for one pupil. What Charles feared the most was ridicule from his peers. The topic of the first group meeting he attended was how to deal with peers' teasing about baldness and the feeling of different-ness that was exacerbated by having no hair. Various group members shared their experiences. One female explained that she had even had her wig pulled off in school and managed to cope with it by directly confronting the boys who were teasing her with information about what caused her baldness. This was a valuable discussion for Charles. But perhaps even more beneficial was the next meeting, held at the bowling alley, where he instantly became the group hero by bowling higher than everyone else by at least a hundred points. To feel accepted and valued by a group of peers was of immeasurable benefit to Charles, giving him a sense of confidence that helped him decide to return to school.

The group serves different purposes for different teenagers; in part, this depends on how they have chosen to cope with their cancer. For example, two of the teenage girls who began the group have been in continuous remission since their diagnoses. Of the two, only one remains a group member, and she is now president of the group. This teenager has chosen to lecture on her experiences with the diagnosis and treatment of her leukemia; her audiences have included classmates and American Cancer Society delegates. Although her cancer no longer actively interferes with her daily life, she has chosen to continue these activities. This is in direct contrast to the other teenager, who dropped out of the group, after attending meetings regularly for the first year of her illness. She is very involved in her school and in extracurricular activities with peers. She feels that her cancer is cured and that coming to the group meetings is a reminder of a problem in her past, which she would like to put permanently behind her. The group meetings were valuable for her only when her cancer was first diagnosed and treated. The first teenager makes more use of learning and teaching about her disease as a way of coping with her cancer, whereas the second one's chief coping mechanism is denial. Both of these teenagers are well adjusted, both academically and socially.

The relationship between two of the male group members helped make one of the most stressful experiences of their treatment more comfortable. Testicular biopsies are routinely conducted on male leukemia patients before they are taken off chemotherapy. For teenage boys, the anxiety and fantasies concerning this procedure are prominent. These two boys were able to schedule their testicular biopsies on the same day, and they spent their preoperative time together, telling jokes and giving one another support at a time when only someone facing the same experience could really understand how they felt. This clearly illustrates the usefulness of relationships between teenage cancer patients, which goes beyond the benefits derived during group meetings.

Difficulties and Proposed Solutions. We have encountered several difficulties during the three and a half years of our teenage group's existence. One frustration, especially for the teenagers, has been the poor attendance at the meetings. Although we send out invitations to approximately sixty-five teenagers, rarely do more than five or six teenagers attend. A problem for some teenagers is the distance they live from Nashville; some have trips of two hours each way. With all of the clinic visits they must make, it is costly and inconvenient to make an extra trip for our meetings. We have scheduled several meetings during regular clinic visits, but since we have no meeting room close to the clinic, such scheduling is difficult given all the other necessary clinic procedures. The teenagers themselves have offered to decorate and furnish a room near the clinic, where they could share space and time with other teens both on their own time as well as during our regular group meetings.

Another major difficulty has been the role and agenda of the group leaders. As a psychologist and psychotherapist, I had an idea about how the group meetings should be structured to best accomplish our stated goal of providing an opportunity for teenagers with cancer to serve as supports and resources for one another. I assumed that an ongoing discussion of common problems and solutions would be the most appropriate technique and would also employ my clinical skills. The teenagers themselves were not as enthusiastic about discussing common concerns and were clearly more interested in having fun. Leaders and teenagers together must resolve these different goals and determine who (that is, the leaders or the teenagers) should take responsibility for organizing and structuring the group meetings. Ultimately, since it is the teenagers' group, I believe that the teenagers' goals should be the top priority.

One final difficulty that we have encountered is that our group meetings tend to attract teenagers who are in their first remission and are far enough into their treatment to be feeling well. Our activity orientation may discourage newly diagnosed teenagers, who are often feeling weak and tired, from attending our meetings. We have thought of establishing two different types of teenage cancer groups. One would be a continuation of what we have now, with a recreational and project orientation and meeting every six weeks. A second group would be more time limited with the meetings held one to two weeks apart. This group would be designed for newly diagnosed teenagers, and the content would be more didactic and focused. These meetings would be held at a time and place convenient for teenagers who are in the hospital as well as recently diagnosed outpatients.

Reflections of a Group Leader. As a consultant to the hematology-oncology team, I have been asked to work primarily with patients, parents, and siblings who are having extreme difficulty coping with patients' illnesses and treatment. Working with the teenagers' group has given me the opportunity to become acquainted with children who are adjusting well to their illness. This allows me to engage in preventive work, warding off the emotional problems that can result from the diagnosis of a life-threatening illness. More specifically, one necessary part of adjusting to a diagnosis of cancer is to express the accompanying inevitable feelings of anger, frustration, and despair. Our group meetings as well as informal contacts between group members encourage such expression. As a psychologist, my understanding of developmental issues facing adolescents and my clinical skills were helpful in working with the teenagers' group. My lack of medical training became an issue only when the teenagers had questions about their illness and treatment. Providing a nurse-clinician as a coleader who had this information and who also knew all of the teenagers has worked well for our group meetings.

Working with teenagers who have cancer can be emotionally draining, especially when a teenager responds poorly to treatment or dies. Loss is a common experience that one shares with these teenagers: loss of health, loss of hair, loss of limbs, and sometimes loss of life. Despite the sadness and anger one feels about this seemingly unjustified suffering, there is nothing as inspiring as seeing firsthand what incredible strength these teenagers have. Witnessing their abilities to face adversity with optimism and to share with and support one another has been an invaluable experience for me, both personally and professionally. I have often found that a minor intervention on my part, such as calling a school principal on behalf of a teenager who needs special consideration, can significantly reduce the stress involved in that teenager's effort to adjust to his or her illness.

In Chapter One, Roback referred to the roles and functions of group leaders. My coleader and I serve in several of these capacities in our teenagers' group. As catalysts and providers of emotional stimulation, we encourage group members to participate in discussions by sharing their experiences and feelings. We accomplish this by asking questions and introducing topics that we know are relevant for particular teenagers. We express support for the stresses associated with the teenagers' illness and show warmth and caring for each group member. We are rarely asked to give information, but when we are (for example, about a teenager who has died), we try to do so honestly and directly. We try to create an atmosphere in which teenagers feel comfortable bringing up anxiety-laden issues. Since we both know most group members, we can facilitate discussions by eliciting from group members helpful suggestions in response to other members' problems. We positively reinforce members' contributions to group discussions, especially when the teenager is disclosing a painful or difficult experience. We openly acknowledge our philosophy that talking about illness-related worries and concerns is essential to adjusting adequately. The group leaders still perform the executive functions of setting rules about when and where the group will meet and how each meeting will be organized, although we had hoped that by having officers the teenagers themselves would carry out more of these functions.

Summary and Conclusions

A group for teenagers with cancer can help them accomplish each of the major developmental tasks that such patients face. With regard to the need to develop autonomy and an ego identity, the group participation gives teenagers a sense of movement away from parents by providing an opportunity to work on feelings related to their illness with persons outside of their families. As the teenagers learn solutions to common problems from one another, they begin to feel a greater sense of control over their lives and hence feel less dependent on adults in their environment. The closeness achieved with peers in such group discussions combats feelings of differentness and isolation. Self-esteem is enhanced, and this confidence can be used in improving relationships with well peers. Talking about what is ahead and seeing other teens with cancer set and achieve educational and vocational goals for themselves keeps the teenagers future oriented.

The group meetings also serve to support adaptive coping mechanisms of teenagers with cancer. We support adaptive denial of the life-threatening nature of the disease to the extent that the teenagers discuss primarily aspects of living with, rather than dying from, their cancer. The activity orientation of our group encourages as normal a teenage existence as possible. The planning of projects and activities to help make the cancer experience less stressful for other teenagers gives group members a sense that they are exerting greater control over their lives.

It is also clear that our group meetings do not directly reach all teenagers with cancer who are treated at the hospital. The meetings seem most useful to newly diagnosed teenagers and teenagers whose diseases have a relatively smooth course. Perhaps teenagers who are doing poorly medically (with the cancer recurring, with serious infections, or in the terminal stages of their illness) are not suited for group interventions. On the other hand, teenagers at significantly different points in their illnesses may need different types of group meetings. Many variations of group work could be tried with teenagers with cancer, because it is clear that, for many, group interventions make a significant difference in their adjustment. If a relatively simple group intervention such as the one described in this chapter can make the experience of cancer during adolescence any less stressful, it is well worth the efforts of health care professionals to set up such programs.

References

Berman, S. J. "Adolescent Coping with Cancer: The Issue of Control." Paper presented at the 88th annual meeting of the American Psychological Association, Montreal, September 1980.

Cunningham, J., Strassberg, D., and Roback, H. "Group Psychotherapy for Medical Patients." *Comprehensive Psychiatry,* 1978, *19* (1), 135-140.

Erikson, E. H. *Identity: Youth and Crisis.* New York: Norton, 1968.

Gardner, G. G. "Adolescents with Cancer: Current Issues and a

Proposal." *Journal of Pediatric Psychology*, 1977, *2* (3), 132-134.

Geist, R. A. "Onset of Chronic Illness in Children and Adolescents: Psychotherapeutic and Consultative Intervention." *American Journal of Orthopsychiatry*, 1979, *49* (1), 4-23.

Heffron, W. A. "Group Therapy Sessions as Part of Treatment of Children with Cancer." In C. Pochedly (Ed.), *Clinical Management of Cancer in Children.* Acton, Mass.: Publishing Sciences Group, 1975.

Kagen-Goodheart, L. "Reentry: Living with Childhood Cancer." *American Journal of Orthopsychiatry*, 1977, *47* (4), 651-658.

Karon, M. "The Physician and the Adolescent with Cancer." *Pediatric Clinics of North America*, 1973, *20* (4), 965-973.

Kellerman, J., and Katz, E. R. "The Adolescent with Cancer: Theoretical, Clinical and Research Issues." *Journal of Pediatric Psychology*, 1977, *2* (3), 127-131.

Koocher, G. P., and O'Malley, J. E. *The Damocles Syndrome: Psychosocial Consequences of Surviving Childhood Cancer.* New York: McGraw-Hill, 1981.

Lazarus, R. S. "The Costs and Benefits of Denial." In J. J. Spinetta and P. Deasy-Spinetta (Eds.), *Living with Childhood Cancer.* St. Louis, Mo.: Mosby, 1981.

Little, S. "Psychology of Physical Illness in Adolescents." *Pediatric Clinics of North America*, 1960, *7* (1), 85-96.

Marten, G. W. "Psychological Effects of Cancer in the Adolescent: Clinical Management and Challenge for Research." In J. L. Schulman and M. J. Kupst (Eds.), *The Child with Cancer: Clinical Approaches to Psychosocial Care.* Springfield, Ill.: Thomas, 1980.

Meeks, J. E. *The Fragile Alliance.* Baltimore, Md.: Williams & Wilkins, 1971.

Moore, D., Holton, C., and Marten, G. "Psychologic Problems in the Management of Adolescents with Malignancy." *Clinical Pediatrics*, 1969, *8*, 464-473.

Nir, Y., and Maslin, B. "Psychological Adjustment of Children with Cancer." In J. G. Goldberg (Ed.), *Psychotherapeutic Treatment of Cancer Patients.* New York: Tree Press, 1981.

312 Group Treatments for Specific Medical Problems

Plumb, M. M., and Holland, J. "Cancer in Adolescents: The Symptom Is the Thing." In B. Schoenberg and others (Eds.), *Anticipatory Grief.* New York: Columbia University Press, 1974.

Sachs, B. "Group Therapy." In J. Kellerman (Ed.), *Psychological Aspects of Childhood Cancer.* Springfield, Ill.: Thomas, 1980.

Schowalter, J. E. "Psychological Reactions to Physical Illness and Hospitalization in Adolescence: A Survey." *Journal of the American Academy of Child Psychiatry,* 1977, *16,* 500-516.

Spinetta, J. J. "Behavioral and Psychological Research in Childhood Cancer: An Overview." *Cancer,* 1982, *50* (9), 1939-1943.

Thomas, J. "Patient Groups for Children Who Have Cancer." In J. L. Schulman and M. J. Kupst (Eds.), *The Child with Cancer: Clinical Approaches to Psychosocial Care.* Springfield, Ill.: Thomas, 1980.

Zeltzer, L. K. "The Adolescent with Cancer." In J. Kellerman (Ed.), *Psychological Aspects of Childhood Cancer.* Springfield, Ill.: Thomas, 1980.

12

12

Stephen B. Shanfield, M.D.
Daniel M. McDonnell, M.S.W

田 田 田 田 田 田 田 田 田 田 田 田 田

Terminal Illnesses

This chapter describes a group therapy experience with dying patients who were hospitalized in the inpatient unit of a hospice.

The Hospice Concept

The inpatient unit of a hospice is a specialized hospital for care of the terminally ill (Shanfield and Kettel, 1980). The hospice itself is a relatively recent and rapidly growing health care system for the dying and their families (Saunders, 1978). Most of the hospice patients have end-stage cancer, although some have progressive neurological diseases such as amytrophic lateral sclerosis. Both these diseases are predictable and have a "death trajectory" that can be noted with some precision (Glaser and Strauss, 1965). The focus of care is palliation rather than cure. The hospice staff, patients, and families all share in the vision of humane care of the terminally ill. This vision is the driving force behind the hospice care delivery system.

Description of Hillhaven Hospice and Its Patients

The group experience took place at Hillhaven Hospice (presently St. Mary's Hospice) in Tucson, Arizona, which opened in April 1974. This was the first free-standing hospice with an

313

inpatient unit, and it operated under the guidelines of nursing home licensure. The average length of stay was twenty-seven days, and most patients died in the hospice. These patients required a greater degree of skilled nursing care than could be provided in the home. Some were admitted for immediate terminal care, but most had a slower trajectory of death. A few were in the hospice because their families needed respite from the difficult and depleting task of caring for them. About 10 percent were admitted for the control of pain, which often had a depressive component (Shanfield and others, 1979a and 1979b).

The hospice facility had twenty-seven rooms. Since the average number of patients was twenty, most patients were in single rooms. Because of the design of the building, socialization outside of the rooms was difficult. Thus a considerable amount of the interaction between staff and patient, family and patient, and patient and patient took place in the patients' rooms (Koff and Ittelson, 1980). In spite of efforts by the staff and family, some patients experienced a sense of social isolation.

Most of the patients were elderly, in their late sixties, and drawn from the middle to lower middle class. Many had not gone beyond high school. This was a cohort phenomenon, since most lived through the Great Depression and were shaped by that experience. This cohort group does not easily talk about psychological issues and has little experience with mental health professionals. It generally needs to maintain a stance of self-reliance, and those of this cohort in the hospice showed resigned acceptance of hard times.

The relationships of the elderly patients with their often midlife children had changed from earlier years. While family members were not living at home, emotional ties were maintained. For some families, the emotional crisis of the illness accentuated existing family problems or reactivated latent ones. But for most, the illness brought families closer together. Most of the elderly patients had families or other loved ones living nearby. Roles were often reversed, and children were an important source of emotional and financial support. Additionally, the actual physical care in the home was in some cases provided by a child, particularly by daughters for their mothers.

Many of the children became the liaison between the parent and the myriad of medical and social services assisting the ill parent. Some parents felt the increased burden taken on by their children, and these concerns came up in the group. Additionally, family support often determined whether patients participated in the group.

For some patients, the expense of treating the illness depleted lifetime savings. Furthermore, how money was handled in a patient's family often changed as a result of the patient's illness. For instance, if a patient had previously made the major decisions about money, the healthy spouse had to learn how to survive financially. This included learning about finance and coping with the many expenses of the illness. How spouses would manage financially was one of the patients' concerns, and this concern surfaced in the group.

Psychological Impact of Impending Death

The level of integration of the meaning of the disease varied among the patients and had important implications for the group. Most, if not all, knew that their disease was terminal. Those with a rapid onset of the disease and a rapid downhill course had not had much time to face the implications of the disease and had the most intense grief. They had a sense of shock and disbelief about the real and potential losses caused by the disease and had not yet integrated the meaning of these concerns.

For the many patients with a steady downhill course, there was an ongoing adjustment to the disabilities caused by the illness. The initial intensity of dealing with the shock of the illness had passed some time before. Most were dealing with many small but important losses caused by the disabilities of the illness and the depletion of energies. Examples included the inability to watch a complete baseball game on television, to sit through a visit with a child who had come from a distant city, to balance a checkbook, or to sit through a full group session. Patients' psychological resources were involved with the exigencies of living, and most patients were preoccupied simply with surviving. Many accepted the losses, but for some each day was a struggle. Some were resigned, and a few were frightened. The patients experienced a narrowing of interests and gradual psychological withdrawal. Patients usually dealt with questions of death and loss in a piecemeal, often subconscious fashion, so that the corresponding pain was intermittent. For most patients, this stage was the end of a process that had begun months or years before.

Rationale for Group Treatment

A small body of literature discusses group interventions, usually on an outpatient basis, for cancer patients and the terminally ill (Ferlic, Goldman, and Kennedy, 1979; Franzino, Geren, and Meiman, 1976; Spiegel, Bloom, and Yalom, 1981; Spiegel and Yalom, 1978; Wood and others, 1978; Yalom and Greaves, 1977). One report is of structured groups on an acute oncology hospital service (Ferlic, Goldman, and Kennedy, 1979). Most are descriptive, but a few are of controlled studies (Spiegel, Bloom, and Yalom, 1981; Wood and others, 1978). They differ from the present report in that most group members seem to be months away from death and are healthier than the hospice patients. Additionally, these reports seem to describe patients in the earlier stages of their disease and the emotional shock of learning about their illness.

There is agreement on the value of group therapy for cancer patients. The groups are helpful for sharing problems and instilling hope, as well as for ventilating painful feelings (Spiegel, Bloom, and Yalom, 1981). Groups provide a sense of universality since the members have similar circumstances and share common dilemmas (Spiegel, Bloom, and Yalom, 1981). Groups can also provide a sense of cohesiveness and belonging, which can decrease feelings of isolation (Spiegel and Yalom, 1978; Yalom and Greaves, 1977). Members of the group can bolster feelings of self-esteem by helping each other. Through seeing others with the same problems and witnessing their solutions, the group members can be provided with a sense of hope and a spirit of revitalization.

Spiegel, Bloom, and Yalom (1981) note that the group therapist mainly used the techniques of focusing and clarification. There was little confrontation and little "here-and-now" work in dealing with interpersonal conflicts. They note that the focus of the group was "on living in the context of dying" (Spiegel and Yalom, 1978), and that it was difficult for the group to deal with the death of one of its members (Spiegel and Yalom, 1978; Yalom and Greaves, 1977).

The group therapy at Hillhaven Hospice evolved to provide psychological support as well as social stimulation. After the initial period of medical treatment, many patients, although ill and in need of continuing nursing care, were alert and able to interact with the staff. For many, the illness had reached a plateau, and many felt socially isolated and even bored. A few, although weak, were able to move about either in a wheelchair or with the aid of a walker and to visit other patients. Many, of course, were not able to leave their beds. The patients and their families were able to participate in a number of ongoing hospice events, including group therapy. In the context of these other supportive involvements, group participation was an important activity for patients.

Hillhaven Hospice Group Experience

Goals. The goals for the group were manifold. The group was to provide a forum for sharing common problems affecting the hospice patients. These problems involved the illness itself, families, finances, and losses of activities, as well as other real and anticipated difficulties. An important goal of the group was to facilitate the integration of past experiences by providing a forum for reminiscing (Butler, 1975). Another goal for the group was to help the patients establish a sense of connection and to improve socialization and decrease social isolation. Finally, a major goal was to have the patients provide support for each other.

Membership and Membership Issues. The group leader was the hospice social worker. The senior author served as a consultant and occasional coleader. The group ran for two years, over which time about seventy patients were members. Membership in the group varied from two to ten patients. Most sessions had three to five patients, which was about one fifth of the hospice population. Although there was no contract with the patients to attend from week to week, the membership maintained a stable core, with one or two new members entering the group each week. Some of the members were quite ill but continued to attend, particularly if they had established a relationship with other group members. Most patients died before attending more than three or four sessions.

The group met weekly for forty to fifty minutes, which was felt to be a reasonable length of time for these very ill patients. The frequency of the meetings was determined by compromise, since the group competed with a number of other hospice events.

Rounding up the patients for the group took considerable effort; a few hours before the morning meeting time, the group leader would remind the nursing staff and the patients about the group. The nurses would be asked to recruit patients for the group. The participation of the nursing staff was critical, since many of the patients needed the nurses' assistance to attend the group. Some patients were able to walk but required supervision. Others had to be transported in wheelchairs or their hospital beds. The meeting was in a large room that could accommodate beds and wheelchairs.

Some patients could not participate in the group. A serious deterrent for them was moderate to severe depression. Many of these individuals were angry, demoralized, and withdrawn; they were not interested in interacting in a group and usually did not attend. Many of these patients were being treated for their depression with antidepressants, but many came to the hospice too late for effective intervention in their depression.

Patients who were in the very last stages of dying or in significant pain were not asked to participate. Others were not able to attend because they were acutely ill but not close to death. Some were delirious or in a coma for days to weeks before their death and could not attend.

The presence of an organic brain syndrome, however, did

not deter participation in the group. Many of these patients found the closeness established in the group valuable. The other group members were quite patient and helpful with these brain-damaged patients. For instance, one member had brain metastases from a primary carcinoma of the lung and was quite confused. He attended the group regularly, and in spite of his disability, he still exuded great personal charm and warmth. He had been a superintendent of a school district and was an inveterate joiner of organizations. He thought that he was at work and that the group was his executive committee. The other patients were quite supportive of him despite his severe cognitive defect. They would gently correct him when he occasionally made a statement indicating his misconceptions about the group. The group helped orient this patient and bolstered his self-esteem by listening to his concerns and providing a sense of connection. The patient seemed to appreciate this interaction.

Some patients were reluctant to participate in a group because of a lifelong aversion to group interaction—they were loners. The group was not appropriate for these individuals. On the other hand, many individuals were gregarious by nature and easily participated in the group.

Some families kept patients from the group, telling the nursing staff that their family member did not wish to attend. The staff would not pursue such statements too aggressively. These often seemed to be families who had difficulty in dealing with their own grief, and they would often instruct the hospice staff not to talk with patients about issues of illness and dying. The families were told that the staff could not control such interactions but respected the families' preferences.

Some members of the immediate family—often daughters and occasionally sons and a few husbands and wives—would attend the group. They were an important source of support for their family members and for other patients. Participation in the group for the family members, although mostly unspoken, was a way of maintaining intimacy with their loved one.

Leadership Roles and Techniques. The therapists provided a forum for discussing the patients' concerns. The main technique employed by group leaders was clarification, which was used to help group members focus on issues. Loss and grief were not discussed unless the patients raised these issues. Remarks by members of the group prompted many other comments in response.

The patients' defenses were not breached. Individuals in the group were considered ahead of the group. There were few process comments about the group and few interpretive comments. The therapists supported and facilitated the patients' interactions. They would help link the members' comments to those made by others and direct comments to help patients capture important past moments. There was little intrusion into interpersonal problems, patients' situational problems, or patients' longstanding psychological difficulties. Indeed, efforts were made not to uncover psychiatric problems.

Thematic Content. A considerable amount of exchange in the group concerned day-to-day life in the hospice. This included discussions of interactions with the hospice staff and, inevitably, the quality of hospice food and hospice services. The patients voiced concerns about their families, especially difficulties such as divorce, separation, or financial setbacks. Additionally, the members discussed past and future home visits and other family events, such as weddings and births.

The patients' place in the life cycle provided a guide to some of the major concerns that surfaced in the group (Erikson, 1968). An important aspect of this stage is a review of past accomplishments and failures (Greenspan and Pollock, 1981). The psychological impact of the illness and impending death intersected with these developmental themes, and the illness commonly accelerated the life review. Many of the concerns revolved around despair over perceived failures, unresolved aspects of past actions, or ambivalence about past or present important relationships. Many, of course, felt good about the course their lives had taken. This process of review was aided by active listening.

Because of various physical problems, some members were not able to discuss issues coherently and logically. The group members were unusually tolerant of these patients, who on occasion went off on tangents or responded inappropriately to issues raised in the group. For instance, a ninety-five-year-old former railroad worker who was hard of hearing responded to another patient who yelled at him, "Do you want some candy?" with "I am" over and over. One of the other group members thought that the patient had interpreted the question to be "Are you a gandy dancer?" (a gandy dancer is a laborer on a railway section gang). This interpretation gave meaning to the patient's statement and went beyond his immediate identity as a deaf old man lying in bed. His fellow group members were able to maintain a sense of connection with the patient and continued to be supportive.

There was little philosophical discussion about death and loss, which were acknowledged but rarely discussed at length. The patients were too ill and preoccupied with maintaining their precarious physical state. Most of the patients had passed the most emotional stage of dealing with their death.

Discussions of death and loss were usually quite brief, even with the leaders' efforts to press for such discussions. There was a sense that the patients were fearful when they dealt with these topics, although they were mentioned regularly. For instance, one individual who attended the group for a number of sessions would open the group with the sardonic statement "I wonder who's going to be next." A few moments of silence followed, and then the group changed the topic without directly responding to what had been said.

Sometimes the patients would inquire about a particular patient who died. On one occasion, a patient asked the therapist what the last moments were like for a particular group member who had died. The group leader noted that the patient had had labored breathing for a few hours and then stopped breathing. The leader asked the patients if they had wondered how death would be for them. The patients nodded; when pushed for an answer, they said they did not know how it would be and went on to another topic. With time the leaders became comfortable in accepting the patients' lead in dealing with these issues.

Grief and loss colored much of the interaction in the group and were implicit in the discussions of family, friends, and past experiences. The patients were weak, sick, dependent, and seemingly helpless, thus creating a sense of psychological fragility in the group. This atmosphere added a special poignancy to the group interaction. Many of the patients' comments could be seen as efforts to anticipate losses. For instance, one patient with a brain tumor would discuss the Indianapolis 500 race. His preoccupation with this event became clear when it was learned that he grew up and lived near the Indianapolis Speedway. His discussion was a form of grieving for what he would not see or hear again. The leader acknowledged that the patient missed his home town and the race.

Grief was implicit in discussions about disability, in which the prominent affect was sadness about lost powers. Some patients would talk about their illness and its progress and inquire about others in the group. The group tended to recognize the many losses brought about by old age and the disease itself. One elderly man who had been an ironworker many years before held up his large, rough, and still calloused hands. He noted that his hands had been his living and that he had climbed and worked on many tall buildings. This was a declaration of his past identity. It was also an effort to come to terms with this lost identity and to establish his present place in the world. Additionally, it established his place in and connection with the group.

Not all discussions in the group centered on morbid issues. Often there were discussions of good times, past and present. These seemed to provide validation and support for an inner sense of continuity—of a good life that was well lived and was continuing to be well lived. Some patients would joke about their illness and its circumstances. For instance, on one occasion the room in which the group was held had just been cleaned and had an odor of disinfectant. A patient noted the pungency of the fumes and said that the fumes were killing him. This was seen as a mature way of dealing with the painful aspects of the disability and eventual death (Shanfield, in press; Vaillant, 1977). The joking allowed the group members to share their common dilemmas and to express their predicament without discomfort.

Group Dynamic Factors. Although there was considerable peer interaction in the group, there was little open conflict with other members or open confrontation with the leaders. This was a reflection of their dependence on the leaders as well as on the hospice for their very survival.

On occasion, individual problems and ambivalences were played out in the group. One patient continually kidded another about his religious beliefs. He would say, "You don't believe in that stuff [that is, heaven and God], do you?" Actually, both patients were very concerned about life beyond death, which they were not able to discuss directly in the group. When the patient who had done the kidding died, his roommate noted that he had been praying. This affirmed the surviving patient's sense of faith. These individuals also had considerable difficulty in getting along with each other, and this would occasionally be discussed in the group. These were some of the few occasions when interpersonal difficulties were discussed in the group.

An important function of the group was to regulate the affect associated with loss, grief, and death, as well as to air these concerns (Scheff, 1977). Although the affect was muted, the group provided a context for discussing this affect. In this sense, the group provided a major supportive function. It also provided a forum for expressing and integrating important life experiences. For those who were demoralized, the group was also ameliorative. The interaction bolstered a sense of self-esteem and helped some restore a sense of meaning and purpose to their lives.

Major causes of the low level of intensity of feeling were the patients' degree of illness and lack of energy. Another cause was the mixture of the group. Many of the members of the group were cognitively impaired and unable to deal with the full range of affect.

The group was, at times, a jarring experience for some patients. Some noted that they were surprised at how sick their fellow members were and wondered if they, too, looked ill. The presence of others who were also close to death seemed to establish a special sense of connection. This was manifested by a ready understanding of the issues of death and loss among the members of the group. This is similar to the notion of universality as a curative factor in the group and served to decrease the sense of isolation common in this situation (Yalom, 1975). The identity of the members would be reasserted by membership in the group ("I am not dead if I see and hear you"). There was, however, little catharsis or outpouring of feelings.

Outcome. The group leaders informally assessed satisfaction through self-reports of patients and families. Many patients felt that the group was helpful and continued to attend the group during their weeks at the hospice. The families of the patients were also a part of the outcome of the group, even though they may not have participated directly. Although some family members were upset about the feelings raised by the group discussions, some greatly benefited from interactions with the patients concerning the issues of death and loss. This value of the group to the family members was an unanticipated outcome. Additionally, some family members maintained contact with family members of other group members after their loved ones died.

Difficulties. The interaction of the group was contrary to the therapists' expectations. From their experience with groups in mental health settings, the therapists anticipated a greater degree of interest as well as more intense affect in dealing with psychological problems. Also, from previous experiences, the therapists expected more intense discussions of grief and loss. Indeed, they were surprised by the slow, subdued pace of the hospice group.

The contract with the therapist was different from that for therapy groups in mental health settings. These individuals had not identified themselves as psychiatric patients, in spite of any difficulties they may have had. Many patients came to the group because it was one of the activities that were part of the hospice support network. Since few patients attended the group for more than a few weeks, developing new themes with continuity from week to week was difficult.

The hospice staff members felt that the dying experience was intensely personal and were committed to providing individualized care. They did not see the group as essential, even though they were asked to recruit for the group. Their mission was to help patients die in comfort and with dignity, and since patients sometimes found the group uncomfortable, the nurses found it difficult to pressure patients to attend. Staff resistance took the forms of "not remembering" the group from week to week, "not remembering" who was in the group unless reminded by the group therapist, or not volunteering individuals to participate in the group.

Some family members were also ambivalent about whether their patient-relatives should attend. For instance, one patient with an expressive aphasia began to cry in the group; his wife expressed concern about this and felt he should not return. He did attend one more meeting and died shortly after. In retrospect, it was felt that he had recognized that death was close and was openly grieving.

Other family members were also upset when patients were tearful or were told of the themes of the group, and they wondered whether their family members should continue to attend. Some family members dissuaded patients from attending.

The group leaders could not deal with certain problems. The few hospice patients who had been in the inpatient unit a long time avoided the group because they had lived longer than expected. They were not as ill or as fragile as most other hospice patients, and they interacted mainly with the staff, avoiding interaction with other patients because the death of fellow patients was traumatic. The few long-term patients who did attend came for only one visit. The hospice staff eventually learned that it was best to discharge such patients and place them in either long-term care facilities or their homes.

Personal Reflections

An early problem for the therapists was their own grief over the many losses experienced while working with the dying (Shanfield, 1981). The losses included the actual deaths of patients as well as more subtle losses resulting from identification with patients and family losses. Inevitably, clinic encounters with the dying and bereaved reminded the therapists of old and unresolved losses in their personal and professional lives (Shan-field, 1981). These responses occasionally intruded into the therapeutic transaction, particularly early in the group, and were manifested in a variety of ways. For instance, a variant of the grief response was a seeming lack of empathy for a patient. This numbing of the therapists' feelings could prevent proper responses to a patient's concerns. On occasion, the therapist would withdraw from the patient, and the patient sometimes lost an opportunity to discuss important issues and concerns. Therapists would sometimes feel intensely about a patient and his or her predicament and become preoccupied with how the patient should work out the problems. This would lead to the impulse to overcontrol or to be unnecessarily intrusive. These countertransference responses caused feelings of therapeutic depletion.

The hospice was a new and pioneering effort in the care of the dying, and the therapists had little clinical experience to guide them. The literature on death and dying was generally not helpful in dealing with this phase of dying. Discussions between the therapists helped to air the inevitable difficulties that surfaced. With time, the therapists became clearer about their own responses and were able to empathize with the patients' losses in an unimpeded manner. They learned that the responses to death and loss were complex and multidimensional (Shanfield, 1979), and they became more efficient in dealing with their own feelings about loss so that there was minimal interference with the therapeutic process. Indeed, the therapists' sensitivity to their own response became an important ingredient of the therapeutic transaction, enabling patients' and therapists' losses to be placed in perspective. This allowed the therapists to use their internal responses to alert them to the patients' responses.

Future Directions

Current legislative efforts limit hospitalization for hospice patients and increase reimbursement for the care of the hospice patient in the home (for example, the Hospice Reimbursement Act of 1983). Under these circumstances, inpatient groups for the dying are difficult to sustain because hospitalized hospice patients are too ill to participate and their life expectancy too short. This is borne out by the experience at St. Mary's Hospice. When the Hillhaven Hospice inpatient facility shifted to an acute care hospital and became St. Mary's Hospice, it operated under acute care licensure guidelines. The average length of stay shortened to eleven days, and 65 percent of the patients died at home. Patients admitted for care around the immediate dying period had a length of stay of five days. The number of patient activities was reduced. Additionally, the patients were often only able to participate in one group because they died soon after. Staff energies were focused on rapid evaluation, treatment, and rapid discharge. Few resources were available for developing an ongoing group.

The logistics of convening a group when patients are close to death outside of a hospital setting are formidable. The patients are bedridden or wheelchair bound and are not able to attend many activities outside of their immediate surroundings. Probably groups for those who are close to dying are best held in long-term settings such as nursing homes and convalescent homes. The principles discussed here can easily be applied to such settings.

Further research is needed on the impact of such groups. It is unclear whether groups that are formed earlier in the disease course can or should be sustained on a long-term basis. Whether such ongoing groups that include actively dying patients can remain viable and sustain the emotional intensity generated by repeated deaths is an unanswered question. The experience at Hillhaven indicates that patients who are not close to death avoid interacting with those patients who are. Certainly the logistics of maintaining a group until death is difficult outside of a closed setting.

Final Comments

Groups for the dying are a specialized treatment modality. They provide an opportunity for dying patients to maintain a sense of connection to and continuity with the larger world—

as well as to achieve a sense of renewal. The therapeutic posture in such groups is supportive, nonintrusive, individually oriented, and facilitative of patients expressing their concerns. Under these circumstances, groups can be an important part of the life of the hospice patient, but the goals for these groups are limited. The authors feel that the traditional therapeutic orientation of helping patients uncover and work through psychological problems is inappropriate for patients close to death and is *not* recommended. Aggressively pushing patients to deal openly with and work through the painful aspects of separation, as a goal of therapy, serves no useful end. Patients can experience such a group as intrusive and as perhaps destructive; for instance, conflicts may arise that cannot be resolved. Furthermore, such a group has the potential of disrupting the relationship of the hospice with the patient, the family, and others involved with the patient, including the family physician.

How important are such groups and under what circumstances should they be organized? Certainly therapeutic groups for the dying in the absence of other activities are not enough. Groups for individuals at the end of their lives should be part of a balanced program that provides social stimulation and support, decreases isolation, and facilitates interaction of the patient with his or her family—activities that all can be quite important. Indeed, priority should be given to sustaining the interaction of patients with their families and friends. In some cases, these other activities may be all that are possible since the patients are so ill and their lives so short. In other cases, therapeutic groups are possible since the patients are generally not as ill and they are more a part of the ongoing social system; but even here such groups should take place within a larger program for patients. All patients but the extremely ill should be included.

References

Butler, R. N. *Why Survive: Growing Old in America.* New York: Harper and Row, 1975.
Erikson, E. H. *Identity, Youth, and Crises.* New York: Norton, 1968.

Ferlic, M., Goldman, A., and Kennedy, B. J. "Group Counseling in Adult Patients with Advanced Cancer." *Cancer,* 1979, *43,* 760-766.

Franzino, M. A., Geren, J. T., and Meiman, G. L. "Group Discussion Among the Terminally Ill." *International Journal of Group Psychotherapy,* 1976, *26,* 43-48.

Glaser, B. G., and Strauss, A. L. *Awareness of Dying.* Chicago: Aldine, 1965.

Greenspan, S. I., and Pollock, G. H. (Eds.). *The Course of Life.* Vol. 3: *Adulthood and the Aging Process.* Washington, D.C.: U.S. Department of Health and Human Services, 1981.

Koff, T. H., and Ittelson, W. "A Post-Occupancy Evaluation of St. Mary's Hospice." Tempe: Department of Business and Public Administration, University of Arizona, 1980. (Mimeograph.)

Saunders, C. M. (Ed.). *The Management of Terminal Disease.* Chicago: Year Book Medical Publishers, 1978.

Scheff, T. J. "The Distancing of Emotion in Ritual." *Current Anthropology,* 1977, *18,* 483-505.

Shanfield, S. B. "Social Determinants of the Death Process." *Arizona Medicine,* 1979, *36,* 602-603.

Shanfield, S. B. "Mourning of the Health Care Professional: An Important Element in Education About Death and Loss." *Death Education,* 1981, *4,* 385-395.

Shanfield, S. B. "Some Observations of a Hospice Psychiatrist." *Hillside Journal of Psychiatry,* in press.

Shanfield, S. B., and Kettel, L. "Hospice Care." *Arizona Medicine,* 1980, *37,* 314-315.

Shanfield, S. B., and others. "Clinical Aspects of Pain Part I." *Arizona Medicine,* 1979a, *36,* 507-509.

Shanfield, S. B., and others. "Clinical Aspects of Pain Part II." *Arizona Medicine,* 1979b, *36,* 585-586.

Spiegel, D., Bloom, R., and Yalom, I. "Group Support for Patients with Metastatic Cancer." *Archives of General Psychiatry,* 1981, *38,* 527-533.

Spiegel, D., and Yalom, I. D. "A Support Group for Dying Patients." *International Journal of Group Psychotherapy,* 1978, *28,* 233-245.

Vaillant, G. E. *Adaptation to Life*. Boston: Little, Brown, 1977.

Wood, P. E., and others. "Group Counseling for Cancer Patients in a Community Hospital." *Psychosomatics*, 1978, *19*, 557-561.

Yalom, I. D. *The Theory and Practice of Group Psychotherapy*. New York: Basic Books, 1975.

Yalom, I. D., and Greaves, C. "Group Therapy with the Terminally Ill." *American Journal of Psychiatry*, 1977, *134*, 396-400.

13

Marcia Pavlou, Ph.D.

⊞ ⊞ ⊞ ⊞ ⊞ ⊞ ⊞ ⊞ ⊞ ⊞ ⊞ ⊞ ⊞

Multiple Sclerosis

Clinical experience suggests that the psychological toll of multiple sclerosis (MS) derives from the medical aspects of the particular condition. The newly diagnosed person first learns that while the life span is essentially normal, very little about the future disease course or symptomatology can be predicted. Life will be lived with the uncertainty of whether the MS will run a very mild course with nonvisible symptoms or progress to severe disability that results in confinement to a wheelchair or bed. Any point along this broad spectrum is equally likely.

Uncertainty defines life with MS. The MS person discovers that the particular symptoms may vary, depending on where in the central nervous system the nerve tissue suffers damage to its ability to conduct nerve impulses. Most commonly, people experience numbness and paresthesia, disturbance to vision, fatigue, and problems with gait, coordination, bladder control, and sexual functioning. Symptoms change over both short and longer periods, and they are often vague and difficult to discriminate from those due to more acute problems and stress. Signals from the body are no longer reliable or interpretable.

The MS person further learns that while specific symptoms may be treated with varying degrees of effectiveness, the capacity to limit and control the basic disease process is very limited. Frustration may begin early when, in the absence of a clear diagnostic test, the person may be told that the problem is anything from a possible brain tumor to hysterical anxiety. Because symptoms in different parts of the body bear no apparent connection, the patient finds it difficult initially to know which kind of specialist to consult. Disappointment in the medical system may increase when, after a diagnostic period that can last for years, the person is told repeatedly, "We don't know, there's not a lot we can do." Research cannot tell the person how or why the MS came to be, and emotionally significant private theories about etiology move in to fill the void. "I got MS because I worked too hard"; "My mother got MS because I was a difficult child"; "I got MS because of my hidden guilt"; "I got MS because of my pregnancy." There is no treatment to provide any hope, nor are there data to support or discount the plethora of fad treatments—such as special diets, snake venom, and special surgeries (Aronson and others, 1982; Counte, Pavlou, and Hartings, 1978)—which seem to generate spontaneously from the pool of wishes for a positive future.

Without prognostic guideposts, the MS person may become obsessive and even hypochondriacal in the constant monitoring of the body for signs of change (Pavlou and Stefoski, in press). Practically, the MS person has difficulty knowing whether to move from a two-story to a one-story house, whether to have another child, whether to prepare for a less physically demanding career, or, more fundamentally, whether it will be possible to remain self-sufficient. With the onset usually occurring in early adulthood, MS strikes at a time when careers, families, and friendships are just getting started and the inability to plan is a particular hindrance.

Stress of and Adaptation to MS

Psychological research confirms that MS is a significant stressor. Shontz (1956) proposed that the ambiguity of the disease creates a basic insecurity, a chronic anxiety, and a constant threat of despair. Chodoff (1959) and Ambrose (1955) describe core feelings of helplessness and doom. Depression is a common reaction to undesirable life events (Silver and Wortman, 1980), and a number of authors have noted a greater incidence of depressive affect in MS people than in normals; also, Canter (1951) reported a mild elevation on the MMPI Depression scale, at a level suggesting apathy and lack of hope rather than true clinical depression. Gilberstadt and Farkas (1961), Shontz (1955), and Wender and Dominik (1972) noted similar though lower scores in groups of long-term MS patients, and they postulated a greater acceptance as experience with the condition increased. Schmidt (1943) reported a reactive depression, though Schwartz and Pierron (1972) found no greater incidence of suicide in MS people. Shontz (1956) and Bolding (1960) observed greater body anxiety in MS populations, and Johnson and Pavlou (1981) reported that MS people endorsed negative statements about their bodies within the context of otherwise intact self-images.

Cognizant of the broader cost of MS, other observers looked at the disease in a family context. In a survey of the social needs of forty-seven nonhospitalized MS patients, Braham and others (1975) noted child behavior problems, poor parent-child relations, and a lack of proper physical care for children in eighteen of twenty families with children under eighteen years of age. Also observed were marital problems in thirty-two of forty-four couples and a problem with spouse reactions to the illness in an equal number.

In a study of children of MS parents, Arnaud (1959) noted that these children demonstrated more anxiety about body function, greater dependency longings, and a higher incidence of a pattern of false maturity (pseudoindependence). However, this author does confirm essentially normal development in the children. Comparing a group of seventy-five adolescent children from MS families with twenty-three controls from non-MS families, Pavlou and Johnson (1981) reported that the children from MS families scored as a group within normal ranges on standard personality tests. However, these young people expressed a unique set of life issues reflecting the MS in the family, including greater worry about family and relatively less concern about matters related to the definition of themselves.

Despite the stress of the disease, its uncertainty and

chronicity also allow for hope. Even the absence of effective medical treatment, while not positive in any way, does promote the search for better ways of living with the condition. Research suggests that the pursuit of improved adaptation is realistic. Matson and Brooks (1977) noted that self-image is improved with greater experience with the illness, and Harrower and Kraus (1951) observed periods in the disease when emotional growth seemed to be maximized. While some authors feel that the ability to recover completely from a chronic disease is overestimated (Silver and Wortman, 1980), rehabilitation psychologists assert that good adaptation to a disability is the norm. These researchers have consistently reported no important correlation between personal distress and the level of disability (Shontz, 1977) and have asserted that good adaptation is possible at nearly any level of medical problem.

Although a comprehensive review of the study of coping is beyond the purview of this chapter, several generalizations concerning problems and findings in the area may help to relate the stresses of MS with the goals of group work. Some investigators have confirmed that general personality stability is a prerequisite and a good predictor of adjustment to disability (Linkowski and Dunn, 1974; Matson and Brooks, 1977; Starr and Heiserman, 1977). Others have asserted that social support provides a buffer against life stress (Cobb, 1976) and that the person who is well integrated into the community or family is likely to adapt more easily to chronic disease. As one author concluded, "Informal support systems (family members, friends, and neighbors) are probably *the* critical way that people in the new generation have adapted to deal with their life problems" (Veroff, Douvan, and Kulka, 1981, p. 19).

In their review, Silver and Wortman (1980) suggest that social support provides a climate in which self-identity changes can occur and an environment that reinforces positive behavior. Others (Pavlou, Counte, and Davis, 1982) postulate that supportive networks help to present and reward useful perceptions of disease. Rehabilitation psychologists emphasize that adaptive success reflects the cognitive statements the person makes about the disease (Shontz, 1975). Adaptation is a learned set of cognitive skills and attitudes. As elaborated in materials circulated to MS patients, people respond to MS in accordance with their interpretation of its personal meaning (Davis, Pavlou, and Hartings, 1977). One person may view MS as a totally disabling condition, while another will decide it is a misfortune creating manageable limitations. Observers point out that cognitive appraisal can change with input from relevant sources (Lazarus, Averill, and Opton, 1974) and presumably from a group of valued peers.

The interaction of MS-related stress with individual adaptive resources creates a characteristic psychological profile for the population of MS people seen in the health care setting. In the author's experience, three groups warrant consideration from a psychological perspective. First, the substantial majority experience increased general stress but no diagnosable psychopathology or inability to function. Patients in this majority acknowledge MS as a continuing and unwelcome mental companion and readily talk about times when the disease consumes most or all of their thoughts. Though investigators in the past sought to identify common responses to the illness, for example, greater dependency or repressed anger (Grinker, Ham, and Robless, 1950; Harrower, 1950), clinical observations suggest that the preillness personality determines response patterns along the total range of psychological possibility. Times of difficulty may be accompanied by unmanageable worry and preoccupation with MS, feelings of hopelessness or great sadness, anger with family and friends, a temptation to abuse alcohol, or psychogenic pain responses.

A second, smaller group experiences acute and more debilitating psychological crises. Patients may appear clinically depressed or hypochondriacal, or they may be unable to manage usual activities. Adaptational crises often occur at times of medical change—the initial diagnosis, the first time there are residual symptoms after a remission, a time when a cane or a wheelchair becomes necessary, the first experience of socially debilitating bladder incontinence, the experience of more than one serious exacerbation in a short period of time, or the occasion when a particular medication stops working. These crises may also occur at periods of social change—the loss of a job, a divorce, or the departure from the home of a supportive adolescent child. Many people, of course, do not experience severe adaptive crises even in the presence of such disease changes and life problems.

Finally, a small minority of MS patients always appear in crisis, are always seriously depressed, or make nearly no adaptive progress over long periods. Preexisting psychopathology is usually observed, though an unusually difficult medical course may have similar consequences. For example, the person with a relentless and rapid downhill course may develop chronic adaptive problems, as may the person with profound disability in speech or other personally critical areas.

Rationale for Group Treatment

The MS group program targeted the majority of people mentioned above who are experiencing disease-related stress but generally have adequate coping resources and personal stability (Pavlou and others, 1979a). Philosophically, we favored a concept that respected the adjustment difficulties of psychiatrically normal individuals under unusual long-term stress (Hartings, Pavlou, and Davis, 1976). As a group, MS people welcomed attention to their adaptive needs, but they also appreciated the understanding of problems as being nonpathological. They demanded the recognition of the hope that their basic psychological health allows.

The group plan addressed the stress factors described earlier and sought to augment the experiences currently believed to be useful in the adaptation process. The groups were designed to build social support both by providing a network of MS people and by assisting in the resolution of issues interfering with relationships outside the group. The groups provided an atmosphere of warmth and general calm in which MS could be discussed in a matter-of-fact way among people who knew about the disease, understood its problems, and gradually came to care. The groups were designed to provide a reference group experience (Adams and Lindemann, 1974) or a setting in which people could acquire some of the cognitive or attitudinal skills necessary to live their lives in a new and different way.

People grow up with expectations and models for how to be husbands or wives, parents, friends, and workers, but few people acquire any experiences that help them form an internal image of having a successful life with a disability. The group could provide a spectrum of attitudes and behaviors from which the person might choose those useful to him. While group leaders believed that the present state of knowledge was not sufficient for them to offer a formula on how to live well with MS, they did promote some general concepts. There was some demand that people consider their ability to control their interpretations of the illness, even though the physical disease process itself could not be altered to any major extent. While there was the usual treatment latitude in facilitating the exploration of emotional pain, there was some expectation that the group experience would be positive and optimistic overall. Unlike approaches for patients with terminal illnesses, which promote emotional investment in immediate experiences, the MS groups in general favored the "pursuit of hope" (Ottenburg, 1978) or the ability to look ahead with strength despite an unpredictable life course.

The MS Group Experience

While the success of the group program reflected the appropriateness of this format for the MS population, it was additionally supported by several features of the clinical setting that housed it. First, the group program was presented as one facet of an integrated health care plan involving the primary medical care providers. Part of an MS center and a large urban medical center complex, the group programs were introduced within the context of treatment efforts addressing the patient's primary concern—his physical health. The groups drew upon the very large patient pool that continuously filtered into the MS center. The center physicians encouraged group enrollment, and the neurologist's participation in selected group meetings reinforced his support for group involvement.

Second, people entered the group with considerable individual preparation and generally with some experience with the psychologist who led the group. For most, the group was introduced at the first MS center appointment during the psychology intake interview, which was a routine part of the initial medical evaluation process. During this interview, the psychologist explores the expectations for the medical appointment, the quality of experience with the physician, current questions and issues regarding MS, and adaptive style. Had she learned about MS or was she trying not to think about it? Had she told people about the disease? What was her style for dealing with other setbacks and misfortunes? What was her greatest concern at this point?

If the psychologist believed the group might be useful for the person, she could discuss the potential utility of the experience within the context of relevant issues introduced in the intake interview. The invitation to the group was focused and personal. The interviewer could be sensitive to the person for whom the groups were not suited and could avoid losing credibility by unempathically recommending group involvement. The psychologist could explain what to expect from the group—that the group was a place to learn about MS and about new ways to live with the condition, that it was designed for psychologically normal people under stress, and that it provided opportunities to give as well as to learn. Positive experience with the psychologist in the individual interview helped to bridge the fears of coming to the dimly understood new experience—the first meeting.

The functioning of the groups was further enhanced by the selection process, which preceded the first meeting. An effort was made to bring a patient into the right group at a point in the adaptive process when the patient would be particularly receptive. Some were not invited to join a group, at least not during the intake interview. Such persons included the person who was very new to the disease and needed time to settle in before being bombarded with the new identity of an MS patient, the person so overwhelmed that he could not share group time, the very private person for whom sharing in general provoked great anxiety, and the rare individual with a severe organic mental problem interfering with comprehension and communication. Some candidates were interested in addressing adaptive problems but were frightened by the possibility of meeting people whose symptoms were worse than their own. They were told that while there was no procedure for matching people according to the state of the disease, the groups tended to attract people with mild or moderate degrees of MS. The psychologist imposed no pressure on such people to join the group, seeking rather to protect potential members by letting them opt out at this point or in early meetings. Often the acknowledgment by the interviewer of the personal meaning of meeting people with more advanced disease helped to alleviate fear.

The New Group

The people who entered the group did so with a blend of rational goals and personal agendas and with a mixture of hope and apprehension. They enthusiastically endorsed the stated goal of the first meeting—to learn about MS. There were always a variety of questions. What is new in research? What about the latest treatment written up in the popular press? Are there any signs or symptoms that can predict the future of the disease? Should I have physical therapy? Would it help to move to a different climate? Is there a greater incidence of MS in children of MS people? They asked for information, certainly important in the adaptive effort (Moos and Tsu, 1977), but, more fundamentally, they asked for hope and reassurance. Sometimes they asked for information when they did not know what else to ask for or when they wanted the medical team to help somehow. Some people came out of curiosity to meet other people who shared this very special life problem. The first desire may have been just to look and see if anyone else was like them. Others came fired by the discouragement or fear that dominated their recent lives. They might not talk about their concerns for some time, but it became clear that more than mild curiosity motivated some to drive for several hours in bad weather, to take work time, or to find babysitters. Still others came for reasons that even they could not consciously articulate. Could they find a cure here? Perhaps if they could learn to handle their feelings, they could also control the disease. A spouse brought a reluctant MS patient, hoping that the group might somehow pry her loose from the depression that had been crippling the family. An MS patient brought a reluctant spouse, hoping that the group could help him to abandon efforts to seek a cure and to see that her symptoms were legitimate. And they came with apprehension—that they would be disappointed again, that they would be frightened by something they saw or heard, that they would not find hope.

The initial meetings were structured to promote the development of a comfortable and cohesive group and the unfolding of topics of particular significance to the attendees. Labeled as an orientation meeting, the first session provided an introduction to MS, to the group concept, and to the group leaders and members. Participants were offered something concrete and clearly relevant, and they were asked for a minimum of self-disclosure and commitment. Attended by eight to fourteen MS people and family members drawn from lists of appropriate new MS center candidates, the meeting was chaired by one or two psychologists known to most of the potential members. A well-known figure in MS treatment and research, the neurologist guest speaker began the meeting with a short lecture on MS—the basic disease process, hypotheses about etiology, symptoms and treatment, current research, and so on. People often find it difficult to sift through dated textbooks and pamphlets, which present all of the worst possibilities in the most graphic terms. People may also have many misconceptions. While a man might have found a physician who could spend time explaining the condition, he might have been too anxious to listen to the details. In thinking through the situation over a period of time, people often find that they need to hear about MS over and over again, to look at each piece of information from several perspectives, and to be open to material at one point that they could not entertain previously. For many people, the group is particularly conducive to absorbing information. They can hear other people introduce questions that they were afraid to ask themselves, and they can offer information that they themselves have acquired. They can begin to see that others have the same questions, and they can respond to the group leader's query, "I wondered what you were thinking when Dr. Q gave that answer?"

The personal meaning of the medical questions may also be examined. For example, one woman asked the neurologist lecturing at one meeting whether MS was genetic. Later group discussion revealed the latent content of this question—the patient had an aunt with the disease, and she was consumed with worry about the future of her children. She had asked a dozen physicians the same question and knew rationally that MS was not genetically transmitted, but she could not move on until this personal meaning was explored. In the group, people could acknowledge the frustration of what they could not find out about MS, and they could lay a foundation for discussing the uncertainty in their lives and their disappointment in medical science. And they could do it with people as vitally interested as themselves.

While facilitating further exploration of the questions and issues presented in the early part of the meeting, the group leader needed to address several tasks in the forty-five minutes remaining after the neurologist left. He needed to build some group feeling and to neutralize any particularly unusual discomfort that had been generated during the meeting. He needed to ensure that people had some understanding of what a group was so that concrete plans for future meetings could be formulated. Techniques were similar to those appropriate in other new groups. The leader might point out similar concerns or experiences of the members or find ways for each person to contribute to the discussion.

Some groups were very lively even at this point and needed little help. If the group leader sensed a high level of tension between some people, he might move in rapidly and comment, "I'll bet everyone has been looking around to see whose symptoms are mild and whose are more severe." People usually felt great relief at labeling this particular anxiety and responded well to the comment that people seem to be scaring themselves with unlikely possibilities. Generally, patients cannot usefully dwell at this point on the possibility of their condition getting worse, just as healthy people cannot benefit from spending a lot of time thinking about their own death. Orientation groups in most cases ended in high spirits. People had survived the first meeting and had tasted the sweetness of feeling less alone. The session had planted the seeds of hope that the emotional burden of MS could be lightened in the group. The group leader introduced the expectation of a fifteen-meeting group contract, asked for a commitment from interested people, and adjourned the group until the next meeting one week later.

The process of the initial group contract reflected the interplay between MS-related internal issues and the group phenomena characteristic of developing small groups (Yalom, 1975). Structurally, the new group consisted of married couples and single people from the orientation meeting, plus enough others to reach the optimal size of nine or ten members. While some people chose only to attend the initial informational session, attrition after the first two meetings was minimal. Members started with the expectation of a time-limited experience, sometimes wondering whether they had enough to say to fill the fifteen ninety-minute sessions. Though the leader style varied somewhat, most leaders conducted groups with an unstructured format, allowing issues to evolve from immediate concerns and current incidents rather than from a list of preplanned topics.

The hallmark of the early groups was the nearly heady sense that "we are not alone," or universality (Yalom, 1975). There was almost a joy in sharing the details of physical symptoms. When were you diagnosed? Do you ever feel buzzing in your legs? Is it harder when you get up in the morning? Did the ACTH help your double vision? Did you ever feel you had it when you were a teenager? Apart from the attraction felt in any small group to come together with an exchange of common experiences, the discussion seemed to reflect a fundamental need to talk about the body. Certainly research has suggested an altered perception of the body above all else in MS patients (Johnson and Pavlou, 1981), and developmental experts have long asserted that the sense of constancy about one's body underlies feelings of identity. In MS, this body self is altered. Limbs might feel different, things might look strange, the experience of hot and cold might be altered, bladder signals might change, and the person might look and feel differently while walking. One is reminded of the experience of a young teenager, whose body changes throw her into turmoil and self-consciousness as she readjusts to her image of who she is.

There are several possible reasons for the relief resulting from group members exchanging notes about symptomatology. Unlike non-MS people, who might be polite and concerned, the other group members were intensely interested in the smallest sensations and in the detailed chronology of the illness. The group might provide people with whom an individual could identify and thus improve his self-definition. "I'm no longer like most others, but I'm like Mary and Rich and Peggy." Finally, the MS patient may experience fewer emotional barriers between himself and other group members. Feeling unfortunate, victimized, burdened, or unlucky, the MS person sometimes experienced the strain of anger and envy with non-MS friends or even family. The discussion of physical symptoms was extremely important, and it could not be hurried over in favor of dealing with material more psychological in content.

Working against the desire to share the MS experience with the group was the fear of becoming afraid and discouraged. As discussed previously, a central psychological event for many MS people is the fear of getting worse, and this fear was often projected onto the group. Whitaker and Lieberman (1969) and Stock (1962) note that most members of new groups fear contagion, or being made worse by sicker members. This fear of contagion was far more apparent in MS groups than in most nonmedical groups. In the first several meetings, members assessed each other, deciding who was better and who was worse. One person said, "When I walked in and saw two wheelchairs, I really got tense, and I thought that seeing people who were worse really might hurt me." One man said he believed that his walking was temporarily worse after the meeting than before, which he attributed to tension resulting from coming to the meeting and seeing people who were physically worse than he was.

Several groups were comprised entirely of individuals with a very mild variety of MS, and the contagion issues in these groups took a different form. In one group, everyone was ambulatory and had nonvisible symptoms. However, five of the men were currently employed and had expressed concern in screening interviews about what they would do if they could no longer work. Two members of the group had recently lost their jobs, and the working men were concerned that the unemployment of the nonworkers might "rub off" in some way. By the third meeting, the nonworkers were sitting together in one corner of the room, talking mostly with each other. Issues of employment were not being discussed at all. Symbolic statements such as "There are some people who upset me so much I would rather not talk about MS with them" reflected a wish to be rid of such members. However, exploring the phenomenon appeared to be quite productive. Particularly apprehensive people discovered that they could confront a fear and master it to some degree. Mildly disabled people came to know sicker members and learned that these members continued to be who they were despite the disability. They then spent less energy avoiding fearful thoughts about the future. Interestingly, groups composed entirely of mildly disabled patients often demonstrated more overall anxiety than heterogeneous groups, because group members had no focus for their fears.

Being ill creates a wish to be cured, and the MS group dealt with their disappointments in physicians. For the family having a member with chronic disease, the medical establishment becomes a part of daily living, and the relationship with the doctor often becomes intense and problematic. Expecting a cure or at least caring from the medical team, the patient finds that the reality may include hassles over appointments, phone calls, and insurance coverage, as well as the all-too-frequent statement "I can't cure you, so I don't want to see you." Group work was sometimes directed at helping the patient to separate reasonable demands from anger about their shattered hopes for a cure and at asking the patient to take some responsibility in structuring the relationship with her doctor so as to maximize positive experiences for both. Patients sometimes moved from a self-centered view of the physicians' position to an understanding of the impact of their feelings of helplessness on the doctor. The group explored patients' rights—the right to active follow-up, the right to call the doctor with questions, the right to get a second opinion, and the right to be informed about treatments. Group members discussed ways to assert these rights successfully, and they also discussed the emotional issues that blocked assertive behavior, for example, the fear of making demands on someone the patient needed.

Disappointment in the wish to be cured was reflected in the group process more broadly. People brought to the group their needs for concrete assistance. A patient needed help pouring coffee, getting to the rest room, or removing his coat. Group meetings, which were conducted in a hospital, began with a lecture by a physician. Group members were patients in a medical sense, and they often expected to continue to function as patients in the group. While people understood that they joined the group to learn about MS and to study and improve their own adaptation, the group sometimes behaved as if members were there to receive answers from the leader. In one group, for example, a woman became irate at the suggestion that one of the group members might call an absent member and remind her of the meeting. She stated, "Why do we have to do everything? Can't you take the responsibility? Doctors never really want to do anything for us." Another man said, "You sold us a bill of goods. I thought by this point we could have learned from you the proper way to live with this disease." The group provided a forum for working out this issue without breaking off the source of care.

Married couples generally joined the MS group as a unit, and patterns of interplay seen in the group paralleled patterns operating in the home. The healthy spouse often said she came to the group to help the MS partner, and spouses were less rapidly integrated into the group. Matching this group phenomenon was the tendency of many MS families to become "MS centered": Nonaffected family members lost sight of their own feelings and desires, as they became immersed in the daily struggle to manage the disease in the patient. While well spouses sometimes became depressed, angry, or demoralized, they progressively lost the ability to express their own needs. "After all," they said, "I don't have MS. It must be so much worse for the one who does."

In one group for spouses only, people expressed great discomfort and disloyalty as their own needs emerged amidst the more comfortable discussion of the problems of the MS partner. Also implicit in the statement "I'm coming to the group to help my MS wife" was the tremendous desire to do something about the MS. Helplessness may be a core feeling in the MS family. Spouses ache with the thought that MS has afflicted their husband or wife, and they may feel more powerless in the face of this disease than under any other circumstances they have experienced. Well spouses not infrequently said in the group, "I feel my wife could do much more to help herself," and thus attempted to cast off the feeling of impotence by blaming the MS person.

While many people were drawn to the group because of concerns for their marriage, the issue of marital problems tended not to be approached in depth until late in the group. Research and clinical observation suggest that most families spend little time talking about the disease (Pavlou and Johnson, 1981), and some people said that they first learned about their spouse's concerns and viewpoints in the group. Certainly, feelings about MS can be strong and basic, and it may be that couples fear that they cannot manage them in the marriage if they think or talk too much. "Will you leave me?" "I am angry that you have this disease." "No, I don't find you so attractive anymore." "I now feel trapped, and I don't even know anymore how I really feel about you." While some groups discussed sexuality, groups usually introduced the topic and then retreated. Again, most couples were experiencing some neurologically based sexual difficulties (Lilius, Valtonen, and Wikstrom, 1976). Because of the level of anxiety and discouragement in this very personal area, this topic may have been difficult to approach with hope for improvement.

Most groups included one or two meetings with children, generally after the parents became fairly comfortable with the situation themselves. Turning one's children loose with two psychologists and a room full of MS people requires some trust! MS people expressed concern about the impact of MS on their children's lives, though clinical research suggests that parents tend not to be entirely accurate in assessing their children's concerns (Pavlou and Johnson, 1981). Most commonly, the joint meetings began with a brief introduction; then the group split into a meeting for parents and another for children. The children's session included a discussion of MS, family drawings, and questions and personal experiences that the children had concerning MS. The two subgroups then reassembled to share experiences of the evening.

While all the common concerns of the children cannot be related here, it can be said that the children tended to be articulate observers of their families and had good questions. Nearly all children said that their parents' depression was a bigger source of difficulty than the physical disability. They tended to feel responsible for their parents, and they especially wanted to find a cure for MS. They tended to be intensely attached but ambivalent about their families, though they felt that MS inhibited the expression of their negative feelings. Some things were particularly frightening—a parent falling frequently, for example. The experience of even one or two meetings was very powerful for children, both in providing a place to discuss a topic not usually discussed and in allowing them to meet other children with an MS parent. The group often revealed the strained communication between parents and children on the topic of MS. The parents expected the psychologist to assess their children's perceptions and feelings and correct them if necessary so that they would not have to deal with their children's concerns directly.

In summary, the development of the new MS group reflected the merger of specific MS issues with the interactional process characteristic of small groups. Following initial fears that the group might increase fear or discouragement, people joined the MS group with a surge of hope. They talked about body symptoms, experiences with doctors, marriage, their children, jobs, friends, and their own feelings. Patients quickly formed bonds with each other because they assumed other members would understand, because other members possessed needed psychological information, and possibly because other members did not evoke the envy and anger of people without a comparable problem.

Following the high spirits of the first few meetings, the group members by the fifth or sixth meeting began to establish a clear function and role. Members felt some disappointment as the wish for rapid improvement was challenged by the reality that problems were genuine and change difficult. They asked "Where are we going?" or "Do we need more structure?"

Group members also began the important process of making comparisons. They compared symptoms. They saw the range of possibilities and noted with relief that MS did not always cause severe disability. Just as important, people began to notice that people sometimes felt or behaved differently than others with the same symptoms. Most patients assumed that their own emotional response followed inevitably from the MS. "Of course I feel hopeless and discouraged. Who wouldn't who had MS?" The group demonstrated the variety of possible reactions and seemed to help members reflect on the possibilities for choice and change. For example, one man was feeling isolated, stigmatized, and unable to tell anyone about his MS. In the group he talked with another man in the same line of business who said, "I don't worry about that—nobody who works for me cares about my MS—they only care if they keep getting their paychecks." The first man then changed his attitude and told his girl friend, his parents, and his business partners. He realized that he could respond differently.

The Later Group

Most groups requested to continue beyond the initial fifteen-session contract. Entering the group with some reservations about whether they had enough to say to fill the meetings, people often felt by the close of the contract that they were just getting started and that MS-related problems were by no means entirely resolved. Problems about termination were also at issue in some groups, and these will be discussed more fully later in the chapter.

A number of groups continued and became long-term groups, depending on the judgment of the group leader as to why the group wanted to continue and on staffing resources. While an occasional group member terminated or another entered, membership in the long-term groups tended to be quite stable. Patterns of development in well-established, ongoing groups were more diverse and less easy to classify than those in newer groups (Yalom, 1975). The discussion below highlights some common characteristics of MS groups but does not reflect the full range of interactions seen in these groups.

The later group gradually shifted from sharing to moving away from the supportive group function. There was greater depth and breadth in the content, a move toward explicit feedback within the group, and work on internal and intrapsychic issues. The discussion of MS symptomatology became increasingly personal. For instance, bladder and bowel accidents and problems generally evoked considerable shame and embarrassment, and they tended not be discussed until people felt comfortable with each other. Two MS people in one group introduced the topic after an experience on the way to the meeting. One woman felt great urgency and knew she would never make it to the bathroom, and the other woman shielded her with her coat while her friend relieved herself into a coffee can in a quiet corner of the parking garage. Bladder problems especially may create a "crisis in trust," forcing MS patients to disclose personal details before they might choose and with people with whom they would normally maintain greater distance. While discussions of bladder problems were sometimes characterized by joking and bravado, they more often tuned directly into the pain and shame of the childhood feelings of "wetting your pants" in front of strangers. People swapped stories of embarrassing incidents, did some problem solving about concrete ways to minimize bad experiences, and felt increasingly close as they shared this sensitive problem. They honed in on their feelings about it, and they sometimes felt greater self-acceptance as they experienced the understanding and acceptance of other group members.

Sometimes a group member expressed concern that MS might impair thinking. Charcot, the first person to define MS as a disease, stated in 1874 that MS is generally accompanied by memory problems and blunting of the emotional faculties (Firth, 1941; Inman, 1948). Another author in 1905 described euphoria as a symptom of MS (Seiffer, 1905) and created a myth about MS that is still prevalent. Subsequent work reported mental change in anywhere from 0 percent to 98 percent of MS patients! Current thinking suggests that while lesions of demyelination may occur at an infinite variety of sites, mental function remains intact in all but a small fraction of people with MS (Pavlou, 1979; Pavlou and others, 1979b). Mental change tends to cluster in patients with severe disability overall, though many people with severe MS do not suffer serious mental loss.

Significant mental impairment in people with mild or moderate varieties of the disease is very unusual. When it does occur, short-term memory and the capacity for new learning tend to deteriorate, with long-term memory and conceptual thinking remaining unaffected. A few patients, most commonly the most severely impaired, display a "pseudobulbar affect," or a change in the expression of emotions. They may laugh or cry more easily but usually not inappropriately. The actual incidence of euphoria is quite low.

The group provided accurate information and debunked myths about mental change. Discussion prompted an exploration of incidents reflecting supposed mental loss, and it sometimes examined the feeling of reduced self-confidence accompanying or contributing to the perception of reduced capacity. While acknowledging the possibility of some organic change, the group leaders encouraged greater trust in intellectual and general functioning. When a group member seemed to exhibit significant mental change, the group worked to isolate its specific effects so that the person felt less generally inept. An exploration of family issues often ensued, as couples struggled to create or maintain a position of prestige and responsibility for the MS person despite the mental alteration.

Marital issues were main topics in long-term MS groups, and they took the group beyond MS problems. As noted earlier, the depth of MS-related feelings made the acknowledgment of marital problems particularly fearsome. A husband and wife protected each other from the probings of the group, and they did not define their marital problems as explicitly as couples seeking marital therapy. With the growing cohesion of the long-term group, however, fears yielded to the more substantial need to work on couples issues. Trying to decrease the apprehension surrounding the topic, group leaders often labeled the discussion of marital issues as a positive outgrowth of the work to create a new life-style.

MS-related marital problems arose directly and indirectly through the group process. One spouse described to the group her increasing rage over the fact that her MS husband would not go to a special clinic in a distant state. The group dealt with the pain of their own as well as this woman's helplessness in the face of the MS, and several couples experienced the comfort and closeness that accompanied the sharing of their common hurt.

Because both spouses and patients often wished to protect each other from the burden of their unacceptable feelings, communication moved slowly. One man was considerably relieved when he finally revealed his embarrassment at being seen with his wife in her wheelchair. The wife responded well to this confession of feelings that she had long sensed, and the couple was relieved of one secret barrier to their being close.

The explicit involvement of the spouses characterized the long-term group, and this phenomenon seemed to parallel the move in families to reestablish a balance of attention to the emotional needs of both partners. Spouses attended meetings even if their MS partners did not, and they revealed a growing perception that their concerns were as legitimate as those of their partners. Couples lost sight of the distinction between MS issues and other family issues, and the group's operating rules broadened to include a wide range of topics.

Strong positive and negative feelings that developed among members of the advanced MS group demanded expression if the experience was to maintain its power and vitality. Though everyone had MS, the life circumstances and viewpoints of group members varied. One group included a Chicago police-man and a liberal schoolteacher, for example, as well as a college professor of history and a semiskilled laborer. Rivalries and conflicts also developed in the advanced group. Sometimes the discussion of marital issues generated frustration; for example, people wanted change in a couple with entrenched difficulties who were occupying a great deal of group time.

The physical deterioration of a member often evoked intense feeling. One group was devastated when one woman with a mild limp became wheelchair bound over a nine-month period. While this rate of disease progression was unusual, people in long-term groups often witnessed physical decline in other members. Someone in one group said, "I can remember . . . when we first met. Sarah walked without a cane, and I was still working." Another group saw a videotape of an earlier meeting and noted with sadness the change in several people. The acknowledgment and acceptance of physical decline appeared to be somewhat healing, as people grieved together over lost abilities and as they saw that people continued to be valued group members even under this most feared circumstance. The prospect of getting worse became a bit less unthinkable, though the change in attitudes was gradual and unstated.

Despite the buildup of tension among members, the MS group moved with great caution into interpersonal feedback. There had been a stampede to link up supportively around the issue of MS, but patients seemed fearful about anything that appeared to threaten the positive ties. People wanted to be gentle, polite, and helpful. All the patients in one group appeared to be intimidated by the occasional angry outbursts of one woman. When asked about their reluctance to discuss it, one person said glibly, "We know each other so well, we could say anything." The group moved to drop the issue. In another group, most members were very hesitant to assist one man who was currently hospitalized in the institution and needed help in coming to the meeting. However, the group denied any conflicts about the man's medical difficulties.

Augmenting the usual group fears about giving and receiving honest feedback was a concern about causing medical deterioration. Someone said of a woman's recent medical setback, "I was always afraid we had said something to upset her. She got worse right after that very 'heavy' meeting we had." The discussion led to an examination of people's perceptions of themselves as fragile and of the communication issues this created in the group and in families. The group talked about the desire to help rather than create additional suffering, and members examined their ideas about the nature of real support.

Interpersonal feedback and a focus on immediate group feelings developed in the advanced groups as a result of substantial effort by the group leader. Group participants tended to view the leader as someone on whom they depended and as an expert about groups. While group members developed strong bonds to each other, they continued to rely on the leader to interpret and understand the group process. The group leader sometimes provided an explicit rationale about why and how to give intragroup feedback, probed the barriers to such discussion, and modeled or structured exercises to facilitate discussion of immediate group feelings. The emergence of the group's ability to give feedback also allowed perceptions of the leader to be examined.

While these perceptions varied greatly, one common view of the group leader was of a supportive figure to whom anger or disagreement could not be expressed without creating emotional danger. One man said, "If we get angry at you, you'll dissolve the group." This group went on to work on the important topic of needing help and about what happened when one felt anger at the helper. Relationships with physicians and family members often reflected this same problem and were characterized by imbalances in interpersonal power. Although group participants tended to view the group leader as a special person who understood the needs of the chronically ill, the group leader invariably displayed some disappointing insensitivity to a particular problem. On one occasion, when workers doing some building construction locked the usual entry, several people were irate about the barriers to their mobility. They chastized the leader for not anticipating the problem and for not understanding the major difficulties it created for them. They went on to vent their anger at the non-MS world and eventually to examine their assumptions about what should be expected, about the source and quality of their feelings of disappointment, and about their own ability to draw more attention to their special needs.

Despite the fact that attention to intrapsychic issues was not a goal of the group, it became obvious in the advanced group that some apparent MS problems were related less to the disease than to entrenched personality difficulties. One woman continually berated friends, acquaintances, and ultimately the group leader and members for expecting too much of her and for thinking less of her because of MS. She said that no one wanted to associate with her because her MS stopped her from achieving anything professionally. It became abundantly clear during the course of the group that MS was not the problem. Before she had MS, this woman believed that her parents valued her only if she made significant achievements and that nothing she did was good enough. In situations like this, the MS group was in a unique position to challenge the belief that MS was the overwhelming life problem. Unlike friends and relatives, other MS group members could not be easily dismissed as lacking empathy or as preaching from a luckier life position. People could deal with some such issues in the group, and they also were usually receptive to additional individual therapy after a successful group experience.

Termination

Group termination had a special meaning in MS groups (Pavlou, Hartings, and Davis, 1978). Group members almost invariably requested to continue beyond the initial fifteen-session contract and, lacking a formal continuation, initiated social and informal meetings after the group terminated. Certainly, in view of the aim to bolster supportive networks, such contacts and meetings were very positive. They may have represented a victory over the excessive reliance on health care professionals and a positive force to band together to fight MS.

However, resistance to termination also seemed related to issues of dependency and loss; termination of the group meant termination of assistance and of a hope for cure and nurturance. One recent group demonstrated dependency-related termination issues most clearly. This group met for the standard fifteen sessions, which it agreed to at the start, and then asked to continue meeting. Interestingly, the members who had been most vocal in lobbying for continuance did not come to the next meeting to negotiate a new contract. The desire to continue seemed to reflect difficulty in facing termination, not a desire to do more work together. Several issues appeared to be involved.

First, this group had demonstrated greater difficulty with dependency and nurturing than any other group. Members declined to drink the coffee provided by the leaders, and a number of members were continually angry at the health care professionals for not doing enough. Members continually looked to the leaders for answers and not to each other to find care or to regulate their own tension levels. Unlike every other group, this group did not attempt to bring snacks for each other, to form car pools, or to phone each other. The discussion was frequently very tense because members did not use humor, avoidance, mutual support, or other mechanisms used by most groups to keep discussion at a generally comfortable level.

Second, the issue of loss was probably involved in most groups. Many writers (Shontz, 1975) have noted that the disabled deal with the losses of physical capacity, wishes and dreams, feelings of invulnerability, and a personal identity based on well-being. MS involves a long series of new symptoms and often a long series of losses. Thus, loss may be a very live issue that colors members' attitudes toward the termination of the group. Other authors have noticed that people may periodically reexperience a critical life event for the rest of their lives (Silver and Wortman, 1980). Because recovery is less than complete, continued or periodic support may be desired.

Outcome

Graduates of the fifteen-session group stated that, above all, they left the group with a sense that "I know I'm not alone." They found it significant that the group really understood and cared and, moreover, that they themselves could assist other members. The group seemed to augment or restore a sense of community with others. In one group, people felt best about the session in which they worked all evening to help one young man think through ways to approach a union committee about an impending job termination. With such group incidents, individuals recalled that they were valuable and had something to contribute. Because MS patients themselves grow up with the common prejudices regarding disability, they often devalue themselves through their own preexisting negative notions. People may feel further devalued by the extent to which they need help, and they do better when they can help another person.

People found the group a place where they could express some of their vague, poorly articulated feelings and fears, which thus lost some of their power and control. The thoughts were shared and accepted by others. People said, "I'm so glad to hear that someone else feels that way," and they seemed to feel less pathological and sometimes less sinful. The single most urgent issue, of course, was the need to come to terms with the sense of uncertainty. Some said that the group had a stabilizing effect on their marriage. They shared some thoughts on a delicate topic, compared themselves with other couples, and learned that other marriages involving an MS partner existed and did well. The couples format appeared particularly useful. Behaviorally, group graduates seemed to talk less about MS, maintain smoother relations with the medical team, know more about MS, and be more resistant to fad treatments. Many people appeared less frantic and less frightened. Of course, there was considerable variability in response and duration of improvement. While group members viewed the experience as useful (Ginther, 1978), and while clinicians have supplied supporting clinical impressions (Barnes, Busse, and Dinken, 1954; Chubon, 1982; Frolichstein, 1979; Marsh, 1979; Power and Rogers, 1979), the outcome has not yet been confirmed by research data.

Members of the advanced group also said that the formation of solid friendships with other group members was the most profound and beneficial single aspect of the group experience. "We have become a family," said one woman. While short-term group participants linked up with each other also, the personal ties in the advanced group were deep and enduring. People with an extensive group involvement felt that they changed significantly as a result of the experience. They looked back on the differences in their attitudes and behavior since their entry into the group. The short-term group could create an atmosphere conducive to personal gains and the consolidation of resources, but it did not involve people long enough to ensure that important changes actually occurred or endured. People in the advanced MS groups appeared less centered on MS and more focused on other life issues and priorities. Certainly the group gave people an opportunity to be together through a series of disease changes. Possibly it created greater comfort when the disease progressed moderately such that non-MS concerns could assume some of their preillness urgency. One short-term group member said, "What do I do now? The group is ending, but my MS will continue." The advanced group allowed people time to separate MS issues from other troublesome personal concerns.

While MS creates stress almost universally, a person's specific feelings are often a function of preillness psychological vulnerabilities. Many group members cited the growth of psychological mindedness and a general openness as a useful outgrowth of the experience. One woman felt her husband had benefited enormously from contact with the group leader, who provided to this very traditional man a model of an adequate male who could talk about feelings and share emotional hurt.

The group experience provided some additional insights about the process of adaptation to MS. First, adaptation appeared to be a gradual, unsteady process, marked by fluctuating distress over an extended period. In a study of chronically ill hemodialysis patients, Reichsman and Levy (1972) noted that "all patients experienced prolonged states of contentment alternating with episodes of depression of varying duration" (p. 862). The MS person who experiences some continuing pain or renewed difficulties should not feel he has failed, nor should the professional with a very limited intervention aim to alleviate adaptive difficulties indefinitely. Periodic interventions may be most useful.

Second, MS people frequently learned to deal quite successfully with the current disease state, but they very infrequently accepted the notion of major future deterioration comfortably. Certainly none of us would be surprised to be told that we had not fully accepted the probability of infirmity in old age or the inevitability of our own deaths. However, MS people and professionals alike often harbor the mistaken notion that acceptance of MS means that hope for future improvement or stability is minimal and that disappointments over the years will have no emotional impact. Family members also resolve some feelings and are troubled by others; this fact may contribute to the limited marital communication in so many families.

Finally, the group experience confirmed the hope that progress in adaptation to the disease is possible and realistic. With adequate assistance, most MS people integrated MS as one of several important facets of themselves and their lives. MS was no longer the prime focus, at least most of the time. The group experience suggested that the growth of this attitude follows not simply by a contemplation of loss, but rather by the active generation of hope—in the body, in one's emotional resilience and flexibility, and in the concern and goodwill of other people.

Common Questions

This chapter concludes with the most common questions that hospital staff and trainees have about the MS program.

Do Groups Hurt People? Medical personnel often express concern about the potential harm of MS groups, particularly that mildly affected patients will be frightened by contact with severely affected ones. The referring physician might be told that sensitive selection of potential group members screens out people for whom the experience might be upsetting. Obviously, a newly diagnosed twenty-five-year-old will not benefit from a group composed of middle-aged wheelchair patients. Allowing easy exit from the group further allows patients to assess the potential benefits and harm for themselves. While a patient might experience upset after a single meeting, it is unlikely that the experience could create significant damage. Also, as noted earlier, experience with people having greater disabilities eases for some the fears of future deterioration. Finally, skilled group leadership can minimize the potential for harm. Just as there is a good way and a bad way to do a lumbar puncture, so there is a good way and a bad way to structure an MS group. The referring physician or any other person with this question can be reassured that the patient will be considered and protected by the professional group leader. Even for a patient who is placed in what seems to be an appropriate group, the group leader is in a position to detect and deal with undue tension and to help the person leave the group if necessary.

What Are the Special Skills or Qualifications Needed to Run an MS Group? The group leader benefits from a solid grounding in the theory and practice of group psychotherapy and in psychological intervention skills. While some special techniques are useful in the MS group, general group skills are invaluable. The group leader benefits from an understanding of the MS experience and the issues that the disease raises so that she can respond to them promptly, detect them in indirect or symbolic form in group process, and not misdiagnose them as general psychopathology. Finally, the group leader should sensitize herself to unknowingly devaluing statements and acts often inflicted by others upon the disabled. For instance, most people with MS strongly object to being designated as "victims," and some object to the word *patient* or *disabled*. Most people also have strong preferences about the way in which help is offered. People feel devalued if they are spoken to very loudly, as if disability in one area means deafness or mental retardation, and if topics such as sexuality are omitted under the assumption that the disabled have no such interest or potential. They are devalued by the view that their lives are unrelieved misery devoid of pleasure and that they must subject themselves to experimental procedures without question. Sometimes the patient group benefits from some consciousness raising about these issues also.

Are There Variations in the Formats of the MS Groups Described Here? While the groups described above represent a general format, one common variation has been in the specific makeup of the group. The groups listed below are among these variations.

Singles Group. For people not currently married, singles groups addressed some special issues. Single people were concerned with dating, the possibility of not marrying, relations with parents, and long-range financial security and the ability for self-care.

Family-Only Group. Groups for family members only were most commonly attended by parents and spouses of patients with severe MS. Seeking much needed support and an outlet to discuss their special life circumstances, family members in these groups talked about the extent to which the stress of MS seemed to alter the mood of the disabled person, fatigue and burnout in themselves, guilt about ambivalent or angry feelings, and, ultimately, the need to consider their own emotional needs.

Wheelchair Group. Patients in wheelchair groups opted to meet without family members, apparently hoping to develop a greater feeling of separateness from helpers. People in such groups dealt with issues relating to stable disability (that is, mobility problems and prejudice from the nondisabled world), handling feelings of anger toward people upon whom they depended, ways that their own frustration affected the ways they requested and received help, and so on.

References

Adams, J., and Lindemann, E. "Coping with Long-Term Disability." In G. Coelho, D. Hamburg, and J. Adams, *Coping and Adaptation.* New York: Basic Books, 1974.

Ambrose, G. "Multiple Sclerosis and Treatment by Hypnotherapy." *Journal of Clinical and Experimental Hypnosis,* 1955, *3,* 203-209.

Arnaud, S. "Some Psychological Characteristics of Children of Multiple Sclerotics." *Psychosomatic Medicine,* 1959, *21,* 8-22.

Aronson, S., and others (Eds.). *Therapeutic Claims in Multiple Sclerosis.* New York: National Multiple Sclerosis Society, 1982.

Barnes, R., Busse, E., and Dinken, H. "The Alleviation of Emotional Problems in Multiple Sclerosis by Group Psychotherapy." *Group Psychotherapy*, 1954, *6*, 193-201.

Bolding, H. "Psychotherapeutic Aspects in the Management of Patients with Multiple Sclerosis." *Disease of the Nervous System*, 1960, *21*, 24-36.

Braham, S., and others. "Evaluation of the Social Needs of Nonhospitalized Chronically Ill Persons. A Study of 47 Patients with Multiple Sclerosis." *Journal of Chronic Disease*, 1975, *28*, 401-419.

Canter, A. "MMPI Profiles in Multiple Sclerosis." *Journal of Consulting Psychology*, 1951, *15*, 253-256.

Chodoff, P. "Adjustment to Disability: Some Observations on Patients with Multiple Sclerosis." *Journal of Chronic Diseases*, 1959, *9*, 653-670.

Chubon, R. "Group Practices in the Rehabilitation of Physically Disabled Persons." In M. Seligman (Ed.), *Group Psychotherapy and Counseling with Special Populations*. Baltimore: University Park Press, 1982.

Cobb, S. "Social Support as a Moderator of Life Stress." *Psychosomatic Medicine*, 1976, *38*, 300-314.

Counte, M., Pavlou, M., and Hartings, M. "The Use of Nonmedical Treatments (Chiropractic, Acupuncture, Miracle Diets, Psychic Surgery) by Multiple Sclerosis Patients." *Sociological Symposium*, 1978, *22*, 87-99.

Davis, F., Pavlou, M., and Hartings, M. *Emotional Aspects of Multiple Sclerosis*. New York: National Multiple Sclerosis Society, 1977.

Firth, D. "The Case of Augustus D'Este." *Proceedings of the Royal Society of Medicine*, 1941, *34*, 7-28.

Frolichstein, S. "Community Groups and Self-Help." In D. Goetz and M. Pavlou (Eds.), *The Vocational Rehabilitation Perspective in Multiple Sclerosis*. Chicago: Rush-Presbyterian St. Luke's Medical Center, 1979.

Gilberstadt, H., and Farkas, E. "Another Look at MMPI Profile Type in Multiple Sclerosis." *Journal of Consulting Psychology*, 1961, *25*, 440-444.

Ginther, J. *But You Look So Well*. Chicago: Nelson Hall, 1978.

Grinker, R., Ham, G., and Robless, F. "Some Psychodynamic

Factors in Multiple Sclerosis." *Proceedings of the Association for Research in Nervous and Mental Disease,* 1950, *28,* 456-460.

Harrower, M. "The Results of Psychometric and Personality Tests in Multiple Sclerosis." *Proceedings of the Association for Research in Nervous and Mental Disease,* 1950, *28,* 461-468.

Harrower, M., and Kraus, J. "Psychological Studies on Patients with Multiple Sclerosis." *Archives of Neurology and Psychiatry,* 1951, *66,* 44-59.

Hartings, M., Pavlou, M., and Davis, F. "Group Counseling of MS Patients in a Program of Comprehensive Care." *Journal of Chronic Disease,* 1976, *29,* 65-73.

Inman, W. "Can Emotional Conflict Induce Disseminated Sclerosis?" *British Journal of Medical Psychology,* 1948, *12,* 135-147.

Johnson, P., and Pavlou, M. "Family and Other Life Concerns of Parents with Multiple Sclerosis." Paper presented at the annual meeting of the American Psychological Association, Los Angeles, August 1981.

Lazarus, R., Averill, S., and Opton, E. "The Psychology of Coping: Issues of Research and Assessment." In Coelho, G., Hamburg, D., and Adams, J. (Eds.), *Coping and Adaptation.* New York: Basic Books, 1974.

Lilius, H., Valtonen, E., and Wikstrom, J. "Sexual Problems in Patients Suffering from Multiple Sclerosis." *Journal of Chronic Disease,* 1976, *29,* 643-647.

Linkowski, W., and Dunn, M. "Self-Concept and Acceptance of Disability." *Rehabilitation Counseling Bulletin,* 1974, *17,* 28-30.

Marsh, G. "MS Individuals as Peer Counselors." In D. Goetz and M. Pavlou (Eds.), *The Vocational Rehabilitation Perspective in Multiple Sclerosis.* Chicago: Rush-Presbyterian St. Luke's Medical Center, 1979.

Matson, R., and Brooks, N. "Adjusting to Multiple Sclerosis: An Exploratory Study." *Social Science and Medicine,* 1977, *11,* 245-250.

Moos, F., and Tsu, V. "The Crisis of Physical Illness: An Overview." In R. Moos (Ed.), *Coping with Physical Illness.* New York: Plenum, 1977.

Ottenburg, M. *The Pursuit of Hope.* New York: Rawson Wade, 1978.

Pavlou, M. "Psychological Aspects of Multiple Sclerosis." In D. Goetz and M. Pavlou (Eds.), *Vocational Rehabilitation Perspectives in Multiple Sclerosis.* Chicago: Rush-Presbyterian St. Luke's Medical Center, 1979.

Pavlou, M., Counte, M., and Davis, F. "Aspects of Coping in Multiple Sclerosis." *Rehabilitation Counseling Bulletin,* 1982, *25,* 138-145.

Pavlou, M., Hartings, M., and Davis, F. "Discussion Groups for Medical Patients: A Vehicle for Improved Coping." *Psychotherapy and Psychosomatics,* 1978, *30,* 105-115.

Pavlou, M., and Johnson, P. "The Adolescent in the Multiple Sclerosis Family." Paper presented at the annual meeting of the American Psychological Association, Los Angeles, August 1981.

Pavlou, M., and Stefoski, D. "The Development of Somatizing Phenomena in Multiple Sclerosis." *Psychotherapy and Psychosomatics,* in press.

Pavlou, M., and others. "A Program of Psychological Service Delivery in a Multiple Sclerosis Center." *Professional Psychology,* 1979a, *10,* 503-510.

Pavlou, M., and others. *Variety and Possibility in Multiple Sclerosis.* Chicago: Bioservice Corporation, 1979b.

Power, P., and Rogers, S. "Group Counseling for Multiple Sclerosis Patients: A Preferred Mode of Treatment for Unique Adaptive Problems." In A. Dell Ortho and R. Lasky (Eds.), *Group Counseling and Physical Disability.* North Scituate, Mass.: Duxbury, 1979.

Reichsman, F., and Levy, N. "Problems in Adaptation to Maintenance Hemodialysis." *Archives of Internal Medicine,* 1972, *130,* 859-865.

Schmidt, E. "Depression as a Psychical Change in M.S." *Psychiatrie, Neurologie und medizenische Psychologie,* 1943, *5,* 265-270. [Also in C. Sugar and R. Nadell, "Mental Symptoms in Multiple Sclerosis: A Study of 28 Cases with Review of the Literature." *Journal of Nervous and Mental Disease,* 1943, *98,* 267-280.]

Schwartz, M., and Pierron, M. "Suicide and Fatal Accidents in Multiple Sclerosis." *Omega: Journal of Death and Dying,* 1972, *3,* 291-293.

Seiffer, W. "Uber Psychische Insbesondre Intelliginz Storungen bei Multipler Sklerose." *Archiv fuer Psychiatrie und Nervenkrankheiten,* 1905, *40,* 252. [Also in C. Sugar and R. Nadell, "Mental Symptoms in Multiple Sclerosis: A Study of 28 Cases with Review of the Literature." *Journal of Nervous and Mental Disease,* 1943, *98,* 267-280.]

Shontz, F. "MMPI Responses of Patients with Multiple Sclerosis." *Journal of Consulting Psychology,* 1955, *19,* 74-76.

Shontz, F. "Some Psychological Problems of Patients with Multiple Sclerosis." *Archives of Physical and Medical Rehabilitation,* 1956, *37,* 218-220.

Shontz, F. *The Psychological Aspects of Physical Illness and Disability.* New York: Macmillan, 1975.

Shontz, F. "Six Principles Relating Disability and Psychological Adjustment." *Rehabilitation Psychology,* 1977, *24,* 207-210.

Silver, R., and Wortman, C. "Coping with Undesirable Life Events." In J. Garber and M. Seligman (Eds.), *Human Helplessness.* New York: Academic Press, 1980.

Starr, P., and Heiserman, K. "Acceptance of Disability by Teenagers with Oral-Facial Clefts." *Rehabilitation Counseling Bulletin,* 1977, *20,* 198-201.

Stock, D. "Interpersonal Concerns During the Early Sessions of Therapy Groups." *International Journal of Group Psychotherapy,* 1962, *12,* 14-26.

Veroff, J., Douvan, E., and Kulka, R. *The American Experience: A Self-Portrait over Two Decades.* New York: Basic Books, 1981.

Wender, M., and Dominik, W. "Psychological Examination in Patients with Multiple Sclerosis." *Psychiatrie, Neurologie und medizenische Psychologie,* 1972, *24,* 384-392. [Also in *Psychological Abstracts,* 1973, *49,* 1017.]

Whitaker, D., and Lieberman, M. *Psychotherapy Through the Group Process*. New York: Atherton Press, 1969.

Yalom, I. *The Theory and Practice of Group Psychotherapy*. New York: Basic Books, 1975.

14

Robert J. Marcovitz, Psy.D.

▦ ▦ ▦ ▦ ▦ ▦ ▦ ▦ ▦ ▦ ▦ ▦ ▦

Sickle Cell Anemia

While sickle cell disease is well known as a disease occurring in blacks, much confusion and misinformation surround it. Sickle cell syndromes are genetically transmitted disorders of the hemoglobin molecules in red blood cells. Although these syndromes occur most often in blacks of African descent, they are also found among natives of Saudi Arabia, India, and a few Mediterranean countries. A person who inherits two abnormal genes (one from each parent) suffers the most severe syndrome, which is full-blown sickle cell anemia. Inheriting an abnormal gene from one parent and a normal gene from the other results in the milder syndrome, sickle cell trait. In the United States, sickle cell trait is found in 8 to 10 percent of blacks, but only 1 in 400 black births results in sickle cell anemia (Forget, 1982).

The primary clinical manifestations of sickle cell anemia are anemia and vaso-occlusive crises. The anemia is usually chronic and may result in easy fatigability, increased susceptibility to infections, and delayed growth. More acutely distressing to sickle cell patients are the sickle cell crises, which occur suddenly (often with no identifiable precipitating event) and are excruciatingly painful. These attacks may last a few hours to a few days and commonly require hospitalization.

The abnormal genes inherited from one or both parents

result in the production of an abnormal hemoglobin molecule called hemoglobin S. Under certain physiological conditions, hemoglobin S assumes a peculiar shape, which in turn causes the red blood cells to assume the characteristic sickle shape. The sickle-shaped cells are unable to pass through the microvasculature of various tissues and organs. Instead, those vessels become blocked, and the resulting reduced perfusion causes the symptoms known as the sickle cell crisis. The specific symptoms depend upon the specific tissue or organ affected. Pains may occur in arms, legs, back, or chest. Repeated occlusive episodes may result in chronic complications such as skin ulcers, kidney damage, deteriorating vision, or arthritis. People with sickle cell trait have only 50 percent hemoglobin S with 50 percent normal hemoglobin. This amount of normal hemoglobin is usually sufficient to save them from the symptoms of sickle cell anemia except when physiological oxygenation is markedly reduced (for example, at high altitudes).

Medical treatment for sickle cell crisis is mostly supportive, since there are no known means to prevent the sickling process. Fluids, oxygen, antibiotics, and analgesics are the principal treatments. The prognosis for sickle cell anemia is variable. While a few patients die in infancy, some patients have been reported to survive into their fifties or sixties. Recent improvements in medical care have raised the life expectancy to the mid-forties, with death usually resulting from heart or kidney problems. Genetic counseling and prenatal diagnosis are the principal means of prevention, but both have their limitations (Forget, 1982).

Psychosocial Impact

In discussing the broader psychosocial aspects of adapting to chronic illness, Krupp (1976) points to the major tasks of the chronic patient. These are acceptance of the illness, the assumption of the sick role, a realistic assessment of limitations, realistic goal setting, and coping with the altered life expectancy. The acceptance of illness means facing time-limited depression, dealing with grief over what is lost, and then proceeding with rehabilitation. Assuming the sick role is defined as

learning to walk the fine line between overdependency and denial of the illness. The individual must comply with the behavior required of the patient role: visiting the doctor, taking medication, maintaining proper nutrition, and obtaining adequate
rest. The realistic assessment of goals and restrictions means
that the patients recognize their limitations yet function at the
highest level possible. Lastly, chronically ill patients must come
to terms with the fact that they will die sooner and with more
suffering than most people.

In a major paper on the psychosocial aspects of sickle cell
disease, Whitten and Fischoff (1974) consider the impact of the
illness at different developmental stages. Of course, feelings of
helplessness and frustration in the face of unpredictable and
painful crises as well as the possibility of undue dependency on
others are major factors throughout the life cycle. In addition,
these authors explain that how the family and the individual
handle the disease during childhood will set the stage for the
success or failure of the adjustment in adulthood.

In the adult, there is a broad range of adjustment. Poor
adjustment may mean isolation, dependency, preoccupation
with disease, addiction to narcotic medication, or a relatively
chronic state of depression. In healthy adjustment, the adult
sickle cell patient must cope with the problems of attaining financial independence and job stability despite the uncertainty
of the illness and easy fatigability. The well-adjusted sickle cell
patient often establishes a satisfactory relationship with someone willing to share the burdens of the illness while also maintaining a positive and supportive attitude toward it. Even well-
adapted patients tend to become depressed due to the lack of a
cure and the inadequate treatment that is available. As the adult
sickle cell patient approaches the decade of average life expectancy, severe depression may become a problem (Whitten and
Fischoff, 1974).

Rationale for the Group Treatment Approach

LePontis (1975) reported on a long-term support group
for adolescent female sickle cell patients. The main issues dis-

cussed were those associated with the adolescent developmental period, such as individual identity and separation from the family. She concluded that the group format was ideal for adolescents because of their need to establish peer relationships to accomplish the adolescent task of separating from the family. The group appeared to prevent isolation, alienation, and undue dependency in the members. Vavasseur (1977), as part of a comprehensive sickle cell treatment program at LAC-USC Medical Center, provided an eight-week, time-limited parent education group for the parents of children with sickle cell anemia. The main function of this group was to meet parents' needs for information, support, and ventilation.

Our initial group experience at the Thomas Jefferson University Hospital was considered to be a pilot project to determine the feasibility and effectiveness of providing a professionally led support group for this population. The author and a staff nurse coled the group.

Thomas Jefferson University Hospital Sickle Cell Patient Group

Location. The Sickle Cell Center of Thomas Jefferson University Hospital's (TJUH's) Cardeza Foundation is located in a large urban medical center that serves both lower- and middle-class blacks, although the former group is larger. The center is staffed by a physician and a nurse. Psychiatric consultation is contracted through the Jefferson Medical College Department of Psychiatry, and the author is the primary consultant.

Group Approach. The general approach used in the Jefferson sickle cell group is ego supportive. These non-insight-oriented groups aim to reduce anxiety rather than mobilize it. The leaders are quite active, the content is structured, and goals are clearly defined (Klein, 1979). Ego-supportive techniques include education, guidance, reassurance, encouragement, the instillation of hope, environmental manipulation, and chemotherapy. This approach tends to be indicated for more acutely anxious, depressed, or otherwise fragile populations and has also been recommended for chronically ill populations.

Goals. The main goals for the group, given the ego-sup-portive approach, were similar to those Udelman and Udelman (1978) used with rheumatoid arthritis patients: (1) educative—sharing knowledge of and mutual experiences with the disease; (2) social-integrative—preventing patients from an overemphasis on the sick role and minimizing potential regression; (3) sup-portive-ventilative—allowing for the controlled expression of anxiety, frustration, and anger; and (4) exploratory-dynamic—dealing with psychogenic aspects of illness or psychosocial se-quelae.

Selection Process, Patient Preparation, and Group Char-acteristics. An initial pool of 15 patients, drawn from the ap-proximately 150 treated by the center, were chosen. Dropouts and no-shows were expected to leave the group at the desirable size of about eight patients. Patients considered for inclusion were those persons perceived by the staff to be motivated to obtain help in coping with the psychosocial impact of their ill-ness, verbal, reliable in keeping their clinic appointments, and compliant with prescribed treatment. Eight of the patients in-vited to join the group tended to bring up psychosocial issues related to their disease when meeting with the center nurse. Four patients invited were similarly motivated and verbal, but they also had obvious situational problems with their illness, such as more frequently recurring crises. Three patients who had made a poor overall adjustment were also invited to the group. Of the fifteen patients selected, twelve agreed to partici-pate in the group.

The center nurse, in consultation with the psychologist, prepared the patients for group membership. She told them that it was an opportunity to discuss with others having the same disorder how to cope with disease-related problems. It was decided not to present the group as "group therapy" to avoid arousing their fears of being mentally ill and thus increasing their resistance. Rather, they were told it was a support group for persons with a common illness. This response usually allayed their initial anxiety.

During the course of the group, the size varied from four to eight members ranging in age from twenty-two to thirty-five. Later, a sixteen-year-old female joined the group. At the start, the group included three males, two of whom were employed and one who was on welfare and adjusting to his illness poorly. None of the males were married. Two of the five females were employed, two were on welfare, and one was supported by a spouse. All of the patients except the married woman were living at home with grandparents, parents, or siblings. Most of the single females were in their twenties and had steady boyfriends. Nine of the twelve who agreed to participate came to the first meeting. Additional new patients were recruited as the group proceeded.

The group met in the midafternoon for one and a half hours weekly over a period of three months. The group terminated primarily because several of the members were not sufficiently motivated to attend the group when the warm spring weather arrived; they recommended that the group resume in September. Other possible issues involved in the termination of the group will be discussed later.

Phases. During the course of the group, three distinct developmental periods seemed to occur, which will be referred to simply as the initial, middle, and termination phases.

The initial phase of this group encompassed approximately the first four sessions. As in most therapeutic groups, much of the time in the initial sessions was devoted to introductions, determining members' expectations of the group, and superficially discussing issues such as job discrimination, solicitousness of one's family, the physical effects of the illness, and the lack of opportunity for contact with other sicklers. Some members wanted the group to assume the task of educating the public about the disease. The members uniformly felt that there was considerable misinformation about the disease in the community at large. During this initial period, two men claimed that they could not arrange time off from work to attend the group and dropped out.

An interesting aspect of this early period was the readiness of the group members to share ideas and feelings associated with the illness. Cohesiveness seemed to build rapidly as a result. There may have been three reasons for this phenomenon. First, there seemed a pressing need to talk about these feelings. Second, the homogeneous nature of the group allowed the universal aspects of their struggle with the disease to surface in a sympathetic atmosphere. Last, there may have been a certain amount of counterdependence or healthy independence that allowed the members to proceed on their own, behaving as if authority were not present. This counterdependent behavior may have been due to reaction formations against dependency that often develop in individuals with this type of chronic disease. It was actually later in the group that members began to make more demands for information and help from the co-leaders.

In the middle phase of the group (approximately four sessions), there was a continuation of the openness and freedom in the discussion that began in the initial phase. Relatively little leader activity was required to open up discussion, engage more quiet members, or point out common issues. Topics that were brought up in the first few sessions were returned to in greater detail and with more feeling. Cohesiveness appeared to be strengthening and reached a peak when one of the members, Jane, was hospitalized during a crisis. The group started discussing their perceptions of isolation and abandonment by family and friends when they had been hospitalized. Another member, Mary, suggested that after the group meeting they go visit Jane. This idea was carried further when the nurse was asked to provide the names of other sickle cell patients in the hospital, and for a few weeks several members made rounds visiting these patients. In the latter part of the middle period, attendance problems resulted from several members having sickle cell crises. Group members expressed intense frustration about the disease process when this happened.

In the final two sessions, the issue of low attendance due to questionable commitment to the group as opposed to the realities of members' illnesses was considered. At this time the group believed that the combined effects of members' illnesses and the nice spring weather were the main causes of difficulty in keeping the group going. After this discussion, the group felt that they would be able to make a stronger commitment in the fall.

Family Group Meeting. In the middle phase, when the members were discussing ways of obtaining more support and understanding from their families, one suggestion was to have a meeting to which family members could come and ask questions about the disease. The group decided to have this meeting in the late afternoon and open it to the entire clinic population. An announcement was sent to the clinic patients. Twenty-five patients and family members attended. Also present were the director, the nurse, and the psychologist. The format was mainly social and informal; it began with the director introducing himself, the nurse, and the psychologist. He then encouraged people to get acquainted and invited families to ask any questions informally by coming up to staff members during the social hour.

Only three of the group members attended with their families. The patients' feedback was good. The family members reported enjoying the meeting and appreciating talking with the doctors and the nurse. The three patients were pleased that their families had sufficient interest and concern to attend. Feedback from the other nongroup patients and families was uniformly positive along the lines previously mentioned. Questions were related to new treatments available, limitations on activities of children with sickle cell disease, and psychosocial problems such as unemployment or frustration concerning the unpredictability of sickle cell crises. Of the members of the group who did not attend, most said they regretted missing it and gave legitimate reasons why they or their family had not attended. Those group members whose family refused to come may have been too embarrassed to come alone.

Role of Leaders. The members initially viewed the psychologist with some anxiety because of their concern about being considered mentally ill. While this is a common concern in groups led by mental health professionals, it seems to be a more extreme problem for certain populations, particularly urban blacks. In the sickle cell group, the members had not presented themselves as having emotional problems. The strong cultural taboo against mental illness that exists in urban black communities was clearly manifested. However, by emphasizing the purpose of the group as providing support, by reassuring group members that we were there to help them and not to judge them, and by assuring them that theirs were understandable reactions to a real disability, the group leaders helped the patients to talk openly about their difficulties. In general, the psychologist tended to be called on as the expert on whether certain experiences and feelings were normal, such as fears of being hospitalized. He was also requested to give advice or guidance for dealing with interpersonal problems.

The nurse from the center had a warm and friendly relationship with most of the patients before the group was formed. She was knowledgeable about the patients' current life situation and the documented physical effects to which they were subject. She also knew which patients tended to be overly reliant on their analgesic medication. Since they viewed her essentially as caring and interested, her presence was an asset from the start. She was also viewed as an expert on the scientific facts regarding the biological disease process and its treatment.

The cotherapy aspects of this situation were relatively straightforward. There was a mutual respect for both leaders' points of view. The willingness of the author and nurse to defer to each other's areas of expertise led to a healthy and comfortable working relationship.

An important part of the role of the leader in a group is what has been termed "executive functions" (see Chapter One). These include setting the time, place, and fee, introducing new members, setting attendance requirements, and providing a certain amount of structure (such as defining the group task). Another important function of the leader is to introduce constructive norms and values as part of the group atmosphere or culture within which the members may operate. This may also include setting limits on behaviors that may be destructive to the group. While this group did not require much limit setting, group norms for equal participation, verbalizing of opinions, listening to each other, and expressing positive and negative feelings about the group were encouraged. In order to foster openness, members were encouraged to bring up illness-related problems, including those they had successfully resolved and those with which they wanted help from the group. Also, discussion was initiated on issues such as commitment to the group and attendance.

Another role of the leader is to build cohesiveness. This effort was facilitated primarily by the leaders pointing out common issues and problems that several group members shared. The norms for expressing positive feelings to the group and for mutual support and caring were a factor in this process.

Education is an important part of an ego-supportive approach. Both leaders took opportunities to educate the patients about known psychological and medical aspects of the disease. Another important function of the group leader is interpreting group phenomena; this has also been called "meaning attribution" (Lieberman, Yalom, and Miles, 1973). Essentially, this is clarifying and understanding members' feelings either at the individual or group level. In an ego-supportive approach, group or individual feelings are brought to awareness superficially and then ameliorated through other supportive techniques, such as education or guidance.

A good example of this technique occurred when one patient (Jane) discussed her fear of death, which surfaced when she was experiencing the acute pain of a sickle cell crisis. Two other patients responded that they tried to think positive thoughts about how the pain would not last. Another patient said that she used hypnotic techniques to control the pain. In an insight-oriented group, it would have been appropriate to confront the other patients' fear of death, but in our group format, the leader used this situation as an opportunity to introduce other members to hypnosis as a pain control technique. In response, the group requested a session devoted to teaching them hypnosis. A simple method to induce hypnosis through relaxation and eye fixation was utilized; mental imagery (a mountain cabin with a fireplace scene) was then used to deepen the trance. While the members were in trance, several ego-strengthening suggestions were given. No special pain control techniques were introduced, since the leaders felt that these should be individualized. The members were offered an opportunity to meet with a skilled hypnotherapist if they wished to learn more details about hypnotic pain control. Since none of the patients ever followed up on this, this session may have been motivated by an unconscious group desire for a magical cure.

Content. Several types of interpersonal problems were discussed in the group. One that surfaced early was public misinformation about sickle cell disease. Several patients related episodes in which friends and acquaintances who learned of their disease expressed concern that the patients might be contagious. To the group, this was a clear example of the lack of understanding that others had regarding their disease. These disclosures also strengthened the feeling that in the group their problems would be understood.

One topic that came up several times concerned the solicitous attitudes of family and friends. Members expressed a negative view of this behavior in others, saying that it made them feel either annoyed or uncomfortable. Rebecca explained that her husband would treat her differently when she was having a crisis. He would bring her things like food and presents or clean up around the house. She verbalized that she disliked being treated as a sick person. Several other patients found solicitousness or overprotectiveness in their parents offensive. Some felt that it was a continuing battle with parents to get them to be less protective. One of the more perceptive patients, Helen, pointed out that the parents' behavior was often due to guilt, that is, feeling that they were to blame for the illness. Other patients could relate to this observation and felt uncomfortable about it, possibly because seeing guilt in their parents provoked their own guilt.

Interestingly, a woman in one of my psychiatric groups was the mother of a sickle cell patient. She poignantly described her anxiety while watching her adolescent son experimenting with the limits of his illness by trying out for the school athletic teams. She could see a connection between his pushing himself and the onset of a crisis. It was hard for her to come to terms with his need to be like other adolescents.

One aspect of the solicitousness discussion concerned pity versus sympathy and empathy. Being pitied was viewed as the underlying component to solicitousness, or, in lay terms, having people feel sorry for you. Being the object of pity was completely unacceptable to the group members. None of them were able to tolerate others feeling sorry for them. They all expressed considerable resentment about the times that this occurred. The group admitted appreciating a certain amount of sympathy or empathy because they felt it showed people cared for them.

This group covered problems with working rather superficially because only one group member, Harriet, was employed, and she had a relatively mild disease process. As mentioned, the two working men had left the group. Two main points were made concerning work. The group felt that a certain amount of job discrimination existed because employers were unlikely to hire a person who listed an illness such as sickle cell anemia on an application. The members also recognized that the uncertainty of interruptions and time off caused by the illness required employers to grant them special treatment, which they knew might not be tolerated. They experienced this ambivalently with a sense of acceptance and a feeling of injustice.

A large part of group time was spent discussing the impact of the illness on their own person. In addition to the hypnosis session, two sessions were devoted almost entirely to the discussion of pain. All of the patients admitted some fear about pain, although only one, as mentioned previously, related it to a fear of dying. More typically, their concern ranged from the fear of having to go to the hospital (abandonment) to having some permanent physical damage. Harriet spoke about her fear of suffering unbearable pain and consequently losing control of her emotions, crying or moaning.

Much of the patients' anxiety related to their lack of control of the painful crises, especially the uncertainty of onset, duration, and intensity. All of them could relate to the extremely subjective nature of the experience of pain. They said, "It's your own pain, no one else's. . . . Other people don't know how it hurts." The ability of the patients to control and manage their painful crises was very important to them and was a factor in their self-esteem and their ability to manage their anxiety. This was well stated by Harriet, who described her embarrassment and guilt following a particularly painful crisis in the hospital when she had cried out and criticized the nurses for not helping her enough.

As explained early in the chapter, the use of analgesics for pain control is a standard supportive procedure in treating sickle cell crises. This includes opiate derivatives, which may be addicting. The use of medications was a hotly debated issue in the group. When this issue was discussed, two patients in the group were thought to be overly dependent on opiates. Harry, for example, had been in the group from the start. He was considered to be functioning overall at a limited level, embracing the sick role beyond what seemed warranted by his physical condition. He frequently visited the emergency room and regularly requested narcotic prescriptions. The other patient, Denise, a sixteen-year-old, came to us from another center after the first six weeks of the group. She was reported to be depressed and drug dependent, requiring large regular doses of narcotics for pain.

One particular discussion in the group centered around crying wolf. It arose out of Jane's complaint about the reactions of the emergency room staff to her visits. She perceived them as viewing her as a drug addict and expressed anger and resentment at their disbelief about her having terrible pain. Several other members corroborated this perception and experience, reporting instances of waiting much longer than seemed necessary for medication or a physician's attention. Rebecca suddenly stated that this problem occurred because of a few patients who asked for medication that they did not really need. The group expressed considerable anger and frustration toward those people who had spoiled things for persons really needing medication. To the coleaders, the discussion seemed to be an indirect attack on Harry, who represented to the group a failure in overcoming the core issue of dependency or, at least, an offender who ruined their credibility in the emergency room. Interestingly, Harry sat quietly throughout the discussion. When asked his feelings about the conversation, he denied having any and made no comment. He attended only two more sessions following this meeting. The other patient, Denise, had joined the discussion on the same side as the rest of the group. She felt that her requests for medications were fully justified because of the severity of her pain.

The psychogenic aspects of sickle cell crisis have been minimally addressed in the literature and are largely unknown. Two of the more psychologically minded members, Denise and Harriet, believed that this was an important factor and reported incidents in which crises had been preceded by important life events, such as transitions or disappointments. Several other members were dubious but did concede that there may have been some vague connection between stress and the onset of their crises. One member, Harry, could see no relationship between emotional factors and his disease.

A physical effect of sickle cell anemia is fatigue, a subject that came up often in the group. There were two broad themes. The first was the members' own ambivalence about their energy level. Essentially, they had to decide how hard to push themselves because they believed in the relationship between exhaustion and crisis onset. A second related problem was their alternating frustration at and acceptance of not being able to do many of the things they wanted.

Several of the emotional aspects of the disease have already been discussed. Broadly, these are helplessness, dependency, depression, isolation, and fear of injury or death. The helplessness-dependency issue presented itself in the group mostly in more adaptive forms, such as counterdependent behavior. One group member, Harry, was probably chronically depressed and was largely out of touch with these feelings. When Denise entered the group, she was clearly depressed. She had gone through several months of recurrent crises and had been hospitalized several times. She felt isolated and disappointed because her alternating need for hospitalization and rest at home pulled her out of school and away from her classmates, whom she had enjoyed and now missed. She talked of the loneliness at home and in the hospital. While friends and family would visit her regularly, this did not make up to her for the loss of her classmates and her inability to interact with them. She felt handicapped in vigorously pursuing her studies and interest in art. She also experienced a lack of contact with other sickle cell patients and was glad for the group opportunity.

Denise's case points up the difficulties adolescent sickle cell patients encounter, especially in the major developmental task of separation-individuation, which occurs at this time (see also Chapter Seven and Chapter Eleven). They may be forced into greater dependency through homebound school programs and isolation from their peer group, which is the main vehicle by which adolescents emancipate themselves. For this reason, it is important to set up aggressive and flexible programs in which a teenager may maintain these critical links and not become isolated and depressed.

Effectiveness. Despite the fact that the group did not become an ongoing one, the cotherapists viewed it as beneficial for the members. Most of the intragroup goals, such as the sharing of mutual experiences, discussing means of coping with problems related to the illness, and providing an ego-supportive atmosphere, were achieved. Also, the broader goal of completing a pilot project with this understudied population was accomplished. The group was successful in generating new ideas regarding pain management and relationship issues important to this population, such as the use of hypnosis, reactions to family overprotectiveness or solicitousness, and the lack of public understanding. Further, it clarified or validated previous beliefs regarding the need of adolescent sickle cell patients for peer group interaction and the difficulties that sickle cell patients encounter when seeking employment. While the long-term effects of the group experience cannot be determined due to a lack of formal follow-up, a few of the members continued friendly relationships after the group ended. Denise, the depressed adolescent, was followed for several more months in individual therapy at the request of her physician. She reported finding the group helpful, and with the continued individual treatment I observed her return to school, resume her contacts with friends, and regain a more normal energy level. She also reduced her use of analgesics.

Therapeutic Factors. Within the group, many of Yalom's therapeutic forces were observed and appeared helpful. The main goal of providing a supportive experience appeared to be validated by the development of cohesiveness and the sense of belonging in the middle phase (sessions 5 through 9) and also by the well-attended meetings during this period. Another positive force previously mentioned was the session with patients and their families. As a result of this session, the sickle cell patients felt better understood by their families.

Other predicted curative factors observed to be important were ventilation and universality. The need to ventilate was evident, since there was never more than a brief silence during the group. Further, the leaders did not experience any major difficulty in engaging patients in conversation or having them express feelings about their illness.

The universality factor (that is, the sharing of a common feeling or experience) appeared to be an important means of reducing members' sense of isolation and being alone with their illness. This could be observed in the group by the members' intent interest in each other's experiences and in expressions such as "That's how I felt," "I can relate to that," and "I feel better hearing that." One factor that seemed to be a source of positive feelings for the members was that of altruism. Most of the members were quite helpful to each other and had ready advice, reassurance, or encouragement to give.

Difficulties. From the outset, many of the prospective members did not follow through with their verbal commitment to attend the group regularly. Certain members would tell the nurse that they would be there and then not show up. When the nurse followed up, something had invariably come up unexpectedly at the last minute. In low-income urban clinic settings, this author has found missed appointments to be a significant and common dilemma. Another aspect of the attendance issue is related to the uncertainty of onset and the frequency of sickle cell crises. At the group sessions, when only two or three patients showed up, invariably one or two group members were in the hospital and another was sick at home. Within the group, toward the latter period, more emotionally charged subjects were discussed, particularly by the depressed teenager. We suspect that some of the patients may have found this anxiety producing. Finally, Harry's dropping out may have reduced cohesiveness in the latter stages of the group. In retrospect, he may have needed more support either from the leaders or by having another patient with similar circumstances in the group.

Our patients as a rule seemed interested in a quick solution to their disease process. For instance, none of the patients actually followed up on the use of hypnosis for pain control after the one-session introduction, and many never made a real commitment to working at the psychosocial aspects of their illness in therapy. Finally, most patients were much better at keeping their clinic appointments where they received medications than in following through with their group involvement, which provided much less immediate relief. Those who remained committed to the group were those well-functioning patients who were able to foresee the long-term benefits of discussing their illness with other patients.

The issue of racial and cultural differences between the white coleaders and the black patients was never openly addressed in this group. This issue is worth investigating, although it is not clear that this was a cause of any of the group problems. After the first few meetings, the flow of material seemed reasonably uninhibited and the idea of discussing this issue was dropped. However, this issue should have been raised in the first or second session if its possible effects were to be fully understood. The patients at some level may have felt that the therapists could not understand their plight because the therapists would never experience sickle cell disease.

Future Directions

A consideration in these groups—one that this author will pursue more aggressively in the future—is the leaders' relationship to the patients' primary physician. The physician-director of the center was very supportive and psychologically minded but also very busy. There were few joint meetings with the psychologist, physician, and nurse. When there were significant problems with the group or a patient, the physician's involvement made the critical difference between success or failure. Patients and family all responded favorably to his suggestions, and his help was invaluable. For instance, when he spoke to patients who were reluctant to attend the group about its possible benefits, their attendance usually improved.

One particular bias of this group occurred in the selection process; relatively healthier patients were invited to join the group. Most of them had adapted fairly well to their core problems of dependency and depression through counterdependent and counterphobic mechanisms. An important future direction for study of this population would be to compare and contrast various groups of sickle cell patients to determine what constitutes successful or unsuccessful adaptation to the condition and to determine how these groups differ in process or content. Also, clarifying the differences between this and other groups of chronically ill populations will lead to better understanding of the condition and more effective psychotherapeutic interventions.

From this experience, a controversy emerged about how to approach this population with a group model. In deciding to use a group model, an important choice is between the time-limited and the ongoing group approach. Given the uncertain course of the illness, a time-limited approach (six to eight weeks) seems best, with structured discussion of topics such as family issues, pain, coping with stress, physical effects, and other problems. Following this initial intervention, an ongoing group could be initiated if a core was available. Otherwise, centers could run this series at six- or twelve-month intervals as necessary. Further research would help clarify this. Similarly, shorter but more frequent educational sessions for parents or families could be organized.

Personal Reflections

The most frustrating part of the group was nonattenders. In one session only two patients were present, and in another the nurse cancelled the session after learning several members were in crisis. In dealing with our frustration and disappointment, my cotherapist and I would usually discuss the validity of various patients' reasons for missing. We would rehash the previous session to better understand what role the group process may have played in the absences or whether there had been deficiencies in our technique. Time and time again we concluded that the patients' illness was the largest single factor—perhaps one patient's reason for missing was questionable, but usually more than one was in the hospital, in the emergency room, or at home in pain. Most helpful to us was the empathic view that by allowing ourselves to become close to these patients, we were sharing some of their experience of unpredictability, pain, and helplessness. We could only try to accept it as they must.

I did not consider the issue of working with black patients a problem. I have worked for nearly eleven years in urban settings where there have been more black than white patients. Most of the group patients were friendly and easy to talk with, and after their initial doubts about me, we seemed to get along. I cannot generalize about whether other professionals would experience greater or lesser difficulty in dealing with sickle cell patients, although the basic cultural differences between white professionals and black sickle cell patients could be an issue.

References

Forget, B. G. "Sickle Cell Anemia and Related Hemoglobinopathies." In J. B. Wyngaarden and L. H. Smith (Eds.), *Cecil Textbook of Medicine.* (16th ed.) Philadelphia: Saunders, 1982.

Klein, R. H. "A Model for Distinguishing Supportive from Insight-Oriented Psychotherapy Groups." In L. London (Ed.), *Exploring Individual and Organizational Boundaries: A Tavistock Open Systems Approach.* New York: Wiley, 1979.

Krupp, N. E. "Adaptation to Chronic Illness." *Postgraduate Medicine,* 1976, *60* (5), 122-125.

LePontis, J. "Adolescents with Sickle Cell Anemia Deal with Life and Death." *Social Work in Health Care,* 1975, *1,* 71-80.

Lieberman, M., Yalom, I., and Miles, M. *Encounter Groups: First Facts.* New York: Basic Books, 1973.

Udelman, H. D., and Udelman, D. L. "Group Therapy with Rheumatoid Arthritis Patients." *American Journal of Psychotherapy,* 1978, *32,* 288-299.

Vavasseur, J. "A Comprehensive Program for Meeting Psychosocial Needs of Sickle Cell Anemia Patients." *Journal of the National Medical Association,* 1977, *69* (5), 335-339.

Whitten, C. F., and Fischoff, J. "Psychosocial Effects of Sickle Cell Disease." *Archives of Internal Medicine,* 1974, *133,* 681-689.

Yalom, I. *The Theory and Practice of Group Therapy.* (2nd ed.) New York: Basic Books, 1975.

Part Two

❖ ❖ ❖ ❖ ❖ ❖ ❖ ❖ ❖ ❖ ❖ ❖ ❖

Support Groups
for Patients' Families

A recurring theme throughout Part One was that the nature of an individual's adaptation to illness profoundly influences, and is influenced by, the family environment. Part Two focuses on support groups for meeting the informational and emotional needs of family members. It is important that family members have realistic expectations concerning a relative's disorder and its psychological sequelae, be educated about approaches that they can use to help their loved one cope with his or her condition, and learn to deal with their own emotional upset over the major disruption of the family unit's equilibrium. As Cassell (1979) states, "In a sense, sickness spreads into the family, causes disruptions, and causes relationships to change in ways of which the members may not be aware. As one must learn to deal with the disconnection of the patient, so must the needs of the family be tended" (p. 109).

Campbell's chapter on group interventions with family members of patients experiencing catastrophic environmental events (Chapter Fifteen) begins Part Two. A major environmen-

tal disaster in recent years was the tank car explosion in the
small town of Waverly, Tennessee, in 1978. Campbell and several colleagues at Vanderbilt Hospital developed a novel approach for working with the families of the Waverly burn victims. In addition to the uniqueness of developing such a treatment
approach to cope with catastrophic life events, other unusual
features of Campbell's particular experience include: (1) These
family members, unlike the relatives of persons suffering from
catastrophic illnesses such as cancer, had someone to blame for
the incident (L & N Railroad); (2) the litigation with the L & N
and the prospect of large settlements likely diverted some of the
family members' attention from their seriously burned relatives;
and (3) most of the families lived in the same small community
of Waverly and knew one another.

In Chapter Sixteen, Walwork describes his crisis intervention group work with parents whose newborn children died before going home from the hospital. He poignantly describes the
impact of such a child's death on family members and the benefits and problems experienced by participants in the Milwaukee
infant death parent support group.

Euster's chapter (Chapter Seventeen) delineates the struggle that relatives face when a loved one becomes a cancer patient. Euster addresses group work with both relatives of hospitalized cancer patients and cancer patients living at home. While
these troubled families share many stresses, there are also
unique problems to be confronted and resolved. This chapter
serves as a worthwhile companion chapter to Chapters Ten,
Eleven, and Twelve.

As noted in the Preface, family members of patients with
a dementing illness such as Alzheimer's disease face some of the
problems of family members of cancer patients and also some
that are unique. Alzheimer patients never experience remissions,
and to date there is no potential for cure. Group efforts are
typically directed toward aging spouses and adult children who
must adjust to many painful realities, including coping with
their loved one's deteriorating mental and behavioral status. In
Chapter Eighteen, Kapust and Weintraub describe their group
experiences with such families in the Boston Beth Israel Hospital's Behavioral Neurology Unit.

In Chapter Nineteen, Chesler and Yoak discuss self-help groups for parents of children with cancer. The authors discuss the psychosocial impact of the disease and its treatment on parents and other family members. The first author is uniquely acquainted with such groups as both a participant and researcher. The authors also discuss important professional and personal issues faced by professionals who want to work with parent self-help groups.

Reference

Cassell, E. J. "Reactions to Physical Illness and Hospitalization." In G. Usdin and J. M. Lewis (Eds.), *Psychiatry in General Medical Practice*. New York: McGraw-Hill, 1979.

15

Thomas W. Campbell, M.D.

▦ ▦ ▦ ▦ ▦ ▦ ▦ ▦ ▦ ▦ ▦ ▦ ▦

Dealing with
the Aftermath
of Catastrophic Events

Historically, famine, war, pestilence, and environmental disasters of all sorts have been faced by small groups, with the family as the primary unit. Natural selection, both in a cultural and a biological sense, may have determined the universality of this situation. The basic hypothesis underlying this chapter is that the presence of an intact, supportive family strengthens the adaptive coping mechanisms of individuals facing the effects of an environmental disaster. If this is true, then intervention through a group made up of several families should be the most effective way to take advantage of the natural supportive resources of these units.

In the last decade, family and group therapies have become widespread as methods of crisis intervention. However, the use of multiple-family groups as a specific crisis intervention technique is rarely reported. Yet I believe that the process of a multiple-family group is so powerful and arises so spontaneously in disasters that attempts to organize and facilitate the process are not described because the phenomenon is so pervasive and so common that it is not ordinarily noticed. This chapter describes the application of a multiple-family group as a crisis intervention technique in the aftermath of a disaster—the Waverly tank car explosion of 1978.

The Waverly Disaster

In 1978, a railroad tank car derailed in the small town of Waverly, Tennessee. It contained propane gasoline, which subsequently exploded and destroyed much of the small town's center. Several people died; many had severe burns. Seven burn patients were admitted to the Vanderbilt Medical Center, which had no specialized burn center at the time. Thus, these patients were cared for in general surgical wards. Since burn patients require much more attention from nurses, surgical house staff, and physical therapists than most hospital patients, the admission of a large number of burn patients demanded extra time and attention from the staff. Consequently, this admission represented a crisis for the entire system as well as to the families and individuals involved. The response of the nursing and medical staff was, as might be expected, to concentrate on the most urgent tasks of caring for their patients' physical health. The priorities of the hospital system were: (1) saving the patients' lives, (2) correcting their physical problems, (3) relieving physical discomfort, and (4) attending to the patients' emotional distress. The psychological distress of the patients' families was not seen as the direct responsibility of the medical or nursing staff. If major problems in the social environment affected the individual patient, then the social worker or nursing staff might have been asked to deal with the specific family members involved.

The constant pressure from patients and families for information and time was seen by the staff as an understandable but irritating demand, since the staff members were already straining to meet higher priorities. The hospital chaplain, social services personnel, and the psychiatric nurse and psychiatry resident working with the Psychiatric Consultation Liaison Services were all involved independently with the patients and families. In one case, three individuals were involved with the same family.

The attending plastic surgeon, the consultation-liaison psychiatrists, representatives of the nursing staff, the hospital chaplain, and social services personnel met and attempted to clarify their respective roles. Nursing services appeared to bear the brunt of the stress within the system. Caring for these severe burn patients generated an enormous amount of pressure on the staff, and the demands of the patients' families for attention and information simply could not be met. Mutual frustration and irritation were already present between the families and the nursing staff.

The particularly demanding care needed to manage the severe burn patients also required a great deal of the medical staff's time. This care was seen as their main priority, and again, explanations and progress reports demanded by the families could not always be provided by the staff. The medical social worker regularly assigned to the unit did not feel that one individual could respond to the needs of seven severely distressed families, as well as carry on routine care for patients in the rest of the service. Because the psychiatrist noted that none of the patients or their families were deemed sufficiently symptomatic to have a psychiatric consultation requested, no means were available in the traditional structure of the hospital to meet the specific needs of this situation. The chaplain felt that he could not answer questions about medical procedures or relieve the emotional distress experienced by these families collectively.

To meet the needs of the affected families, the psychiatrist proposed the idea of a multiple-family group to provide an intervention for the families, thus simultaneously using the staff's time more efficiently and relieving the system crisis. Such a group would take much of the stress off of the families and the hospital staff. According to this proposal, the multiple-family group would be used as a crisis intervention technique, and it would focus its activities according to the principles of crisis intervention.

The Multiple-Family Group

The psychiatrist and the hospital chaplain coled the group. The presence of the chaplain, who had already met most of the families individually, made the idea of being in the group more acceptable; that is, it diluted the notion of mental problems that the presence of a psychiatrist suggested to these rural southern families. On the other hand, because of his dual role as mental health professional and physician, the psychiatrist was able to function as an intermediary between the medical staff, the families, and other social agencies, and he provided some expertise in running multiple-family groups.

The format was a ninety-minute meeting once a week with two sessions the first week. In the first thirty minutes, the group was given accurate information according to the tenets of crisis information. Initially the attending plastic surgeon provided this information. Subsequently, representatives of the medical staff, the nursing service, and physical therapy, and eventually the recovered burn patients themselves were invited to be present for the initial thirty minutes, during which there was a brief presentation and a question-and-answer session.

The remaining sixty minutes was restricted to the families and the group leaders; a more traditional group therapy model was followed in which the families were encouraged to discuss their feelings and reactions to the material presented, the medical progress of the patients, and their own concerns.

The group consisted of representatives of the seven families. The membership was essentially consistent from week to week with a variation of only one or two individuals. The membership averaged twelve to fourteen persons and consisted of wives, a mother, two sisters, and two adult children.

It is important to note that this group was not primarily didactic in nature. The opening thirty-minute session was primarily a means of disseminating accurate information to the group. This served to decrease distortion, eliminate rumors, and decrease demands on staff time to provide the same information.

Didactic groups have a long history of predating group

therapy (Pratt, 1906). They are characterized by highly structured formats in which information is presented in a highly cognitive, somewhat formal manner. Emotional issues, if addressed,
are seen as secondary reactions to the patients' primary physical
difficulties. In contrast, we wanted to use part of the didactic
group format in the service of one of the basic principles of crisis intervention—giving out information. At the same time, we
also wanted to use and interpret the group process and mutual
support that developed spontaneously in the families and organize it around a crisis intervention model.

Group Processes (Content and Stages). The members of
the group were rather homogeneous. Several individuals knew
each other, and most of them had grown up in the same small
southern town and shared the same cultural and religious viewpoints. There was also a general understanding that the railroad
would provide financial assistance for the individuals injured in
the blast. Hence, certain financial considerations (such as paying for medical care) were not as important as they would normally be.

The group process might roughly be divided into an initial phase, an intermediate phase, and a final phase.

Initial Phase. In the initial or opening phase, group members commonly used denial in a number of ways. Most specifically, during this period, there was a denial of individual anxiety, either on the part of the family or the patient. This denial,
which could be seen as an initial response to life-threatening
catastrophe, was characterized by such statements as "He
doesn't seem to be worried a bit. I saw him laughing while they
were changing his dressings just like his old self. He had that
twinkle in his eye." Family members would deny their own
anxiety by such comments as "Well, I'm just glad I'm able to
be here when he needs me. I'm not really the sort of person that
gets upset by little things."

Discussion in these opening group sessions always focused
on the individual burn patients. Family members rarely spoke
about their own emotions, feelings, or needs. Their attitudes
could be described as a kind of anxious optimism. This was
manifested in the hovering behavior noted by the nursing staff

prior to the group; smiling but anxious family members were seen in the lounge or the hall at all hours of the day or night, hovering around any of the nursing staff who happened to pass by, asking for some word on a patient's progress or status. They felt confident in the medical staff, and they vigorously defended this faith against anything that might disturb it. They seemed to require the sense of well-being that came from knowing that their loved ones were getting the best possible care.

One wife related at length the relief and gratitude she felt when her husband was transferred to Vanderbilt Hospital rather than another hospital in the community where some other victims were treated, because "This is where they teach doctors how to be doctors and the ones that teach them have to be the best." Many commented about what a marvelous place Vanderbilt was. Many family members related stories of near miraculous treatments and cures of individuals performed by the doctors at the Vanderbilt medical center after non-Vanderbilt physicians had been unable to help.

We were struck by the lack of criticism of the hospital staff, even though the situation was clearly frustrating and difficult for all concerned. The occasional criticisms that did arise tended to be directed toward two staff members not directly responsible for patient care. For example, in one instance, a surgical resident was felt to be condescending and rude to a family member. In discussing this, the family members quickly noted with some relief that the resident was transferred to another service and was no longer responsible for the patient's care. They also felt that the attending physician would have "chewed him out" if he had been aware of the resident's behavior.

This combination of denial and the idealization of physician and nursing staff competency served a defensive function: It reassured family members about the likelihood of the recovery of their loved ones. The interventions of the leaders at this point were supportive, focusing on conveying the notion that anxiety and stress in the family members were normal and expected. The group leaders drew frequent parallels between the psychological healing that needed to take place in the family members and the physical healing in the patients, and they emphasized that everyone involved could be expected to experience and was experiencing their own pain. This sort of intervention seemed to legitimize discussion of individual anxiety as the group progressed, and it helped the individuals accept the notion that their distress was a normal, predictable response to the crisis and not a pathological inability to be strong.

Intermediate Phase. After the life-threatening crisis was over and it was clear that none of the patients was going to die, the emphasis and concerns of the group shifted, and the group entered an intermediate phase. At this point the focus became the stress for both the patients and the families that is associated with extended hospitalization. This began the discussion of concerns about the future expressed in terms of chronic psychological stress and adapting to long-term sequelae.

The certainty of the patients' recovery, which by no means meant total recovery, allowed the family members to express their own concerns more readily. Individuals began to voice anxieties, somatic complaints, and difficulty with sleeping, as well as problems with children and increasing conflicts with the nursing staff. It was not clear whether these complaints represented a response to the patients' progress or to the encouragement to express personal concerns in the group. However, it was at this point that the transition from a purely didactic group model became more apparent.

Direct discussion of personal feelings and the stresses on the family members themselves now emerged. The group members appeared to provide direct emotional support for each other, and the group leaders were able to recognize and interpret the major dynamics of smoldering conflicts between family members and the nursing staff.

One example involved a case of a burn patient whose family members were unable to show affection through touching or holding the patient because of medical precautions. Administering to simple needs such as feeding and assisting in some nursing needs provided the only direct contact available to the family. The family recognized that they wanted to administer these services themselves because of their need to nurture and have contact with their relative, and this enabled them to dis-

cuss this need constructively with the nursing staff. At first, the
nursing staff had seen the family's insistent requests to be involved in feeding and caring for the patient as interference and
an intrusion on their professional responsibilities. After feedback from the group, the nursing staff delegated specific tasks
to the family, and much of the conflict expressed in the group
disappeared.

Another example of family stress involved a construction
worker whose hands were severely burned. It became clear that
even with multiple grafts, he could not return to his previous
work. This became a source of great anxiety for his wife, who
began speaking of her concerns, such as looming financial problems for the family and her doubts about her ability to find or
hold down a job. Two other wives in the group who were working were able to help this woman. They described their own
similar feelings before they started working, and they reassured
this woman that it was possible to work and carry on the responsibilities of being a wife and mother, describing in detail
how they did it themselves. One of the wives' daughters was
also helpful in describing her reactions to having a working
mother. Together, these people were able to provide some practical suggestions and empathic support for the woman, as well
as serving as role models.

Final Phase. Concerns about posthospital adaptation
characterized the final phase of the group. This again paralleled
the clinical course of the burn patients. The completion of the
grafting and the general progress of the patients clearly indicated that discharge was imminent. The major issues for family
members at this time tended to be a growing recognition of the
problems of disfigurement and scarring and the severe disruption in their lives brought on by the disaster.

It was striking that issues concerning anger at the railroad
or the financial settlement were never openly discussed in the
group, nor could the group leaders discern any related issues.
Most group members seemed to feel that the financial settlement would be generous and adequate and that there was no
reason to be concerned about it. There may have been some element of denial and magical expectation in this belief. The fami-

lies were more concerned about the impact of the burns and the effects of the trauma on the patients and how the family members would deal with those effects when the patients returned home.

The chance for the group to meet with a recovered burn patient and his wife at this point was a valuable experience. The group had the opportunity to come to terms with such ongoing problems as the burn victim's sensitivity to sun and the painfulness of grafted skin (for example, patients experience difficulty putting their hands in the pockets of clothing for some years after grafting). The group was also able to deal with the problems related to the emotional reactions of extended family members and friends to the new appearance of the burn patients. All of this seemed to have a marked impact on the group, and it brought into sharp focus some of the issues that they would face when their patients returned home.

One patient who had been utilizing primarily traditional religious support systems and who relied upon the chaplain during his hospitalization began to experience intense anxiety as his discharge date came up. The chaplain attributed this heightened distress to the patient's difficulty in assigning a meaning to his experience within the context of his religious background and the magical expectation that he would be cured completely through faith in his religious beliefs and the medical staff. A similar state of marked anxiety was observed in his wife and mother. This family, which was involved with a fundamentalist church, employed a very closed and rigid style of communication. The expression of doubts about the future was considered as a loss of faith or a denial of the family's religious values.

Other group members interpreted the events differently. Their similar backgrounds and the cohesiveness of the group enabled the family to hear and accept these differing perspectives. The notion that the anxiety was both understandable and acceptable and that every other family also wrestled with the meaning of the event reassured the troubled family, provided models, and allowed them to discuss their feelings and concerns with others in new ways.

The group terminated as the first burn patients were dis-

charged. This decision was based purely on medical considerations and logistics. Given the outcome, discussed below, termination was a mistake. The group should have continued until
the patients had satisfactorily reentered their families and their
community. A transition was noted in the group process from
the opening phase of the group, when phrases like "if only"
and "what if" were very common. In the terminal phase of the
group, this speculation seemed to be replaced by a sense of a
special bond among the families and patients. Reports from social workers and medical staff who had frequent contact with
patients and families in the outpatient clinic where they came
for follow-up indicated that these bonds persisted for some
years after termination of the group.

The Therapeutic Process and Outcome. Several general
benefits of the group sessions were observed. These may be
categorized according to the same three phases noted in the
group process. During the first stage, providing information and
support were the most critical interventions. This stage occurred
during the initial hospitalization and during the initial stage of
the life-threatening crisis. There was a marked decrease in the
anxiety of the families as they became better informed about
the burn treatment and its possible complications. Mispercep-
tions diminished and a general improvement in communication
was noted by the medical and nursing staff. This seemed to result directly from the dispersal of information in the group,
where the same information was heard by everyone at the same
time.

For example, it was difficult for families to understand
the need for tube-feeding to maintain a positive nitrogen balance. It was also difficult for them to understand the painful
treatments that the patients resisted, such as whirlpool baths
or passive and active walking exercises to prevent contractures.
Because of the presence of one of the nurses during the initial
phase of the group, valuable feedback about the necessity of
these various procedures could be provided. It helped the families to see the difficulties that members of the nursing staff and
physical therapy had in inflicting pain on their patients during
these procedures. Thus, the families came to see the staff as
caring and human rather than sadistic.

A striking result of this phase for the hospital system was the reduction in stress experienced by the medical and nursing staff. The time required for lengthy, repetitious explanations was reduced, and the nursing and medical staff had more time to meet their increased patient care responsibilities. Less demand for individual attention from the staff was noted as the level of friction between families and staff decreased as a result of the group.

In addition to information giving and support, emphasizing the common experience improved the cohesiveness of the group. The emphasis on the naturalness of psychological distress and the similarity of the symptoms among patients was important in preparing the families for the more open discussion of these issues that emerged in the intermediate stage. The recurring conjectures about "what if" and "if only" concerning the accident and attempts to find meaning in their experiences were also seen as a generalized phenomenon that promoted cohesiveness among the group members.

The intervention in the intermediate stage shifted more toward psychological issues. The increasing cohesiveness of the group and the decreasing anxieties about the survival of the patients facilitated this shift. The staff interventions focusing on the psychological healing processes and the naturalness of psychological distress in both patients and their families also encouraged the discussion of these issues.

Finally, in the final stage, focusing the group on the anticipated problems raised by the patients' reentry into the family was markedly facilitated by bringing in recovered burn patients. Again, the families were of considerable help to each other in discussing how they would handle the reactions of strangers and family members to the patients when they returned, what attitudes to take, whether they should be concerned about being overprotective of the patients, whether they should encourage the patients to talk about their feelings and experiences, how the accident would change the relationships between the patients and other family members, and so on. In retrospect, the problems that developed in these families after the group terminated indicate that anticipating the difficulties involved in reentry does not prevent the severe distress associated with these phenomena from emerging. This will be discussed later in the chapter.

Short-Term Follow-up. During the group, no patients or family members developed sufficient overt symptomology to require psychiatric consultation or treatment. However, after the patients were discharged, five individuals (including both patients and family members) sought treatment for major problems largely attributable to the emotional trauma caused by the disaster. These problems are described below.

Approximately one year after discharge, one patient, Mr. A., developed a major depression with vegetative symptoms requiring antidepressants and psychotherapy. This individual was struggling with a loss of status and self-esteem resulting from his inability to use his hands. Mr. A. was a mechanic and derived a large part of his livelihood from operating a service station. He maintained and repaired cars and household appliances for family members as well as customers. With the loss of income and the ability to do these things for his family, he felt worthless and inadequate.

Mrs. B. sought treatment for depression and marital difficulty. She ultimately sought a separation and divorce. While significant conflicts existed before the disaster, the increasing withdrawal and uncommunicativeness of her husband, who seemed to be struggling with a reactive depression, proved insurmountable.

Another patient, Mr. J., was readmitted for regrafting and became increasingly and profoundly regressed, unable to feed himself, and uncommunicative, and he required a psychiatric consultation. His symptoms cleared dramatically when the physician who had cared for him during his first admission returned from vacation. Mr. J. had developed a very intense, idealized relationship with this physician, and he did well after discharge.

Still another patient, Mr. M., was admitted for complications caused by excessive alcohol intake. This seemed an attempt to self-medicate for his anxiety and depression, which were generated by problems due to his reentry into the family and community.

Finally, Mrs. O. was admitted for an exacerbation of a

chronic medical problem, diabetes. This was felt to be secondary to stress and her failure to follow daily medical regimens involving diet and insulin injections, which she had previously managed without difficulty. Her attending physician felt this to be an unconscious communication about her own distress and neediness.

These developments after discharge from the hospital following an apparently effective short-term intervention point to a disparity between physical and psychological recovery. In some cases, discharge may have allowed other family members to express their distress or to seek help after a period of holding themselves together for the sake of the severely burned patients. For other families, the necessary long-term adaptation to burns did not occur until healing was complete and they were forced to adjust to their relative's scarring and permanent disabilities.

This experience impresses us with the need for ongoing support after hospital discharge. Specifically, crisis intervention should continue until the crisis in psychological terms is resolved. The individual patient and family needs should determine the end of treatment and support, not external events such as hospital discharge. We think the completion of healing in these burn patients may have precipitated a period of intense distress that forced them to confront realities previously masked by magical expectations of having no scars. The attempt to work with these issues prior to hospital discharge within the family group did not dramatically affect the intensity of the experience when the families and patients finally had to deal with these issues.

A parallel exists with the failure of anticipatory grief work to prevent any acute grief reactions in the families of the terminally ill, as noted by Glick and Parkes (1974). These authors note the disparity between the duration of distress actually reported by these widows and the prevailing notion that grief is resolved in a few weeks or months. We think a parallel may be drawn between extended mourning and the psychological effects of a traumatic event such as was caused by the Waverly explosion. Both represent normal (though unusual) responses that have predictable symptoms and that are generally underestimated both in degree and duration by professionals and society at large.

Countertransference Reactions

Working with a multiple-family group is complex and anxiety producing for the therapist. This increased anxiety can be explained in part by the complexity of the data in a multiple-family group compared with therapy for an individual, a single family, or a group composed of unrelated individuals. Multiple-family groups require that data be processed from all these sources at the same time. Specifically, one must pay attention to the responses of the individual, to the family as a system, and then to the processes of the group as a whole and the family as a subunit of that group. For this reason, the use of a cotherapist has generally been helpful.

Some differences within the group discussed here were particularly outstanding. The most striking feature was the sense of drama and excitement that the background of the explosion and fire created. The therapist's wish to be accepted and to feel a part of the unfolding newsworthy events was quite strong. In such a situation, the therapist's interest and curiosity may cause him or her to fail to identify verbalizations by group members about the disaster as being defensive in nature. Consequently, although such utterances do not reflect genuine efforts at working through the trauma, they are reinforced by the therapist's keen interest in them.

Additionally, there may be a strong tendency among mental health professionals whose major orientation is psychodynamic to interpret defenses too quickly and to "deal with what's really going on" when, according to the principles of crisis intervention, a more supportive technique is indicated, at least during the period of acute crisis.

Reflections on the Use of the Multiple-Family Model

In an early study, Morley and Brown (1969) compared the advantages and disadvantages of using groups as a crisis intervention technique, which they based on their experiences with an open-ended group for low-income individuals in crisis. They noted several advantages to this model: (1) Many patients are more willing to participate in a group setting about a specific problem than to enter psychiatric treatment; (2) many individuals are unable or unwilling to contract for long-term help for a specific problem; and (3) the universality of the crisis creates a common ground between the patient and the therapist. Disadvantages were some loss of group process as a tool and the loss of spontaneity.

In our group, the didactic phase provided a structure and a focus within which we attempted to deal with emotional factors. The use of a psychiatrist and a chaplain as coleaders appeared to legitimize emotional issues as well as decrease the tendency to intellectualize, a characterisitic of didactic groups in general. We felt that some of the unique characteristics of this group (the sharing of the same crisis in time and type of injury by members of the same community and the extent of informal contact outside the group) compensated for many of the disadvantages of crisis intervention groups previously noted by Morley and Brown (1969). Additionally, the didactic group format met the informational component of the crisis intervention for the families involved. At the same time, the group's ability to use some of the advantages of therapeutic group settings (the mutual support, the suggestions of alternative means of coping, and the expression of usually unacceptable feelings) was not impaired.

Our basic premise is that individuals cope best when they have supportive, involved families. The corollary is that using crisis intervention groups to support family units is a maximally efficient way to assist large groups of individuals in a minimal amount of professional time. The data to support or refute this premise are, at the present time, meager.

The measure of the success of the crisis intervention group described here was based largely on the clinical impression of the staff involved. Nonparticipating staff in the hospital also perceived the group as an effective intervention, although no objective measurements were available to support these observations. However, it was quite clear that the intervention helped reduce stress on the nursing and medical staffs. Anxiety

among the individual family members appeared to be significantly reduced, and they appeared to adapt psychologically to
living with the sequelae of chronic burns better than did family
members of patients with severe burns who were not in the
group. This judgment is based on the observations of group
leaders as well as the nursing staff and the medical staff, who
were able to observe the patients in the outpatient clinic and at
follow-up. According to these staff members, families who were
in the group seemed more comfortable, asked fewer questions,
and were more accepting of the burn patients than other families were. The absence of a control group and some objective
index of distress both before and after the intervention limits
the usefulness of these observational findings.

The therapeutic benefit as measured on a number of
parameters has been noted objectively in an outcome study of
crisis intervention groups for individuals, but data for groups
like the one discussed here are unavailable. Using similar parameters to measure individual distress in a future application of
this group model should yield useful data.

A number of publications emphasize the importance of
helping patients cope with disasters (Block, Silber, and Perry,
1956; Faberow and Gordon, 1981; Silber, Perry, and Bloch,
1957; Titchener and Kapp, 1976). However, documentation of
the impact of family support is surprisingly small. Increased
fear and the need for affiliation as a consequence of a natural
disaster have been documented (Strumpfer, 1970), which supports the notion that groups and family groups in particular
meet specific individual needs. However, Bromet, Schulberg,
and Dunn (1982) failed to demonstrate a dependent relationship between social network and psychiatric distress in mothers
following the Three Mile Island incident. In Bromet's study, although women who experienced low distress reported that their
social networks were qualitatively better, this could not be demonstrated as an independent variable. We conclude that documentation of the degree and manner of assistance with which
families help individuals to cope with disaster or crisis is not yet
available.

Conversely, there is evidence that at least in some situations, crises are destructive to family units. For example, among the Love Canal families, there was a 40 percent rate of separation or divorce among the 1978 evacuees (Holden, 1980). Some investigators have emphasized preserving the family unit after crisis and thus its vital role of support (Block, Silber, and Perry, 1956; Faberow and Gordon, 1981; Silber, Perry, and Bloch, 1957; Titchener and Kapp, 1976). Rapaport (1958), adapting a concept from Piaget, emphasizes the importance of family and community in supplying the "nutrient stimuli" for certain superego functions that sustain individual and cultural values. When the support of family and community is removed, most individuals respond with a variety of regressive and maladaptive behaviors. This is a parallel phenomenon to the altered cognition and perception seen in sensory deprivation experiments. Numerous examples exist, from North Korean brainwashing techniques to the Patty Hearst case (Rapaport, 1958).

Multiple-family groups for crisis interventions hold promise as a technique for improving individual coping ability as well as supporting the family unit. They would appear to be more effective where there is a common crisis experienced by all the families involved. They are especially useful in a hospital setting, where the structure and focus on individual patients limit the intervention available for other family members or the family unit.

Future Directions

In order to further develop the crisis intervention group as a clinical tool for families, research should be aimed at documenting the group's influence on individual and family emotional responses, adaptation to crisis, and the family's ability to provide support to its members. Finally, it should be emphasized that there is a ripple effect of a disaster on individuals, the family units of which they are a part, and the institutions and systems that make up their community and society. To look at it too closely or too narrowly is to miss seeing part of the phenomenon.

References

Block, H., Silber, E., and Perry, S. "Some Factors in the Emotional Reaction of Children to Disaster." *American Journal of Psychiatry,* 1956, *113,* 416-422.

Bromet, E., Schulberg, H., and Dunn, L. "Reactions of Psychiatric Patients to the Three Mile Island Nuclear Accident." *Archives of General Psychiatry,* 1982, *39,* 725-730.

Donovan, J. M., and McElroy, C. M. "The Crisis Group—An Outcome Study." *American Journal of Psychiatry,* 1979, *136,* 906-910.

Faberow, N., and Gordon, N. *Manual for Child Health Workers in Major Disasters.* Department of Health and Human Services Publication No. (ADM) 81-1070. Washington, D.C.: U.S. Government Printing Office, 1981.

Glick, I. O., and Parkes, C. M. *The First Year of Bereavement.* New York: Wiley, 1974.

Hill, R., and Hansen, D. "Families in Disaster." In G. Baker and D. Chapman (Eds.), *Man and Society in Disaster.* New York: Basic Books, 1962.

Holden, C. "Love Canal Residents Under Stress." *Science,* 1980, *208,* 1242-1244.

Morley, W. E., and Brown, V. B. "The Crisis Intervention Group: A Natural Mating or a Marriage of Convenience?" *Psychotherapy: Theory, Research, and Practice,* 1969, *6,* 31-36.

Pratt, J. H. "The Home Sanitorium Treatment of Consumptives." *Boston Medical Surgical Journal,* 1906, *154,* 210-216.

Rapaport, D. "The Theory of Ego Anatomy: A Generalization." *Bulletin of the Menninger Clinic,* 1958, *22,* 26.

Silber, E., Perry, S., and Bloch, D. "Patterns of Parent-Child Interaction in a Disaster." *Psychiatry,* 1957, *21,* 159-167.

Strumpfer, D. "Fear and Affiliation During a Disaster." *Journal of the Society of Psychology,* 1970, *82,* 263-268.

Titchener, J., and Kapp, F. "Family and Character Change at Buffalo Creek." *American Journal of Psychiatry,* 1976, *133,* 295-299.

16

Edward Walwork, A.C.S.W.

▦ ▦ ▦ ▦ ▦ ▦ ▦ ▦ ▦ ▦ ▦ ▦ ▦

Coping with the Death of a Newborn

The birth of an infant is usually eagerly anticipated. The family expects the event to be a time of joy. The maternal-infant relationship commences in utero, grows with quickening, and blossoms with the birth of the baby. When a newborn dies, the joy is dashed and replaced by grief, sorrow, and often feelings of failure. Although the fields of perinatology and neonatology have made tremendous advances, deaths in the neonatal intensive care unit still occur and families continue to require support.

The neonate is a unique member of the hospital patient population. Although each baby is an individual with a separate prognosis, the neonatal intensive care unit population shares a common characteristic. Every patient in this type of special care unit has been hospitalized since birth, never having been cared for at home by the family. The length of the infant's life in the neonatal intensive care unit varies with the severity of the medical problem and the aggressiveness of care by the health care delivery team. Some infants who are born alive live only a few minutes, while others live for hours, days, weeks, or months, all within the confines of the hospital. The intensity of the parental grief reaction is not proportionate to the length of the newborn's life.

Any family with a sick infant in the neonatal intensive care unit has legitimate needs for support and counseling. The author is the medical social worker assigned to the neonatal intensive care unit (NICU) at Milwaukee County Medical Complex in Milwaukee, Wisconsin. The role of the medical social worker is to deal with the psychosocial needs of families whose infants are hospitalized. The Milwaukee County Medical Complex is a tertiary-level health care facility providing specialty care in many areas. Its NICU was developed in 1967, and the author assumed the position of medical social worker with the unit in 1977. Much of the work described in this chapter occurred before the author joined the unit. The initiation and success of a bereaved-parents program at Milwaukee County Hospital were accomplished through the efforts and dedication of previous medical social workers.

Families experience stress and anxiety throughout their infants' stay in a neonatal intensive care unit, since the quality of life of their children is often a primary concern. This chapter, however, addresses the unique needs of a subgroup of NICU families—those who experience the death of a newborn.

Major Causes of Neonatal Death

Before addressing the psychosocial aspects of families experiencing the death of their newborns, it is important to describe the major causes of neonatal death. These descriptions may be helpful in understanding the impact such deaths have on family members.

Many neonatal deaths are associated with prematurity. The term gestation of pregnancy is forty weeks; however, NICUs care for infants from twenty-four weeks gestational age onward. Infants whose birth weight is less than 1,000 grams and whose gestational age is less than thirty weeks are more likely to have underdeveloped lungs than older and larger premature babies. Deaths of these premature infants can occur because of hyaline membrane disease (the premature lung disease) despite maximum respiratory support (provided by a ventilator, endo-tracheal tubes, and so on). Most other causes of death of pre-mature infants are related to the brain. Premature infants have a multitude of fragile vessels in the ventricles of the brain. These vessels sometimes hemorrhage, and the subsequent bleed-ing into the brain is associated with neonatal death. Seizures in the neonatal period, whether related to interventricular hemor-rhage or other causes, can be a factor leading to the patient's death.

Other neonates who die in the neonatal intensive care unit may be term or postterm infants who have experienced birth trauma resulting in birth asphyxia, accompanying seizures, or brain death. Perinatal events such as a prolapsed umbilical cord, placental abruption, or placenta previa can lead to anoxia and subsequent neonatal death. These infants are not prema-ture babies. Because they are term or postterm, they may look like any other newborn.

Sepsis or infection, whether viral or bacterial, is another cause of neonatal death. Treatments exist, but they are not al-ways successful, and some newborns succumb to an overwhelm-ing infection.

Birth defects, also known as congenital anomalies, occur in a portion of the newborn population. Defects such as hypo-plastic kidneys, certain heart defects, and certain central ner-vous system defects can all lead to death in newborns.

Another major category of causes of neonatal death is the elective withdrawal of life support systems or withholding the use of these supports. The types of infant that might be in-cluded in this category are those whose prognoses are terminal regardless of the extent of treatment provided and those who are brain-dead or ventilator dependent. Also included are in-fants whose quality of life would be compromised by institu-tional dependency. Neonates whose prognosis includes profound mental retardation, severe cerebral palsy, or uncontrollable seizures might be considered as candidates for the elective with-drawal of treatment. In general, the withdrawal of treatment is considered when an infant's prognosis indicates a lifetime of de-pendency, even for the most basic of human needs.

412   Support Groups for Patients' Families

This area involves many moral, legal, and ethical issues, and laws regarding withholding or withdrawing life support vary by state. In some states, such as Wisconsin, the law has not addressed this issue with regard to newborns. Opinions vary as to the use of extraordinary measures, and families involved in such a circumstance must make an agonizing decision. There are neonatal centers where the physician unilaterally decides to withhold or withdraw support for an infant. Some ethicists espouse an implied contract between the physician and the patient, in this case the infant, and thereby eliminate the rights of the parents to decisions regarding their child.

In this author's experience, however, parents need and want to be involved in decision making, even though it is difficult and painful, and the infant and parents should be treated as a unit or system. In this view, the treatment contract exists between the physician and the family. In spite of moral and legal controversies, the fact exists that in NICUs around the country, elective withdrawal or withholding of life supports does occur and is a cause of death.

Psychosocial Needs of the Family of the Critically Ill Newborn

In the NICU the infant is the focus of physical care; however, the family is the focus of psychosocial care. Apart from attempts to satisfy the infant's needs for sensory stimulation at appropriate times (that is, auditory, olfactory, tactile, visual, and kinesthetic), very little is done to provide for the infant's emotional well-being. The family is considered the focus of psychosocial care, for indeed, at this point, these are the individuals who need help in coping with the emotional upheaval.

Even before coping with a newborn's death, the family must cope with a critically ill newborn. The birth of an infant who requires intensive care is a crisis for the family and places them in a state of disequilibrium. Initial stages of shock and denial may be followed by a period of grieving. The fact that most critically ill newborns are cared for in isolettes places a Plexiglas barrier between parent and child. Fear of the death of the child places a psychological barrier between parent and child, as the parent tries to protect himself or herself from emotional pain.

In addition to these psychological and physical barriers to bonding with a critically ill newborn, there are often additional physical barriers. Since perinatal care is regionalized and neonatal intensive care is available only in tertiary-level centers, mothers who deliver at community hospitals are initially deprived of contact with their newborn. The neonate in critical condition is transported by ambulance, helicopter, or airplane to a regional intensive care unit. Not until the mother is discharged from her own postpartum course may she be able to have contact with her sick newborn.

In the case of a premature infant, parents initially grieve the loss of the infant they anticipated and then adjust their image to the infant they have actually produced. Commonly there is anticipatory grief of the possible loss of this child. The anxiety that accompanies having a critically ill newborn often produces fear of the worst, which is often worse than the situation that actually exists.

The experience of having a newborn who is critically ill produces high levels of stress within the family. The mother, who has just delivered a baby, has her own discomfort, which drains the emotional energy needed to cope with the crisis of her sick infant. The normal postpartum period produces hormonal changes as the body readjusts to a state of nonpregnancy. The "postpartum blues" are then complicated by the stress of having a sick newborn. The father of an infant transported to a tertiary-level center is stressed by having to decide whether he should remain with and comfort his wife or go to the neonatal intensive care unit to be with his baby. The high cost of neonatal intensive care places financial stress on the family as well.

During the time that an infant is in intensive care, the family must restructure its priorities. Schedules are set and arranged around visits to the hospital. The time spent at the hospital varies with the baby's problems. Because the parents' work schedules are often disturbed by medical crises, the experience

is very disruptive to a family's life-style. Not until the newborn
is home from the hospital can some semblance of order be reestablished in the family's life.

Decisions about surgery or terminating life supports place
a couple under great stress. The extended family may or may
not be helpful in these situations. Additional stress might also
surface if the parents are not supportive of each other or if they
have differing opinions. The ability to communicate effectively
with one another is especially critical at this time.

When a newborn dies, as in any situation where there is a
great loss, the family is devastated. Parents may initially be in a
state of shock and disbelief. Statements such as "No, not my
baby" or "It can't be" indicate the family's use of the defense
mechanism of denial. Families need this until they are emotionally able to cope with the reality of the situation. A very normal
reaction in parents to the death of a newborn is guilt. Mothers
particularly tend to ruminate about their pregnancies and often
experience irrational thoughts about events that occurred or did
not occur that may have led to either premature delivery or the
infant's eventual death. Some parents feel guilty over sexual activity during the pregnancy, over being emotionally upset during the pregnancy, or over rejection of the mother's altered
body image during the pregnancy. Many families after the death
of a newborn have strong feelings of anger. These feelings of resentment can be directed at God, at family members, or at the
physician, whether an obstetrician or pediatrician. The most
destructive form of anger is directed inward by the family at
themselves.

Parents experiencing neonatal death cope with a period
of intense suffering. Physiological reactions include a lump in
the throat, chest tightness, aching arms, and subsequently the
release given by tears and sobs. This stage is experienced by
individuals at different times. Grief appears to come in waves,
interspersed by periods of relatively calm relief.

The death of a newborn can affect the marital relationship as well as the individual parent. Since men and women
usually grieve differently, there can be misunderstandings between partners. One partner may feel that since the other may

be ready to return to activities and social contacts sooner than the other, the love for the lost child was not as great. The husband may feel that his wife is overreacting with prolonged periods of depression. Since one parent may not wish to upset the other by discussing their loss, necessary communication and support may be hindered.

One effect of the infant's death on the parents can be manifested in the couple's sexual relationship. Although physical intimacy is a source of comfort to the parents, depression can lead to a lack of desire for sexual contact. The act of intercourse is directly related to pregnancy, and the fear of experiencing another pregnancy and subsequent neonatal death can be a barrier to a fulfilling sexual relationship.

Siblings of the infant will react to the loss. Their reactions will vary according to age, past experience, and how the event is handled by the parents. A wide range of responses is normal, from incessant talking about the death to a refusal to speak of it at all. Many children wish to know why the death occurred and if the baby will be coming back. Younger children may confuse wishes with events and need reassurance that wishes could not have caused or prevented the baby's death. If the parents use the concept of illness to explain the infant's death, siblings may need to be reassured repeatedly of their own wellness. All children will grieve and must be allowed to do so.

Using the Group Approach with Bereaved Parents

Families who experience the death of a newborn are plunged into a state of crisis. During crisis, there is a feeling of disequilibrium within the family; normal methods of coping are not effective, and the family searches to achieve a state of equilibrium again. This strong need tends to make the family more receptive to support offered by a group. During the period immediately following the death of an infant, the parents often have the support of hospital staff, extended family, and friends; however, as weeks go by there is an increasing amount of isolation from both professionals and the peer group. This isolation can occur despite the parents' continuing need for support.

Parents who have had an infant in an NICU for any length of time often develop very close relationships with the NICU staff. After the death of the child, the parents lose not only their loved one but also those who knew the infant best. This dual loss and accompanying feelings of isolation cause many parents to reach out to a group. The experience of having had a helping relationship with professional staff during a critical illness and death facilitates the parents' acceptance of other forms of on-going help.

The death of an infant who has never been home, never been cared for by the family, and perhaps never even validated as an individual human being is not an event that is understood by the community. Those individuals who have never experienced the phenomenon or have never known families who have lost a newborn do not appear to understand the period of bereavement that the parents experience. Superficial statements such as "You're young, you can always have another baby" or "It was a good thing you never brought him home" indicate a lack of understanding of the bereavement process experienced by the parents. This lack of understanding by the community in general is one of the strongest rationales for utilizing a group approach with parents experiencing neonatal death, since the opportunity to be understood by other families who have also suffered a similar loss is an attractive support.

People who have difficulty coping with a major life event may benefit from individual supportive guidance; however, because of pride or fear of being considered unable to handle grief or because of other reasons, some people resist reaching out and seeking help. Our society places great value on one's ability to cope with life's stresses. A group of bereaved parents collectively seeking support provides a less stigmatized source of help. The decrease in stigmatization is especially evident in self-help groups, because the power and control of the group are initially perceived by potential group members as being held by those like themselves.

The support and acceptance received in a group setting allow bereaved parents to present and discuss issues or thoughts generally considered taboo in the general population. Such issues often include feelings of resentment toward other mothers who have had successful pregnancies and healthy children and feelings of anger toward others who have either said something insensitive to the bereaved parent or else avoided them completely.

Since each group member in a bereaved-parents group has experienced the death of his or her child, it is legitimate for members to place demands on each other for reality testing. Parents cannot use the defense that the others do not know what it feels like or that they do not understand. Since a group is a protected environment representing a segment of the larger community, it provides a relatively safe milieu for testing new behaviors. Members of the group can accept certain coping patterns and reject others; anger is acceptable but denial and threats of suicide are not. Role playing within the group, such as trying out more assertive methods of behavior to be used with family members, friends, and health care providers, is a valuable practice before incorporating these new methods into the personal repertoire of the individual parent. The group setting exposes parents to a variety of methods of coping with loss. After exposure, the parent can attempt to use different methods outside the group, perhaps after testing them out in the group.

The fact that a group is a strong source of mutual assistance makes it an appropriate modality for intervention with bereaved parents. A bereaved-parents group offers an opportunity for mutual assistance, and each member derives satisfaction and positive reinforcement from helping others while also obtaining the help and support they need. The fact that a group is comprised of a number of individuals provides an opportunity for greater variety in types of helping relationships than is possible in a one-to-one relationship.

Notwithstanding differences in leaders' styles and effectiveness, the group approach promotes a feeling of equality among the group members, including the leader. The power, in a therapeutic sense, is derived from the group collectively, not from a sanctioned therapist. Because of the multiplicity of helping relationships and the egalitarian nature of a group approach,

the transference phenomenon experienced in a one-to-one therapeutic relationship is greatly reduced. It is more difficult to
project feelings and thoughts from one's life experiences onto a
group of people than it is to transfer them onto an individual.

One of the most important considerations in initiating a
successful group from the therapist's point of view is the sanc-
tion and approval of the agency, facility, or other system. This
gives the leader freedom to make important decisions regarding
location, group size, group duration, and so on. One of the most
salable factors in the group approach is the use of time. Group
counseling is more efficient in its use of professional time than
individual intervention, so more families can be reached, especially during those periods when demands on the worker's time
are great.

A Model Protocol for Dealing with Neonatal Death

An effective multidisciplinary relationship between the
physician, nurse, and social worker in the NICU at the Milwaukee County Medical Complex helped to establish a protocol for
dealing with neonatal death. Specifically, the social worker
meets with the family (whom he usually knows from a screening
assessment interview) at the time of the infant's death or dying.
Additionally, the social worker schedules appointments for the
family to meet with him and the physician approximately two
months after the death of the child and again at six months
after.

The purpose of meeting at the time of the death is to provide support, comfort, and information that can be accepted at
that time. The information needed by the family at that time
concerns the types of burial available, the possibility of donat-
ing the baby's body, the types of memorial services available,
how to notify family and friends of the death, and whether to
have an autopsy. In addition, parents are informed of the approximate costs involved for various decisions. Decision making,
however, does not have to be immediate. Parents often need to
be encouraged to express their grief—they need to be told that
it is normal and helpful to cry or scream and that they do not

have to "be strong." Parents may want to be alone with their baby at this time, or they may wish one of the staff to remain with them. Additionally, parents should be given the opportunity to hold their deceased baby if they wish. This is especially important, since they may never have had the chance to do so before.

In the meeting two months after the death, parents are reassured about the normalcy of their grief response. A wide range in the intensity of grieving and the duration of grieving stages is normal. This meeting also gives parents a chance to ask questions and to receive an interpretation of autopsy results. At the time of death, parents are often in a state of shock and do not hear or recall things that have been said. The individual meeting may clarify and emphasize information already discussed at the time of the infant's death.

Most parents at this time have questions and anxieties about future pregnancies. During the meeting, these concerns are addressed and as much reassurance as is warranted is given to the family about the likelihood of another traumatic birth experience. Regardless of the amount of reassurance given a family, a future pregnancy will be a time of anxiety because of the previous experience. The uniqueness of the deceased infant should be emphasized, as should be the fact that any future child will not replace the lost infant but be loved as a unique individual. Parents are advised to allow themselves time to work through their grief reaction before assuming the stress of another pregnancy.

Individual meetings with the physician, nurse, and social worker are time consuming for these already busy professionals, but they are of vital importance to the families. The families' need to talk through their experiences is evidenced by the length of individual meetings and the fact that parents unhesitatingly travel up to sixty or seventy miles to meet with the staff.

The meeting with a family held six months postdeath provides the family with an opportunity to recall and discuss their baby. Most parents are at a different stage of the grieving process at this time. The experience is bittersweet; time does not erase sorrow over the loss, but parents are often able to speak of having the joy of loving their baby, as brief as the experience may have been. The meeting also provides an opportunity to assess the family's grief reaction and to refer them to ongoing therapy if pathological grief responses are noted. The staff (physician, nurse, and social worker) also derives an indirect benefit from meeting with families postdeath—seeing a family survive and adjust to such a tremendous loss is therapeutic to a highly stressed professional.

Bereaved-Parents Group at
Milwaukee County Medical Complex

The time constraints on the professional staff pose a problem in meeting with families after the death of a newborn. In the early years of the NICU at the Milwaukee County Medical Complex, many bereaved parents expressed a need for ongoing support after the death of their infant. A previous social worker and the physician met with several sets of parents who were interested in a bereaved-parents support group and supported their request. The families formed the group to provide the additional support that they felt they needed; the group approach was felt to be most feasible because it served a greater number of families.

According to records kept on the initiation of the group, the core group was apparently selected by accepting all those parents who approached the staff with the idea of a support group. The social worker became the group leader and helped identify and formulate a group purpose: to provide ongoing support to one another and to help newly bereaved parents cope with their loss. The parents comprising the initial core group were past the shock phase of the grief reaction, and this factor was considered when recruiting new group members. Although the core parents still had unmet needs themselves, the purpose of their involvement was to help others.

The initial core group consisted of five couples (ten individuals). This group was homogeneous (married, generally middle class, and Caucasian), although this was not intentional. The

past the shock phase
core group

homogeneous nature of the group, as well as the clustering around a common theme, helped stabilize the project, and the core group members were quick to support one another.

The role of the social worker in the beginning phase of the group's life was that of facilitator. The social worker made the necessary practical arrangements and reserved a meeting room in the hospital that was large enough to accommodate ten people comfortably. The room was located on a different floor from the NICU. After consulting with the core parents, the social worker planned the time, length, and frequency of meetings. The group met once a month at 7:00 P.M. for two hours. The therapist notified parents of the meetings and subsequently provided ongoing referrals. As facilitator, the social worker suggested topics for group discussion and encouraged individuals to become involved in the group process.

During the initial phase, the therapist set ground rules. Information shared within the group was to be confidential, and the purpose of the group meetings was to provide bereaved families with emotional support and an avenue for ventilation. The group was free to discuss details of their own infant's death, but since each infant's circumstances were unique, the group was not to give medical advice about newborns to one another.

The bereaved-parents group was planned to be long term and open ended. The core group members committed themselves for an unspecified period of time; however, as the group life developed, parents initiated and terminated involvement in the group according to their own needs. New members joined the group as old members terminated, and the group process continued.

After several group meetings in the hospital, the group elected to meet in the members' homes on a rotating basis. Not only did this remove the obstacle of coming to an emotionally charged place, but the change in meeting place increased the group's power, since they now were on their own turf.

One of the many topics discussed was how to handle holidays. Couples who had already experienced a holiday after the death of their baby gave personal accounts of their experiences to newly bereaved parents in the group. One parent recounted that all of Christmas Day was tearful and depressing, especially since the holiday celebrates birth. The way she was able to make it through the day was not to attempt or expect to be happy or jovial but to accept her sadness while reminding herself that the holiday was only one day.

Another theme discussed was handling the reactions of friends and relatives. One mother ventilated her anger about a relative who told her that she now had a little angel in heaven. The mother recounted that she did not want an angel in heaven and how cruel and insensitive this comment seemed to her. The group supported her and validated her feelings while suggesting responses such as "That isn't the way I feel about it" or "It doesn't help me to think about my baby's death that way," which are direct and clear statements that avoid arguments which might be upsetting.

Evolution into a Citywide Self-Help Group

The first year of the bereaved-parents group proved to be a period of evolution. The change in meeting place and its attendant increase in the group's power and control had important implications for the future of the group. Although it had been initiated for parents whose infants had died in the Milwaukee County Medical Complex, the group was expanded to accept referrals from all hospitals in the Milwaukee area. This enlarged the group from a moderate size of ten individuals to a large group of twenty-six to thirty. It also precluded the social worker serving as group leader, since the hospital's social service department did not provide service to other hospitals' patients. As a result, the social worker acted only as a consultant to the group.

As the group's identity emerged and its power and control grew, members of the group began to assume leadership roles. The group was clearly evolving from a therapist-led group into a self-help group. Subsequently, the direct support of the Milwaukee County Medical Complex was withdrawn, and the group obtained financial support and legitimization from the Childbirth Education Association.

As the group evolved into a self-help group, the group purpose expanded. The emotional support to newly bereaved parents in a group setting remained the primary purpose; however, in order to supplement the services offered in the monthly group meeting, a volunteer phone counselor network was established. This involved training parents to deal effectively with newly bereaved parents on a one-to-one basis. In addition to the telephone contact program, a visitation program was established whereby a group parent would visit a newly bereaved parent, either at home or in the hospital, to provide individual support.

The bereaved-parents self-help group also added a task and goal orientation to the existing purpose of providing group help to one another. Since the group size had increased dramatically, it became possible to set up committees within the organization. A library committee of the bereaved parents self-help group developed a bibliography of literature dealing with infant death and grief reactions in families, which it then organized and printed for distribution to group members. Many of the books and articles included in the bibliography were obtained, and the library committee established a lending library for parents. The library committee also reviewed and acquired new texts for the lending library.

One of the most helpful tasks that the entire self-help group accomplished was compiling and reproducing a Bereaved Parents' Information Packet for dissemination to newly bereaved parents. The booklet in the packet discusses such topics as hospital procedures following the death of a newborn (such as autopsies and the disposition of the infant's body), a funeral for the baby, grief, reactions of friends and relatives to the baby's death, helping the other children when the infant dies, and thinking about another pregnancy. The packet contains a bibliography and information about the bereaved-parents group. The Bereaved Parents' Information Packet has been distributed to hospital nurseries throughout the Milwaukee area.

The bereaved-parents support group, functioning as a self-help group, also established an educational committee, which has developed an outreach program to contact physicians, nurses, and other allied health care professionals to inform them of the group's existence and its role. The educational committee has presented lectures and in-service training sessions to perinatal hospital staff, including physicians, nurses, social workers, and chaplains. They have also done in-service training with public health nurses, who have a community-level involvement with newly bereaved families and other helping professionals.

Strengths and Limitations of the Self-Help Format

In overview, the transformation of the bereaved-parents support group to a self-help group has had positive and negative results. The group now has an expanded mission and continues its original purpose, serving a need rarely met by the professional community. However, there are problems encountered in such a group. Since the group is open ended and ongoing, the membership is ever changing, which decreases group stability. The group's continued existence depends on constant referrals of newly bereaved families, but this random recruitment leads to a certain loss of control. At times the group can be too large to promote any intimacy among group members. Also, a large group can be very intimidating to vulnerable new parents and make it difficult for them to feel secure. Finally, a large group makes it difficult for each member to get individual attention.

In addition, because of the random recruitment, the issue of whether a group experience is appropriate for an individual is ignored. Not all newly bereaved parents should receive group help; a one-to-one therapeutic relationship is more appropriate for some parents. Parents do have a life before losing their child, and each parent brings a unique set of life experiences into the crisis situation of neonatal death. Parents with existing psychoses or histories of depression are not appropriate for a self-help group. Not only can group members with preexisting pathologies be hurt by the group, but they can also be destructive to the group itself.

The skill of the group leader is one of the keys to the success of the group. Without a professional group leader, group-related problems may not be addressed. More verbal parents

may tend to monopolize the group session, depriving less assertive parents of the opportunity of talking through issues. Individuals who are particularly vulnerable may be scapegoated by
the group if the group leader does not make appropriate interventions.

Although the pattern of grief reactions in most parents
is similar, occasionally a parent may experience a pathological
grief response, such as an overwhelming denial of the death or
suicidal ideation. Without a professional leader, pathology may
be overlooked or even reinforced by the group. The leader
needs to identify pathology, know how to deal with the affected individual, and direct the person to a competent professional for individual therapy. A self-help group leader may not
recognize pathology or have the confidence or ability to channel the individual to alternative sources of help.

The bereaved-parents group in Milwaukee was initiated
with a professional leader; however, it evolved into a self-help
group. The change in goals of the group as it evolved from a
professionally led group to a self-help one perhaps accounts for
the group's continued existence. The group is currently more
task- and goal-oriented than therapeutic. Although the group
functions independently, the group's effectiveness would be improved if it consulted a professional counselor or therapist.
Such a consultant could train the parents in group facilitation
and peer counseling and educate them about (1) relating to parents who are grieving the death of their baby, (2) setting limits
in working with parents, (3) recognizing normal and abnormal
grief, and (4) using interview techniques. Such training would
transform parents with good intentions into peer counselors,
but they should realize that old pain will be recalled. In addition to training peer group counselors, the professional consultant should be available to help peer counselors decide whether
to refer parents to individual therapy and where to refer them.
The consultant should be available to supervise peer counselors
in any area where they have doubts about their own competence.

Unfortunately, employing a consultant can create rivalry
for power and control, since once a self-help group functions

without a consultant, it is difficult to incorporate a consultant from outside the group. An effective consultant will need to establish a relationship with the group leaders based on mutual trust and a respect for the consultant's knowledge. The consultant will need to convey to the group leaders that he or she values their thoughts and opinions. This will increase the leaders' feelings of self-worth and enhance the relationship between the leaders and the consultant.

The bereaved-parents support group has not yet addressed termination and related issues since the group is ongoing and open-ended. A form of termination has occurred, however—the termination of leadership. As times passes, leaders terminate their involvement with the group and new leaders take over. Events such as a new pregnancy, moving out of state, or a new career may cause a leader to leave the group. Such times of transition create a crisis of change within the group, as a feeling of loss recurs. The crisis can be one of loss or of opportunity. The group experiences a metamorphosis, with some members terminating involvement and others increasing theirs. The transition of group leadership, then, provides an opportunity for personal and group growth in the face of challenge.

There has not been any measurement of the effectiveness of the group in Milwaukee. It is difficult to assess the current effectiveness of the group, since peer leaders control the group. The author has heard positive statements from parents participating in the group when he has met them at the two-month and six-month follow-up visits.

Conclusion

In summary, the family experiencing the death of a newborn is in a unique situation. Most pregnancies end successfully, and most deaths that have been experienced by others have been the deaths of individuals known to the community. The death of a hoped-for child is a loss of what could have been. The camaraderie felt by bereaved parents who undergo this experience naturally leads to a group experience. Families who experience neonatal death, just like other medical-surgical patients and their families, need the reassurance that they are not alone. A traumatic or tragic event, whatever it might be, has happened to others and will happen again. Other patients and families have adapted and coped, and through group support, reassurance, and modeling, so will each individual who experiences a medical or surgical crisis. Through this sharing of experience, the support group can be a powerful therapeutic intervention for all kinds of medical-surgical patients and their families.

References

Borg, S., and Lasker, J. *When Pregnancy Fails.* Boston: Beacon Press, 1981.

Duff, R. S., and Campbell, A. G. M. "Moral and Ethical Dilemmas in the Special Care Nursery." *New England Journal of Medicine,* 1973, *289,* 890.

Freeman, J. M. "Is There a Right to Die Quickly?" *Journal of Pediatrics,* 1972, *80,* 904-905.

Klaus, M. H., and Kennell, J. H. *Maternal-Infant Bonding: The Impact of Early Separation or Loss on Family Development.* St. Louis, Mo.: Mosby, 1976.

Kubler-Ross, E., and others. *On Death and Dying.* New York: Macmillan, 1969.

Marshall, R. E., Kasman, C., and Cape, L. S. *Coping with Caring for Sick Newborns.* Philadelphia: Saunders, 1982.

Nance, S., and others. *Premature Babies: A Handbook for Parents.* New York: Arbor House, 1982.

Sager, C. H., and Singer-Kaplan, H. (Eds.). *Progress in Group and Family Therapy.* New York: Brunner/Mazel, 1972.

Schwartz, W., and Zelba, S. (Eds.). *The Practice of Group Work.* New York: Columbia University Press, 1971.

17

Sona Euster, A.C.S.W.

▦ ▦ ▦ ▦ ▦ ▦ ▦ ▦ ▦ ▦ ▦ ▦ ▦

Adjusting to an Adult
Family Member's Cancer

Cancer is a catastrophic, devastating, and chronic illness. Its emotional effect on those experiencing it has been well explored and documented (see Chapter Ten). In addition, however, there is a significant emotional impact on the family members of cancer patients. This chapter explores that impact and identifies two group intervention programs developed to assist relatives in coping with this difficult experience.

In developing groups for relatives of cancer patients, there are two major populations to address: relatives of hospitalized patients and relatives of patients living at home. Stresses for these groups are at times very similar but at other times quite different.

Relatives of Hospitalized Cancer Patients

Relatives of hospitalized cancer patients often deal with responses to the diagnosis of cancer as well as to its treatment. The first hospitalization of a loved one is usually the time when a definitive diagnosis is made and primary treatment initiated.

Patients, of course, have their own responses; emotionally, they react with shock and disbelief as well as with fear, anger, and a sense of despair. There is also a reaction to the often mutilating, disfiguring treatment, such as a disturbance of body image or a loss of self-esteem.

Family members experience two responses at this time. They are dealing with their own reaction to the diagnosis and treatment as well as attempting to cope with the patient's response. In reaction to the diagnosis of cancer, relatives often mirror the patient's response. They may find the diagnosis difficult to believe. Statements such as "Are you sure? Perhaps there has been some mistake?" are common. Once shock subsides, emotional reactions are multiple and often quite changeable. Anger about the illness is rampant, and a sense of unfairness and injustice reigns. There is also fear about the future and a dread that a loved one will die. Guilt is a palpable, tangible response. There is a sense of "This should have happened to me. Why am I still healthy?"

Concerns about how to communicate with other family members are also raised. How to inform children, parents, and grandparents becomes a significant issue for the first relatives to be informed of the diagnosis. Often relatives, in an attempt to sort out their reactions, appear to contradict themselves or to rationalize in illogical ways.

Mr. M., a forty-five-year-old man, became quite tearful and distraught upon learning of his wife's breast cancer and mastectomy. In attempting to verbalize his concerns, he cried about the "death sentence" she had just received and about his impending loss. In the next breath, he spoke of the surgeon's excellent reputation and his certainty that "they had gotten it all." He spoke of how devastated his wife would be, then of how strong she was and how well she would cope. He spoke of his anger, his sense of injustice, and the bad timing of this situation. Finally, he mobilized his defenses and stated that "everything would work out."

Mr. M.'s response is not atypical. Faced with an overwhelming situation, he experienced a wide gamut of responses and pieced them together in a manner suitable and useful to himself.

Relatives must also face and cope with the patient's reaction to diagnosis and treatment. They are uncertain how to respond. Suddenly they feel isolated from the loved one and are faced with a myriad of questions about how to act in the patient's presence. If the patient is very depressed, relatives often feel frustrated by their inability to ease the depression. If a patient denies the reality of the medical condition, family members are unsure whether to accept the denial or to confront it directly. Relatives may also choose to deny, and this defense may be challenged if the patient's orientation is toward reality. Relatives may then wish to avoid communication with the patient.

Family members are also confronted by real physical changes in their loved one. Will a husband be comfortable looking at his wife's mastectomy scar? Will a daughter allow her father to hug her with one arm as easily as she did when he had two? Relatives fear that they will respond to physical mutilation and alteration in the wrong way. They expect perfection from themselves in dealing with these difficult realities, and guilt is an ever present response.

When a patient is hospitalized, particularly for the initial diagnosis and treatment, relatives are generally unfamiliar with the hospital system. Even a small community hospital appears to be a large, impersonal institution. This sense of being lost in a massive complex is exacerbated if treatment occurs in a major medical center. Relatives may feel isolated and confused. Very often they do not have an ongoing relationship with the physician, who is a cancer specialist and whom they have met only once. They are hesitant to approach him with questions and unsure about what questions to ask.

In a short period of time, they may be exposed to a large number of diverse health professionals. They are unclear about the roles of each and how they can be of help. Hospital personnel often seem abrupt and too busy to be disturbed. These observations contribute to a feeling of powerlessness and a sense of frustration. Relatives feel uncertain about the systems available for obtaining medical information. Does one speak only to the physician? How does one locate her? Is it permissible to discuss the patient's condition with a nurse? Does she have accurate information? What does the x-ray technician know? These questions and the lack of answers are usually overwhelming.

Finally, should accurate medical information be obtained, questions about its meaning arise. What exactly is leukemia? What is the difference between radiation and chemotherapy? What is the exact meaning of the phrase "a good chance for cure"? Relatives are unclear about a multitude of facts and their implications and are hesitant to ask questions and unsure about what to say.

All of these problems in dealing with hospital systems contribute to relatives' feelings of impotence. There is a sense of unreality—of being thrust into a foreign and hostile environment without a tour guide. Feelings of mastery and competence diminish and are replaced with a sense of loss of control. Adaptation to the medical system is difficult and requires a familiarity and assertiveness that are developed, in part, through professional intervention.

Veterans of the hospital routine are often patients and family members who are dealing with metastatic disease and ongoing treatment. These patients experience responses similar to those when newly diagnosed but there is an additional sense of doom and despair. The "cure" has not materialized, and the illness has become a day-to-day reality. Patients experience frustration with medical care and a pervasive fatigue. They are tired of being sick, tired of treatment, tired of pain. This fatigue often alternates with hopes of remission.

Relatives experience a similar sense of frustration and fatigue. They are tired of the repeated hospitalizations and the treatment regimes. They are tired of seeing a loved one in pain. Family members reach a point where they look forward to an end—either cure or death. They desire an end not only to the emotional turmoil of illness but also to the environmental pressures created by it. Financial pressures begin to build as medical expenses continue to rise. The patient may have been employed before the onset of the disease, and the prolonged loss of income can strain the family's financial situation. During hospitalization, a homemaker may be required to assist in running the household. Transportation for visits is often difficult and expensive.

Finally, the initial lack of knowledge of the hospital setting may have turned into painful familiarity and a sense of boredom. There is a desire to escape from the routine, the sterility, and the illness that pervade any medical institution. All of these reactions mobilize feelings of guilt. Relatives may feel they are wicked or unworthy for having wishes for the patient's death. They feel they should somehow be stronger, more patient, and more giving. Ultimately, there is a sense of being trapped and having nowhere to turn.

Relatives of Cancer Patients Living at Home

Relatives of cancer patients living at home experience responses similar to those described above. These may be exacerbated, however, by the continued presence of the patient in the household. The family members experience no relief; they are constantly viewing the illness and disability of the loved one. They live daily with the strains of caring for the patient, whether the needs are minor or more involved. The continued stress of an ill family member creates feelings of anger in the relatives. They are angry at the demands of the patient and perhaps at having to sacrifice personal desires to meet those demands. Concomitant with the anger is the ever present guilt—"A more loving wife would not be resentful" or "Better children would play less noisily."

All of the emotional responses outlined are complicated by the alterations in normal family life that occur when chronic illness is present. While this disruption varies in degree depending upon how ill the patient is and how the family copes with stress, changes in family functioning almost always arise. Relatives experience social isolation. They may not see friends as often because the patient does not feel up to it, because friends withdraw from the illness, or because they must remain at home to care for the patient. There is a sense that their world is shrinking, being reduced to work, school, or the household and the sickroom.

The illness may necessitate role reversal or alteration. The patient's inability to continue in an established role creates a significant stress for the patient and the other family members. When the breadwinner is stricken, the financial base of the family is threatened. Other money earners may be recruited, but this creates disequilibrium due to role changes and may also make fewer people available to care for the patient at home. Child care may suffer, particularly when the mother is ill. If the disease strikes a child, parents may tend to neglect other siblings or become inconsistent in their parenting. Siblings may begin to act out or withdraw, manifesting their resentment, jealousy, and guilt. In all situations, family members may have to function in roles previously unknown or unacceptable.

Additionally, outsiders may be called on to perform certain functions. Whether these be grandparents, aunts and uncles, or paid strangers, the presence of individuals not normally part of the family circle creates feelings of incompetence and loss of self-sufficiency in immediate family members. There is also resentment about the family's privacy being invaded.

Sexual dysfunction may occur. Partners may experience sexual deprivation due to a spouse's illness or an inability to perform sexually due to stress. There may be a decrease in libido, and anxiety caused by this problem adds additional pressure.

All of the difficulties created by having a cancer patient in the home are exacerbated over time. As the cancer becomes more of a chronic illness, the stresses within the family build. Situations that are tolerable for a few weeks become less so after months and perhaps intolerable over years. Over time, relatives feel depleted. Inner resources become drained, and it appears that there is nothing left to give. Also, over time, support systems weaken. Friends become tired of hearing about illness; distant relatives are not so willing to offer help. Community agencies may have time limits that halt assistance. This feeling of isolation is compounded by the distance of the family from the health care provider. When the patient is at home, there is anxiety about emergencies, reaching the physician, and getting to the hospital. As a result of these pressures, family members feel alone, unsupported, and drained. They live with a daily burden that might well be overwhelming. Their ability to cope successfully is decreased, and they are at a loss for sources of aid.

Rationale for a Group Treatment Approach

Because of the stresses and needs of relatives of cancer patients, the group treatment approach seems viable. Whether patients are hospitalized or living at home, relatives need to decrease their sense of isolation and recognize their difficult positions. The group as a source of mutual aid affords such comfort. While literature on the group approach has little discussion about this particular population, the modality is recognized as a way to ease the stresses of coping with family illness. Bloom and Lynch (1979) discussed their group approach in working with relatives of patients in intensive care. The authors report that a group format proved beneficial in that it was able "to provide emotional support to families at times of crisis" (p. 50), to lessen family members' isolation, and to give relatives the opportunity to share their concerns with other families in a similar situation.

Bailis, Lambert, and Bernstein (1978) used the group modality with relatives of hospitalized psychiatric patients. They found it an effective means for enabling relatives to tolerate, rather than displace, their complex emotions. Also, the group became a primary force in permitting family members to recognize their own needs rather than to focus exclusively on those of their ill relatives.

The most similar approach to a cancer population has been documented by Johnson and Stark (1980). They implemented a group program for cancer patients and their relatives during treatment at an acute-care teaching hospital. The group provided clarification of medical information, orientation to the medical complex, and an opportunity for patients and family members to discuss their emotional responses to the illness and treatment.

As is evident from much of the literature and from a knowledge of this population, the onset of the illness and its concomitant problems may be viewed as a crisis or series of crises. As defined by Rapoport (1962), a crisis is a situation perceived by an individual as a disruption to his or her life-style; it appears difficult to resolve with past coping mechanisms.

For family members of cancer patients, disequilibrium is present at each stage of the disease process from diagnosis to death. Changes are continual; there seems little constancy in the family's world. We have already discussed the impact of the initial diagnosis and treatment. After this crisis is resolved, families may function adequately until recurrence or metastasis is detected. At this time, again, the family's delicate psychological equilibrium is shattered. Relatives must cope with various stages of treatment, repeated hospitalizations, possible remissions, and, ultimately, the patient's death. How is this possible? What mechanisms assist human beings in coping with such traumatic life disruptions?

Rapoport (1962, p. 29) has identified three steps necessary for crisis resolution. These are:

1. the correct cognitive perception of the situation, which is aided by seeking new knowledge and being conscious of the problem at all times,
2. management of affect by being aware of feelings and by discharging and mastering tension through appropriate verbalization, and
3. seeking and using help with actual tasks and feelings by using interpersonal and institutional resources.

Group interventions with relatives of cancer patients enable them to work at the above steps. Crisis resolution is learned at the stage of initial diagnosis and may be employed at each crisis of the illness. Through participation in a group, family members at various stages of the disease lessen their sense of isolation. They receive correct information about their situation, and they are permitted and encouraged to express and explore their emotional responses so that they may begin to master them. Finally, they begin to utilize help from peers (other group members) and the professional group leader.

Groups for Relatives of Hospitalized Cancer Patients

The first group to be discussed was developed for relatives of hospitalized cancer patients. The group, following an open-ended format, meets weekly for one hour. It is open to relatives of all patients on a particular hospital unit. The patients have various cancer diagnoses and are at various stages of treatment. The group is coled by a registered nurse and a social worker. Relatives are informed of the group through notices posted on the unit, through conversations with the nursing staff, and through individual recruitment by the coleaders a short time before each weekly session begins.

Goals. The group was designed with many goals for treatment. Members may begin the process of crisis resolution during group participation. They may also begin the process of problem formulation and identification of the problem-solving process. Often relatives are so overwhelmed by their situations that they are unable to articulate their problems. Through discussion in the group, formulating these problems and methods for approaching them become clearer. A common example is a parent who is unsure of how or what to tell children about a spouse's illness. This dilemma may feel like an overwhelming burden, in part because the dilemma is unclear. The group may assist the member in clearly formulating the problem, such as "How do I tell my nine- and eleven-year-old sons that their mother has breast cancer?" The group may then begin to formulate and rehearse solutions.

Communication is often a problem for people in crisis, and improved communication skills are a goal of the group. Assisting individuals in verbalizing concerns and stating fears and fantasies enables them to regain some sense of control and ultimately improves communication with the patient and with members of the nuclear family.

Mr. T. was agitated during a group session. When questioned, he explained that he knew that his wife was going to show him her mastectomy scar that evening and he was terrified about his own reaction. He discussed his squeamishness and fear that any revulsion he might show would devastate his wife.

The group members helped him to identify his fears and to rehearse ways of talking to his wife about this painful issue. At the end of the session, he was visibly relaxed and stated that he felt he was more able to handle the evening's communication with his wife.

A final treatment goal of this group is to help members distinguish adaptive and maladaptive behaviors and coping mechanisms in order to promote the use of successful ones. In crisis, individuals often lose sight of past successful problem-solving mechanisms and require assistance in retrieving them. They also require aid in seeing maladaptive behaviors so that these can be controlled and possibly discarded.

Leadership Roles and Techniques. To achieve these goals, group leaders employ various methodologies. The focus of the group is twofold—educational and therapeutic. Therefore, one method of goal achievement is to provide accurate, understandable medical information when indicated. The sessions are not didactic in emphasis or format; rather, clarifying misconceptions and providing sufficient information to ensure mastery are the underpinnings of the group method.

It is also vital to create an open forum for group members. Group leaders are responsible for communicating the acceptance of all verbalizations and for permitting the expression of negative as well as positive responses. To achieve such open and honest communication within such a short time, group leaders' interventions must be direct. Group purpose must be clearly stated, and the group must unhesitatingly explore and interpret members' responses. Group leaders must communicate to members through words and actions that they do not fear painful material and are willing and able to assist in resolving difficulties. Group leaders must also be skilled in using confrontation as a means to resolve problems. Group members respond to the mirroring of their behaviors and the mutual exploration of unsuccessful coping patterns. Through this kind of intervention, group leaders also become role models for other members.

Role modeling is particularly useful when discussing communication with physicians. Mrs. R. complained throughout a group meeting that she could never get hold of her son's surgeon. She was angry and frustrated, and the group leader did not allow her to sit with these feelings. She questioned Mrs. R. about the specifics of her contacts and gently confronted her with the reality that she had not tried very hard. Mrs. R. acknowledged this and shared her anxiety about talking to the doctor, which derived from her discomfort at not knowing what to say. Using the group leader as a role model, Mrs. R. rehearsed her questions and approaches to the physician.

This role modeling is extremely significant in an open-ended, short-term group such as this. The population changes each week so that every session essentially begins anew. Group leaders must set the stage quickly for the discussion to follow. The initial interaction of each meeting is necessarily with the coleaders, as members address their concerns and responses to the leaders. These concerns are often specific medical questions.

The subject of these questions ranges from the details of a particular surgery to the cure rate for a particular type of cancer. Permitting a brief question-and-answer period serves a dual purpose. It clarifies the facts, which are necessary for mastery, and it allows group members to open up and orient themselves to one another safely. Medical facts are an unthreatening subject upon which to begin formulating trust and cohesion within the group.

In order to prevent the session from becoming solely didactic, it is important to interpret the underlying emotional concerns after questions are answered. For example, after providing whatever numbers are available in response to a question on cure rates, the group leader might remark, "It must be quite frightening to contemplate the idea that some cancers are not cured." If some group members have been present for previous sessions, they may assume this responsibility and assist in educating new members in the group process. If all members are new, the group leaders must move the discussion in the direction of problem formulation.

Since most group members at each session are newcomers, the group essentially remains at the phase of identifying problems and formulating tentative solutions. The problem-solving process, however, is accelerated by the exchange of ideas of different members. This is particularly true when some group members are coping with the initial diagnosis while others are dealing with ongoing treatment and metastatic disease. Newcomers to the illness may have a fresh perspective to offer those whose resources have been drained over time. Conversely, those who have attended previous meetings can share the benefit of their experience.

During one session, Mrs. W. raised her concerns about how difficult her visits with her hospitalized thirty-six-year-old daughter, who had advanced cancer, had become. She declared herself "at her wits' end." She felt she must be at the hospital at every possible moment, but the visits became empty silences or, worse, arguments. Through discussion with some other group members dealing with the newness of hospitalization and visiting routines, Mrs. W. was helped to see that her constant presence only underscored her daughter's sense of helplessness and uselessness. Both the mother and daughter needed to maintain some independence and individualization despite the severity of the illness. Enmeshed in her own pain and the enormity of her burden, Mrs. W. required the perspective of those new to the problem to help her formulate a solution.

In this example, as in many others, group leaders emphasized the use of other group members as resources. The thrust of all interventions is fostering mutual aid to resolve problems.

Therapeutic Factors. One of the major therapeutic forces in this group is the mutual aid derived from interacting with other group members. Not only does this assist in dealing with specific problematic issues but it also enhances group members' sense of self-worth and self-esteem. Relatives of cancer patients often lose sight of their capabilities; they focus on what they are not doing or what they should be doing better. By offering assistance to others and having that assistance recognized and valued, they begin to see themselves and therefore their actions in a more positive and realistic light.

Another significant therapeutic force at work in this group is the focus of the coleaders on here-and-now issues, coupled with persistent, direct exploration of painful material. By assisting group members in discussing the realities associated with having a relative with cancer, numerous situations become less overwhelming for the group members. What is verbalized and examined is ultimately less frightening and burdensome than what is hidden.

Finally, of great therapeutic importance is the permission given to relatives to react to their loved one's illness. This is in and of itself a gift. Relatives often feel they have no right to react personally, since they are not ill. Fortunate enough to retain their health, they are not entitled to any selfish responses. Through participation in the group, they see their reactions as human and therefore not unique.

J. S., a seventeen-year-old daughter of a breast cancer patient, used the group session to share her feelings of guilt. She had spent the entire previous night crying because she would not be able to attend a long-awaited school dance because of her mother's hospitalization. She was angry at life's injustice but immediately felt guilty. What right had she to be so selfish when her mother was critically ill? No one in the group judged her response negatively, and the group supported her healthy desire to function as normally as possible. She was also given realistic hope—there would be other parties. Members' concerns and emotions are accepted without judgment by individuals in similar situations as well as by the professional staff. This atmosphere of nonjudgmental acceptance promotes adaptation and mastery of major crisis situations.

Difficulties. While this weekly family group encourages group members to make productive adaptations, there have been difficulties in the group's ongoing implementation. There is a constant lack of in-depth group cohesion due to the changing population and time limitations of the meeting. To counter this problem, group leaders must actively participate in each session's process in order to foster mutual aid. Coleaders do not have the luxury of the group taking responsibility for itself as they would if it were a closed group that met over time. This is not a major drawback, but it does require significant energy and enthusiasm on the part of the coleaders at all times.

Also due to time limitations, certain issues may be raised during group session but remain unresolved. This phenomenon can leave group members with a sense of unfinished business. For this reason, leaders must verbalize this potential problem in the group and provide individual follow-up where indicated.

Following up on certain individuals is crucial if this type of group is to succeed. Group members may require individual attention for various reasons. One is certainly for continued problem resolution if the process is unfinished at the end of the group session. A second is that certain members may have concerns or difficulties that are not appropriate for group intervention. Also, certain issues that would ordinarily be addressed in the next group session must be handled more immediately because the patient is about to be discharged from the hospital. Group leaders must realize that the time commitment to the group program goes beyond the hour spent in the group. Leaders must be available on an individual basis to group members as well as to subgroups of family constellations.

Termination. Because the group is open ended, termination is not a significant issue for members or leaders. Only for members with unsolved problems is termination a factor, and this problem may be resolved through individual contact. In a sense, since the group is an ongoing program of the hospital unit, there is no termination. This group has a life of its own, reinforced by the constancy of the coleaders. Members enter, leave, and may well enter again in future weeks or months.

Outcome. This group program has met with a good deal of success. Three treatment outcomes have emerged consistently. Members regain a sense of control over themselves and their situations, there is evidence of improved familial communication, and there is a solid beginning in formulating the issues that family members must address in order to cope with a loved one's cancer. The responses of group members, patients, and staff members have provided the evidence of these outcomes. All three groups have commented on improved family functioning and regained control as a result of family members' participation in the group. Physicians and nurses have been particularly sensitive to the group effect on certain relatives. Surgeons, specifically, have been impressed by what they view as "more appropriate behavior and more focused questioning" by family members with whom they interact. Instead of a relative asking, "Will my husband be cured?" (a question very difficult to answer at the time of diagnosis), a wife is more likely to ask, "How large a tumor was it? Is further therapy indicated?" These specific questions are much easier for the medical staff to answer.

The strength of this program is that service is provided at times of crisis, when it is most needed. Thus, intervention may be both therapeutic and preventive. Much of the benefit derived from problem formulation during a patient's hospitalization is preventive. By anticipating problems, family members often avoid them. Situations are acknowledged and explored before they become explosive and unmanageable. In the example of Mrs. W., her exploration of her problem in visiting her daughter provided a solution before the relationship with her daughter deteriorated to the point at which damage would have been irrevocable.

Group for Relatives of Cancer Patients Living at Home

To meet the needs of relatives of cancer patients who are living at home, a second group was initiated. This group focused on a select population: husbands of women with advanced breast cancer. This group met weekly for an hour and a half. It met consistently for about two years with minor changes in membership. Coled by a social worker and the women's oncologist, the group ran concurrently with one for the patients.

The patients' group consisted of approximately ten women with advanced breast cancer, all of whom were receiving chemotherapy. The group met weekly to assist the patients in coping with the side effects of the treatment and the impact of a chronic, progressive illness.

Goals. As in the first group, the coleaders for the spouses' group agreed on several treatment goals. It was expected that participation in the group would partially, if not totally, resolve problems created by the chronic and degenerative illness of one's spouse. Communication between spouses and among family members would improve, and husbands would increase their medical knowledge and understanding. They would begin the process of anticipating the grief work necessary for healthy mourning. Given these goals, the group process would assist members in recognizing and distinguishing both adaptive and maladaptive behavior patterns. They would identify successful coping mechanisms and utilize these to alter maladaptive behaviors.

Leadership Roles and Techniques. The methodology employed to achieve the above treatment goals consisted of the creation of an open forum in which members had to participate in a problem-solving process. The use of the group and its cohesive forces was the primary source of treatment. Through participation, members increased their psychosocial network. This expanded peer group provided an opportunity to explore honestly the realities of living with a chronically ill partner. The exploration was facilitated by group coleaders, who interpreted comments and confronted group members as indicated.

Phases and Content. In the two years of its existence, the group moved through three major phases. During the initial phase, which lasted perhaps three to four months, group members tended to focus on the patients' needs and problems. The husbands found it extremely uncomfortable to talk about themselves and continually raised questions about their wives' situations. They spoke of the pain that the women experienced, the frustration that the illness created for the women, and the sorrow that the husbands felt for the patients. The husbands also expressed concern about the medical condition. Week after week new questions arose about cancer-related news items. Each medical treatment, test, or office visit was questioned and analyzed. The covert message of these questions, "How long does my wife have to live?", was never expressed and was denied when even hinted at by group leaders.

Also apparent during this initial phase was a strong dependence upon group leaders, particularly the physician. Members looked to him for guidance not only about medical concerns but also about group norms and behaviors. A significant portion of the work during the initial phase was assisting members in understanding the roles of the coleaders, particularly through demonstration. As members became more aware of the group process, they began to let go of their need for concrete, factual discussions. They used the social worker's behavior, her more emotionally laden discussion, and her challenging of the physician's authoritarian stance as a role model and began to explore psychosocial issues that were of concern to them.

This slight shift in the group process led to the longer, productive, ongoing phase of the group, which lasted over a year. During this period, subgroups formed. Of the ten regular members, six clearly divided into two subgroups. The basis for forming these subgroups appeared to be similarities in age, professional status, and socioeconomic background. The subgroups did not in any way impede group process. They were evidenced primarily during the brief social exchanges before sessions began and in references to contacts between sessions. The subgroups appeared to have hastened the cohesion that developed among members. The closeness established in the subgroup enabled members to risk themselves more easily in the entire group. It seemed as though the subgroup members were assured of the support of one or two allies and therefore could allow themselves to present as vulnerable and unsure to the rest of the group.

As the process of problem-solving progressed, group members evidenced less need for the coleadership and a greater reliance and dependence on one another. They utilized the questions and comments of the coleaders but no longer depended on them for direction. The members clearly developed expectations of one another participating in the group process and held each other accountable to fulfill those expectations.

These expectations were primarily related to the discussion of personal material. During the ongoing phase of this group, the focus on patient problems became unacceptable. Members wanted to use the group for themselves and demanded that kind of work from one another. Discussion centered on their own difficulties in coping with the illness, their frustrations, guilt, and anger.

During one session, Mr. R. commented on how difficult it was for his wife to be wheelchair bound. Another member asked, "What is it like for you?" Initially, Mr. R.'s response was that it was really much more of a problem for his wife. Other members refused to accept this and demanded that he address his own depression, sorrow, and anger at the latest health crisis in his family. Ultimately, he did speak of the burden he was experiencing due to her inability to walk and his need to find ways of coping with this. Thus, much time was spent supporting the husbands' need to occasionally remove themselves physically and emotionally from the all-consuming realities of sickness at home.

Coping problems and how they were manifested shifted periodically, often due in part to the realities of the patients' physical condition. A major medical setback for one of the women created upheaval for her husband, who would use the group to mobilize himself to deal with the crisis. The ongoing phase of the group, in fact, became very much a support network for the husbands, as they experienced over time the day-to-day realities of their wives' deterioration. The group became a much needed haven, a source of comfort as well as aid, where painful issues were not dismissed but explored with an eye toward problem resolution.

The group entered the termination phase as patients began to die. The confrontation with death indicated to group members that the group itself would not continue forever. This was discussed openly, and the husbands agreed to meet "as long as needed." The implicit meaning of this phrase was clear to all —until all their wives had died. During this phase, the work of the group was less progress oriented. The members dealt with tangible losses over and over again, and mourning became the primary focus. Throughout the mourning process, the husbands evidenced a tremendous need for support from other members and the coleaders. What was remarkable was that the support was always present. No matter how drained and personally devastated an individual might be, he was able to assist another member during a group session. The strength and caring evidenced by these men were striking and pointed not only to their individual resources but also to the benefits derived from their work in the group over a year and a half.

Therapeutic Factors. The therapeutic forces operative in the group over this time period are perhaps obvious from the above discussion. The mutual aid factor cannot be overemphasized. Coupled with the professionals' focus on problem solving, this created a milieu that fostered growth and a healthy adaptation to a most devastating life event.

Difficulties. As with any new project, the formation and implementation of this group had a number of problems. Initially recruitment was a significant issue. While the target population was clear to the coleaders (the husbands of the patients already participating in a patients' group), overcoming the husbands' resistance to attending took a great deal of time, skill, and energy. Their objections centered on the distance they lived from the medical center and their need to remain at home to care for their spouses. These objections were overcome through patient, consistent individual exploration of these obstacles until solutions were found. Coleaders initially found it more productive not to deal directly with the underlying emotional resistance to participation. Focusing on the logistical obstacles and attempting to overcome them ultimately yielded a membership of about ten.

Another difficulty evidenced by this group was the members' resistance to remaining in treatment as spouses began to die. There was overt questioning of the value of exposing oneself to such pain. "Why do I need to come here and see a preview of what will happen to me?" This resistance was never completely overcome, but time and again members chose to continue with the group, finding that the support and problem solving outweighed the pain experienced during the group process.

Another significant factor about this group was the need for ongoing professional help outside the group context. Due to the critical nature of the patients' illness and both professionals' involvement with the total family, situations arose that demanded other kinds of therapeutic contacts. For both spouses and patients, individual counseling was indicated for brief periods. Marital counseling was also necessary in some cases.

One couple independently shared their marital discord

with the group leader. The husband was having an affair with another woman and had told his wife about it. Both were angry, guilty, and immobilized by the intensity of their responses. Neither was willing to deal with this issue during a group session. They agreed to meet regularly with the group leaders, setting a goal of improved communication and respect during the last phases of her illness. The social worker conducted most of the counseling. The work was stimulating and rewarding, but the time demands were great. These time demands need to be considered in establishing this kind of program.

Termination. Termination was a particularly difficult issue for this group and must be explored. In reality, members were dealing with two losses that contributed to their termination in the group—the loss of a spouse as well as the loss of other group members. This double loss is extremely difficult to counteract. One solution is to assist the widowers in utilizing the group for bereavement. There was ambivalence to this approach, however. Although the husbands who had already lost their wives were anxious to derive support from the group, their desire and need to forget the hospital and the issues related to illness were very great. It was difficult for them to return to the medical center and to discuss the concerns of members whose wives were still alive. This need to forget ultimately prevailed, and the widowers did not remain with the group for more than one or two sessions.

This dropping out led to a staggered termination for the group as a whole. An individual's time in the group was determined by his wife's death, and thus the group's continuance was determined by how long the wives remained alive. This uncertainty and continual need to address termination created strains in the group. It did not destroy the process or the program but was a significant factor during the last months of the treatment process.

Outcome. The overall evaluation of this group was positive. Members and their wives supported the program. During participation, the couples commented on how the group assisted them in coping with the severity of the illness and its effects on their family life. Contact with the men some months after the group had ended also revealed positive responses. While the pain was not eliminated, the widowers felt that it had been lessened because of the group and that the last months of their marriages had been more productive and healthier than they might have been otherwise.

The advantages of the group program for these men were considerable. The group provided an outside support network for members at a time when family supports were dwindling due to the constant strain. It helped members to anticipate grief work and mourning, which promoted healthier resolution of the spouses' death. Finally, group membership established interpersonal and professional resources that the men were able to draw upon after their wives had died. While the group did not continue, relationships established within it were maintained. A number of the men are still close and still see each other.

The program was not without shortcomings. The most significant shortcoming is built into this kind of group. The common factor among the members is the terminal illness of their spouse. This painful reality cannot help but create resistance periodically in the life of the group. This resistance must be addressed, and the group must be willing to tolerate the questioning of the group's value over time. The other major shortcoming of this program is its open-ended format. Since it depends in great part upon the life span of the patients, there is an uncertainty about its duration, which creates additional strain for members. As has been shown, this strain can be overcome and therapeutic value derived from the program.

Personal Reactions

Working as a professional with relatives of cancer patients is a diverse, complex, and intense experience. Numerous issues are raised. Countertransference is a major issue. Due to the catastrophic nature of the illness, group leaders immediately form strong bonds with members. Since cancer is an illness that tends to dominate a family's experience, professionals may become caught up in the overwhelming, omnipresent specter of the disease and lose objectivity at times. There may also be a conscious or unconscious desire to rescue group members. This may be evidenced by attempting to provide quick, easy solutions or by hesitating to confront maladaptive behavior. As a result of this deep caring, the professional may experience a personal sense of loss when the relationship terminates.

In addition to these countertransference issues, professional issues are raised for group leaders. Since leading these kinds of groups requires significant contact with both patients and family members, questions of role arise. There may be conflict about who is one's client, the patient or the relative. Since one's role shifts depending on the degree of illness, whether the patient is hospitalized, and so on, one must be alert to these demands. One's role may also become unclear at times. Is one simply a group leader? Marriage counselor? Individual therapist? All of the above? How does a professional wear so many hats and remain clear and objective? Over time, the professional may also begin to overidentify with one individual. The attachment may become too strong, and objectivity may be seriously hampered. As a professional, one must commit oneself in these situations to self-examination and self-awareness. One must receive supervision or consultation for these groups in order to prevent personal responses from interfering in the therapeutic process.

One of the arguments for the coleadership of these groups is based on the need to examine the professional's role objectively. Coleaders may provide checks and balances for one another. One professional's overinvolvement with a particular individual or family may be recognized and pointed out by the other. Coleaders may assess each other's performance, explore intervention techniques together, and support one another at stressful times during group process.

Coleadership, however, also presents fertile ground for conflict, both professional and personal. Coleaders from different professional disciplines have different training and experience. They may not understand the other's role completely, or they may disagree with it. It is imperative that coleaders communicate their missions, thoughts, and goals before initiating any group program. Poor communication between coleaders is a group's worst enemy.

Coleaders must commit considerable time and energy to

explore and enhance their relationship. This may, of course, give rise to personal conflicts, as coleaders discover that they simply do not like one another. This creates a real burden for them and possibly for the group members. Even in this case, however, open, honest communication will ease the situation.

Coleadership in a group situation is a difficult, albeit valuable approach. For groups with family members of cancer patients, it is an approach very much to be considered. However, professionals must consider it with an awareness of possible problems and pitfalls and a willingness to address these consistently and constructively.

Having embarked upon a treatment relationship with this population and having experienced the problems and conflicts inherent in this work, the professional must take stock of his or her response. In my opinion, there are significant rewards in this work. It provides an excellent opportunity for professional growth, since these groups are a constant challenge to one's skill and commitment. They continually create new opportunities for developing innovative treatment techniques. One is constantly searching for better ways to assist with problems and to develop programs that meet the expressed needs of family members.

In addition, these groups provide a tremendous sense of fulfillment. One feels a personal closeness with the clients and a real sense of having made a difference in peoples' lives. Cancer is a family illness, and knowing that one has had a positive and lasting impact upon family life is one's greatest reward.

Future Directions

Since this work provides the professional with the challenge of new program development, one must ask oneself, "What is the next step to take?" Still needed are other groups for relatives of cancer outpatients. One viable approach would be to establish a short-term, closed group for relatives of cancer patients without regard to the patients' specific diagnoses. The group would meet for eight sessions, contracting around specific goals such as improving communication with the patient or assessing the impact of the illness on the group members' daily life. As new issues arose, the group could recontract around suitable goals for an additional eight sessions.

There are certainly numerous possibilities for group intervention. The use of the group modality for family members of cancer patients is a valuable and exciting method of intervention, allowing members to use professional and interpersonal supports and creating a forum for fostering healthy, growth-promoting behavior with which to handle a family crisis.

References

Bailis, S., Lambert, S., and Bernstein, S. "The Legacy of the Group: A Study of Group Therapy with a Transient Membership." *Social Work in Health Care*, 1978, *3* (4), 405-418.

Bloom, N. D., and Lynch, J. G. "Group Work in a Hospital Waiting Room." *Health and Social Work*, 1979, *4* (3), 49-63.

D'Afflitti, J. G., and Weitz, C. W. "Rehabilitating the Stroke Patient Through Patient-Family Groups." *International Journal of Group Psychotherapy*, 1974, *24*, 328-333.

Ferlic, M., Goldman, A., and Kennedy, B. J. "Group Counseling in Adult Patients with Advanced Cancer." *Cancer*, 1979, *43*, 760-766.

Foster, Z., and Mendel, S. "Mutual-Help Group for Patients: Taking Steps Toward Change." *Health and Social Work*, 1979, *4* (3), 83-97.

Grunebaum, H. "A Soft-Hearted Review of Hard-Nosed Research on Groups." *International Journal of Group Psychotherapy*, 1975, *25* (2), 185-197.

Hartford, M. E. "Groups in the Human Services: Some Facts and Fancies." *Social Work with Groups*, 1978, *1* (1), 7-13.

Johnson, E. M., and Stark, D. E. "A Group Program for Cancer Patients and Their Family Members in an Acute Care Teaching Hospital." *Social Work in Health Care*, 1980, *5* (4), 335-349.

Kornfeld, M. S., and Siegel, I. M. "Parental Group Therapy in the Management of a Fatal Childhood Disease." *Health and Social Work*, 1979, *4* (3), 100-118.

Lang, N. C. "The Selection of the Small Group for Service Delivery: An Exploration of the Literature on Group Use in Social Work." *Social Work with Groups,* 1978, *1* (3), 347-363.

Mantell, J. E., Alexander, E. S., and Kleinman, M. A. "Social Work and Self Help Groups." *Health and Social Work,* 1976, *1* (1), 86-100.

Rapoport, L. "The State of Crisis: Some Theoretical Considerations." *Social Service Review,* 1962, *36* (2), 22-31.

Ross, J. W. "Coping with Childhood Cancer: Group Intervention as an Aid to Parents in Crisis." *Social Work in Health Care,* 1979, *4* (4), 381-391.

West, M., McJivaine, R., and Sells, C. J. "An Interdisciplinary Health Care Setting's Experience with Groups for Parents of Children Having Specific Disabilities." *Social Work in Health Care,* 1979, *4* (3), 287-298.

Wood, P. E., and others. "Group Counseling for Cancer Patients in a Community Hospital." *Journal of Psychosomatic Medicine,* 1978, *19* (9), 555-561.

Yalom, I. D. *The Theory and Practice of Group Psychotherapy.* New York: Basic Books, 1975.

Yalom, I. D., and Greaves, C. "Group Therapy with the Terminally Ill." *American Journal of Psychiatry,* 1977, *134* (4), 396-400.

18

Lissa Robins Kapust, A.C.S.W.
Sandra Weintraub, Ph.D.

田 田 田 田 田 田 田 田 田 田 田 田 田

Living with a Family Member Suffering from Alzheimer's Disease

The elderly are a rapidly expanding segment of the nation's population. As life expectancy increases, the illnesses of old age will affect more and more people. Senile dementia, particularly Alzheimer's disease, has recently been in the spotlight as a leading cause of decreased productivity in the elderly. As dementia becomes more widespread, health care providers must meet not only the medical needs of the patients but also the emotional and informational needs of their families.

The term *dementia* refers to a broad class of diseases of the brain in which there is a progressive, irreversible deterioration of brain cells resulting in the loss of mental competence. Dementia affects 5 to 10 percent of the population over the age of sixty-five; the proportion increases to 25 percent of people over eighty. Although less common under the age of sixty-five, dementia can affect individuals in their fifties. Dementia is suspected when a patient experiences forgetfulness, but there may be other early signs. Difficulty in thinking of the words one wants to use, spatial disorientation, trouble with addition and subtraction, and subtle signs of social inappropriateness can also signal the onset of dementia. Characteristically, patients with dementia are physically healthy; there is little outward sign of the devastating illness that is slowly eroding their mental faculties and personality. Many patients are unaware of their failing competence, since the ability to monitor one's own behavior is often lost during the course of the illness. Ultimately, the patient can no longer perform routine activities, such as dressing and cooking, and becomes entirely dependent on others for survival.

The most prevalent cause of dementia is Alzheimer's disease (Katzman, 1976). It is identified by specific pathological changes in the brain consisting of the formation of senile plaques and neurofibrillar tangles (see Tomlinson, Blessed, and Roth, 1968). Changes in the neurochemistry of the brain, specifically in the cholinergic system, are also evident (Davies and Maloney, 1976). A number of other illnesses share with Alzheimer's disease a progressive course of behavioral decline. These illnesses, which include Parkinson's disease, Huntington's disease, and multi-infarct dementia, have a similar impact on the patient and his or her family.

Because there is no cure or effective treatment for dementia, family support is one service that can offer relief to care givers,* who often feel powerless. Further, because dementia has been poorly understood by the public and health professionals, the need for education about the disease and its course is critical. In our experience, one of the best ways to provide support and information to families of patients with dementia is in support groups. Support groups satisfy the need that family care givers have to meet others who have common interests and problems. Educational sessions allow them to acquire technical information about dementia. Support groups for families of pa-

---

*In this chapter, "care givers" refers to family members rather than health care personnel, since family members usually provide most of the care for patients with dementia.

tients with dementia have dramatically increased over the past five years and have employed a variety of approaches. Some groups are directed by laypersons; others are led by health care professionals. In this chapter, we present a rationale for and description of a treatment program that we have developed over several years of experience with demented patients and their families.

Impact of the Illness

Family members of patients with dementia are not viewed as the primary patients—rightly so, since they are not medically ill. However, the impact of the illness on the family is often ignored by those involved with the medical care of the patient. They are likely to overlook what Fengler and Goodrich (1979) have labeled "the hidden patients." Fengler and Goodrich identified one group of hidden patients, the wives of elderly disabled men, who may themselves be physically healthy but who suffer from isolation, loneliness, and economic hardship. These wives are overwhelmed by the stress of assuming their spouses' responsibilities. The families of patients with dementia who cope with similar issues can also be considered hidden patients.

Care givers struggle with two fundamental losses: the patient's loss of competence and skill and their own loss of a spouse or parent. Both losses are intensified by the fact that they occur over a protracted period of time, lasting from five to fifteen years. The gradual loss of a loved one has been labeled "the ongoing funeral" (Kapust, 1982). In response to these losses, care givers universally experience feelings of sadness, anger, and frustration, vacillating from one to another as they attempt to understand and accept what has happened. Care givers often struggle alone; their loss is not always apparent to outsiders, since the patient's healthy physical state and preserved social graces belie the erosion of thinking that is taking place.

While loss is the underlying theme, many practical issues are presented by the patient's behavioral changes as well. There are changes in roles within the family requiring adjustment to new responsibilities. The social structure enjoyed by the family may change as friends desert them or other family members withdraw their support. As the illness progresses, changes in the patient's symptoms and skills necessitate altering management strategies. Families need guidance and suggestions for restructuring the patient's environment and for locating community resources. Ultimately, care givers may have to face the difficult emotional and financial decision of nursing home placement.

Rationale for Group Treatment Approach

Our group treatment approach was shaped by five years of experience with families of patients with dementia. In individual work with families, we repeatedly encountered similar emotional responses and questions of practical management. Despite the prevalence of these themes, each family experienced isolation and the feeling that their dilemma was unique. Group treatment seemed to be a reasonable service to offer people who expressed the wish to meet others in similar circumstances. We were also struck by the variety of strategies that families had devised on their own. Through the group, families would be able to pass their strategies on to others.

There are many characteristics shared by care givers that promote group unity. Spouses are often elderly and are faced with the issues encountered with advancing age—failing health, financial strains, and isolation. Overwhelmed by the patient's requirements for care, they find it difficult to learn new roles as they assume the total burden of responsibility for the household. They are grieved by the loss of their partners' competence, and many feel cheated out of their retirement, a period they had looked forward to as a time of rest and enjoyment. Adult children find their energies divided between resolving their own life crises and planning for the future of a parent. Group members are eager to learn more about the illness and need advice on how to manage daily situations.

A variety of approaches for counseling and providing support for families living with cognitively and behaviorally impaired patients have been described (Bergmann and others, 1978;

Elliott, 1979; Farkas, 1980; Kapust, 1982; LaVorgna, 1979; Lazarus and others, 1981; Lezak, 1978; Rabins, Mace, and Lucas, 1982). Support groups can offer families an emotional outlet as well as assistance in managing the patient at home. Support from families, friends, or a treatment milieu can be important in reducing stress and vulnerability to illness in care givers (Caplan, 1981) and can also diminish the family's sense of burden in providing care at home (Zarit, Reever, and Bach-Peterson, 1980). Bergmann and associates have further determined that patients cared for by their families do not enter institutions as early as those who are not. Therefore, providing families with a support system may delay early institutionalization and enhance their ability to cope with a dementing illness.

There are few objective data on the effectiveness of group treatment. Lazarus and others (1981) compared responses of group participants to nonparticipants on several measures of psychological well-being. Nonparticipants showed no change in their responses to these measures over a ten-week interval. However, group participants receiving treatment during that time showed significant changes. On one of the measures, Rotter's (1966) internal versus external locus of control, group participants' posttreatment responses indicated that they felt more in control of their own lives and less at the mercy of fate.

Group Treatment Approach

The treatment approach described here is tailored to meet the special needs of families caring for patients with dementia. The chronic and progressive nature of the illness requires an approach emphasizing flexibility and adjustment to a constantly changing situation. In addition, since the group offers support rather than psychotherapy, the approach differs from traditional group practice in several distinctive ways. Most notably, the groups are time limited. Each group meets weekly for eight sessions and meetings last for one and a half hours. The principal reason is that group members, who rely on neighbors or relatives to supervise the confused patient at home while they attend the meetings, are better able to make the necessary arrangements for a limited number of meetings. A short-term contract is welcomed by care givers who are often overwhelmed by the responsibilities for patient care. Further, our early experience with open-ended groups revealed that relatives felt that an indefinite commitment made too great a demand at a time when their physical and emotional energies were depleted.

Some groups have requested follow-up sessions after the regular sessions were concluded. Not all group members choose to participate in these meetings. However, for those members who do wish to continue meeting, follow-up sessions scheduled at monthly intervals can meet members' emotional needs and continued commitment to group treatment. Although we initially offered only daytime groups, we recently added evening groups. This change was in response to requests from working relatives who want to attend group after work hours. Evening sessions are also preferred by some care givers because they can more easily arrange for someone to stay with the patient in the evening. Meetings are scheduled for the early evening (7:00 P.M. to 8:30 P.M.) so that relatives can return home early. Daytime groups are also carefully scheduled (10:00 A.M. to 11:30 A.M.) so that care givers can get the patient up and ready in the morning and still return home by lunchtime.

The group is coled by two therapists, a clinical social worker and a neuropsychologist. This combination blends various skills and interests. The clinical social worker is experienced in individual, family, and group treatment. Because of her primary role as a family worker in the behavioral neurology unit, she can readily make referrals of appropriate members. In the group session, she listens closely to emotional issues raised by members and to group process. Her comments in the group are often responses to these affective components. The neuropsychologist is primarily involved in research on dementia and in administering to patients the battery of neuropsychological tests used in making the diagnosis of dementia. In the group, she provides information about the disease and addresses the myriad of medical questions raised by family members. Over the years of coleading groups together, the boundaries between the areas of professional expertise have become somewhat blurred, as each group leader assumes some knowledge and skills possessed by the other.

Groups are limited to a maximum of ten and a minimum of five members, with most groups averaging about seven. Groups larger than ten do not allow ample time for members to interact adequately during the eight one-and-a-half-hour sessions. Members comment that groups of fewer than five feel too small. In determining group size, leaders keep in mind that some members will have difficulty attending all of the sessions, either because of their own health problems, a crisis for the patient, or complications in plans for patient supervision. It is not unusual to have one or two members absent from each session.

Group members consist primarily of individuals whose parents or spouses have been diagnosed in our own unit or in another facility. However, occasionally other care givers and relatives have attended groups. Participants have included a paid companion who wanted to better understand the patient she cared for, siblings, and the spouse of a patient's daughter. It is important that group leaders establish flexible admission criteria that accommodate the many variations found in living and caring arrangements.

An attempt is made to mix spouses and adult children in each group. Spouses who may be in conflict with their own adult children over support and assistance in caring for the patient can hear the other side of the story from adult children in the group, and vice versa.

In each group there is usually a fair representation of family members attending patients at different stages of the illness. Patients in early or intermediate stages are usually cared for at home, while more severely affected patients are often institutionalized. The mix of different severity levels as well as patient location allows group members to look forward and backward. Those with relatives still at home can become prepared for what lies ahead. Those with relatives in a nursing home can recall what it was like to have the patient at home. These com-

parisons are critical in coping with the gradual loss they are experiencing.

Referrals come from a variety of sources, including hospi-
tal- and community-based physicians, local home care agencies,
the Visiting Nurse Association, mental health facilities, and self-
referrals. The media play an important role in focusing attention on the multifaceted problems of dementia and the availability of support groups to serve family members.

Each family member referred to the group first meets individually with the clinical social worker. This evaluation session is used to screen appropriate referrals. Interested members
have an opportunity to meet with a group leader who gives an
overview of the group and discusses mechanics of the group, including fee structure, dates and times of groups, and related
issues. Participants' expectations about the group are elicited.
Often the group leader has to clarify for the potential member
what the group realistically can and cannot do. For example,
relatives may express the unrealistic hope that their attendance
at group will make their spouses better or take away their sadness about the situation. The evaluation session sometimes reveals prospective group members who may have complex psychiatric histories or who may themselves be showing signs of
confusion and forgetfulness. In such cases we may determine
that an alternative treatment strategy is preferable or perhaps
even urgent and that a support group would be inappropriate at
that time. However, in our experience most family members are
appropriate for the group and can benefit from what it offers.

At the first meeting, group members receive a schedule of
topics to be covered in the eight sessions. This format ensures
that all relevant topics are covered and stimulates preparation
for each session. Members are assured that the schedule is flexible and can easily be adjusted to accommodate individuals'
needs as they arise. Scheduled topics include the patients' medical workup, practical problems of patient management, emotional reactions to the illness, changing roles within the family,
utilization of community resources, and thoughts about the
future.

Treatment Phases

Introduction. The initial phase of the family support group can be characterized as "show and tell." In the first group session, members introduce themselves. Even though leaders suggest that members tell the group something about themselves, the conversation inevitably turns to the patients. The care givers, often feeling little identity apart from the sick spouse or parent, have difficulty turning the focus of attention on themselves. In early sessions, members need to tell the story about how they learned of the diagnosis, the course of the illness, and the problems that they now face in caring for the patient. Group members are eager to share their stories with an audience of sympathetic listeners, especially after the unempathic or critical responses they may have received from relatives or friends. Family and friends may minimize the situation, telling care givers "It could be worse" or "Don't lose your patience." In addition, being carefully listened and responded to in the group is a relief after hours at home with the noncommunicative patient. In the initial group meetings, all of the members have the opportunity to be in the spotlight and to tell their story in their own way. Group leaders, attentive to the particular way in which the story is told, gather important clues on issues with which each participant is struggling and coping.

Reactions to Loss. One aspect of Alzheimer's disease that contributes significantly to the family's emotional response is the phenomenon of psychological death. A death of spirit and intellect precedes the physical death of the demented patient. The family has lost the person they once knew. Yet the patient lives·and continues to make demands on the physical, emotional, and financial resources of the care givers. Cath (1978, p. 28), reflecting on the aging process, poignantly describes this: "Witnessing the death of a beloved ego is even more intolerable than the experience of physical death. Senility represents a progressive and agonizingly slow death of the human side of existence, for its ultimate residue is no longer recognizable as a person."

Group members frequently express some sense that psychological death is taking place. One member said that life with the patient was like "the funeral that never ends." Another, whose husband ultimately had to be institutionalized, spoke sadly of her wish that her husband might have died quickly from "a nice, clean heart attack" rather than suffering with dementia. One woman, reflecting on her ambiguous social situation, called herself a "walking widow." References and images of death in response to the patients' failing competence contribute to sadness, guilt, and anxiety for care givers.

In one meeting, a member who had spoken for several weeks about his wife's compromised status brought an article on euthanasia to the group. At first he spoke philosophically about the moral and ethical aspects surrounding the controversial issue of euthanasia. With help from the group leader, he was able to translate this to his own situation. He painfully spoke about his wife, who was now "a stranger" to him. He admitted, with guilt, that there were times when he wished she were dead rather than alive in such an altered condition. Other group members echoed similar feelings. Group leaders pointed out that these feelings were understandable and that wishes of death were not deeds. Emphasizing the important distinction between a wish and an act brought sighs of relief from family members who felt less guilty.

The grief experienced by the family of a demented patient is incomplete, since healthy resolution of the mourning process includes a sense of psychological closure and acceptance, which this situation does not allow. Because patients with dementia tend to be generally healthy and may live for many years, the agony feels endless for the family. The group provides a format for the protracted grieving that occurs in such circumstances. Mourning occurs in stages, each marked by further progression of the dementia. First, a wife may grieve over her husband's early retirement and the ensuing loss of income and status in the community. Later, she grieves over his inability to share responsibility for household management. With further deterioration, she grieves for his changing personality and habits. Ultimately, she expresses that she now lives and sleeps with a stranger, not the man she married. She realizes not only that her husband is different but also that he frequently has to be cared for like a child.

As members begin to share their stories, leaders clarify themes common to the group. Sadness and loss are the feelings usually expressed in early meetings. It is not unusual to have a group of members openly weeping. Often one member's tears will pave the way for a flood of group sadness. In early sessions, some members apologize for this expression of sadness. Leaders respond by stating that the group is a place where they can openly share with others how badly they are feeling and assuring them that grief is a natural response to their difficult situations.

Listening to one another express their grief in group, members begin to prepare for what lies ahead. The process of grieving occurs in conjunction with the process of accommodating. Group members slowly learn to live with and manage the patient at each new level. Group leaders highlight the two important themes of loss and accommodation that continue for the family until the patient's death.

Group members feel heightened sadness around important holidays, times for family gatherings when memories of the past are rekindled. The group can help members make practical decisions about how to handle these difficult times, as the following example demonstrates.

Mrs. W. talked about "a ticklish situation." Her children were planning a large party to celebrate their parents' fiftieth anniversary. Mrs. W.'s husband was moderately demented, and she worried that the commotion of a large party would upset him. She doubted that he would remember friends' names, which would be an embarrassment. As she talked further, she was able to express her own ambivalence. She was feeling sad and frightened about her husband's declining social and intellectual abilities, and the future looked bleak. Mrs. W. felt that there was little to celebrate at this point in her life. She was not sure how to suggest to her enthusiastic children that their plans for a large party might be an added burden for her. With group help, Mrs. W. was able to work out a compromise with her children. They planned a small dinner to commemorate the event, limiting invitations to family and close friends. This solution allowed her children to recognize an important event without adding to her anxiety. Later, she reported that it had been a lovely party that provided her with some moments of pleasure.

As Thanksgiving approached in one group, members talked about their plans. Some members living far away from family and isolated from friends sadly anticipated spending the holiday alone. Others spoke of changes in the way in which the holiday would be celebrated, as in the case of Mrs. C. Mrs. C, who had adult children in the area, talked about her dread of the family gathering. In response to Mrs. C.'s complaints that "everything was getting to be too much" because of her husband's illness, the dinner had been hosted for the past few years by her son's family. Although relieved to have the burden of preparing the meal lifted from her, she tearfully reflected upon Thanksgiving dinners in the past when the family gathered at her home. She would organize and prepare the meal while her husband acted as host. She remembered Mr. C., seated at the head of the table, assuredly carving the turkey. Now, because of his illness, his role in the family was greatly diminished. Mrs. C., with the group's understanding, was able to mourn for her husband's losses and consequently for losses that she, too, endured. Each group member related to some bittersweet aspect of the approaching holiday.

Shifting Roles and the Social Predicament. As part of the grieving process, family members learn to accept shifting roles in the family resulting from the patient's altered physical, intellectual, and emotional competence. Role reversals disrupt the family, as years of interactive patterns and precedents must be undone. The once stable family is in a crisis of disequilibrium. The process of establishing a new balance will be strongly influenced by the quality of family relationships before the illness and the problem-solving strategies used by the family. Role shifts will affect relationships between spouses, between the patient and his or her adult children, grandchildren, and other extended family members who help care for the patient.

Adult children are often in the role of parent to their parents. They may express ambivalence about "taking over." When a parent becomes demented, the adult child may be called on to assist the care-taking parent in making plans. The adult child, now in a powerful decision-making role with regard to the demented parent, may feel overwhelmed with guilt and anxiety. Children may feel the need to make financial sacrifices or to make more time available to the patient or to the healthy parent. These additional demands may be poorly timed for adult children who are involved with their own families. These adult offspring may be caught up in the crises of their own adolescent children, or all their children may have finally left the home and they are now looking forward to some peace and quiet. They understandably resent the task of resuming the parenting role, this time for their aging parents. Institutionalization may be viewed as a punitive, retaliatory act against the parent (Cath, 1978). The group can help the adult child understand both the practical and psychodynamic aspects of this role reversal.

The older husband or wife who becomes the primary care giver for a demented spouse faces significant role changes as well. The group offers the healthy spouse an opportunity to discuss this much changed life-style. The practical problems of assuming the new responsibilities necessary for day-to-day living are usually brought up first. For example, a wife may be frightened about having to assume the role of financial planning, which had always been managed by her husband. Or, it may be the care-giving husband who now needs to learn to shop in the grocery store and prepare meals. The need to learn new skills comes at a time when care-giving spouses are already feeling overwhelmed. They must successfully assume new roles or face a threat to their independent life-styles. Group members are resourceful in guiding each other to outside professionals or service providers who might assist with a specific task. For example, a husband, worried about keeping the house clean, was directed by group members to a local homemaker agency that could offer help.

The uncertain social situation of care-giving spouses is openly addressed in the group. It is difficult for these spouses to entertain friends if the patient is irritable or agitated. The care-taking spouse may feel isolated and alone, perceiving the social world as being couple oriented. It is not uncommon to hear group members express the sentiment, "I don't feel married and I don't feel single." Pursuing activities alone seems awkward and uncomfortable. Group members mourn for the lost marital relationship; the dementing illness has robbed them of a mate, best friend, and companion. Frustrated and distressed by their ambiguous position, some group members contemplate separation or divorce, but the idea of leaving a vulnerable husband or wife usually provokes guilt.

In addition to having to face the lost companionship, the care-giving spouse must accept changes in how love is given and received. The healthy spouse continues to wish for closeness and affection. However, the emotionally withdrawn patient may lack sexual interest, while the agitated patient may make incessant, inappropriate demands. The illness may alter the patient's personality to such an extent that the spouse may find it hard to react with genuine feelings of warmth and affection. These sentiments were expressed by one member who spoke of her sense of revulsion toward her husband, who was now incontinent and drooled. While she was committed to providing for his physical care, she admitted that she now viewed him as "a retarded child, requiring mothering, not sexuality."

Older spouses may be reluctant at first to discuss sexuality in a group setting. Once they feel comfortable with one another, they are able to talk about the changes in this aspect of their relationship brought about by the illness. In group meetings, one member's open and direct expression of sexual issues prompts other group members to share similar experiences. Adult children in the group are curious as they hear about this aspect of the altered marital relationship that may also be affecting their own parents. Thus, they learn from older group members about issues that may be too sensitive for their own parents to share with them.

Lacking affection, the healthy spouse hopes for some expression of thanks for his care-giving efforts. Sadly, the confused patient is often unable to respond. Instead, the efforts of the emotionally needy care giver are met by hostility, paranoia, or apathy. Group members try to respond to this unmet need by providing praise for each other's efforts. They share the understanding that the absence of thanks is a result of the illness, not a conscious rejection by the patient.

The Expression of Anger. Once group members have demonstrated to each other that they are basically loving and devoted family members, they feel more comfortable about expressing angry feelings. Anger may be directed toward the spouse, health care providers, the illness, or God for having unfairly delivered such a burden. Anger is sometimes expressed in the group about the medical workup. They report that the illness was misdiagnosed for many years or that they were "handed the diagnosis like a death sentence" by insensitive health care professionals. The sense of helplessness experienced by the family is intensified, since there is no treatment or active program of intervention for dementia. Family members trying to learn about what lies ahead are further frustrated as they discover that they will witness progressive deterioration in the condition of their loved one.

Anger is a frequent response of care givers when demands for patient care become physically and emotionally exhausting. This is particularly true for the elderly care giver coping with his or her own health problems and other life crises. Paying for important support services may put further stress on the family. If institutionalization becomes necessary, family members must struggle not only with their guilt and sadness but also with the very real financial burden imposed by that decision. Often nursing home costs require the healthy spouse to compromise his or her life-style such as by selling a home or limiting travel plans to visit friends and family.

The decisions within the family about who assumes primary responsibility for the patient's care are likely to stir up feelings of anger and resentment. If spouses are the primary care givers, they may be angry with adult children for not doing more and compare today's youth with their upbringing. Adult children caring for a patient may resent siblings for abandoning responsibility or may be angry about changes in their life-style necessitated by the parent's care. Further fueling the care-giving children's anger may be the idealized attitude of the patient toward the siblings not involved in daily care. The patients may praise these siblings while heaping insults on the children providing the ongoing care.

Practical Problem-Solving Phase. Group members also ask for practical help and suggestions related to patient management. Leaders designate two sessions on the agenda for this important matter. Family members continually present management problems from the earliest sessions, even though structured discussion of problem solving does not occur until the fifth and sixth sessions. Leaders turn to group members as the proven experts in solving practical problems. When one care giver has a problem, another family member usually has a helpful suggestion. In each family group, leaders learn new creative strategies that have been successfully utilized by care givers. The leaders participate with family members in problem-solving endeavors. Leaders may share simple models of behavior therapy and environmental manipulation with care givers, who can then implement changes at home.

In one group, members sought suggestions for dealing with problems related to personal hygiene. For one member, getting her husband to bathe regularly had become a major source of conflict. Another member described her solution to a similar problem. She had enlisted the cooperation of the patient's physician, who agreed to prescribe regular bathing as part of the patient's health maintenance plan. He sent the patient home with a prescription specifying the frequency of bathing. This prescription was displayed in the bathroom and served as a reminder to the patient. The order to bathe was more easily accepted by the patient when it came from the doctor rather than from a family member.

Considerable time and energy are spent discussing activities of daily living. Typical questions posed include: How can I get my husband involved in some activity or hobby so that he doesn't spend the whole day in bed? How can I help my mother arrange her kitchen in a way that minimizes her confusion and ensures maximum safety? Should I travel to Florida this winter with my confused wife? Group members encourage one another to utilize available community resources. Often these resources, such as homemakers or adult day health centers (that is, structured programs for the disabled elderly staffed by professional workers), can help provide much needed relief to the family members. When patients can no longer assume legal or financial responsibilities themselves, family members want information on issues related to power of attorney and guardianship.

Finally, family members request assistance in making appropriate inquiries for nursing home placement. During one of the eight group sessions, we invite the nursing home liaison coordinator from our hospital to address the group. Group members frequently feel intimidated by nursing home administrators and the interview process. The coordinator counters this attitude by reminding members that they are consumers of this service and should approach the task of finding a nursing home as they might approach any other major financial and emotional decision. She encourages group members to approach their search for a nursing home in an active and systematic manner.

Not all the members feel ready to contemplate nursing home placement. However, they may refer back to the presentation at some point in the future, as did a young woman with a family who had quit her job as a nurse to care for her father in her home. She refused to consider institutionalization. At a follow-up session, several months after the eight-week program had ended, she announced that she had placed her father in a nursing home. She described the process she went through, using the list of questions that had been generated in the group session with the nursing home coordinator. She was astonished at how this framework had facilitated her search and decreased her anxiety concerning the adequacy of her father's care. One overriding concern was that her father, who tended to become agitated at night, would be excessively medicated or physically restrained. With delight she told the group that she felt confident enough to ask the administrator directly how she would deal with this problem. She was relieved when her question was met with an honest answer that satisfied her criterion for compassionate care for her father.

Resolution. As the support group progresses, family

members understand the patients' illness and their own reactions to it better. They recognize fully that the future will mean continued adaptation to a deteriorating situation. As one group member summarized, "Just when you think you have the situation under control, there's a new bend in the road. Each day brings new changes and new problems to solve. You think you won't be able to cope with the patient slipping to a lower level, but you just have to manage." For some group members, difficult decisions regarding the patient's care and their own life plans are made in the final sessions. Often these decisions had been postponed because of guilt, depression, or a lack of accurate information.

Over the eight weeks of group meetings, sessions become a time in the week that members eagerly anticipate. As groups begin to think about termination, some members may request follow-up sessions, wanting to stay in touch with each other in a formal and structured way. Reluctant to give up the relationships and the atmosphere of support, members agree to less frequent follow-up sessions. Group leaders recognize the importance of these sessions, since care givers are coping with a continuously changing situation.

After several follow-up meetings, members may begin to drop out or attend less frequently. Some report that they have located informal support systems closer to home. They feel that they are coping adequately and no longer need the group. When leaders sense this disengagement, they urge remaining members to return for a final meeting. Group leaders bring closure to the group, acknowledging with members the ongoing challenges they each face.

As with other therapies, some benefits are realized after treatment ends. Several months after the conclusion of the sessions, one member reported to a group leader that he had finally sold his large home, where he was living by himself, and moved into a more manageable apartment. This decision was significant, since it represented his acceptance of the fact that his severely demented and institutionalized wife would not regain her health and could not return home to live.

Therapeutic Forces

Validation of feelings and the sharing of experience are significant therapeutic forces in providing relief for this group of care givers. Family members express audible sighs of relief in early group meetings as they realize that they are not alone in their reactions to a dementing illness. The isolated family member frequently remarks, "I feel so much better talking with others. I thought I was going crazy, too." Freedom to express anger and frustration also provides relief.

The emphasis on education serves an important purpose in a dementia support group, since members often come to group with myths, misinformation, or no information about the illness. Without a clear understanding about possible causes, symptomatology, and the course of the disease, family members cannot interact effectively with the patient or make realistic plans for him or her. After one group session that focused on the probable causes of dementia, a member blurted out her relief to learn that physical changes in the brain were responsible for her husband's dementia and not his trumpet playing. For years she harbored the thought that he had literally blown his brains out playing the trumpet. In another group, a member secretly wondered whether a marital dispute many years ago had somehow caused her husband's problems. Some family members are concerned that dementia is a mental illness similar to schizophrenia or retardation and are embarrassed by the association. In addition, they worry about genetic factors and the implication for other family members.

As family members learn about a dementing illness, understand their reactions, and make plans for themselves and the patient, they have the opportunity to gain insight into their own behavior. Family members talk about the quality of the relationship with the patient that predated the illness and they discuss relevant family dynamics. From these discussions, they begin to understand how prior experiences and interactions bear on the current situation. In one group, a daughter talked at length about her longstanding difficult relationship with her

mother. The old conflicts, which had been put aside, were rekindled. She tearfully stated, "I thought I had all this mother
stuff worked out!"

In addition, group members may point out to other members aspects of their behavior that they were unaware of. In one
group, a member spoke about how dependent she was on her
husband prior to his illness for all planning and decision making.
Now, in a decision-making role, she felt that her ideas and opinions were not valid. Group members viewed her differently.
They saw her as a competent woman, stating that they felt she
underrated herself. This helped her begin to alter how she perceived herself.

Participating in group meetings is an activity that counters the feeling of doing nothing. In part, the helplessness experienced by family members is brought about by the lack of
active treatment interventions for the demented patient. Care
givers express the feeling that coming to the sessions keeps them
linked up with an academic research and teaching hospital.
Should a treatment or cure be discovered, they want to be in
contact with clinicians who can then help the patient. This
wishful fantasy reflects the positive transference that group
members experience toward the group leaders. Some members
have had upsetting experiences with other professionals whom
they perceived to be insensitive and uninformed about dementia. Group leaders, in a position to be empathic and helpful with
practical management issues, are generally seen in a favorable
light.

Isolated care givers benefit from socializing with other
group members. The informal group begins when members who
arrive early drink a cup of coffee together and catch up with the
events of the past week. At the end of the formal group session,
some members linger in small groups to talk or adjourn to the
cafeteria for a quick bite to eat. Being able to talk or snack in a
relaxed fashion is a luxury that they are not afforded in their
care-giving roles at home. Group members may exchange phone
numbers and set up an informal support hotline. Members report in group that during the week they may have telephoned
one another for support at a stressful time. They are grateful

to have someone who can just listen to them or give some helpful suggestions with a problem. In one group, a few members attended an educational luncheon and lecture sponsored by the local Alzheimer's Disease and Related Disorders Association.

Group discussions aid care givers by helping them prepare for the future. A family member caring for a patient in the early stages of the illness learns about what problems to anticipate from members caring for patients at more advanced stages of the disease. Family members begin important planning with this knowledge. For example, anticipating that the patient with dementia may soon be unable to drive, a couple may choose to give up a rural home for one closer to public transportation. Or an adult child may begin to recognize that her father is not managing well in his independent living situation. Drawing on experiences of other group members, she may begin to explore the feasibility of building an addition to her home for her father. Thinking and planning ahead allows family members to make careful decisions about the patient's care before a crisis arises. Knowing that long-range plans have been explored allows family members to cope more effectively with their current situation.

Usual Treatment Outcome and Predictors of Success

Both short-term and long-term treatment outcomes can be evaluated. Structured rating forms allow us to assess short-term goals. Group members are asked to complete these at the end of the eight-week sessions. It is evident from the responses that the majority of members find participation to be stimulating and beneficial. Many participants emphasize the significance of learning the facts about the illness. They note that they feel better equipped to cope with situations as they arise.

Long-term benefits are more difficult to assess, particularly if members are lost to follow-up. However, from those members who continue to participate in monthly follow-up meetings, we have gathered evidence that what is learned in group carries over into periods when the group does not meet. Members feel that they have developed a framework for understanding their own feelings and the patient's behavior. One woman whose mother was showing early signs of dementia when the group formally terminated returned after the summer to a follow-up meeting. She told the group that her mother had suffered a stroke over the summer and that she had been contemplating having her mother live with her. In previous group sessions, she had expressed concern about the difficulties of taking care of her mother in her home all by herself. She said, "I kept hearing all your [the group's] comments and warnings about taking my mother to my house." She ultimately decided to enlist the aid of a companion to provide the additional support the patient needed. Her case demonstrates the fact that members seem to carry with them other opinions to which they can appeal when they feel blinded by their own anxieties.

Several factors influence the outcome of treatment. Participants' expectations before joining the group can alter their experience and affect whether they feel the treatment has been useful. Group composition also influences treatment outcome. Members seem to benefit more from heterogeneous groups. Homogeneous groups can reduce the likelihood of discussing certain issues while overemphasizing others. Groups that consist entirely of spouses or of adult children may lack the elements of conflict and comparison that naturally arise in a heterogeneous group. Generally, fewer men than women participate in these groups; when this occurs, the male perspective may either be challenged or absent. One group was conducted in which all the participants were elderly and in poor health themselves. They were also significantly depressed, and an overwhelming degree of sadness was expressed during these meetings. It was difficult to introduce new themes for discussion, and some members questioned how much they were gaining from their participation.

Effectiveness of the Method

The group treatment approach just outlined has not yet been rigorously tested. We are in the process of collecting pre- and posttreatment questionnaires to determine how effective the treatment is in meeting the goals we have set. The questionnaire contains ten factual questions about dementia and ten questions about how group members are managing with practical and emotional issues. Unlike the measures used by Lazarus and others (1981), our questionnaire focuses directly on treatment aims rather than on participant personality factors, which may or may not change with treatment. Preliminary results suggest that our goals of educating care givers, providing useful management strategies, and allowing an emotional outlet are met and perceived by the group as useful. The results of this study will appear in a future report.

Difficulties

The approach we describe is not without its difficulties. Some participants feel the need for more prolonged treatment and follow-up. They are reluctant to terminate the sessions either because they feel they could derive more benefit from additional sessions or because they find it difficult to end their contact with other group members. Some members begin to meet informally outside the group. Others choose to have individual treatment sessions after the group terminates. Yet others join another series of sessions after several months have elapsed. We have attempted to deal with this need for continuation by offering monthly or bimonthly follow-up sessions. However, the break in the continuity of weekly sessions produces a loss of momentum, and the attrition factor in the follow-up period is often significant.

Groups for families of patients with dementia present special problems. Care givers often have difficulty in making arrangements to come to the meetings. Elderly spouses may have failing health and find it hard to arrange for transportation. Also, they may be the sole care providers and may be unable to leave the patient unattended while at the meeting. These difficulties are managed by directly assisting the members in arranging for transportation or recruiting a suitable companion for the patients while spouses are at the meeting. We are currently working with the volunteer service in our hospital so that it can

assist with this problem. Volunteer companions are being recruited to stay with patients who accompany the group members to the hospital.

In the course of solving one set of problems, others may
be created. Evening groups tend to be made up entirely of adult
children, removing the spouses' perspective as an element in the
treatment process. The converse is sometimes true of daytime
sessions, where the majority of participants are spouses. In composing groups, we attempt to include as much variety as possible with respect to the age and sex of the participants, the severity of the illness in the patient, and patient location.

When a group is homogeneous, we attempt to introduce
other perspectives in our discussions. Very frequently members
from one homogeneous group will ask us how members of another group are doing. One group made up entirely of adult
children asked us about the concerns of spouses of patients.
This gave us the opportunity to explore their fantasies and their
concerns about their own healthy parents.

Occasionally members of the group convey intensely hostile feelings toward their patient. This occurs most often when
the premorbid relationship between the spouse or adult child
and the patient had a long history of conflict and ambivalence.
Other group members may react with puzzlement, fear, or
counterhostility. A woman in one of our groups who expressed
intense anger toward her husband described an unsatisfactory
relationship that had prompted her to consider divorce several
years earlier. She had sought psychiatric treatment for depression in the past. She saw her husband's illness as an additional
burden to an already explosive situation. However, none of the
other members in the group shared her experience or intensity
of feelings, and she became set apart from the rest. She ultimately decided to drop out of the group. We helped to arrange
individual treatment for her with a psychiatrist. Group members were encouraged to express their reactions to this member
after her departure from the group. This event promoted a lot
of active group discussion. In some cases this allowed care givers
to examine angry feelings that they had never openly expressed.

Future Directions for Group Work

After experimenting with different treatment models, we have arrived at an approach that we believe is well suited to the needs of family members. It also allows group leaders to provide a comprehensive support framework in a short time. With each new group, however, we discover additional services that could be offered to care givers in the context of the group. As previously mentioned, we have devoted one session to a discussion with the nursing home liaison in our hospital, who provides members with guidelines for choosing a nursing home. Occasionally we will engage the group in an activity that stimulates controversy and discussion. In a recent follow-up session, we showed a film on Alzheimer's disease that featured research carried on in our hospital. The producer of the film, which was prepared for television, attended the group session. Members discussed with her the content of the film and also the importance of publicizing the facts about Alzheimer's disease.

At the request of families, we are now thinking about offering patient-family groups. Some patients in the earliest stages of the illness may be aware of their failing abilities and may become depressed and apathetic. Family members finding it difficult to respond to these feelings have suggested that they would like to include such patients in group meetings. Treatment would focus on allowing patients to express their feelings and on assisting family members in accepting and responding to these expressions.

In our individual work with families, we have seen some benefits of patient participation. In one family meeting, a woman with Alzheimer's disease who was still functioning rather well at home asked her husband not to take over for her completely. She had begun to feel suffocated by his assumption of activities that she was still able to perform. Her ability to express this openly decreased the tension in the relationship. She was able to verbalize her frustration and sadness comfortably, and together they were able to contemplate their future.

Health care professionals wishing to offer support group

services must consider rigorous methods of evaluating treatment. Objective data are essential in order to compare treatment versus no treatment or different approaches with each group. Objective information not only is necessary in establishing the validity of a method of treatment but also can help group members define what they have accomplished in the course of treatment. Methodology is also needed to determine the long-term effects of treatment after members are no longer participating in the groups. It would be useful to know, for example, whether the decision about institutionalization, which may be made months after treatment, is facilitated by having participated in the group.

Personal Reflections

Like the families of demented patients, health care providers experience feelings of helplessness when dealing with this illness. It is a discouraging task for professionals to document and diagnose a dementing illness with little to offer the afflicted patient. Without treatment or curative interventions, being able to offer the support group to families affords health care providers an important sense of doing something.

As group leaders, we become increasingly convinced at the conclusion of each eight-week program that we have a valuable service to offer families. We derive personal satisfaction from helping care givers understand and begin to resolve the life crisis into which they are thrown by a dementing illness. Our work with families has given us the opportunity to meet many interesting and devoted care givers. Family members, able to maintain a sense of humor through the tears, exhibit an outlook that is most admirable. Many group members who have taken the program keep in touch with the group leaders during clinic visits for the patient, by letter, or by phone. It is especially rewarding when we learn from family members that issues concerning the patient and his or her illness are reasonably settled and that the care givers are now moving on with their own lives.

Coordinating the family support group and working with

an elderly population of patients brings issues of aging into sharp focus for us. Older group members painfully articulate their loneliness, discouragement, fears of illness and disease, disgust with their wrinkled, aged faces and failing bodies, and their fury with God for not treating them better in their old age. At an age when we are finally beginning to feel settled in our professional and personal lives, we find it difficult at times to listen to such discussions. Group discussions, in addition to stirring up anxiety about our aging process, raise questions about our commitment and responsibilities to our own aging parents. Furthermore, we wonder how our own marriages and close relationships would hold up under the stress of a dementing illness.

We identify with adult children when they openly express their emotional struggles with an ill parent, while older group members may remind us by their gestures, appearance, or speech of our own parents. These strong feelings and identifications are regularly dealt with in an open way after each meeting. We set aside time to reflect on our own reactions to group themes and individual members. Periodic supervision is also helpful in guiding our work. Understanding these countertransference feelings can result in personal and professional growth for the group leaders.

References

Bergmann, K., and others. "Management of the Demented Elderly in the Community." *British Journal of Psychiatry,* 1978, *132,* 441-449.

Caplan, G. "Mastery of Stress: Psychosocial Aspects." *American Journal of Psychiatry,* 1981, *138,* 413-420.

Cath, S. H. "The Geriatric Patient and His Family: The Institutionalization of a Parent—A Nadir of Life." *Journal of Geriatric Psychiatry,* 1978, *1,* 25-46.

Davies, P., and Maloney, A. J. F. "Selective Loss of Central Cholinergic Neurons in Alzheimer's Disease." *Lancet,* 1976, *2,* 1403.

Elliott, J. "Care for the Demented: It May Be Up to the Family." *Medical News,* 1979, *241,* 231.

Farkas, S. W. "Impact of Chronic Illness on the Patient's Spouse." *Health and Social Work,* 1980, *5,* 39-46.

Fengler, A. P., and Goodrich, N. "Wives of Elderly Disabled Men: The Hidden Patients." *The Gerontologist,* 1979, *19,* 175-183.

Kapust, L. R. "Living with Dementia: The Ongoing Funeral." *Social Work in Health Care,* 1982, 7, 79-91.

Katzman, R. "The Prevalence and Malignancy of Alzheimer's Disease." *Archives of Neurology,* 1976, *30,* 217-218.

LaVorgna, D. "Group Treatment for Wives of Patients with Alzheimer's Disease." *Social Work in Health Care,* 1979, *5,* 219-221.

Lazarus, L. W., and others. "A Pilot Study of an Alzheimer Patients' Relatives Discussion Group." *The Gerontologist,* 1981, *21,* 353-358.

Lezak, M. "Living with the Characterologically Altered Brain-Injured Patient." *Journal of Clinical Psychiatry,* 1978, *39,* 592-598.

Rabins, P. V., Mace, N. L., and Lucas, M. J. "The Impact of Dementia on the Family." *Journal of the American Medical Association,* 1982, *248,* 333-335.

Rotter, J. B. "Generalized Expectancies for Internal Versus External Control of Reinforcement." *Psychology Monographs,* 1966, *80,* 1-28.

Tomlinson, B. E., Blessed, G., and Roth, M. "Observations on the Brains of Demented Old People." *Journal of the Neurological Sciences,* 1968, *11,* 205-242.

Zarit, S. H., Reever, K. E., and Bach-Peterson, J. "Relatives of the Impaired Elderly: Correlates of Feelings of Burden." *Gerontology,* 1980, *20,* 649-655.

19   Mark A. Chesler, Ph.D.
      Margaret Yoak, M.A., M.S.

▦ ▦ ▦ ▦ ▦ ▦ ▦ ▦ ▦ ▦ ▦ ▦ ▦

Self-Help Groups
for Parents
of Children with Cancer

Self-help groups concerned with health care have grown rapidly
in the past decade. These groups offer opportunities for professionals and consumers to act together to improve the quality of
psychosocial care during medical treatment, as well as to develop mechanisms for pioneering changes in the delivery of health
care. At the same time, such groups often present a challenge to
the local medical establishment, to traditional professional
roles, and to typical relationships between professionals and the
patients or consumers of medical care.

Numerous treatises exist on health-related self-help groups,
but few discuss groups formed around children's illnesses. In
this chapter we examine self-help groups formed by or for families of children with cancer. We first discuss the stresses experienced by these families and the kinds of social support they
seem to need and want. Then we examine the specific resources
and activities of self-help groups and how they help people deal

with these stresses and provide this support. Self-help groups established to help people deal with health-related stresses should be examined in the context of the particular stresses and the coping patterns and support systems people utilize in dealing with stress. The chapter concludes with a discussion of some useful roles for health care professionals in such groups. In order to illuminate our discussion, we have included reports from our studies with families of children with cancer and with self-help groups formed by or for such families (Chesler and Yoak, 1983; Chesler and others, 1981).*

Stresses of Childhood Cancer

Several recent reports from the National Cancer Institute (1981) and the American Cancer Society (1982) indicate rapid rises over the past two decades in the percentages of children with cancer who are surviving several years beyond diagnosis. In 1979 the National Conference on the Care of the Child with Cancer projected a cure rate of 40 to 50 percent for children with acute lymphocytic leukemia and from 30 to 90 percent for the other most common forms of childhood cancer (D'Angio, 1980; see also Siegel, 1980; Simone and others, 1978). Thus, what was once an almost universally fatal childhood disease is no longer so. For instance, Wilbur (1975, p. 809) notes that "many people . . . treat children with cancer as though they will all have a fatal outcome. Out of this has evolved a particular emphasis on helping families and children prepare for their ex-

*Chesler and others (1981) conducted interviews with ninety-four parents of children with cancer who were treated at a major midwestern hospital, expressly focusing on their reports of stressful experiences, coping strategies, and social support systems (including participation in a local self-help group). Chesler and Yoak (1983) conducted interviews with parents and professionals active in a nationwide sample of thirty self-help or support groups of families of children with cancer. We appreciate the contributions of our colleague, Oscar Barbarin, in these studies and especially in developing the ideas underlying Table 1. We also appreciate the support of the Rackham Graduate School of the University of Michigan, which provided a faculty research grant that contributed to the funding of this work.

pected death. The expectation of a frequently successful outcome with eradication of disease, and a recognition of the importance of rehabilitation, has just begun to emerge."

Whether preparing for chronic illness and death or, as is now increasingly common, long-term treatment and potential recovery or rehabilitation, families of children with cancer encounter many stresses in the care and management of the child and family. Many more families and the medical community itself are concerned with enhancing the quality of life of those affected by childhood cancer. Such enhancement requires dealing with a series of stresses, which begin with diagnosis and continue after death or after all treatment has ceased and recovery or cure is evident.

Diagnosis: First Encounters with Long-Term Stress

The major stresses associated with childhood cancer usually begin with the formal diagnosis. At this point, whether in an instant or over a period of hours and days, life is turned upside down. Parents' prior reality is shattered, and they enter a new reality, with new definitions of their children, themselves, and their world. From whatever level of consciousness they respond, these parents know that they are embarking on a long and difficult struggle. They may hope for a good outcome and perhaps a rapid return to a normal existence, while recognizing that their life can never return to what it was before.

A number of research studies emphasize the shock accompanying this diagnostic period (D. Adams, 1979; Binger and others, 1969; Hamburg and Adams, 1967; Knapp and Hansen, 1973; Koch, Hermann, and Donaldson, 1974; McCollum and Schwartz, 1972; Ross, 1978). A review of some parents' comments provides direct personal evidence of their trauma, sense of unreality, and often despair:

> For a while I didn't deal with it; nothing they told me sunk in. They had to tell me three times before I was grasping it. They told me things and two minutes later I couldn't tell you what they told me in terms of medicine, treatment, and stuff.

> When I heard the diagnosis, I left the room. I
> ran. I don't know where I went. I know I ended up
> on the seventh floor. I know that I was trying to
> dial numbers and couldn't see the phone. I know I
> must have called four people before I was aware of
> what I was doing. I was so totally alone I didn't
> know how to function. I was going up and down
> the stairs of the hospital. It certainly was the worst
> day of my life. I thought the day that my dad fell
> dead was the worst experience of my life, but this
> was the worst.

These feelings continue. They may abate over time and
be moderated by experience, hope, and recovery, but they return throughout the course of treatment. After all, cancer in
children is not a one-time event; it is a chronically life-threatening disease. Chesler and his colleagues (1981) asked a sample of
parents of children with cancer to fill out a self-anchored scale
indicating the times and events of greatest stress during their experience with the child's illness.

The precise nature of this question and composite repre-
sentations of parents' answers are presented in Figure 1. Although the data indicate that the diagnosis is one of the greatest
stress periods for parents, other events were also reported as potent (Futterman and Hoffman, 1973; National Cancer Institute,
1980; Ross, 1978). The dotted lines in Figure 1 indicate that
while not very many parents mentioned that their child experienced surgery or relapse, these events were more stressful than
the diagnosis for those who did. Parents of children who died
indicated that the relapse was even more potent and took on
continuing importance, since it often was the start of a down-
ward trend. The parents of deceased children also identified
deterioration (the terminal phase) and anniversaries such as
birthdays and important family events as potent stresses (Lascari and Stehbens, 1973).

The rise and fall of these stress points reflect portions of
what D. Adams has called the typical "illness cycle" (1979, pp.
17-21). Some observers, noting a rhythm to families' stress at
different phases of the child's illness or their adjustment to ill-

Figure 1. Composite Stress Chart of Parents of Children with Cancer.

Here is a chart, a timeline, that can be used to describe the time that has elapsed from before you learned the diagnosis until now.

1. Mark on this line the critical events or stages in your experience with your child's cancer. Indicate the approximate date of each.

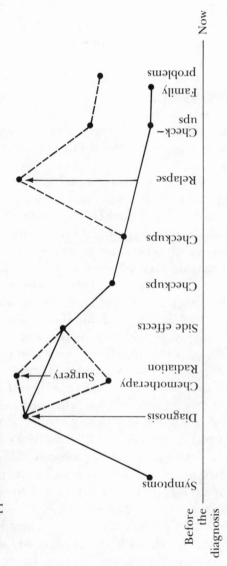

2. Which of these events or stages were most stressful? Draw an arrow for each event, indicating with a high line the highest stress times or events, and with a low line the lower stress times or events.

Key: – – – – Events or stresses reported by a minority of parents

────── Events or stresses reported by all parents

ness, suggest providing different kinds of help or social services
at various points (Kaplan and others, 1973; Obetz and others,
1980; Ross, 1978).

Categories of Stress

The medical situation of the child with cancer is clearly
the major generator of personal and family stress, but it is by
no means the only problem requiring resolution. Nor does it
take a singular form; many different stresses are created by the
medical and social complexities of this chronic and serious illness.

One set of stressors is *intellectual* in nature and requires
parents to understand and master massive amounts of new and
complex information about their child's condition. A second set
of stressors is *instrumental* or practical in nature and involves
parents in finding or generating solutions to the day-to-day
problems of arranging their personal and family life around the
treatment of a child with cancer. There is also a range of *interpersonal* stresses that parents experience, as old relationships are
disrupted and tested and new relationships created in response
to their child's illness. In addition, there is a variety of personal
emotional stresses, psychological and psychosomatic pressures
that parents experience when faced with this threat to their
child's life and their own normal living pattern. Finally, parents
often experience *existential* stresses, challenges to their understanding or evaluation of the meaning of their careers and lives
as the normal order of life and death is cast into doubt.

Intellectual Stressors. Part of what is difficult and even
shocking for parents of children with cancer is the need to assimilate a great deal of new information and to learn their way
around the unfamiliar organization of the hospital. If parents
are to be involved in the long-term care of chronically and seriously ill children, they must have adequate and detailed information about symptoms, disease progress, danger signals, and
treatment procedures and options. Gathering and understanding
information may be critical to the child's survival, as well as to
parents' own emotional stability and integrity. Futterman and

Hoffman (1973) emphasize the latter issue as they note that some parents "use intellectual mastery to gain some sense of control, as though knowledge actually were power" (p. 133).

As parents try to cope with and act upon intellectual stress, they sometimes encounter a medical system that exacerbates the information gap. Their tasks are made more difficult when medical information is withheld from them or when it is presented in ways that are unfamiliar to parents with a lay lifestyle and culture. Thus, parents of chronically and seriously ill children are faced with the need to make a rapid entry into a different culture, with new rules, roles, and language. The particular vocabulary, jargon, and even style of the medical system often make it more difficult for parents to understand what is happening to them and their child. Consider the following parental reports:

> There was a communication gap between the doctor and us parents. The hematology staff would tell the residents who would tell the medical students who would tell the residents again. By funneling the information through in this way, sometimes it is not all gotten, and there is a chance it will get muddled. Therefore, a more direct communication and relationship between parents and doctor would be helpful.

> When I brought a book on hematology and wanted to discuss something in it with a nurse, she tended to discourage rather than encourage my reading from other sources. None of them could understand why I wanted second opinions on some of the treatments.

Instrumental Stressors. As the child with cancer is treated or perhaps hospitalized for chemotherapy or surgery, parents must often establish new patterns of family life and new divisions of labor that permit them to care for the ill child, as well as to care for other family members, continue their jobs, manage transportation to the hospital, and ensure that household chores are accomplished.

Parents who must deal with the medical system on a long-term basis begin to develop an awareness of medical records, hospital billing procedures, and insurance forms. They often monitor the daily care of their child.

> Doctors keep changing, and many come in without having even bothered to sit down and read the records, and don't know what's going on. You have to keep constantly telling them things over and over. You feel you have to be there or she won't get taken care of.

For children with cancer treated on an outpatient basis, who come only occasionally to a clinic, parents become front-line care givers. Then they must become proficient in recognizing symptoms, monitoring dosages and compliance, and providing care, which has traditionally been defined as a medical prerogative (Futterman and Hoffman, 1973).

Current regimens for the treatment of childhood cancer do not leave many reasonable decisions in parents' hands, at least not at the beginning of treatment; relatively proven treatment modes comprise standard courses of initial treatment. But parents may be asked to participate in research studies or experimental treatment programs and may need to select a treatment facility before they have mastered the intellectual challenges just posed. Later, if the child's situation should deteriorate, parents often become involved in making choices about whether or when to cease treatment, where and how their child should die, and so on.

For some parents, managing the financial stress of childhood cancer also represents a major practical problem. Parents who report the financial impact of the disease as "somewhat serious" or "serious" tend to be concentrated disproportionately in lower-income groups, and some report that they have to make major changes in their life-styles in order to cope with new financial problems.

> We had to sell our house because he [the child] went through most of my health insurance

policy in six months. Recently, my husband's been laid off again, and we're going through the financial strain again.

The bills are bad. I work, but I'm still in debt.

We know enough about the meaning of socioeconomic status in American life to know that people's lives are affected by these factors in a variety of subtle ways. Financial resources make a difference in the life experiences of all families and are especially critical when problems arise. Several students of stressful life events suggest that lower-income families are exposed to more unfavorable living conditions and stress of all sorts in our society (Dohrenwend, 1970; Myers, Lindenthat, and Pepper, 1974; Pearlin and Schooler, 1978). The addition of childhood cancer makes an already difficult life situation more difficult and magnifies many of the practical problems of everyday living.

Interpersonal Stressors. Dealing with the child's adjustment to the disease and treatment and to the many new routines the treatment requires creates many stressful family situations (Kaplan and others, 1973). For instance, although most parents report that their spouse is very supportive during this time, new divisions of labor and new family roles may create stress. If mothers and fathers have very different contacts with doctors and other sources of medical information, they may experience an imbalance in normal family expertise and roles. Parents who are quite depressed or angry may be unable to have intimate times with their partners, which can strain the marriage. It is also typical for siblings to develop feelings of curiosity and concern about their brother or sister's illness, to question why this person was selected for this fate, and to experience jealousy or anger about reallocations of time and attention in the family (Gogan and others, 1977; Sourkes, 1980; Spinetta and others, 1976). In some families, siblings act as safety valves, acting out or blowing off when internal family tension becomes too great. In other instances, they act as "reality challengers," indicating to parents when they are paying too much attention to the ill child. If childhood cancer and its associated stresses disturb the family's prior patterns, it can threaten the interpersonal relationships between the ill child and his or her siblings and between parents and all their children.

One of the critical tasks that the parents of a chronically ill child must face is going public—sharing the new reality, and as much of its meaning as they wish, with their extended family and friends. This is a self-redefining act; in performing it, parents inform themselves and others of a life-changing status that they have just assumed. Not knowing how they should behave in public with their seriously ill child, concern about how others will react, and a desire to give the right impression to others, all create awkward social situations. As Goffman (1968) notes, people who are close to a stigmatized person are often treated by others as stigmatized themselves. Moreover, they often internalize the same reaction to stigma. No one likes being labeled or stigmatized, and parental denial or silence with friends about their child's illness may be a way to avoid further social stress.

As parents turn their attention to the other people and relationships in their lives, each person or group becomes a potential stressor; sometimes their reactions increase the stress parents already experience (Cassileth and Hamilton, 1979; Hymovich, 1976; Kaplan and others, 1973; E. Katz, 1980; Voysey, 1972; Wortman and Dunkel-Schetter, 1979). Thus, despite many reports of increased closeness to friends, some parents report stress and distress associated with friends' responses and reactions to their child's illness.

> You go back to work and everything's pretty calm for a while. And people at work don't know what to say. So they're afraid to say anything.

> Some of the people who we thought would be our best friends never showed up for at least a couple of months after. That was particularly tough at the time, because you expected them to be right there at your doorstep. As you get through

this stage, the crisis stage, you find out that the
reason they weren't there is because they couldn't
handle it themselves.

In addition to managing relationships with friends and co-
workers, parents also must deal with representatives of other
social institutions. Parents of school-age children sometimes experience difficulty in creating effective partnerships between
the medical staff and the school as their child reenters the educational environment (Barbarin and Chesler, 1982). If princi-
pals, teachers, and parents of classmates are frightened or awkward in dealing with the child who has cancer in school, classmates are also likely to be uncomfortable. Any of these situations can add social stress and strain to the existing medical
stresses of childhood cancer.

Emotional Stressors. As the quotations from the parents
and the data in Figure 1 indicate, the diagnostic encounter often has an overwhelming emotional impact. Even after this initial period, and even as the child "recovers," every symptom,
every side effect, and every checkup may carry a dangerous
message. Parents continue to be concerned about the uncertain
progress of the disease because there is seldom a time in the
near future when anything is certain. For most, the uncertain
waiting, hoping that a relapse will not occur, lasts for years.

> I worry when he says, "Mom, my stomach
> hurts." And I worry what's going on there. But as
> time goes on, you learn what to worry about and
> what not to.

> Regular CAT scans worry me, because they
> show potential progress of the disease, and each
> subsequent scan has been stressful. It is hard for
> me to wait for the results from the tests because
> they could show evidence of the disease.

The fact that a child's life is threatened, and that this
threat will exist for a long time, undoubtedly creates chronic
emotional stress. Constant alertness to small signs of recurrent
disease, constant adaptation to new treatments and their side

effects, and the prolonged effects of constant worry tax the
mind and heart and body. Many parents report signs of personal
psychosomatic illness, as in their own aches and pains, sleepless-
ness, fatigue, loss or gain of weight, and so on. Some become
easily irritable, provoked by otherwise minor events in their
lives; others become depressed and anxious.

Parents cope with the personal and emotional impacts of
childhood cancer in a variety of ways: Some undertake active
problem solving, while others become passive and reactive.
Some try to ward off worry by denying potential ill effects for
their child:

> I try to keep my mind off it. I don't watch
> TV shows or anything pertaining to it. I shut them
> right off. For instance, my brother called and
> started telling me about *Brian's Song*. He'd seen it
> and it made him cry, and he asked if I had watched
> it. I said, "No." He said, "Don't you want to hear
> about it?", and I said, "No." So he shut up. Why
> hurt yourself by watching that garbage?

> I deny the possibility of a relapse. I refuse to
> believe it's possible.

Other parents try to think positively:

> I think positively. I think in terms of her
> growing up and going to school and getting better
> and doing the things that a normal child would do.
> We're preparing for her future.

Since parents are often front-line care givers and know that
their own reactions are transmitted to their child, their management of their own internal feelings is critical. It may affect the
eventual mental health of their child with cancer as well as other children and adults in the family.

Existential Stressors. Many parents find it stressful to fit
the experience of childhood cancer into their prior understanding of life and death. Serious and chronic childhood illness is,
after all, a challenge to how most people understand and organ-

ize their views of the world as well as their patterns of daily living (Spinetta, Swarner, and Sheposh, 1981). Death is conceived of as occurring mostly to the elderly, perhaps to the evil or warlike, but certainly not to the young and innocent. That it happens, and happens personally, may disrupt one's view of normal existence and one's faith in an orderly and just world.

For some people, this experience is attributed to environmental or hereditary factors, although those factors are seldom specified with much clarity or confidence.

> I think one of the problems is that our technology has developed so much, and I think the private sector has been using contaminants irresponsibly.

> It's hereditary, because there is a lot of cancer in our family.

Others feel it is due to an act of God or of fate (Kushner, 1982):

> We feel that our lives are controlled by God, and that He allowed this for a learning process.

> For a while I thought the Man upstairs was punishing me for something I've done.

And some people give up trying to discover meaning in what appears to be a meaningless event or situation.

These efforts to make sense out of an experience that appears to violate normal expectations about life and death often require parents to question the meaning or direction of their own lives. Attempts to resolve these issues within the realms of normal experience seem quite difficult and often challenge existing religious or spiritual beliefs. Some parents report altering their religious beliefs and practices, and others indicate considering major changes in their career patterns, personal priorities, and goals for the future. Dealing with this disorder in one's understanding of life and death and the meaning of life itself can be stressful.

Coping and the Search for Social Support

Parents experience these stresses of childhood cancer in different ways and to different degrees; moreover, they come to this experience with different backgrounds, values, and skills. Thus, they cope in a variety of ways. The general literature on coping with stress suggests a wide variety of options, including active and passive styles (Lazarus, 1966) and attempts to reduce the source of stress or to provide a buffer against its effects (Lazarus and Launier, 1981; Pearlin and Schooler, 1978). Some literature emphasizes a transactional approach, suggesting that coping patterns are related to and should be seen in the context of the specific nature of the stress experienced (Coyne and Holroyd, 1983).

With particular reference to the five categories of stress emanating from childhood cancer, some parents respond by seeking intellectual mastery—by gaining information and understanding about the disease and its treatment (D. Adams, 1979; Friedman and others, 1963; Hamburg and Adams, 1967; Hamovitch, 1964; Lascari and Stehbens, 1973). Such information may help them cope with their own anxieties, loss of control, and sense of shock. Other parents report trying to solve the immediate practical problems with which they are faced, so they arrange transportation and child care, find substitutes for themselves at work, or actively participate in the medical care of their children.

Still others, not necessarily excluding those above, respond to interpersonal stress by altering social relationships or seeking help from family members and friends who can be part of a supportive social structure. Similarly, some try to establish relationships with health care practitioners, extending themselves to physicians, nurses, and social workers and seeking help and support from them. Many respond to their potential emotional imbalance by attending to their psychological or physical needs, being alert to their eating and sleeping habits, making sure they stay healthy, and deliberately trying to control despair and optimism, realism and fantasy, and hope and terror. In this effort, some parents seek professional counseling or therapy, availing themselves of social workers' or psychologists' professional services on an individual or family basis. Still others deal with existential stresses by testing and often reinforcing their religious beliefs or by redefining their purpose in life, marshalling new spiritual or worldly resources to provide meaning to their new roles and situations.

Regardless of the specific stresses involved and the coping styles employed, almost all of the stresses and coping patterns involve the use of some form of social support. In the first two columns of Table 1, we list the five major classes of stress and coping tasks for parents of children with childhood cancer. The third and fourth columns identify some of the forms and agents of social support relevant to each major category of stress and coping task. The research in general indicates that social support can buffer individuals from the full impact of stress and help them recover from the effects of unavoidable stress (Bloom, Ross, and Burnell, 1978; DiMatteo and Hays, 1981; Gottlieb, 1981; Hirsch, 1980; Pilisuk and Froland, 1978). However, the process of giving and receiving support is quite complex, and many persons indicate that they do not find what they need when they feel they need it (Sontag, 1979; Wagner, 1981). Moreover, several observers discuss how the stigma of cancer may make it even more difficult for friends and family members to offer effective support (Sontag, 1979; Wortman and Dunkel-Schetter, 1979).

One way in which social support is useful for parents dealing with the stresses associated with childhood cancer is by providing information. For instance, although several parents indicate that they did not receive enough information from the medical staff, others report how helpful the medical staff was in supporting them intellectually.

> What impressed me most was the time they took to answer my dumb, stupid questions. Whatever it might be, they took that time.

> On my request, one doctor told a nurse to xerox information from a pediatric oncology book for me. The nurse did it and I received great information. That doctor was a help.

Table 1. Stress and Social Support for Parents of Children with Cancer.

Category of Stress	Relevant Coping Tasks and Strategies	Forms of Social Support	Agents of Social Support	Self-Help Group Activities
Intellectual	Getting information about cancer and treatment procedures Interpreting medical jargon Protecting against information overload Getting information about the hospital	Information Ideas Books, newsletters	Medical staff Social service staff Scientists	Lectures by staff Writing handbooks Establishing library of articles Printing newsletters Information sharing by parents
Instrumental	Getting help at home (child care, housekeeping) Getting help at work Negotiating with hospital Making financial plans Solving other problems Caring for the sick child	Problem-solving activities Practical assistance at home or work Financial aid Transportation Negotiations with the hospital	Social service staff Family members Friends Neighbors and coworkers Institutional representatives	Collecting and distributing funds for wigs, prostheses, parking Providing transportation Arranging parent lodging Efforts to improve local medical care Fund raising for research or added services
Interpersonal	Maintaining relationships with family members and friends Creating new social roles Talking and sharing with others Relating to the medical staff Informing others (and avoiding stigma)	Affection Listening Caring Being there	Family members Close friends Medical and social service staff	Reference group processes Meeting new people Having someone to talk with

Emotional	Getting counseling Finding love and affirmation Dealing with hope, anger, fear, and despair Stabilizing self Monitoring somatic reactions Feeling efficacious in providing care	Affirmation Counseling Clarifying feelings	Close friends Spouse Social service staff	Professional counseling Peer counseling Sharing intimate feelings
Existential	Seeking meaning and explanations for the illness Creating new social identity Relating to God and fate Reordering life plans and dreams	Reflection on God and fate Creating a community	Clergy Philosophers	Talking about religious beliefs Sharing the struggle

On some occasions, nonmedical personnel, friends, and acquaintances can also provide helpful information.

> Another family of a child with cancer was
> over one day, and I told them about my son's
> strange behavior and pains. They said it happened
> to their child, too, and that it was one of the drugs.
> Then we knew what to do.

A second kind of social support may help in meeting particular instrumental needs. For instance, parents report that many family members and friends help with key household or care-taking tasks, such as cleaning the house, cooking dinner while they are at the hospital, providing transportation, entertaining siblings, visiting the ill child, filling in for an employed parent, and so on.

> His side of the family was helpful with the
> practical things like babysitting, cleaning the
> house, taking us out.

> Our friends and neighbors brought over food
> for the kids. Our kids spent the night with neighbors
> lots of times. The neighbors took them places.

> Neighbors would come over and spend the
> night with our sick child so we could get some
> sleep.

A third kind of support, sometimes the most important kind, helps relieve the stresses created by unstable or unresponsive interpersonal relationships. For instance, many parents report being grateful that some people were "just there" and that an interpersonal network existed. This kind of help may be especially difficult to provide, for the well-intentioned giver may feel that he or she is not really doing much, but such a presence is important nevertheless.

> They called and inquired about how he was
> doing. If we needed their help in any way, we just

had to let them know. They didn't want to keep
pestering us, but if we needed them all we had to
do was to pick up the phone and they'd get it
done.

A fourth form of support aids in helping parents to maintain emotional balance. House (1981) refers to this kind of support as oriented either toward love and caring or to empathic
feedback and comments to the parents on "how well they are
doing." Family members and close friends especially may be
able to help parents identify the extent to which they are not
"going crazy," are doing well, or are keeping things in perspective.

They gave me a shoulder to lean on, they
cried with me and were very understanding ...
[They] stayed by my side.

One friend would go out for coffee with me
and just talk. Mostly this guy just listened. He was
somebody I could talk to and he'd sit and listen.
Knowing he was there was great.

I did talk to a social worker, and you need
that to keep a perspective. A lot of times I could
get insight this way.

A final form of social support relieves the existential
stresses parents report. Often the agents of such support are the
clergy, friends, or even the ill child.

I had more success with the pastor at the
church than I did with any medical professional.

Clergy helped us deal with why God let this
happen to our child. But my daughter, before she
died, helped us more than any doctor, clergy, or
reading.

Most of these sources and forms of social support are
available in the medical, family, and community environments

surrounding the families of children with cancer. Recently, however, we have seen a new way of organizing social support emerge that has direct relevance for many parents in their efforts to cope with these particular stresses—self-help and mutual support groups. We now turn to an examination of these groups' roles and functioning.

The Unique Resources and Activities of Self-Help Groups

Groups of people who are in similar situations, coping with similar stresses, sometimes organize mutual support or self-help groups (Collins and Pancoast, 1976; Gartner and Riessman, 1977; A. Katz, 1981; Katz and Bender, 1976; Killilea, 1976; Lieberman and others, 1979; Powell, 1975; Tracy and Gussow, 1976). These organized groups develop to aid people coping with prolonged, serious stresses that affect their own social identity and role or those of other family members.

A self-help group has been defined in different ways, but most literature defines it as an identifiable group of people, in a similar situation or with common needs, coming together voluntarily to help each other cope with a chronic problem. The focus on doing for themselves distinguishes self-help groups from other support groups run or guided by professionals. As Smith and Pillemer (1983) note, many support and service groups "involve people not suffering from an alterable, pressing personal problem attempting to help those who do suffer from such a problem" (p. 206). In the case of pure self-help groups, the people with the problem are the ones helping people who suffer from the same problem.

Within this loose definition, there still is great variety, but some of the health-related groups that most observers would agree fit this prototype include: Reach for Recovery, Mended Hearts, Osto-Mates, Make Today Count, and Living One Day at a Time.

Some scholars argue that dissatisfaction with the bureaucratic and technological paradigms and practices of modern medicine alienates consumers and prompts the formation of self-help groups (Back and Taylor, 1976). Indeed, the active posture and the reciprocity of support generated in typical self-help groups may be an antidote to the nonreciprocal and passive roles forced on patients by most medical and social service professionals (Gartner and Riessman, 1977). Other scholars find no link between such dissatisfaction and active membership in self-help groups, suggesting instead that some people seek self-help groups as an alternate form of social connection and mutual aid, not necessarily as a compensation for negative feelings about current medical practice (Banhoff, 1979; Lieberman, 1979; Tracy and Gussow, 1976).

Relatively little research is available on self-help groups for families of ill children, and even less on children with cancer. The self-help anthologies referred to earlier discuss only one group related to these concerns, and that group serves parents of children who have died from a variety of causes (Society of Compassionate Friends). Informal reports indicate that self-help groups have been organized at many children's cancer centers. In fact, the Candlelighters Foundation, a national clearinghouse of self-help groups of families of children with cancer, estimates that over 200 such groups are currently in existence.

Since there are no detailed reports or direct observations, it is hard to know much about these local groups and to distinguish between various kinds of self-help groups and professionally led discussion groups, support groups, group therapy sessions, and so on. However, Stolberg and Cunningham (1980) do state several important facts: Eighteen of the twenty-one children's cancer centers responding to their inquiry reported some kind of parent support group, most of which were initiated and staffed by professional social service workers. Several other reports describe groups for families of children with cancer that were organized by medical or social service professionals (D. Adams, 1979; Belle-Isle and Conradt, 1979; Heffron, 1975; Kartha and Ertel, 1976; Knapp and Hansen, 1973; Martinson and Jorgens, 1976; Ross, 1979; Sachs, 1980).

The dominance of professionally led groups in the literature is explained partly by the professional authorship and readership of these articles and journals. Many other groups of families of children with cancer exist that are not initiated or led by

professionals. There probably are key differences between groups
organized and led by parents themselves (not necessarily without professionals but less dependent on them) and those organized by professionals, but as yet little systematic research is
available on this point. The groups we examined include some
that are very much run by parents themselves (pure self-help),
some very much run or guided by professionals (pure support),
and many with a mixture of professional and parental leadership and control. Unless otherwise noted, we refer to all of these
groups as being engaged in self-help activities.

What Do Parent Self-Help Groups Do?

The literature and our own study of self-help groups of
families of children with cancer (Chesler and Yoak, 1983) suggest that there are several different kinds of group foci and thus
different kinds of help that parents provide to and receive from
one another. Five different kinds of activities seem to be most
popular: Each of these forms of social support appears to respond to different stresses and coping strategies.

One focus of activity and one kind of group is educational
or informational in nature, helping to inform parents about the
disease and its side effects, potential child-rearing and discipline
issues, and the nature of the hospital and hospital staff (M.
Adams, 1978; Belle-Isle and Conradt, 1979; Gilder and others,
1976; Heffron, 1975; Kartha and Ertel, 1976; Martinson, 1976).

Other people are going to be experiencing
processes that us "advanced parents" have gone
through. The whole concept is to prepare them, to
get them to ask questions and learn more about the
disease and treatment and understand it better.

It's a good idea for families to get together
and to answer questions. The doctor helped, but I
still had a lot of questions. Talking to another parent of an amputee helped.

Information and education are the most common group
focus, which is adopted by almost all groups at some time dur-

ing their history. In some cases, parents educate each other about these matters; in other cases, an outside speaker addresses the group. Inviting local physicians to speak to the group is often a particularly attractive option, one that may help recruit previously inactive parents. Moreover, such an invitation may help link the treatment center and medical staff more strongly with a larger group of parents. Some self-help groups publish regular newsletters with medical information, and others develop handbooks for parents of newly diagnosed or newly hospitalized children.

A second major focus of some groups is instrumental aid to parents. By helping to solve problems of transportation and child care, for instance, self-help groups provide some of the same material assistance offered by friends and family members. Personpower is the most readily available resource for such services, but many groups also become involved in raising funds to support their activities. Some raise small amounts of money in casual ways, mostly to support their own newsletters and social events. Other groups raise more substantial funds, primarily to purchase prostheses for children who were not adequately covered by insurance, to buffer the high costs of transportation, parking, or child care for families, or to pay for in-room television for hospitalized patients. Still other groups undertake major fund-raising efforts to finance transporting children to specialty treatment centers, to subsidize or construct low-cost lodging near the treatment center, or to support research at the medical center.

In another form of instrumental support, some groups try to make changes in the operation of the staff or treatment center (Gilder and others, 1976). For instance, some groups try to solve problems in the local delivery of health services by suggesting or demanding modification in the policies or staffing structure of clinics and wards, providing feedback to the medical system on services to families, helping the hospital improve its services, funding special medical programs, or holding certain services accountable to consumer scrutiny. These groups usually work closely with health care professionals, but on occasion they advocate changes despite professional resistance. In most instances (but by no means all), both professionals and parents report that they eventually experience satisfaction with the collaboration such advocacy generates and with the outcomes of changed procedures.

A third major focus of group activity is interpersonal networks—friends and social relations. Some groups feel their primary activity is to provide an arena within which people with a similar experience can gather and talk with one another (Belle-Isle and Conradt, 1979; Martinson, 1976). Staying at a light level, people may ask for help if they wish, but they concentrate on keeping in touch and in having a good time with one another. Groups of this sort may provide a subtler kind of support as well—parents may serve as referents for one another, as points of comparison for defining or understanding appropriate behavior in a new situation (Powell, 1975; Silverman, 1976). According to one parent:

> It helps to talk to people. Knowing that other people have gone through it helps. Sometimes I think I felt isolated, like this was only happening to me.

Another parent indicates how a newsletter links one to others as well as serves as a source of medical information:

> The newsletter is a great form of communication for people going through what I did, especially for some families who are from out of town and don't have friends nearby to help.

Sharing feelings and emotional support with other parents is a fourth major focus of many groups. Here the objective is to provide an arena in which parents can share their joys and pains, their hopes and despairs, and discuss their emotional responses to childhood cancer. The problems may cover quite a range: dealing with spouses' and family members' feelings, preparing for death, fighting depression, coping with the diagnosis or a relapse, understanding the medical staff, getting ready to come off treatment, being afraid, bringing up an ill child, dealing with the ill child's siblings, and so on (D. Adams, 1979; Belle-Isle and Conradt, 1979; Gilder and others, 1976; Heffron, 1975; Kartha and Ertel, 1976). The topics of these meetings may be quite similar to those of the information and education sessions, but the purpose and style are quite different: Here the goal is for parents to share their experiences and feelings with one another.

> I went to the meeting and shared my experiences with them. When I see someone else who is going through the same thing I am and they can handle it, then I can conquer it too.

> It would be helpful to have someone who has been through this at the very beginning. No one else knows what you're going through until they've been there. You can tell someone who's been through it how you feel and ask should you or do you have the right to feel that way?

The two-way street of giving and receiving help is a vital part of self-help groups for parents of children with cancer. For instance, Leiken and Hassakis (1973) explain this aspect of self-help groups in terms of their report that "the most frequently used helpful coping mechanism was the 'doing defense'" (p. 55). One example of this mechanism involves people helping other children and parents with similar problems; Riessman and his colleagues (Dory and Riessman, 1982; Gartner and Riessman, 1977; Riessman, 1965) refer to this as the "helper-therapy principle." As one parent notes:

> The leukemia group which I am working with gives me something positive to do. I feel I am helping someone down the road and changing things in a positive, constructive manner.

Other authors have indicated how helping others may enable people to work through some of their own difficulties (Silverman, 1976) or to announce and act on the assumption that they are doing well and have extra energy and resources to share with others. In some cases, parents provide such active emotional support to one another directly; in other cases, a social worker, nurse, or other staff member facilitates these discussions and promotes openness and sharing among group members.

A fifth focus of some groups is the existential challenge referred to earlier. Although this seldom forms the major purpose of any group, it is an issue that arises at some time within most groups. In this context, parents share their understanding of the role that their struggle with childhood cancer plays in their lives. For some, especially for parents of terminally ill or deceased children, the group exploration centers on the meaning of life after death and testaments to their own spiritual faith and commitment. For others, discussion focuses on their secular philosophy and how it has changed as a result of their experiences. As parents see how others have incorporated the meaning of these events in their own lives, they may be aided in discovering more effective answers for themselves.

Each of these foci may be appropriate, depending in part on how parents cope and what stage their child is in of the illness or treatment cycle. For instance, parents who are trying to cope with intellectual stress may find information sessions and activities most appropriate. Others who have difficulty managing the many practical and instrumental tasks associated with the treatment of childhood cancer may want help or advice on how others have dealt with these matters. For those parents in dire financial straits, the benefits provided by fund-raising activities may be most important. Parents who wish to share, express, and reflect on their feelings may be best served by groups that promote emotional sharing and intimate engagement. Parents who wish to know and meet others in similar situations may be most interested in a group that talks easily and comfortably with one another or that plays and has picnics or potluck dinners together.

In addition, the appropriateness of each focus for a self-help group depends on the treatment center or the community. Parents may start up a group or participate in an existing one to make up for deficiencies in available care. By the same token, the availability of certain community services (American Cancer Society support, Ronald McDonald Houses, and meetings of the Society of Compassionate Friends) makes some foci for groups less important for parents who already have access to such resources.

Although many groups address several of these foci, most emphasize one or two in particular. Thus, different groups appeal to parents with different desires or needs. Clearly, parents are not likely to become active in groups that do not meet their needs. Aside from this self-selection, a subtler process of socialization may occur, whereby parents who enter a group for one purpose become bonded to other members and alter their needs or coping styles in order to fit with the main focus of the group. Thus, parents who enter seeking information may become comfortable and active in a group emphasizing feelings, and parents originally not committed to fund raising may engage in such activities when a group in which they have close friends decides to move in this direction. In addition, some parents who want to participate in a group not currently oriented to their needs and styles may exert influence on other members to change the focus of the group. The potential interaction or fit between the activities of self-help groups and parents' major stresses, coping patterns, and social support mechanisms in dealing with childhood cancer is illustrated in the last column of Table 1.

Some groups deal with the problem of attaining a balance among these purposes by forming subgroups, some of which meet (perhaps once a month) to receive and share information and some of which meet (every two weeks or so) to share feelings or emotional problems, and some of which meet (once or twice a year) to socialize and have a holiday party, summer picnic, or child-centered activity. At a more formal level, some groups have developed parallel structures, separating incorporated fund-raising activities from subgroups where they share information and discuss feelings. Some groups have leadership struggles or subgroups committed to different activity priorities. As a result of such struggles, some people and activities may dominate the life of the group, and other people may leave the group or become inactive.

Are Self-Help Groups for All Parents of Children with Cancer?

Despite the range of social support found in self-help groups and their relevance for different coping styles, not all parents search for such support or find it useful or helpful. Thus, self-help groups are not for everyone, and people decide to become active or inactive through various patterns of self-selection and socialization. One reason parents may elect not to participate in a self-help group is simply time and energy. Coping with the stresses of childhood cancer, particularly at certain stages (diagnosis, relapse, and termination) may be too time consuming to allow meeting with others; the priority might be to be with one's child as much as possible. While interpersonal support may still be sought, regular meetings and participating in an organized group may be a low priority. In addition, families living a substantial distance from the self-help group's meeting place may find it difficult or costly to travel to attend meetings, and some parents may not be available during regular meeting times.

In addition to these considerations, some parents find that their own style of coping is not compatible with any of the various activities or forms of social support available in self-help groups. For instance, the two parents quoted below note their unwillingness to talk with strangers about these issues. The third indicates her unwillingness to risk thinking about and talking about (or hearing others talk about) painful issues.

> I've never been a "go-to-meeting person," so I never went. I do like to run my mouth, but not in groups, especially with people I don't know.

> Personally, I don't feel the need to get together with other people in the same boat and get reassurance. I'm a loner.

> It would bring back things that I'd really rather not even try to remember.

A common issue faced by many groups is whether parents

of deceased children should be encouraged to be active in the same group as parents of living children. Arguments in favor of both sets of parents being part of the same self-help group include the following: (1) Parents of deceased children still have ties to the hospital and to other parents, and they might be sadder and lonelier if these ties were cut; (2) parents of deceased children have organizational skills and energy that groups need; (3) parents of deceased children can help prepare others for the possibility of death; and (4) parents of living children can benefit from the model of parents of deceased children—that life continues even after the death of a child.

The major arguments against such integrated groups include the following: (1) New parents may be frightened by meeting parents of children who have died; (2) parents of deceased children may be at different stages of their lives and not interested in talking about the same things as parents of living children with cancer; (3) parents of deceased children may find it too painful to meet with and see parents of living children; and (4) it may be too guilt provoking for parents of living children to take joy in their situation in front of parents of deceased children. Of course, only the parents themselves can decide whether parents of deceased children should be involved and whether they can benefit.

Roles of Professionals in Self-Help Groups

One of the key issues in self-help groups is their relationship with the medical system and with health care professionals. We have already indicated various observers' views of how consumers' orientations toward the modern health care bureaucracy may affect self-help group activity. In addition, other scholars have discussed the drawbacks and benefits of collaboration with professionals (Gartner and Riessman, 1977; Kleinman, Mantell, and Alexander, 1976). It is clear that the needs and orientations of parents are not the only important variables in understanding groups' relationships with medical systems. Tracy and Gussow (1976) indicate the importance of professionals' attitudes as well, noting that many physicians worry about self-help groups sharing misinformation or superstitions, pressuring group members unwisely, raising patients' expectations, or just plain intruding into the carefully controlled physician-patient relationship. For instance, with particular regard to support groups for parents of children with cancer, Belle-Isle and Conradt (1979, p. 49) warn that "the danger of parents inappropriately sharing their concerns and unwittingly increasing each other's emotional burdens is a constant threat. With professional guidance this danger should be significantly less as staff participants are present to correct misinformation and control inappropriate exchanges." Almost the same statement is made by Binger and others (1969) and Kartha and Ertel (1976). Although many of the professionals we interviewed expressed similar concerns, few of them (and very few parents) actually had seen or experienced such dangers in organized groups, whether those groups were led by parents or professionals. Moreover, several reports indicate that many staff members recognize and support the value of even relatively autonomous self-help groups. Thus, the issues go beyond a simple dichotomy of conflict versus collaboration or trust versus nontrust and require a better understanding of how such groups "work out an articulation with institutionalized medicine" (Tracy and Gussow, 1976, p. 396).

It seems obvious that professionals' attitudes and their resulting actions make a difference for the future of local self-help groups. Depending on their attitudes and prior experiences, professionals can engage in actions that provide or fail to provide important resources to self-help groups. Some of these important resources are quite tangible (such as access to members and the availability of meeting rooms), while others are relatively intangible (such as reputation and credibility); all may affect a group's ability to recruit members, to provide resources, to affect the hospital or community, and otherwise to sustain operations.

For instance, physicians cannot literally keep parents who want to get together from getting together, but they can make it easier or more difficult for them to find and rely upon one another. Medical staff members, especially nurses and physicians, are in very powerful positions with respect to patients and patient families. They are perceived (often rightly so) to have life and death power over children with cancer, and some parents report being afraid to challenge, confront, or displease them, fearing repercussions to their child. In addition, staff members' status and authority in the medical system provide them with control over key resources essential for self-help groups. How they use their power and make these resources available determines how they can help families respond to stress, meet coping tasks, and gain the social support they require. While these stresses, coping tasks, and social support mechanisms may differ for each family, and indeed for each family member, certain classes of resources are especially relevant for the operations of family self-help groups.

One set of resources to which medical staff members have special access is information. These resources are particularly relevant for families responding to the intellectual stresses of childhood cancer and for self-help groups trying to develop educational and informational activities. Nurses and physicians especially have technical information about cancer and its treatment and access to materials and libraries where such materials are stored. To provide this information in ways that laypeople can understand more easily, professionals have written articles for group newsletters and presented lectures, discussions, and panels at meetings. In addition to information about the disease and its treatment, professionals (perhaps especially psychologists and social workers) have special expertise in family coping mechanisms and have shared information personally or through written materials about the coping tasks families may face and how others have resolved these tasks. Finally, a key aspect of information shared by professionals is their special knowledge about the staff and the operations of the local treatment facility. Social workers also often have information about financial and social services that may be available in the community or the school system. Groups trying to help members get services or trying to improve service availability need such information.

A second set of resources available to the professional staff may be particularly relevant to meeting some of the prac-

tical needs of parents and the related activities of self-help
groups. The problem of identifying one's own needs, either
ahead of time or as they are occurring, is a serious issue for
many families. Professionals have been helpful in identifying
these needs and providing special programs for training group
members to aid each other. The staff may also have access to financial support for the family or to agencies and services that
may be able to provide such support. In some cases, where self-
help groups have raised funds to support wigs, prostheses, and
incidental expenses for families, the professional staff has been
involved in helping to identify needy families and distribute
these funds. Groups that anticipate raising large amounts of
money must often collaborate with the medical staff to legitimize their effort, gain tax-exempt status, and help tap major
local sources of funds. In some facilities, the professional staff
has also helped establish good working relations between parent
groups and local educational agencies, especially parents of
school-aged children with cancer. In a number of cases, medical
staff members have even aided self-help groups' efforts to conduct in-service training sessions or conferences for school staffs.
Thus, the staff's links to other resources in the hospital and the
community can make additional sets of resources available to
local groups.

        Professionals frequently have the resources to help groups
gain recognition, run good meetings, and keep their records in
order. For instance, if some parents are fearful or cautious
about joining a group of "nonexperts," professionals may help
allay their fears and assure them that the self-help group is a
credible and valuable source of support. Establishing an effective and vigorous referral system through which parents of newly diagnosed children are placed into contact with self-help
group members is another example of practical help provided
by professionals. Some groups, especially those led by parents
who do not have skills in organizational leadership, have found
social workers' skills in group processes very helpful in developing sound procedures for electing officers, effective ways to run
meetings, efforts to gain tax-exempt status, and so on.

        The professional staff generally has resources for dealing
with the interpersonal stresses that family members face and for

helping the group generate programs to deal with these stresses. Staff access to hospital or clinic records enables them to put parents who can help each other in touch with one another. This is an especially useful function when the group wants to establish a one-to-one visitation program for parents who have faced or are facing similar problems (such as age of child, diagnosis, or treatment). By encouraging parents to attend self-help group meetings, and thus making the parents accessible to other parents' resources, professionals strengthen the person, the family, and the self-help group simultaneously. Parents who have not clarified their interpersonal needs or who have not thought seriously about the stigma and problems of being open about their children's illness may need such encouragement.

The staff's resources for aiding parents to deal with their emotional stress have also taken the form of group therapy or counseling sessions, either during scheduled meetings of the self-help group or at special meetings. Some professionals have encouraged self-help groups to provide such counseling as part of their meetings and activities. In these instances, professionals have also provided parent group members with special training in counseling and responding to others' emotional needs.

Finally, professional staff members may have resources that help parents deal with the existential stresses associated with childhood cancer. Their contacts with clergy and with physicians who can identify causes of cancer have helped groups develop programs that offer new perspectives on questions of fate and the meaning of illness. To the extent that all group members can share their experiences on this dimension, parents may be able to see their unique dilemmas from a broader perspective. As a result, they may be able to overcome feelings of isolation and feel part of a larger community of people who are suffering with chronic and serious illness.

Role Dilemmas of Pediatric and Oncology Staff Members

Usually, the health care professional who takes the leading role in developing or working with a parent self-help group is the staff social worker. In some cases it is a nurse or clinical nurse practitioner. Whichever staff member serves this purpose, it is a role fraught with tension and difficulty, and interviews with these staff members have highlighted several issues worthy of attention. Adequate understanding of these issues, by parents as well as other staff members, might facilitate the process of collaboration.

Some observers emphasize a complementarity of interests between self-help groups and the medical professionals who work with them (Lenrow and Burch, 1981; Lieberman and others, 1979). These researchers document consumers' positive views of health care systems, professionals' positive outlook on self-help groups, and ways in which providers and consumers can collaborate. For instance, Lenrow and Burch argue that collaboration can be fostered when both professional helpers and their clients understand they each have "equally important resources to contribute to their common task" (1981, p. 234). Of course, disagreement about what "equally important resources" and "their common task" are may lead to conflict. When Kleinman, Mantell, and Alexander (1976) examine these issues in the context of a case study of a particular self-help group and a particular agency, they conclude not only that conflicts exist but also that the differences in power and values between professionals and self-help volunteers are irreconcilable. If, as some scholars argue, self-help groups are composed of persons who are dissatisfied with modern medical care or consider traditional services a failure, conflict between parents and professionals should be the norm (A. Katz, 1981). However, if the following differences and conflicts are understood and dealt with by all parties, the results may be quite positive. If such differences and conflicts are denied or ignored, everyone involved may miss the opportunity (and challenge) to work through important issues with honesty and clarity.

Some of the dilemmas that staff members face in working with parent self-help groups are rooted in basic differences in their role definitions and experiences (Reinharz, 1981). Staff members, of course, are not parents of children with cancer. They are often locked into the role of giving help, while parents are fixed in the reciprocal role of receiving help. Moreover, staff members' knowledge is based on technical training and experience that is quite different from that of parents. Whereas parents' knowledge is likely to be experiential and individually unique, staff members' knowledge is more likely to be academic, abstract, and universal, applicable to a wider range of cases. The staff member is primarily accountable to other staff members, perhaps to an institutional hierarchy; parents are accountable to themselves and their children. The role of family relations differs as well: The staff member's family generally provides a respite from the issues of childhood cancer; for the parent of an ill child, the family is one more setting in which children's cancer is a preeminent factor. Conversely, a parent's role is usually removed from the hospital and direct contact with childhood cancer; the staff member's job role focuses directly on these issues.

The nature of these differences establishes some operating dilemmas for staff members. First, their role is often unclear—to themselves, their employers, and self-help groups. Are they supposed to consider themselves part of the group or not? Are they insiders or outsiders? Are they regular members or people with a special role? In actual practice, when self-help group members share their feelings, should social workers and nurses share theirs as well? If professionals work with some self-help group members in an individual therapy situation, how do they relate to these same people in the group context? How can they help link parents with one another for mutual support without violating professional norms of confidentiality?

Second, staff members' unclear role is often made even more confusing by ambivalent support from the medical staff. In some treatment centers, the social worker's or clinical nurse's function is not at all clear. Physicians may expect them primarily to control misbehaving patients and to process insurance forms. Any other activities they may engage in may be seen as performed of their own initiative and therefore as not part of their formal obligations. They may even be termed "deviant" for spending time after hours with parent groups. Even more subtly, if the social worker or clinical nurse does elect to work with self-help groups, they may be held responsible by the rest of the staff for what the group decides to do. If the group does things the staff feels good about, all well and good. But if the self-help group starts to do things the staff does not condone, the professional participants may be called upon to account for such behavior and to control it.

Third, staff members who work closely with a parent group must often act as translators. This calls for familiarity in the different vocabularies of laypeople and the medical staff. In addition, professionals may feel compelled to defend or express loyalty to the medical staff in front of parents. In those circumstances where groups challenge the health care organization, close relations between professionals and group members may blunt the challenge, for better or worse. On the other hand, some professionals may find themselves defending parent activism before the medical staff. Several observers have indicated circumstances under which professionals working with parents and parent groups communicate to other staff members regarding parents' needs, just as they educate parent groups to the workings of the medical staff (McCollum and Schwartz, 1972; Ross, 1980; Stuetzer, 1980). There is much less discussion of how profesionals may mediate actual conflicts between parent groups and the medical staff (Chesler and Barbarin, in press). Any of these roles as advocate, mutual educator, or mediator may strain the identification of the professional as a servant of parents' needs and as the agent of the medical facility and staff. This issue is made more poignant by the reality that the professionals working most directly with parent self-help groups generally occupy the lowest status roles within the medical staff. Consequently, they often are barely tolerated and meagerly rewarded, have little influence at staff meetings, and are buffeted by the medical staff's crises.

Fourth, we indicated previously that some health care professionals are concerned about the danger that autonomous parent groups may pose by inappropriately sharing their concerns and increasing each other's emotional burdens. It is impossible to assess the degree of real danger involved here, but it is clear (from our own interviews and from the literature) that some medical staff members worry about this issue—certainly more than do parents active in groups. Because of professionals' training and orientation, they may assume greater dangers than actually exist, and these assumptions may be heightened when the goals or activities of self-help groups are not clear or not agreed on.

In fact, some staff members may become confused or threatened by group activities in which parents provide emotional support and help to one another. Such parents may appear to be invading social workers' turf and providing services that the professionals have been trained to perform. On the other hand, some professionals worry that parents will avoid the real issues and not do the hard work of dealing with the impact of childhood cancer. Staff members who feel they know what parents need may be caught in a particular bind if parents appear to need and want something else. Thus, professionals working with such groups may find their own assumptions creating dilemmas of trust and concern about letting a group meet without their protective presence. Even more importantly, professional protectionism may express itself in other subtle ways: warnings against certain activities, refusal to permit some activities without professional supervision, cautious referrals of newly diagnosed parents to groups that professionals cannot guide or control, and general tension about group autonomy and independence.

In a similar vein, professionals who feel they know which parents need or are ready for a self-help group may face difficult decisions. Should they exercise this knowledge or intuition and only refer those parents who appear needy and ready to the group? Or should they refer and encourage all parents to the self-help group, trusting the parents and the group to discover who needs what and is ready for what? If everyone is referred, what do staff members do about a parent they think is not being served well by the group? How can freedom of information, clients' right to choose, consumers' need to organize, and professionals' responsibility for services, formal and informal, be reconciled?

Fifth, staff members who care about these issues may find it difficult not to take an active leadership role in the group, despite values to the contrary. After all, staff members who are strongly committed to good psychosocial care can provide some of that care in the self-help group setting. The professional is likely to be a central person in the network, one who knows most of the parents and is known by most of them; most parents in a group that is just starting do not know many other parents. Since the staff members have access to so many of the other useful resources in the medical system (materials, mailing lists, funds, and rooms), even when they do not want to exercise task leadership they may be trapped into assuming this role. In addition, parents' uncertainty about their own skills or their unwillingness to commit enough time may foster group dependence on available and committed professionals.

In the midst of a caring group, staff members occasionally may feel uncared for. Caring for others and reaching out to share skills with others, staff members may feel left out if parents do not express affection and appreciation in return (such as by observing their birthdays, weddings, and other events). Of course, staff members are trained to be cautious and a bit distant and to avoid such emotional dependency upon their clients. But caring is a very human feeling, and not to acknowledge and deal with these feelings ignores the human side of professional work. The natural reciprocity of caring in human relations is made most difficult by strictly adhering to roles that distinguish between the givers and receivers of help. Separated from parents by these role definitions and often lacking the support from peers and supervisors on the medical staff, staff members may become very lonely. When and how can they ask parents for reciprocity in caring? If this is difficult or impossible to do, how do these staff members avoid emotional isolation and burnout (Freudenberger, 1974; Klagsbrun, 1970; Maslach, 1976; Rothenberg, 1967; Vachon, Lyall, and Freeman, 1978)?

Most discussions of the coping strategies that health care professionals use to prevent or reduce burnout focus on support from family, friends, and colleagues. Unfortunately, little attention has been given to the support that professionals may receive from their clients or patients, especially when they have been active together in a long-term support group. In some groups, parents recognize the dilemmas facing the professionals with whom they work closely, perhaps because staff members share or deliberately educate parents about them. Under these circumstances, parents and professionals may develop a pattern in which they support and take care of each other and thus improve the quality of work and life for everyone involved in providing health care to children.

Conclusion

Self-help groups formed by and for families of children with cancer combine aspects of small voluntary organizations and of support systems for people undergoing chronic and severe stress. As such, their organizational principles arise from the nature of parents' stressful situations and the coping strategies parents use to gain social support in dealing with those stresses. In addition, these organizations are grounded in the group dynamics typically generated by people utilizing social support networks to accomplish personal and group tasks (Smith and Pillemer, 1983; Toch, 1965). They are also influenced by the institutional structure and resources of the local medical system and the medical staff's energy and outlook on self-help groups.

The experience of childhood cancer imposes long-term stress on parents and family members. For those family members who elect to seek social support, self-help groups can be a useful and growth-producing aid. In these groups, parents may find others who help them deal with the intellectual, instrumental, interpersonal, emotional, and existential stresses caused by their situation. Not all people desire to be part of or benefit from parent self-help groups. Those that elect to be active appear to have a coping strategy that seeks and uses help from others, especially others in similar situations. Moreover, they often express a commitment to contribute to others' welfare, perhaps even to alter the environments in which they find themselves.

Professionals working with such groups must often wrestle with problems of leadership and control. Some observers argue that support groups should always be run or guided by professional staff members to prevent inappropriate sharing or burdens on parents who are already vulnerable. Other observers suggest that parent groups should be relatively autonomous to provide parents with a feeling they can cope on their own, and help others cope, even in the midst of crisis. Several dilemmas for professionals arising from these self-help groups center on questions of their proper role, degree of emotional openness, institutional loyalty, and ideological assumptions about the helping process. If parents and professionals can share and work through these dilemmas together, they may be able to create exciting new partnerships in the psychosocial care of ill children and their families.

References

Adams, D. *Childhood Malignancy: The Psychosocial Care of the Child and His Family*. Springfield, Ill.: Thomas, 1979.

Adams, M. "Helping the Parents of Children with Malignancy." *Journal of Pediatrics*, 1978, *93* (5), 734-738.

American Cancer Society. *Cancer Facts and Figures*. New York: American Cancer Society, 1982.

Back, K., and Taylor, R. "Self-Help Groups: Tool or Symbol." *Journal of Applied Behavioral Sciences*, 1976, *12* (3), 295-309.

Banhoff, E. "Widow Groups as an Alternative to Informal Social Support." In M. A. Lieberman and others (Eds.), *Self-Help Groups for Coping with Crisis: Origins, Members, Processes, and Impact*. San Francisco: Jossey-Bass, 1979.

Barbarin, O., and Chesler, M. *The School Experience of Children with Cancer: News of Parents, Educators, Adolescents, and Physicians*. Ann Arbor, Mich.: Center for Research on Social Organization, 1982.

Belle-Isle, J., and Conradt, B. "Report of a Discussion Group for Parents of Children with Leukemia." *Maternal-Child Nursing Journal*, 1979, *8* (1), 49-58.

Binger, C., and others. "Childhood Leukemia: Emotional Impact on Patient and Family." *New England Journal of Medicine*, 1969, *280*, 414-418.

Bloom, J., Ross, R., and Burnell, G. "The Effect of Social Support on Patient Adjustment After Breast Surgery." *Patient Counseling and Health Education,* 1978, *1* (2), 50-59.

Cassileth, B., and Hamilton, J. "The Family with Cancer." In B. Cassileth (Ed.), *The Cancer Patient: Social and Medical Aspects of Care.* Philadelphia: Lea and Febiger, 1979.

Chesler, M., and Barbarin, O. "Problems Between the Medical Staff and Parents of Children with Cancer." *Health and Social Work,* in press.

Chesler, M., and Yoak, M. *The Organization of Self-Help Groups for Families of Children with Cancer.* Ann Arbor, Mich.: Center for Research on Social Organization, 1983.

Chesler, M., and others. *Role of Informal Networks and Medical Care Organizations in Helping Families Cope with Childhood Cancer.* Ann Arbor, Mich.: Center for Research on Social Organization, August 1981.

Collins, A., and Pancoast, D. *Natural Helping Networks.* Washington, D.C.: National Association of Social Workers, 1976.

Coyne, J., and Holroyd, K. "Stress, Coping and Illness: A Transactional Perspective." In T. Millon, C. Green, and R. Meagher (Eds.), *Handbook of Health Care and Clinical Psychology.* New York: Plenum, 1983.

D'Angio, G. "Late Sequelae After Cure of Childhood Cancer." *Hospital Practice,* 1980, *11,* 109-121.

DiMatteo, R., and Hays, R. "Social Support and Serious Illness." In B. Gottlieb (Ed.), *Social Networks and Social Support.* Beverly Hills, Calif.: Sage, 1981.

Dohrenwend, B. "Social Class and Stressful Events." In E. Hare and J. Wing (Eds.), *Psychiatric Epidemiology.* New York: Oxford University Press, 1970.

Dory, F., and Riessman, F. "Training Professionals in Organizing Self-Help Groups." *Citizen Participation,* 1982, *3* (3), 27-28.

Freudenberger, H. "Staff Burn-out." *Journal of Social Issues,* 1974, *30,* 159-165.

Friedman, S., and others. "Behavioral Observations on Parents Anticipating the Death of a Child." *Pediatrics,* 1963, *32* (4), 610-625.

Futterman, E., and Hoffman, I. "Crisis and Adaptation in the Families of Fatally Ill Children." In J. Anthony and C. Koupernick (Eds.), *The Child in His Family: The Impact of Death and Disease*. Vol. 2. New York: Wiley, 1973.

Gartner, A., and Riessman, F. *Self-Help in the Human Services*. San Francisco: Jossey-Bass, 1977.

Gilder, R., and others. "Group Therapy for Parents of Children with Leukemia." *American Journal of Psychotherapy*, 1976, *30*, 276-287.

Goffman, E. *Stigma: Notes on the Management of Spoiled Identity*. London: Penguin Books, 1968.

Gogan, J., and others. "Impact of Childhood Cancer on Siblings." *Health and Social Work*, 1977, *2*, 41-57.

Gottlieb, B. (Ed.). *Social Networks and Social Support*. Beverly Hills, Calif.: Sage, 1981.

Hamburg, D., and Adams, J. "A Perspective on Coping Behavior: Seeking and Utilizing Information in Major Transitions." *Archives of General Psychiatry*, 1967, *17*, 277-284.

Hamovitch, M. *The Parent and the Fatally Ill Child*. Durante, Calif.: City of Hope Medical Center, 1964.

Heffron, W. "Group Therapy Sessions as Part of Treatment of Children with Cancer." In C. Pockedly (Ed.), *Clinical Management of Cancer in Children*. Acton, Mass.: Science Group, 1975.

Hirsch, B. "Natural Support Systems and Coping with Major Life Changes." *American Journal of Community Psychology*, 1980, *8*, 159-172.

House, J. *Work, Stress and Social Support*. Reading, Mass.: Addison-Wesley, 1981.

Hymovich, D. "Parents of Sick Children: Their Needs and Tasks." *Pediatric Clinics of North America*, 1976, *23*, 225-232.

Kaplan, D., and others. "Family Mediation of Stress." *Social Work*, 1973, *18* (4), 60-69.

Kartha, M., and Ertel, I. "Short-Term Group Therapy for Mothers of Leukemic Children." *Clinical Pediatrics*, 1976, *15*, 803-806.

Katz, A. "Self-Help and Mutual Aid: An Emerging Social Movement?" *Annual Review of Sociology*, 1981, *7*, 129-155.

Katz, A., and Bender, E. "Self-Help Groups in Western Society: History and Prospects." *Journal of Applied Behavioral Sciences,* 1976, *12* (3), 265-282.

Katz, E. "Illness Impact and Social Reintegration." In J. Kellerman (Ed.), *Psychological Aspects of Childhood Cancer.* Springfield, Ill.: Thomas, 1980.

Killilea, M. "Mutual Help Organizations: Interpretations in the Literature." In G. Caplan and M. Killilea (Eds.), *Support Systems and Mutual Help.* New York: Grune & Stratton, 1976.

King, S., and Meyers, R. "Developing Self-Help Groups: Integrating Group Work and Community Organization Strategies." *Social Development Issues,* 1981, *5* (2-3), 33-46.

Klagsbrun, S. "Cancer, Emotions and Nurses." *American Journal of Psychiatry,* 1970, *126,* 1273-1244.

Kleinman, H., Mantell, J., and Alexander, E. "Collaboration and Its Discontents: The Perils of Partnership." *Journal of Applied Behavioral Sciences,* 1976, *12* (3), 403-409.

Knapp, V., and Hansen, H. "Helping the Parents of Children with Leukemia." *Social Work,* 1973, *18* (4), 70-75.

Koch, C., Hermann, J., and Donaldson, M. "Supportive Care of the Child with Cancer and His Family." *Seminars in Oncology,* 1974, *1,* 1.

Koocher, G., and others. *The Damocles Syndrome: Psychological Consequences of Surviving Childhood Cancer.* New York: McGraw-Hill, 1980.

Kupst, M., and others. "Family Coping with Childhood Leukemia: One Year After Diagnosis." *Journal of Pediatric Psychology,* 1982, 7 (2), 157-174.

Kushner, H. *When Bad Things Happen to Good People.* New York: Schocken, 1982.

Lascari, A., and Stehbens, J. "The Reactions of Families to Childhood Leukemia." *Clinical Pediatrics,* 1973, *12,* 210-214.

Lazarus, R. *Psychological Stress and the Coping Process.* New York: McGraw-Hill, 1966.

Lazarus, R., and Launier, R. "Stress-Related Transactions Between Person and Environment." In L. Pearlin and M. Lewis (Eds.), *Perspectives in Interactional Psychology.* New York: Plenum, 1981.

Leiken, S., and Hassakis, P. "Psychological Study of Parents of Children with Cystic Fibrosis." In J. Anthony and C. Koupernick (Eds.), *The Child in His Family: Impact of Disease and Death.* Vol. 2. New York: Wiley, 1973.

Lenrow, P., and Burch, R. "Mutual Aid or Professional Services: Opposing or Complementary." In B. Gottlieb (Ed.), *Social Networks and Social Support.* Beverly Hills, Calif.: Sage, 1981.

Lieberman, M. A. "Help-Seeking and Self-Help Groups." In M. A. Lieberman and others (Eds.), *Self-Help Groups for Coping with Crisis: Origins, Members, Processes, and Impact.* San Francisco: Jossey-Bass, 1979.

Lieberman, M. A., and others (Eds.). *Self-Help Groups for Coping with Crisis: Origins, Members, Processes, and Impact.* San Francisco: Jossey-Bass, 1979.

McCollum, A., and Schwartz, A. "Social Work and the Mourning Patient." *Social Work,* 1972, *17*, 25-36.

Martinson, I. "The Child with Leukemia: Parents Help Each Other." *American Journal of Nursing,* 1976, *76* (7), 1120-1122.

Martinson, I., and Jorgens, C. "Report of a Parent Support Group." In I. Martinson (Ed.), *Home Care for the Dying Child.* New York: Appleton-Century-Crofts, 1976.

Maslach, C. "Burned-out." *Human Behavior,* 1976, *5*, 17-22.

Myers, J., Lindenthat, J., and Pepper, M. "Social Class, Life Events and Psychiatric Symptoms." In B. Dohrenwend and B. Dohrenwend (Eds.), *Stressful Life Events: Their Nature and Effects.* New York: Wiley, 1974.

National Cancer Institute. *Coping with Cancer.* Bethesda, Md.: National Cancer Institute, U.S. Department of Health and Human Services, 1980.

National Cancer Institute. *Decade of Discovery.* Publication 81-2323. Rockville, Md.: National Cancer Institute, U.S. Department of Health and Human Services, 1981.

Obetz, S., and others. "Children Who Survive Malignant Disease: Emotional Adaptation of the Children and Their Families." In J. Schulman and M. Kupst (Eds.), *The Child with Cancer.* Springfield, Ill.: Thomas, 1980.

Pearlin, L., and Schooler, C. "The Structure of Coping." *Journal of Health and Social Behavior,* 1978, *19*, 2-21.

Pilisuk, M., and Froland, C. "Kinship, Social Networks, Social Support and Health." *Social Science and Medicine,* 1978, *12B,* 273-280.

Powell, T. "The Use of Self-Help Groups as Supportive Reference Communities." *American Journal of Orthopsychiatry,* 1975, *45* (5), 756-764.

Reinharz, S. "The Paradox of Professional Involvement in Alternative Settings." *Journal of Alternative Human Services,* 1981, *1,* 21-24.

Riessman, F. "The 'Helper-Therapy' Principle." *Social Work,* 1965, *10* (2), 27-32.

Ross, J. "Social Work Intervention with Families of Children with Cancer: The Changing Critical Phases." *Social Work in Health Care,* 1978, *3,* 257-272.

Ross, J. "Coping with Childhood Cancer: Group Intervention as an Aid to Parents in Crisis." *Social Work in Health Care,* 1979, *4* (4), 381-391.

Ross, J. "Childhood Cancer: The Parents, the Patients, the Professional." *Issues in Comprehensive Pediatric Nursing,* 1980, *4,* 7-16.

Rothenberg, M. "Reactions of Those Who Treat Children with Cancer." *Pediatrics,* 1967, *40,* 507.

Sachs, B. "Group Therapy." In J. Kellerman (Ed.), *Psychological Aspects of Childhood Cancer.* Springfield, Ill.: Thomas, 1980.

Siegel, S. "The Current Outlook of Childhood Cancer—The Medical Background." In J. Kellerman (Ed.), *Psychological Aspects of Childhood Cancer.* Springfield, Ill.: Thomas, 1980.

Silverman, P. "Mutual Help." In R. Hirschowitz and B. Levy (Eds.), *The Changing Mental Health Scene.* New York: Spectrum, 1976.

Simone, J., and others. "Three to Ten Years After Cessation of Therapy in Children with Leukemia." *Cancer,* 1978, *42,* 839-844.

Smith, D., and Pillemer, K. "Self-Help Groups as Social Movement Organizations: Social Structure and Social Change." In L. Kriesberg (Ed.), *Research in Social Movements: Conflict and Change.* New York: JAI Press, 1983.

Sontag, S. "Illness as Metaphor." *Cancer News,* 1979, *33* (1), 6-12.

Sourkes, B. "Siblings of the Pediatric Cancer Patient." In J. Kellerman (Ed.), *Psychological Aspects of Childhood Cancer.* Springfield, Ill.: Thomas, 1980.

Spinetta, J., Swarner, J., and Sheposh, J. "Effective Parental Coping Following the Death of a Child from Cancer." *Journal of Pediatric Psychology,* 1981, *6* (3), 251–263.

Spinetta, J., and others. *Emotional Aspects of Childhood Cancer and Leukemia.* San Diego, Calif.: Leukemia Society of America, 1976.

Stolberg, A., and Cunningham, J. "Support Groups for Parents of Leukemic Children." In J. Schulman and M. Kupst (Eds.), *The Child with Cancer.* Springfield, Ill.: Thomas, 1980.

Stuetzer, C. "Support Systems for Professionals." In J. Schulman and M. Kupst (Eds.), *The Child with Cancer.* Springfield, Ill.: Thomas, 1980.

Toch, H. *The Social Psychology of Social Movements.* Indianapolis, Ind.: Bobbs-Merrill, 1965.

Tracy, C., and Gussow, Z. "Self-Help Health Groups: A Grass Roots Response to a Need for Services." *Journal of Applied Behavioral Sciences,* 1976, *12* (3), 381–397.

Vachon, M., Lyall, W., and Freeman, S. "Measurement and Management of Stress in Health Professionals Working with Advanced Cancer Patients." *Death Education,* 1978, *1,* 365–375.

Voysey, M. "Impression Management by Parents with Disabled Children." *Journal of Health and Social Behavior,* 1972, *13* (1), 80–89.

Wagner, J. "Fathers of Seriously Ill Children." Unpublished manuscript, Shands Teaching Hospital, University of Florida, 1981.

Wilbur, J. "Rehabilitation of Children with Cancer." *Cancer,* 1975, *36,* 809–812.

Wortman, C., and Dunkel-Schetter, C. "Interpersonal Relationships and Cancer: A Theoretical Analysis." *Journal of Social Issues,* 1979, *35* (1), 120–155.

20

Howard B. Roback, Ph.D.

▦ ▦ ▦ ▦ ▦ ▦ ▦ ▦ ▦ ▦ ▦ ▦

Conclusion: Critical Issues in Group Approaches to Disease Management

The preceding chapters present a variety of group applications designed to meet the informational and emotional needs of medical-surgical patients and their families. Among the populations addressed in this volume are people whose bodies have been invaded by progressive disease, people whose organ systems have failed, people who have lost a limb as a consequence of accident or disease, people who have transformed psychological hurt into physical pain, and people who have confronted imminent death. This volume is based on the premise that a group format is a preferred mode of intervention for helping the vast majority of such persons and their families cope with the complex constellation of emotions and concerns associated with their particular circumstances.

527

The diversity of populations, approaches, and experiences described in the preceding chapters is readily apparent to the reader. Not as easily discerned are the common issues that confront all group leaders working with different medical-surgical patient populations. In this concluding section, I shall attempt to identify the clinical, research and theoretical, and personal issues that are relevant for all group leaders.

Clinical Issues

Treatment Goals. Although treatment goals vary according to the patient population, the particular therapist, and the therapeutic setting, the overriding goals expressed in this volume include helping patients to adjust to life-style changes imposed by the disorder and helping patients to maintain as much personal responsibility for their lives as possible. Also important are giving patients a genuine sense of participation in the treatment process, helping them adjust to living with some degree of discomfort, and teaching them coping strategies. Finally, these groups provide patients with a place to ventilate feelings safely and to acquire accurate information about their conditions.

Contributors working with family units emphasize helping family members cope with their complex feelings toward the patient, with the disruption in their social activities, and with the role reversals occurring within the family as a result of the patient's medical condition. In addition, the group provides a forum for expressing emotional reactions and gives family members the opportunity to observe and learn from other families' coping styles.

The foregoing patient and family goals seem to apply regardless of therapist orientation or the nature of the patient's disability.

Selection Factors. As a rule, the selection criteria used by therapists for screening possible members for groups of medical-surgical patients and their families appear to be less stringent than those used by group therapists working with psychiatric outpatients. The former group of therapists place less emphasis on an individual's general level of self-disclosure, capacity for self-reflection, ability to tolerate aggression from others, and so forth. Therapists working with inpatient units often extend broad invitations to all patients on the unit capable of participating constructively in the group sessions (excluding only psychotic or brain-damaged individuals). The decision of whether to attend the sessions is left up to the patients and their respective family members, for as Jerse, Whitman, and Gustafson indicate in Chapter Ten, numerous complex internal and external conditions come into play when individuals face such a situation. When group participants demonstrate the need for more intensive or individualized therapeutic care, Jerse and her associates follow the typical practice of referring such persons elsewhere for treatment.

Most therapists who conduct disease management groups for outpatients also tend to have lax selection criteria, perhaps because they view their missions as twofold: (1) providing treatment for patients in acute turmoil and (2) offering preventive counseling for persons whose early adjustment to the stresses of their disorder appears satisfactory. Family members who are too angry, depressed, or confused or who have unrealistic expectations of the group are also excluded (see Kapust and Weintraub, Chapter Eighteen).

Treatment Techniques. Although their preferred mode of intervention varies, many therapists employ treatment strategies geared to specific group phases. Campbell (Chapter Fifteen), working with the families of burn victims, is representative of those therapists who view providing information and support as being most helpful to the families during the initial phase of a group (at the time of hospitalization and life-threatening crisis), while in later phases the focus of the group requires other types of intervention, such as reflection and interpretation. Jerse and associates (Chapter Ten) emphasize that therapist interventions vary not only with the group phase but also within the course of a particular group session. Armstrong (Chapter Seven) describes the effective therapist as active and flexible and as one who utilizes a multimodal approach to the care of his or her patients.

On the whole, most therapists tend to utilize educational

approaches such as audiovisual aids and written materials (for example, Chapters Five and Seven) and didactic lectures about the patients' illness presented by medical specialists (Chapter Thirteen). In addition, they employ supportive approaches, including encouraging the group in projects it wishes to undertake (such as the pamphlet written by the adolescent cancer patients described in Chapter Eleven), crisis intervention techniques when necessary (as described in Chapters Fifteen and Seventeen), and a potpourri of other strategies (see Chapter Nine) aimed at improving the stress reduction skills of patients and families.

The diversity of therapeutic interventions described in this section have the common, overriding theme of helping patients (and families) to achieve a greater sense of control over their environment and fate. While the lack of empirically supportive data for individual intervention methods or programs may reflect the state of the art, such supporting documentation will hopefully be forthcoming.

Practical Problems. Practical problems for group therapists working with medical-surgical patients include membership issues, irregular attendance, dropouts, special types of difficult intratherapy events, heavy demands on the therapist's time, and termination issues.

Some patients hesitate to participate in any form of treatment viewed as psychiatric. Ford (Chapter Two) has made several excellent recommendations for overcoming this resistance. For example, the name of the group should emphasize a medical rather than psychiatric focus, meetings should take place within medical and surgical clinics, and the therapist should meet individually with a patient several times before the patient enters the group in order to establish some rapport with the patient. On the other hand, many patients acknowledge the problems and stress that confront them in adjusting to their disease (see Pavlou, Chapter Thirteen) and are grateful rather than offended when offered the opportunity to join a group.

Irregular attendance and premature termination have been cited as serious hindrances to developing cohesiveness in any treatment group (Cunningham, Strassberg, and Roback,

1978). With respect to membership arrangements in closed groups, Ford (Chapter Two) suggests that the therapist's policies should be communicated to (and agreed upon by) potential members before they attend the first group meeting, including policies on attendance, fee arrangements for missed sessions, the number of sessions patients are expected to attend, and so forth. Irregular attendance and dropouts are not as detrimental to open-ended groups as they are to closed groups, since patient turnover is normal anyway. However, a constantly changing membership makes it difficult to deal with process issues.

Not surprisingly, many of the difficulties that occur in groups (such as the monopolizing patients, competitiveness, subgrouping, and scapegoating) also occur in groups for medical-surgical patients and their families. In psychiatric groups, these events are often the essence of group process, while in disease management groups these issues are obstacles to the attainment of the group's objectives. Recommendations to the group leader for managing such problems are particularly emphasized in Chapter Ten.

For instance, in dealing with monopolists who insist on conveying their particular story in endless detail, Jerse and associates recommend a redirecting comment such as "We're getting a bit off the track from feelings." My preference is a somewhat similar statement, such as "I'd like you to tell me more about how you *feel* about these matters." The monopolist's behavior is typically fueled by anxiety, which could be escalated by a comment that is construed as a criticism or a put-down. Readers are referred to other sources (Dinkmeyer and Muro, 1971, pp. 197-212; Ohlsen, 1970, pp. 164-192) for additional suggestions for managing difficult patients and group events.

Special problems of particular relevance to disease management groups are described in the present volume: overidentification with the group (Chapter Three), overuse of the defense mechanism of denial, fears of deterioration or contagion (see Chapter Thirteen for a particularly good discussion of this phenomenon), anger at the medical establishment for not effecting a cure (Chapter Thirteen), or feelings brought about by major medical reversals and repeated losses (Chapter Seventeen).

Readers are directed to the referenced chapters for more detail about these specific problems and methods for coping with them.

Several therapists commented on time constraints and the needs of some patients and families for individual sessions with the group leader. This situation presents a particularly difficult dilemma for group leaders, who must provide many additional hospital services. One group leader (Euster, Chapter Seventeen) notes that time limitations often leave the therapist with a sense of unfinished business. She believes that group members may legitimately require individual assistance following a group session for dealing with unique concerns or difficulties that are not appropriate for group intervention. Thus, she recommends that leaders be available for individual interventions to particular group members as well as to various members of their families.

My view of this matter is that most patient-related issues can be handled in group sessions if the therapist conveys that expectation to the members and gently encourages them to adhere to this expectation in all but the most unusual or extreme circumstances.

Due to constant member turnover, termination in open-ended groups is not as important an issue as in closed groups. Yet several authors noted the difficulty that some patients and families have in terminating groups. One therapist (Pavlou, Chapter Thirteen) perceived the members as viewing termination as the "termination of assistance and of a hope for cure and nurturance." She also discussed the meaning of termination to people who have already experienced the loss of physical capability, wishes and dreams, personal identity as a healthy person, and feelings of invulnerability. This sensitive discussion of the topic of termination should underscore the necessity of exploring and understanding the unique significance attached to this event by individuals for whom loss is already a major issue.

Some leaders recommend monthly or bimonthly follow-up sessions to prolong gains achieved and to diminish potential termination difficulties (Chapter Eighteen), while others report on the formation of self-help groups. As Walwork (Chapter Sixteen) points out, even within self-help groups there is a reactivation of the feeling of loss during periods of leadership transition. However, this change can provide the opportunity for personal and group growth in the face of challenge. Other contributors also note that some members tend to continue relationships with one another informally after termination, while other members may seek individual counseling.

I fully share Kapust and Weintraub's (Chapter Eighteen) recommendation that to counter termination problems, therapists should offer patients the opportunity of monthly follow-up sessions. This periodic follow-up also provides a mechanism for care should a change in the patient's condition require a psychological "booster shot."

Therapeutic Factors. Although the nature of the group approach used and the type of patient population served will greatly influence what therapeutic factors are in operation, I was struck by the frequent references to the therapeutic factors cited by Yalom (see Chapter One) and other prominent theorists. This reflects an important consensus about the significance of these factors.

Over seventy-five years after Pratt's (1907) observation that a major therapeutic factor in his didactic-inspirational group work with tuberculosis patients was the finding of a "common bond in a common disease," contemporary group leaders working with medical patients continue to cite universality as an important therapeutic ingredient. Pavlou (Chapter Thirteen) points out that the hallmark of the early treatment sessions is a "We are not alone" feeling that promotes cohesiveness within the group. Such positive feelings tend to combat the undeniable sense of isolation experienced by many patients with serious medical problems.

The opportunity to share and compare one's experiences with those of others in similar situations improves one's problem-solving strategies. As a specific example, Eisenberg's (Chapter Five) spinal-cord-injured patients shared experiences in reestablishing a sexual component to relationships, acquiring new vocational skills, and dealing with solicitous, though well meaning, persons. Through gaining such information, patients often feel more able to find solutions to future problems.

Based on her group work with adolescent cancer patients,

Lewis (Chapter Eleven) noted that for the newly diagnosed teen, contact with others who are successfully battling a similar disease process fosters a more optimistic view of one's own chances for survival and ability to cope with treatment requirements and resulting life-style changes. It goes without saying that the opposite side to such optimism is a deep feeling of hopelessness and despair; even the most hopeful patient is never far away from lapsing into the latter feelings during private moments.

Jerse, Whitman, and Gustafson (Chapter Ten) point out that "many patients and family members have no forum for expressing and working through the flood of feelings, changing family dynamics, and painful experiences that having cancer induces. They often find that their existing support network cannot handle the situation." Pavlou (Chapter Thirteen) presents a particularly good example of patients communicating highly personal concerns when she describes a group of multiple sclerosis patients talking about embarrassing bladder problems. Although these discussions were at times purposefully lighthearted and humorous, more frequently patients "tuned directly into the pain and shame of the childhood feelings of 'wetting your pants.' " This author also poignantly describes the relief experienced by a patient's spouse when he was finally able to disclose his embarrassment at being seen in public with his wife in a wheelchair. This disclosure relieved the family unit of one "secret barrier to their being close."

In a supportive group context, persons are often able to convey thoughts otherwise considered taboo in the larger society. As an example, Walwork (Chapter Sixteen) mentions that in a bereaved-parents group, discussions often include feelings of resentment toward other mothers who have experienced a successful pregnancy and a healthy child.

The labeling and sharing of potent and pervasive feelings (such as embarrassment, anger, fright, and powerlessness) with other persons in similar situations enable individuals to make the first step in learning how to channel such affect constructively. It is essential, however, that the therapist be sufficiently skilled in handling such emotions that they do not overwhelm certain group members and cause these members to terminate prematurely.

Analagous to the therapeutic function of sharing common experiences among group members is the beneficial effect of the group leader presenting information about the specific medical illness. This information debunks myths and faulty beliefs commonly held by patients and family members, as is well demonstrated in Chapter Eighteen by Kapust and Weintraub. These authors present the example of a woman whose husband suffered from Alzheimer's disease. Following a group session that focused on the probable physical causes of dementia, this particular woman blurted out that she had secretly harbored the thought that her musician spouse had literally "blown his brains out playing the trumpet." Another woman had secretly wondered whether a marital dispute a number of years earlier had somehow contributed to her husband developing Alzheimer's disease.

Patients also have many unexpressed beliefs about their disorder, such as the fear of many multiple sclerosis patients (Chapter Thirteen) that their disorder will seriously impair their mental faculties over time. Such erroneous beliefs can be corrected through educational means. Nevertheless, even in strict didactic sessions, care givers should be attuned to the emotional component of members' questions. Understanding this emotional state can help lead to further discussions exploring feelings as well as cognitions.

The therapeutic factors presented above are not an exhaustive listing of the important change mechanisms presented by the contributors. Additional factors cited by contributors included developing insight into how long-standing family relationship patterns influence the familial response to the patient's illness (Chapter Eighteen) and improved patient reality testing (see Chapters Ten and Sixteen).

While skillful and perceptive therapists have acknowledged the contribution of these factors to their successful therapeutic groups, issues such as the relative importance of these factors, the stage at which they are most important, the degree of overlap between factors, and the underlying components comprising these broad constructs must be explored. These questions are addressed in an excellent paper by Marcovitz (who authored Chapter Fourteen) and Smith (1983).

Research and Theoretical Issues

Group Therapeutic Effectiveness. I share Strupp's (1979) view that clinicians need to address the questions about psychotherapeutic practice being asked by legislators, insurance companies, and the patient. These questions include: Are these treatments effective? If so, for whom and under what conditions? What are the extent, meaning, and significance of therapeutic change? What risks does the patient undertake? In our book *Group Psychotherapy Research* (Roback, Abramowitz, and Strassberg, 1979), we emphasized the importance of documenting the cost-effectiveness of these interventions with specific populations. Without such documentation, the field is unlikely to continue to receive support from public and private funding agencies.

The contributors to this volume were identified by their professional colleagues as providers of exemplary psychosocial care for a designated medical-surgical population or associated family units. Although few of the contributors would identify themselves as psychotherapy researchers, many authors have attempted to provide some kind of follow-up on the efficacy of their therapeutic approach. These outcome assessments typically did not involve the testing of a theoretical hypothesis. For instance, most of the authors present subjective therapist and patient reports of clinical effectiveness. A few contributors (Chapters Six and Eighteen) have tried to evaluate the quality of their interventions through structured interviews or the use of questionnaires.

The most systematic research on the effectiveness of a specific group program was conducted by Razin (Chapter Nine). He assessed participants on behavioral, physiological, and self-report affective and cognitive measures, both before and after treatment. Although the reported findings are promising, Razin recommends important refinements in future protocols.

In a comprehensive discussion of methodological issues in research on coping with chronic disease, Watson and Kendall (1983) point out that chronic disease patient groups are often viewed as homogeneous populations when, in fact, they may be heterogeneous with regard to factors such as etiology, severity, and duration of the disease. The authors also point out that the reliability of medical diagnoses should not be taken for granted, that coping is a multifaceted concept that cannot be assessed by a single measure, that samples of patients seen at one site may not be representative of a total chronic disease population, and that it is important to find appropriate control samples and take into account the confounding effect of improper comparison groups and placebo effects.

Another methodological issue concerns the appropriate perspective from which to conduct the assessment of outcome. Should it be the patient's primary care physician, the patient's family, the patient, or some independent evaluator? Cunningham and associates (1978) stress that questions such as the latter are not easily answered. The nature and specific goals of a particular intervention group will in part determine how, and by whom, outcome would be most appropriately measured (Mally and Ogston, 1964; Schoenberg and Senescu, 1966).

Contributors to this volume clearly recognize the lack of documentable data on efficacy in the field and encourage controlled studies to measure the potency of their treatment approach as a major future direction. In the absence of such important data, readers should not accept uncritically the penetrating clinical insights of the authors but rather should test the observations and hypotheses in order to acquire important cumulative process and outcome data.

Readers interested in learning the basic steps in designing a group psychotherapy outcome protocol are referred to a 1975 article by Diamond and Shapiro. Although geared toward the study of encounter group effectiveness, the Diamond and Shapiro paper appears equally useful for assessing group therapy outcome. Models of group therapy studies can be found in Roback, Abramowitz, and Strassberg (1979), Bednar and Lawlis (1971), Lieberman, Yalom, and Miles (1973), and Malan and others (1976). These references should provide interested readers with the basic methodology and design considerations for conducting process, outcome effectiveness, follow-up, and comparative research.

Negative Effects. In contrast to the substantial literature on negative effects of individual psychotherapy (Strupp, Hadley, and Gomes-Schwartz, 1977), very little has been written about negative changes in group psychotherapy apart from the encounter group literature. Bergin (1971) estimates a 10 percent deterioration rate for traditional individual psychotherapy, while others suggest that the deterioration rate for conventional group therapy might be higher (Bednar and Lawlis, 1971; Hartley, Roback, and Abramowitz, 1976).

Walwork (Chapter Sixteen) makes several important points about negative effects. Self-help groups may preclude the assessment of the appropriateness of an individual to a group experience. Individuals with previously existing psychoses or histories of depression "can be hurt by the group, but they can also be destructive to the group itself." For such individuals, more intensive individual treatment may be indicated. In addition, the absence of a professional leader may cause psychopathology to be overlooked or occasionally even reinforced by the group.

Pattison (Chapter Eight) discusses the negative effects of psychodynamic group therapy on hospitalized patients with chronic lung disease. Emotional upset in such patients can lead to respiratory distress that can be life threatening. In leading such a group, Pattison recognized the legitimacy of the patients' fears that the affective emphasis of the treatment was making their condition worse and shifted to a disease-oriented, didactic emphasis with favorable results.

Shanfield and McDonnell (Chapter Twelve) reported that hospice inpatients who had outlived their predicted life span were at risk for repeated grief reactions to the deaths of fellow patients. It became necessary to transfer such patients either to a long-term care facility or to their families. The potential harm of group therapy to terminally ill patients or patients with life-threatening medical conditions needs to be carefully evaluated.

Professional and Personal Issues

Working with Chronically Ill Patients. This book has focused on groups for medical-surgical patients and their families. If the editor had no length constraints, he would have included a section on groups for hospital staff members. Working on a day-to-day basis with seriously ill and dying patients takes its toll, as reflected in absenteeism, staff turnover, burnout, emotional withdrawal, and depression (Eisendrath, 1981; Eisendrath and Dunkel, 1979). Group therapists working with such patients and their families must also contend with job-related stress. I will comment on three areas of stress cited in this volume: personal reactions to working with specific populations, interdisciplinary tensions, and staff-family tensions.

Regardless of theoretical discipline, therapists in the course of their training hear about the importance of maintaining professional distance from their patients. This stance seems particularly difficult to assume with medical-surgical patients and their families, because therapists are confronted with the realization of their own vulnerability to disease. Thus, the individuals whom they are protecting are not only the patients but also themselves. In addition, it is difficult to maintain such objectivity when the patients have played no identifiable role in what happened to them—for instance, anyone can have a car accident and suffer an irreversible injury, such as spinal cord damage, or fall victim to a dreaded illness such as cancer.

Kapust and Weintraub (Chapter Eighteen) squarely address the difficulties of listening to older group members "painfully articulate their loneliness, discouragement, fears of illness and disease, disgust with their wrinkled, aged faces and failing bodies, and their fury with God for not treating them better in their old age." These authors, both in their thirties, comment on the similarities between themselves and certain group members who at a similar age were fully in charge of their lives and careers. Kapust and Weintraub also point out how this stirs up anxiety about the aging process (as well as questions about their responsibilities to their own aging parents). The authors cope with such feelings through open discussion with one another following each group session. They state, "We set aside time to reflect on our own reactions to group themes and individual members. . . . Understanding these countertransference feelings can result in personal and professional growth for the group leaders."

In her discussion of work with cancer patients and their families, Euster (Chapter Seventeen) stated, "Due to the catastrophic nature of the illness, group leaders immediately form strong bonds with members. . . . The professional may experience a personal sense of loss when the relationship terminates." Euster shares Kapust and Weintraub's conviction that coleaders must provide feedback to one another.

The comments above and those conveyed by other authors are extremely relevant in alerting therapists to the profound personal effect of working with the populations discussed in this volume. Contributors also note the great sense of personal satisfaction they experience when they see their group members take charge of their lives and how gratifying it is to see that such gains have been maintained at follow-up.

Interdisciplinary Tensions. Most authors who felt comfortable speaking about interdisciplinary relationships addressed their value in cotherapist-led groups but rarely wrote about their interactions with the primary physician. Some contributors (Marcovitz, Chapter Fourteen) noted that the primary physician was helpful as a trouble shooter but did not have enough time for regular meetings with the group therapist. I sense that many contributors feel disappointed that such ongoing meetings are not held between the primary physician and themselves.

Armstrong (Chapter Seven) provides a persuasive discussion on how primary physicians can detract from the effectiveness of a treatment group. Consequently, he will not conduct such groups unless the primary care giver (1) subscribes to the leader's group goals, (2) includes the group therapist in patient-care meetings, (3) announces to patients the existence of the group, (4) encourages patients considered suitable to attend the group, and (5) helps to avoid splitting by encouraging patients to talk directly to the group leader about group concerns. Armstrong's strong feelings result from his having encountered in some physicians little psychological-mindedness and little appreciation of the value of psychotherapy. Clearly, this psychotherapist wants his groups to have a good start and, before putting an enormous effort into them, wants to ensure that he has the full support of the primary physician.

Staff-Family Tensions. Chesler and Yoak (Chapter Nineteen) discuss sources of tension between staff members working with family support groups and the family members themselves. They believe that conflicts often arise from subtle difficulties in role definition. For instance, a staff person may be threatened or confused by parents who are providing emotional support to one another, perceiving them as invading the professional person's domain. The professional and family members may disagree about the desirable therapeutic strategies with the result that the staff person feels left out. Since care givers may also experience half-hearted support from the medical staff, their role may prove a very lonely one. Chesler and Yoak recommend that professionals educate families from the beginning about possible sources of tension that could arise in their working together.

A Few Closing Words

"Progress in any field of science seems to evolve from the interaction of several basic ingredients, such as fertile ideas and theoretical formulations, useful methods and techniques of procedure, and a passion for serious work in their pursuit" (Waskow and Parloff, 1975, p. v). The present volume presents the current thinking and approaches of skilled professionals dedicated to improving the quality of life of persons with medical problems through the use of group methods. However, this book will fall short of its goals if it does not also stimulate readers to advance the field through collaborative research.

References

Bednar, R., and Lawlis, G. "Empirical Research in Group Psychotherapy." In A. Bergin and S. Garfield (Eds.), *Handbook of Psychotherapy and Behavioral Change.* New York: Wiley, 1971.

Bergin, A. "The Evaluation of Therapeutic Outcomes." In A. Bergin and S. Garfield (Eds.), *Handbook of Psychotherapy and Behavioral Change.* New York: Wiley, 1971.

Cunningham, J., Strassberg, D., and Roback, H. "Group Psychotherapy for Medical Patients." *Comprehensive Psychiatry,* 1978, *19,* 135-140.

Diamond, M., and Shapiro, J. "Method and Paradigm in Encounter Group Research." *Journal of Humanistic Psychology,* 1975, *15,* 59-70.

→ Dinkmeyer, D., and Muro, J. *Group Counseling: Theory and Practice.* Itasca, Ill.: Peacock, 1971.

Eisendrath, S. "Psychiatric Liaison Support Groups for General Hospital Staffs." *Psychosomatics,* 1981, *22.*

Eisendrath, S., and Dunkel, J. "Psychological Issues in Intensive Care Unit Staff." *Heart and Lung,* 1979, *8,* 751-756.

Hartley, D., Roback, H., and Abramowitz, S. "Deterioration Effects in Encounter Groups." *American Psychologist,* 1976, *31,* 247-255.

Lieberman, M., Yalom, I., and Miles, M. *Encounter Groups: First Facts.* New York: Basic Books, 1973.

Malan, D., and others. "Group Psychotherapy: A Long-Term Follow-Up Study." *Archives of General Psychiatry,* 1976, *33,* 1303-1315.

Mally, M., and Ogston, W. "Untreatables." *International Journal of Group Psychotherapy,* 1964, *14,* 369-374.

Marcovitz, R., and Smith, J. "Patients' Perceptions of Curative Factors in Short-Term Group Psychotherapy." *International Journal of Group Psychotherapy,* 1983, *33,* 21-39.

→ Ohlsen, M. *Group Counseling.* New York: Holt, Rinehart and Winston, 1970.

Pratt, J. H. "The Class Method of Treating Consumption in the Homes of the Poor." *Journal of the American Medical Association,* 1907, *49,* 755-759.

Roback, H., Abramowitz, S., and Strassberg, D. (Eds.). *Group Psychotherapy Research.* New York: Krieger, 1979.

Schoenberg, B., and Senescu, R. "Group Psychotherapy for Patients with Chronic Multiple Complaints." *Journal of Chronic Diseases,* 1966, *19,* 649-657.

Strupp, H. "Foreword." In H. Roback, S. Abramowitz, and D. Strassberg (Eds.), *Group Psychotherapy Research.* New York: Krieger, 1979.

Strupp, H., Hadley, S., and Gomes-Schwartz, B. *Psychotherapy for Better or Worse: The Problem of Negative Effects.* New York: Aronson, 1977.

Waskow, I., and Parloff, M. (Eds.). *Psychotherapy Change Measures.* Rockville, Md.: National Institute of Mental Health, 1975.

Watson, D., and Kendall, P. "Methodological Issues in Research on Coping with Chronic Disease." In T. Burish and L. Bradley (Eds.), *Coping with Chronic Disease.* New York: Academic Press, 1983.

Name Index

Subject Index

A

Acceptance, and dying, 253

Adaptation, in spinal cord injury, 114

Adolescent cancer patients: analysis of, 285-312; autonomy for, 287-288, 300; background on, 285-286; control by, 292-293; coping mechanisms of, 291-293; denial by, 291, 299, 300, 306; developmental tasks for, 286-291; effectiveness of group for, 304-306; examples of, 288, 290-291, 292-293, 305-306; future orientation of, 290-291; group difficulties of, 306-307; group meetings and benefits for, 298-304; group treatment approaches for, 295-297; impact of disease on, 286; leaders for, 307-309; overcompensation by, 292; peer role models for, 293; psychosocial-psychosexual development of, 288-290; rationale for group work with, 293-294; reflections on, 307-309; structure of group for, 298; summary and conclusions on, 309-310; universality for, 303-305; Vanderbilt group for, 297-309

Adolescents: renal disease group for, 174-180; with sickle cell anemia, 369, 376-377, 380

Affiliation: as group objective, 15-17; stress as stimulant of, 16-17

Alberta, University of, renal disease group at, 170-171

Alexithymia. See Hypochondriasis

Altruism: in anorexia nervosa groups, 67; in cancer patient group, 256; as group mechanism, 12-13; in sickle cell group, 381

Alzheimer's Disease and Related Disorders Association, 473

Alzheimer's disease families: analysis of, 453-480; anger in, 467-468, 476; background on, 453-455; and characteristics of disease, 454; difficulties of group for, 475-476; future groups for, 477-478; and grief, 462-463; and group membership, 459-460, 474; group treatment approach for, 457-460; and impact of illness, 455-456; and incidence of disease, 453; and information giving, 471; and loss, 455, 461-464; and nursing home placement, 469; outcomes of group for, 473-474; personal reflections on, 478-479; problem-solving phase for,

ment, 336-337; and reference
groups, 17-18; and social support, 334, 336, 354, 356-357;
stress of and adaptation to, 332-
336; techniques in groups for,
341-342; termination for, 354-
355; and universality, 342-343,
355-356
Myocardial infarction (MI): background on, 217; cardiac stress
management program for, 234-
242; group interventions for,
222, 223-226, 229, 230, 234-
245; impact of, 220-221

N

National Cancer Institute, 482,
484, 524
National Conference on the Care of
the Child with Cancer, 482
National Kidney Foundation, 179,
181
Neonatal death: analysis of coping
with, 409-427; and anger, 414,
422; background on, 409-410;
causes of, 410-412; and grief,
413, 414-415, 425; and group
approach for parents, 415-418;
and group consultant, 425-426;
leadership for, 417-418, 421,
424-425; and life support withdrawal, 411-412; and limitations
and strengths of group, 424-426;
and marital relationship, 414-
415; model protocol for dealing
with, 418-422; and mutual assistance, 417; and psychosocial
needs of family, 412-415; purposes of group for, 423-424; and
reality testing, 417; self-help
group for, 422-426; and stress,
413-414; summary on, 426-427;
and termination of group, 426
Nosie-30 scale, 203
Novaco Anger Scale, 244, 245

O

Ohio State University Hospital, spinal cord injuries group at, 119

Osto-Mates, 500
Overcompensation, by adolescent
cancer patients, 292

P

Pain. *See* Chronic pain
Paradoxical intention, for somatiza-
tion, 49
Parents. *See* Families
Patients: psychological responses
of, 3-7; tasks of, 367-368
Phantom pains, in amputation
group, 142
Projection: by multiple sclerosis
group, 343; by patients, 5
Psychodrama, in chronic pain group,
91, 93
Psychodynamic therapy. *See* In-
sight therapy

R

Rational-emotive therapy, for coronary artery disease, 228-229
Reach for Recovery, 500
Reactance theory, and loss of control, 4
Regression, by patients, 5
Renal disease, end-stage: adolescent group for, 174-180; analysis of, 159-189; background on,
159-163; clinic as group for,
163-165; comments on groups
for, 180-181; comprehensive
group program for, 172-174; and
dependency, 178; developments
in treating, 161-162; etiology of,
159-160; and family functioning,
167-168; and family group, 171;
funding for therapy for, 169-170;
group therapy for, 168-170; insight therapy for, 171; and lifeboat culture of clinic, 165; literature review on, 170-172; medical and somatic adjustment to,
167; and physician support for
group, 173-174; and private-pub-
lic boundary, 163-165; and pro-